A FIELD GUIDE TO

EASTERN TREES

EASTERN UNITED STATES AND
CANADA, INCLUDING THE MIDWEST

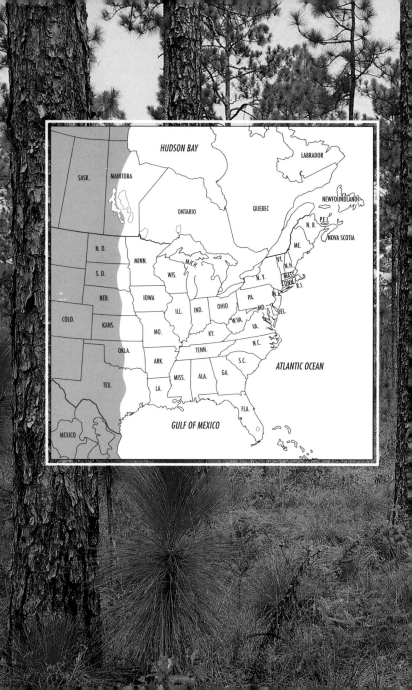

THE PETERSON FIELD GUIDE SERIES®

A FIELD GUIDE TO

EASTERN TREES

EASTERN UNITED STATES AND
CANADA, INCLUDING
THE MIDWEST

GEORGE A. PETRIDES

Illustrated by
JANET WEHR

FIRST EDITION, *Expanded*

SPONSORED BY THE NATIONAL AUDUBON SOCIETY,
THE NATIONAL WILDLIFE FEDERATION, AND
THE ROGER TORY PETERSON INSTITUTE

HOUGHTON MIFFLIN COMPANY
BOSTON   NEW YORK

For information about permission to reproduce selections from this
book, write to Permissions, Houghton Mifflin Company,
215 Park Avenue South, New York, NY 10003

PETERSON FIELD GUIDES and PETERSON FIELD GUIDE SERIES
are registered trademarks of Houghton Mifflin Company.

LIBRARY OF CONGRESS CATALOGING-IN-PUBLICATION DATA

Petrides, George A.
A field guide to eastern trees : eastern United States and Canada,
including the Midwest / George A. Petrides ; illustrated by Janet Wehr.
    p.   cm. — (The Peterson field guide series; 11)
"Sponsored by the National Audubon Society, the
National Wildlife Federation, and the Roger Tory Peterson Institute."
Includes bibliographical references (p.   ) and index.
ISBN 0-395-90455-2
  1. Trees — East (U.S.) — Identification.   2. Trees — Canada,
Eastern — Identification.   3. Trees — East (U.S.) — Pictorial works.
4. Trees — Canada, Eastern — Pictorial works.   I. Title.   II. Series.
    QK115.P46 1998   582.16'0974 — DC21   98-13625

Book design by Anne Chalmers
Typeface: Linotype-Hell Fairfield; Futura Condensed (Adobe)

PRINTED IN THE UNITED STATES OF AMERICA

QWT 14 13 12

T O

MIRIAM

Editor's Note

With more than 400 species, this completely new version of Dr. Petrides' *Field Guide* supersedes his previous book by including all states east of the Great Plains down to the Gulf Coast. However, it confines its coverage to trees; the shrubs and woody vines are not included.

A Field Guide to the Birds, the first book in the Peterson Field Guide Series, was published in 1934, and the principle on which it was founded—a schematic treatment pointing out the visual or field differences between species—proved a sound one. Checklist or phylogenetic order was often subordinated to an artificial but more practical arrangement of the figures on the plates, so as to make things easier for the tyro. For example, the chimney swift was placed with the swallows, and ducklike birds such as the coot were placed near the ducks.

It was inevitable that Field Guides to botanical subjects should follow. In fact, as far back as 1941 I had planned to do a book on trees and had actually started when I learned that Dr. George Petrides was deep in a very similar project. Upon examining his work I concluded that his version adhered to the basic principles of the Field Guide system even more than mine, so I switched my time budget to wildflowers, offering him bits of supplementary material—tree silhouettes, drawings of fruits and flowers, etc.—that would have gone into my own book on trees. He had based his approach mostly on leaf, twig, and bud characters.

A veteran field naturalist with a record of teaching and research, Dr. Petrides served first in the National Park Service and the U.S. Fish and Wildlife Service and then at Michigan State University. He had long felt the need for an approach to plant recognition that the public and his students in ecology and game management would understand. It is well enough to be tutored in basic plant taxonomy, but more often than not the student, even after considerable training, is still confused when confronted by problems of identification.

Dr. Petrides' first book, *A Field Guide to Trees and Shrubs,* published in 1958, covered the trees, shrubs, and woody vines that grow wild in the northeastern and north-central United States and in southeastern and south-central Canada. It was in a sense a pictorial key, using obvious similarities and differences of form and structure by which the beginner could quickly run down his tree, shrub, or vine. True, some botanists may have raised their eyebrows because the plants were not in the traditional order of their relationships, but there were many formal botanies so arranged; it would have been pointless to produce another. This innovative Field Guide was an effective shortcut. Actually, the student could also learn the relationships (even if indirectly) because a key in the appendices made things quite clear. The leaf and twig plates were the ingenious and painstaking labor of Dr. Petrides, while the other figures (silhouettes, drawings on the legend pages, etc.) were mine. A much revised second edition appeared in 1972.

In this completely new version, a total of 455 species, including all North American trees that occur east of the Great Plains, are treated. Also included are 133 confined basically to the state of Florida. If all exotics were included (such as those in suburbia, parks, and botanical gardens) there would be many more. Nevertheless, those trees of foreign origin that are now widely established and on their own are included.

The new illustrations, artfully painted by Janet Wehr, are less schematic and more representational in treatment than the leaf and twig diagrams in the previous book, but retain the comparative approach and are equally effective in putting across their message.

Do not leave this book at home on the library shelf: take it along on your woodland rambles or on your drives in the countryside. In the ecology-oriented years ahead this handy book will inform you about the green mantle of plants that clothe our "small blue planet," the only home we've got.

ROGER TORY PETERSON

PREFACE

This Field Guide differs from the earlier *Field Guide to Trees and Shrubs* (Petrides 1958, 1972) in three basic ways: It deals only with trees; it covers a larger geographic area—all of the eastern United States and Canada, rather than just the northeastern and north-central United States and eastern Canada—and it offers detailed and beautiful paintings in full color, supplemented by black-and-white drawings. The identification charts facing the color plates are another new feature, as are the maps showing the geographical range of each species. As in the previous book, trees that look alike are grouped together, both in the text and in the color plates. Characteristics essential for identification are described for trees in both summer and winter condition. Secondary characteristics considered desirable to confirm identification are also noted, together with items of general interest. The guide describes field marks without using technical jargon.

The geographical area treated includes all of eastern Canada and the United States east of the Great Plains. The territory extends westward through the eastern portions of Manitoba, North Dakota, South Dakota, Nebraska, Kansas, Oklahoma, and Texas. Essentially all of the trees growing naturally east of the Black Hills and Rocky Mountains are covered. Most, but not all, of the species found in central and south Texas have been included. (All are also included in my *Field Guide to Western Trees.*)The area is limited elsewhere by the coastlines of the Atlantic Ocean and the Gulf of Mexico. Inasmuch as many of the species described occur beyond this circumscribed territory, however, the guide is useful in a broader geographical area.

Within the region described above, all native trees are considered as well as trees of foreign origin that regularly survive and reproduce successfully. The only exceptions are the hawthorns (*Crataegus*), whose many species and hybrids are not always identifiable even by specialists. The guide discusses examples from this group, however. In addition, a few frequently encountered and widely cultivated trees introduced from abroad are included as space allows.

Botanical varieties and forms below the rank of species are not considered unless they differ markedly from the typical species. The discussion encompasses 455 species in 210 genera, including three hawthorns; three varieties of full species also are considered to be sufficiently distinctive from their parent forms to be included and given separate accounts.

The above total includes 133 species that basically occur in our region only in Florida. Most of these trees are found only in the most southern (tropical) portion of the state. Several trees that occur only in Florida have been selected for full color and text treatment. Most, however, are assembled on Plates F-7 through F-46D (pp. 130–151). Segregation of the Florida-only species makes it possible to simplify the identification of unknown plants both in Florida and farther north.

I have retained the definition of a tree used by U.S. Forest Service authorities: a woody plant attaining a height of 13 feet or more and having a single trunk at least three inches in diameter at breast height (4½ feet).

This book avoids technical botanical terms. It is sometimes claimed that anyone seriously interested in the subject will be willing to learn such terminology. Moreover, certain terms are necessary to prevent unduly long descriptions. Still, there seems to be little point in describing a leaf shape as "cordate," for instance, when a botanical glossary defines the word merely as meaning "heart-shaped." One might as well say "heart-shaped" from the beginning. Similarly, "stoloniferous" means "with runners," "coriaceous" is "leathery," "cuneate" means "wedge-shaped," "ovate" is "egg-shaped," "lanceolate" means "lance-shaped," "denticulate" is "with fine teeth," and so on. Many botanical terms, in short, can be translated easily into plain English with no loss in accuracy. In adopting a simplified terminology for this book, I trust that I have avoided the dangers of oversimplification and loss of accuracy and that I will have promoted interest in plant identification.

Persons wishing to identify unknown plants are often baffled by botanical manuals and sometimes even by books described as popular guides. Several difficulties are commonly encountered. First, the technical language used may be enough to damp enthusiasm. Second, a "popular" book may not include all species, and the layperson may feel uncertain that the specimen is really the plant indicated. Third, in some books final identification depends on floral characteristics, though the specimen at hand may not be in bloom. Sometimes, too, identification depends on leaf characteristics not visible on specimens in winter. This field guide seeks to avoid such pitfalls by making only limited use of technical terms, by including all trees that grow wild in the area covered, and by stressing characteristics of twigs and leaves that are present the year round.

The reasons for learning about trees vary from the purely recreational to the strictly serious. Many human ills are related to the destruction of plants. Like all other creatures, we depend totally on green plants, which convert inorganic chemicals into organic foods and also help to maintain essential atmospheric gases in a healthful balance.

In any area the presence or absence of certain plant species or their tendencies to increase or decrease may reflect erosion, over-exploitation, or pollution in that particular spot. In addition to serving as indicators of environmental quality, trees and shrubs play immensely important aesthetic and monetary roles because of their beauty. Anyone who doubts that ecology and economics are interlinked has only to consult a forester, a soils scientist, a watershed biologist, a wildlife ecologist, a fisheries limnologist, or a hydrologist. Simpler yet, though, he can ask any urban dweller or real estate broker about the positive effect of green space on morale and property values.

A number of people assisted generously at several points in the preparation of this book. John Beaman and his successor, Alan Prather, curators of the herbarium in the Department of Botany at Michigan State University, provided office space and gave me access to the remarkably complete and thoroughly catalogued collections in their care. Robert K. Jansen, now at the University of Connecticut, extended similar courtesies. George W. Parmelee, curator of woody plants at Michigan State University, made available his extensive living collections of labeled specimens. David Johnson and his wife, Nancy Murray Johnson, now at the New York Botanical Garden, were most kind in allowing me to draw upon their extensive knowledge and their photographic files of tropical species. Niles Kevern, chairman, Department of Fisheries and Wildlife, Michigan State University, and his staff allowed me to use office equipment. The curatorial graduate assistant, Martha Case, was most kind and efficient in locating needed specimens. Her predecessors Cheryl Crowder and Lucille McCook were also very helpful. Edward G. Voss of the University of Michigan Herbarium loaned several specimens.

Janet Wehr not only produced the fine illustrations for the book but also assisted in the preparation of the index and frequently helped with other details. Her son, Peter Wehr, made the computer map renditions, which have now been electronically colored by Larry Rosche. Susan Hazard, word processor extraordinaire, coped magnificently with difficult handwritten manuscript copy. Marcia Brubeck did a fine job assisting in the final editing. She revised a number of complex statements in a clear and concise manner. Harry Foster and Lisa White of Houghton Mifflin Company were most helpful in providing overall editorial guidance.

   In my review of tropical, subtropical, and other trees peculiar to Florida, I was greatly aided by Angus Gholson, who maintains the Gholson Herbarium at Chattahoochee, Florida. Roger W. Sanders, taxonomist at the Fairchild Tropical Gardens near Miami, generously let me preview his manuscript treatment of the Florida palms in a book then in preparation. Jim Watson, herbarium assistant, also reviewed the materials for Plates 47 and 48 and made a number of useful suggestions. Roger L. Hammer, director of the Castellow Hammock Nature Center at Goulds, Florida, generously made me the beneficiary of his detailed knowledge of regional taxo-nomic field botany.

GEORGE A. PETRIDES

CONTENTS

ILLUSTRATED PLAN
OF THE SIX MAIN SECTIONS

Figure 1

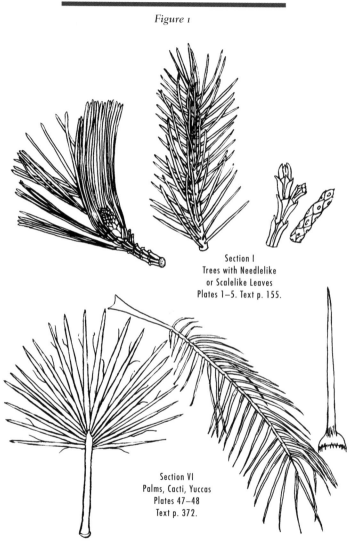

Section I
Trees with Needlelike
or Scalelike Leaves
Plates 1–5. Text p. 155.

Section VI
Palms, Cacti, Yuccas
Plates 47–48
Text p. 372.

LEAVES OPPOSITE OR IN WHORLS

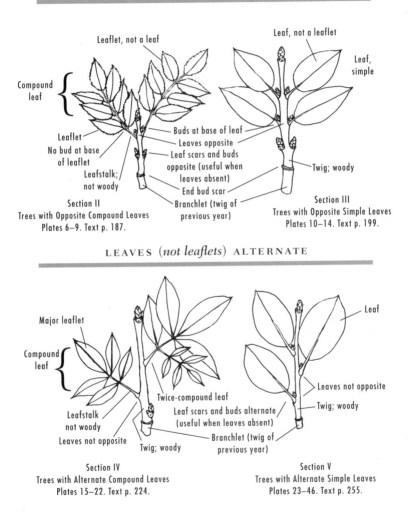

Leaflet, not a leaf

Leaf, not a leaflet

Leaf, simple

Compound leaf

Leaflet
No bud at base of leaflet

Leafstalk; not woody

Buds at base of leaf
Leaves opposite
Leaf scars and buds opposite (useful when leaves absent)
End bud scar
Branchlet (twig of previous year)

Twig; woody

Section II
Trees with Opposite Compound Leaves
Plates 6–9. Text p. 187.

Section III
Trees with Opposite Simple Leaves
Plates 10–14. Text p. 199.

LEAVES (*not leaflets*) ALTERNATE

Major leaflet

Compound leaf

Leafstalk not woody

Leaves not opposite

Twice-compound leaf
Leaf scars and buds alternate (useful when leaves absent)
Branchlet (twig of previous year)

Twig; woody

Leaf

Leaves not opposite

Twig; woody

Section IV
Trees with Alternate Compound Leaves
Plates 15–22. Text p. 224.

Section V
Trees with Alternate Simple Leaves
Plates 23–46. Text p. 255.

A FIELD GUIDE TO

EASTERN TREES

EASTERN UNITED STATES AND
CANADA, INCLUDING THE MIDWEST

HOW TO USE THIS BOOK

PLEASE READ THIS SECTION: People using field guides tend naturally to head straight for the illustrations, either ignoring the introduction and text or simply skimming them. Anyone who seriously wants to identify trees, however, should not overlook this part of the book. The following pages explain the difference between opposite and alternate leaves and between compound and simple leaves. Here, too, are definitions of other terms that will reappear in later sections. Even the word "twig" has an essential specific meaning that may be new to you!

GENERAL ORGANIZATION: The text is divided into six principal sections, beginning with the most easily recognized types of trees:

  I. Trees with needlelike or scalelike leaves
 II. Trees with opposite compound leaves
III. Trees with opposite simple leaves
 IV. Trees with alternate compound leaves
  V. Trees with alternate simple leaves
 VI. Trees with parallel-veined leaves (palms, yuccas, cacti)
Sections II–VI contain the broad-leaved plants.

The six basic leaf types and arrangements are illustrated on pp. xvi–xvii and can be learned in a few minutes. In summer, plants can readily be assigned to one of these sections. In winter, plants without leaves can be placed in the combined opposite-leaved categories (Sections II and III) or in the alternate-leaved categories (Sections IV and V), according to leaf-scar arrangements (drawings of leaf types and arrangements precede the text for each section).

Within each principal section trees are organized in subgroups, beginning with the most recognizable characteristics (thorns, lobed leaves, toothed leaves, etc.) and ending with species having the fewest obvious distinguishing features. It is a good idea to work from front to back within the book as a whole and within each section.

The identification charts and other keys, which are explained below under "Identifying Unknown Plants," will further help you identify species. Appendix A provides a comprehensive winter key to all non-evergreen species. A summary of family and other relationships of eastern trees appears as Appendix B. The meanings of some terms are summarized in the Glossary. A rule on the back cover permits conversion of inches to millimeters. The References include works cited and other publications of interest. The complete scientific names of trees found only in Florida are listed at the end of the book.

LEAF TYPES AND PATTERNS

When they are in leaf, all woody plants fall into one of the six major categories described above under General Organization and illustrated in Fig. 1 on pp. xvi–xvii.

Plants whose leaves are obviously not needlelike or scalelike are *broad-leaved plants*. Foresters often call them *hardwoods*, in contrast with the needle-bearing *softwoods*.

A *simple leaf* has only a single blade and is joined by its stalk to a woody *twig*. A distinct leaf scar remains on the twig when the leaf and its leafstalk fall or are plucked.

Compound leaves are divided into three (rarely two) to several dozen *leaflets*. The leaflet of a compound leaf is attached by its stalk to the midrib of the leaf. This midrib is not especially woody and exhibits only an indefinite mark when the leaflet is plucked. The midrib of the compound leaf is attached by its stalk to the woody twig, and as with the simple leaf, a definite *leaf scar* (see Fig. 2A) remains when the leafstalk drops or is removed. In a relatively few species (Pls. 15 and 22), the major leaflets of the compound leaf are themselves divided into minor (sub-)leaflets. Such leaves are *twice-compound* and may involve 4 to 800 or more minor leaflets.

Both compound and simple leaves may vary in shape, size, texture, and other characteristics, but despite all variations, these two main leaf types are fundamental.

Opposite leaves may be either compound or simple and occur in opposing pairs along the twigs. *Whorled leaves* occur less frequently as three or more leaves arise together. Their leaf scars tend to encircle the twigs at intervals. The few plants with whorled leaves have been included in the opposite-leaved category.

Alternate leaves are arranged singly at intervals along the twigs. One should be careful not to misidentify the opposite leaflets of some compound leaves, even of alternate compound leaves, as

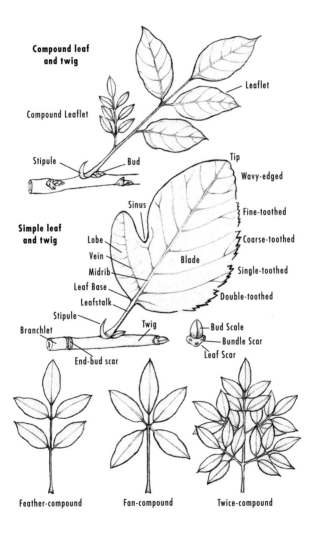

Compound leaf and twig

Leaflet

Compound Leaflet

Stipule

Bud

Simple leaf and twig

Tip

Wavy-edged

Fine-toothed

Coarse-toothed

Sinus

Single-toothed

Lobe

Vein

Blade

Midrib

Double-toothed

Leaf Base

Leafstalk

Stipule

Twig

Branchlet

Bud Scale

Bundle Scar

Leaf Scar

End-bud scar

Feather-compound

Fan-compound

Twice-compound

Fig. 2A. Leaf and Twig Terminology

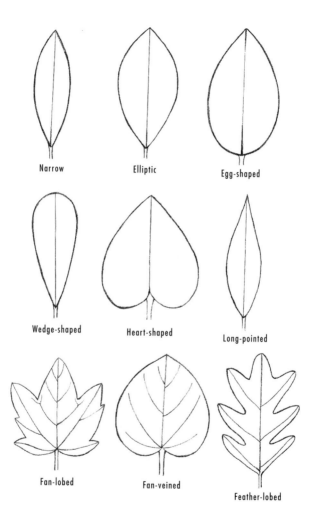

Narrow   Elliptic   Egg-shaped

Wedge-shaped   Heart-shaped   Long-pointed

Fan-lobed   Fan-veined   Feather-lobed

Fig. 2 B. Leaf shapes

opposite simple leaves. Furthermore, some alternate-leaved plants bear *spur branches,* on which leaves are densely clustered (see Fig. 3). These can be mistaken for opposite or whorled leaves if one is not careful to select strong-growing specimen twigs for study (see Identifying Unknown Plants, p. 11). Leaflets of both compound and simple leaves have essentially the same parts.

Leaf shape within a species normally varies somewhat. This book illustrates and describes typical leaf shapes and the usual range of variation

Twig and Bud Types

A *twig* is not just any small division of a branch but the end portion—the part that constitutes the newest growth. It is separated from the *branchlet,* the growth of the previous year, by a series of encircling *end-bud scars.*

In winter, *non-evergreen* broad-leaved plants compose two main groups: (1) those of Sections II and III, with leaf scars arranged on the twigs in opposing pairs, or, much less commonly, in whorls of three or more, and (2) those of Sections IV and V, with leaf scars arranged singly on the twigs in a more or less scattered pattern (see Fig. 3).

It is not always possible to distinguish between the leaf scars of compound and simple leaves, though those of compound leaves are often larger and have more than three bundle scars. Further subdivisions within the opposite- or alternate-leaved groups reflect the number of bundle scars, the type of buds, the type of pith, the presence of milky sap, and other characters. Bud descriptions apply to mature winter buds. The term *chambered pith* is used here to include all types of segmented, transversely divided pith, including pith that is diaphragmed and partitioned. The main characteristics of winter twigs and buds are illustrated in Fig. 3. Unless otherwise specified, bark characteristics are mentioned only with regard to the trunk bark.

I have designated end buds true or false (see Fig. 3) reluctantly, since the distinction is not always obvious. Ideally, there will be a small but evident bud scar next to a false end bud. Some books mention end buds as present or absent rather than as true or false. In this volume, true end buds and clear sap may be considered to be present unless otherwise stated. Central end buds are lacking in several species with opposite buds, as shown on Pl. 7.

Plates

Each plate shows plants that most resemble each other in leaf and twig characteristics. These plants may or may not be related.

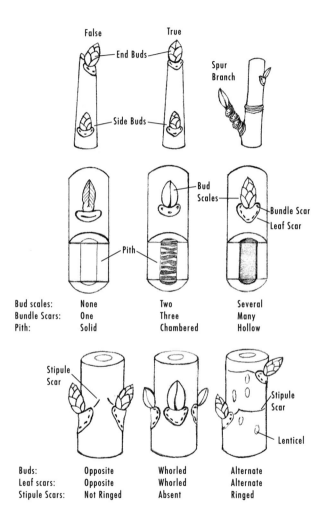

Fig. 3. *Twig and Bud Terminology*

Wherever possible, however, related species have been depicted on plates as close to one another in sequence as possible, given the main objective of grouping plants similar in appearance.

The reader will recognize that not all specimens precisely resemble the illustrations, but the pictures do offer the designated critical points of identification. Stipules (see Fig. 2A) have been illustrated only when they are of diagnostic value, since they often drop early.

On any one plate, the leaves of the several species have been drawn to indicate their relative size. There may be differences in scale, however, for plants shown on different plates. Leaf and plant sizes are given in the text. The illustrations of twigs, buds, and other small parts have often been enlarged to make their details more readily evident.

As noted above, many tropical and semitropical species appear in our area only in Florida. To facilitate tree identifications in both regions, most of these plants are grouped on a series of F-plates beginning on p. 130.

IDENTIFICATION CHARTS

Opposite each plate is a matrix-type identification chart. Scanning the charts enables a quick appraisal of species differences. The charts provide a large amount of information in a compact form. They offer an improved approach to "keying out" a plant in that they present a summary of species characteristics for easy comparison. Trees can rarely be identified by a single field mark, and key features are not always present or may not be readily apparent on the specimen at hand (whether the end bud is false or true, for instance). Thus, having a series of field marks to cross-check can be crucial to correct identification. The plates and appropriate identification charts alone may be enough to identify an unknown tree.

The charts indicate whether a species does (+) or does not (−) possess a particular characteristic or whether it possesses that characteristic in an intermediate or variable (±) form. In a few cases, the chart will indicate (o) that the characteristic cannot apply to a particular species. In general the charts list first the features most important for identification. One should therefore read the plus-or-minus columns from left to right. Additional descriptive notes indicate further distinctive characteristics. The distribution data given in the charts represent merely a general guide to assist in identification; the reader should refer to the more detailed maps in the text.

The scientific names listed in the identification tables lack the authors' names. These appear in the text or, for species occurring only in Florida, on pp. 381–384. Species not illustrated on the associated plate (with names in parentheses on the chart) are similar to those shown.

BOTANICAL KEYS

The identification charts offer advantages when a dozen or so species are to be compared. However, in cases where either a very few or a large number of species must be classified, the charts are not appropriate. In such instances, as at the beginning of each section in the text and in Appendix A, traditional botanical keys are employed. The keys to plant identification may seem formidable at first but should be treated rather like a book's table of contents: their function is merely to divide the subject matter, in this case plant species, into subsections, further sub-subsections, and eventually species or groups of species.

For the most part, keys attempt to divide the many species into two groups. Each group in turn is then divided in two. This process is repeated again and again until species or groups of species are named.

In such a key, the person trying to identify a tree chooses first between the two number ones, then between the two number twos, the two number threes, and so on. Using a key is simply a matter of following a trail that forks repeatedly but typically offers only two paths at any single fork. The seeker continues to make choices between the options that bear the same number, making certain at each point that the choice made fits the plant being identified, until an end point is reached.

SPECIES DESCRIPTIONS

PLANT NAMES: Both common and scientific names are given for each species. Although for many species common names are well established, the same name or a similar one is sometimes also applied to a different, even unrelated species. In our area, for instance, Ironwood is used as the common name for at least seven species in six genera. Species names which include the name of another unrelated group, for example Osage-orange or Baldcypress, are either hyphenated or joined together to indicate that they are not true members of the group.

The Flora of North America (Morin 1993, 1997), now in development, is becoming the basic reference for plant names and classification in the region. The scientific names accepted by the specialists who compiled the first volumes of this continuing series are used in this book. For species not yet reached by the

Flora, I relied mainly on Little (1979). Full citations are given on pages 404–406.

The common names suggested by Little (1979) proved not to be in use in southern (tropical) Florida for many species found there. In these cases I have supplied the names employed by local botanists and confirmed either by Everglades National Park authorities (Stevenson 1969) or by Long and Lakela (1971) or Tomlinson (1980). Several species listed in Morin (1997) but found at only one limited locality or area are not included.

Scientific names have three essential parts: the name of the *genus* (plural, *genera*), the name of the *species* (plural, *species*), and the name or names, commonly abbreviated, of the botanist(s) who assigned the scientific names. In the case of *Quercus rubra* L., for example, the initial stands for Carolus Linnaeus, who is regarded as the father of systematic botany.

Varieties are recognizably distinct subpopulations of a species. In most instances, the distinction is minor. Only a few varieties in our area (Pondcypress, Lombardy Poplar, Cherrybark Oak) are sufficiently distinctive to require separate identification. In such a case, the varietal name and the name of the authority (or authorities) responsible for it follow the basic scientific name of the species—for example, *Taxodium distichum* (L.) Rich. var. *imbricarium* (Nutt.) Croom for Pondcypress.

A main purpose of scientific nomenclature is standardization so that botanists anywhere in the world may discuss a plant with the assurance that they are indeed talking about the same species. Scientific nomenclature is an international cataloguing system that, within certain limits, also indicates plant relationships. Scientific names may change, however, as authorities decide that a species is more closely related to members of a genus different from that to which it was first assigned, that plants once considered to belong to two species should instead be regarded as two varieties of a single species, that a species originally thought to be new has already been named, and so forth.

The rules of botanical nomenclature are much too involved to be fully explained here. The reader will probably find scientific names of value principally as they make it possible to locate the same species in other reference books.

In the United States and Canada nowadays, scientific names tend to be anglicized when spoken, and most pronunciations are acceptable. Anyone who can say *hibiscus* or *hydrangea, sassafras* or *magnolia*, is already using scientific names. In speech, the authors' names are usually omitted.

RECOGNITION: This guide limits plant descriptions largely to identification characteristics. A statement of the general growth habits of the species is followed by characteristics of foliage, twigs, and bark. Individual specimens of a species inevitably vary. Where individual differences may cause confusion in identification, their extent has been indicated in the text. I have attempted to describe degrees of hairiness where it was possible to do so, but the exact extent of hairiness in leaves and twigs is sometimes difficult to indicate in words. Nearly all leaves will show some fine hairs if they are examined closely under a hand lens. Plants described in the text or on the plates as being hairy are usually markedly so. On "hairless" plants, hairiness is not conspicuous. A hand lens is useful in ascertaining the abundance of hairlike structures. Descriptions of bark refer to the mature bark of large stems unless otherwise indicated.

Measurements are given for leaf lengths, plant heights, and trunk diameters. Minimum and maximum leaf lengths are generalizations for normal leaves and include the length of the leafstalk unless otherwise stated. Sprouts of some species bear abnormally large leaves. The common minimum height and diameter for mature trees are followed by the common maximum for each measurement and, in parentheses, the exceptional maximum. Diameters are for tree trunks at breast height (about 4½ feet above the ground—the forester's diameter at breast height). All these figures are given as only general guides. The several maximum measurements are not usually all evident on a single specimen. The "largest" Jack Pine recorded by the American Forestry Association, for example, is only 27 feet tall, although it is 42 inches in circumference. All measurements are given in feet, inches, and fractions rather than in metric-system units, since English units are more widely familiar in our area.

Flower and fruit data have been supplied only to the extent that, as general identification characteristics, they usefully supplement vegetative characteristics. Further details are provided only for those species not easily recognized by leaf and twig characteristics alone. A tree's fruit clusters, not usually mentioned, are of the same type as the clusters described for the flowers. The extreme dates given for flowering and fruiting may need to be modified by a month or so, depending on locality. Where fruiting dates are lacking, dates for the flowers will indicate at least the earliest possible time when fruits might appear. Fruit colors apply to ripe fruits only. The habitat named indicates the vegetation type in which the species is usually found.

General statements regarding the distinctiveness of certain species' characteristics apply to the geographic area of the book.

SIMILAR SPECIES: Critical differences are discussed for species that most closely resemble one another when they are in foliage and when they are leafless.

DISTRIBUTION: Maps showing the limits of distribution in the eastern areas north of Mexico have been published for most tree species in several volumes of the *Atlas of United States Trees* (Little 1971, 1977, 1978). I have followed these maps in preparing the book. For a few species, however, the range is described verbally, with distributional limits reported from northeast to northwest and southeast to southwest.

REMARKS: General observations accompany descriptions of plants that serve as sources of lumber, fuel, medicine, food, drink, poison, fiber, ornament, tannin, and Christmas trees, or are of special value in soil and wildlife management. References to wildlife are usually limited to game birds and to mammals of chipmunk size or larger.

IDENTIFYING UNKNOWN PLANTS

Before attempting to identify unknown plants, one should first learn the general appearance of Poison-ivy, Poison-sumac, and, in southern Florida, Poisonwood and several others (Fig. 4, p. 17). Once their main characteristics are known, these sources of skin irritants can easily be avoided.

It is better to make identifications in the field than to collect specimens for later identification at home. In the wild, additional materials are available, and growth habits are evident. If field identification is impractical, then ample twig specimens, with leaves when they are available, may be gathered and either carried fresh or pressed. *Good specimens are essential for correct identification.* Dwarfed, twisted, or gnarled twigs should be avoided. Abnormally large sucker shoots may not show typical hairiness characteristics, but otherwise strong, quick-growing twigs should be collected for study. On such twigs, the leaves and leaf scars are larger and all details are more evident.

In summer, the first step in identifying an unknown plant is to place it in one of the six main groups, according to leaf type and arrangement (see Fig. 1):

1. Leaves needlelike or scalelike.	**Section I, p. 155**
1. Leaves broad. 2	
2. Leaves opposite or whorled. 3	
2. Leaves alternate. 4	
3. Leaves compound.	**Section II, p. 187**
3. Leaves simple.	**Section III, p. 199**
4. Leaves compound.	**Section IV, p. 224**
4. Leaves simple.	**Section V, p. 255**
1. Palms, yuccas, cacti.	**Section VI, p. 372**

You should turn next to the proper section, scan the plates, and select the species most like the unknown one. It is important to review the facing *identification charts* next and to follow up by checking the *distribution map* and reading the *text description* of the species. You should verify that the specimen and its geographic range and description agree, or else make another attempt to run it down. The text portion on similar species may also help you interpret identification marks.

You may of course prefer to disregard the sectional leaf keys and the identification charts and to rely upon spotting the proper illustration, since the plates themselves are a pictorial key. It is often possible to proceed in this way if the species falls in Sections I through IV or in Section VI. Relatively few plants have needlelike, compound, opposite, or palm-frond leaves. Approximately half of eastern trees, however, have alternate simple leaves and fall into Section V. Unless a Section V specimen has other quite distinctive characteristics, probably you should follow the keys, tables, maps, and so on.

In winter, unless the plant is evergreen, you must either find leaf remains on or under the specimen (and run some risk of picking up part of another tree) or rely on twig and other winter characteristics. If you find dried leaves, you can attempt to proceed as you would in summer. Otherwise you should look for good twig specimens. Both the identification charts and the winter botanical key (Appendix A) should be used.

Some plants may be difficult to identify for a month or so in early spring, when buds have burst but leaves are small and new twigs soft.

Everyone would like to discover a rare specimen. Before you conclude that you have found a species outside its usual range or have unearthed something entirely new to science, however, recheck carefully to verify that you do not have a case of mistaken identity. If it still seems likely that the plant is something unusual, you might collect a specimen (with flowers or fruits, if possible, and always with notes indicating the exact location, date of collection, and your own name and address), carefully press it, dry it, and forward it to the department of botany at your state or provincial university or agricultural college with a request for confirmation of identification.

EQUIPMENT

Fortunately, plant identification requires little paraphernalia. Only two items are essential: a field guide or manual and a hand lens. *A good hand lens is as essential to the botanical naturalist as binoculars are to the birder.* The hand lens is especially helpful in ascertaining twig characteristics but is also essential for assessing leaf hairiness, leafstalk glands, etc. Furthermore the lens discloses hidden beauty in small blossoms and in other plant parts. Lenses for general use should magnify 6x to 10x. Hand lenses are inexpensive and practically indestructible. Those manufactured by well-known optical companies are generally worth the slightly higher price usually asked for them.

As previously noted, it is *strongly suggested that identification be made in the field,* where additional specimens and supplementary data are available. When you need to collect specimens, however, a large plastic bag will preserve them until they can be pressed. A roll of newspapers held by a strap, or even a large magazine, may also do well as a field carrier if specimens are being carried for early identification, but serious collectors will want to acquire a plant press, available from any biological supply house.

In a press, plants are placed within newspaper pages, which are inserted between blotters and placed between sheets of corrugated cardboard. The entire series is packaged between wooden frames and securely tied by straps. Specimens will dry more quickly in dry weather when the press is mounted outside a moving car. A stream of heated air blown through the press will also hasten drying. Otherwise it will occasionally be necessary to replace newspapers and blotters to permit thorough drying and to prevent molds from invading the collection.

Plant Succession

Every plant species, through evolutionary processes, has become something of a specialist. Each one lives in a certain type of *habitat* and thrives under a particular set of climatic, soil, and water conditions. On a newly available site, local conditions are varied, and seeds or other reproductive parts of several species usually manage to be present. As a result a *plant community* composed of several species becomes established. Once they are entrenched most plants and plant communities alter the site so that it becomes less and less suitable for them with the passage of time. (We are not the only species that fouls its nest!) Increasing fertility due to root decay and leaf fall, for example, may invite competition from species originally unable to become established on the site. Alternatively, increasing shade may prevent seedlings from surviving even though they are next to, or are even surrounded by, their parents. These factors and others bring about *succession* as plant communities and the soils they occupy pass through a series of stages until a stable community of plants and mature soil structure finally develops. This end product—a mature and relatively permanent community—is the *climax* plant association.

Primary plant succession occurs when community development begins and develops from a bare surface or in open water. Primary succession may begin on such areas as cliff faces, rockslides, gravel slopes, road cuts, dunes, lava flows, peat deposits, or gully sides or on shallow lake bottoms, in bogs, or on river bars and deltas. In such places *pioneer* communities become established and are eventually succeeded by other plant communities, each of which tends to be more intermediate in its moisture requirements than its predecessor. That is, within the limits set by climate, succeeding communities beginning in a wet environment live on progressively drier sites, while those in a dry environment live on moister sites, with the climax community occurring on neither wet nor dry sites but on intermediate, moist ones.

Secondary plant succession occurs when a plant community is entirely or partly killed or removed, exposing soil that has already advanced to some degree toward maturity. Such plant destruction might be accomplished by fire, trampling, drainage, windthrow, lumbering, cultivation, or other means. The secondary plant community series that follows a change in the original vegetation generally differs from the primary successional series.

Species in developmental stages of plant succession may be geographically more widespread than those of the climax stage. They may even take a part in succession in regions with different climax types. Some species may occupy somewhat different habitats and successional stages in different portions of their ranges, whereas others are restricted to only a portion of a single climax area.

Knowledge of local successional stages is essential in studies of land use, soil conservation, forestry, wildlife management, and outdoor recreation. The amateur botanist will find it an interesting and valuable project to prepare a plant succession chart for his or her locality; see Oosting (1956).

CLIMAX VEGETATION TYPES

From north to south and from east to west in our area, major differences in the character of the climax vegetation are evident. These major units are mostly characterized by distinctive vegetative *life forms* (evergreen trees, deciduous trees, grasses, etc.) and are termed *plant formations*. On the *tundra* of the far North and the mountaintops of eastern Canada and New England grow sedges, grasses, lichens, herbs, and low and creeping shrubs. The northern evergreen or *boreal forest* that covers most of Canada and part of the northern United States is dominated by White Spruce and Balsam Fir, although Tamarack (American Larch) becomes prominent along its northern edge. The *hemlock-hardwood* forest of the Great Lakes area — a formation of mixed conifers and broad-leaved trees — is sometimes also designated the *lake forest*. Its dominant species include Hemlock, Beech, Sugar Maple, Yellow Birch, and White Pine.

Over most of our area is the broad-leaved *deciduous forest*. Several principal climax associations occur in this formation: (1) Mixed Mesophytic (Beech–Sugar Maple–Tuliptree–White Oak–Red Oak–Hemlock) in southern mountain valleys and some lowlands; (2) Beech–Sugar Maple in moist deep soils; (3) Oak-Hickory or Oak-Pine (and formerly Oak-Chestnut) mostly in drier areas; and (4) Sugar Maple–Basswood in parts of Wisconsin and Minnesota. On the flat coastal plain in the Southeast is a portion of the *southeastern evergreen forest*, principally of Loblolly and Shortleaf pines. In extreme southern Florida, numerous *tropical hardwood* trees occur that have wider distributions in the West Indies and American tropics. No climax forest types which involve these species, however, have been described. *Prairie* formations occur in the western part of our area, with woody species important only in valley bottoms.

Poisonous Plants

Only a few species among wild plants in our area irritate the skin. Especially in tropical southern Florida, there are still other irritating species (see Fig. 4, p. 17). The four below, however, are most widespread. All have alternate compound leaves and small, dry, *white or yellowish* fruits. They should be avoided!

POISON-SUMAC *Toxicodendron vernix*   **FIG. 4**

This shrub or small tree has large leaves consisting of 7–13 pointed leaflets which are *not* toothed. It has small white fruits and occurs mostly in open, *swampy* places. See Fig. 4.

POISON-IVY   **FIG. 4**

Toxicodendron radicans (L.) Kuntze or *Rhus radicans* L.

This plant is not a tree but a small erect shrub or tree-climbing vine frequently encountered in the field. Learn to recognize the three-parted leaves, which are variably toothed but have a pointed end leaflet on a longer stalk than the side ones. The stems of old vines may be densely black-fibrous, while young stems are merely brown-hairless.

POISON-OAK   **NOT ILLUS.**
Toxicodendron toxicarium (Salisb.) Gillis or *Rhus toxicodendron* L.
    This plant is very similar to Poison-ivy but more southern and
always erect. It has leaflets that are mostly blunt-tipped.

FLORIDA POISONWOOD   **FIG. 4, PL. F-46B**
Metopium toxiferum (L.) Krug & Urban
    This species does not occur north of central Florida. Its mostly
triangular and leathery evergreen leaves are usually marked with
black spots.

PLANTS POISONOUS TO TOUCH

The 2 tree species shown here have alternate feather-compound leaves. Poison-ivy also is illustrated because it too must be shunned and commonly grows as a vine on trees. Though members of the cashew family, all should be avoided![1]

SPECIES AND REMARKS	Growing to tree size	Only a shrub or vine	Leaflets per leaf	Leaflets toothed	Leaflets wavy-edged	Leaves leathery, evergreen	Twigs stout	Fruit color[2]
POISON-SUMAC *Toxicodendron vernix* Mostly shrubby. Mostly wet places.	+	–	7–13	–	–	–	+	W
POISON-IVY *Toxicodendron radicans* End leaflet long-stalked. Widespread.	–	+	3	±	±	–	–	W
FLORIDA POISONWOOD[1] *Metopium toxiferum* Leaves black-spotted. Bark flaking.	+	–	3–7	–	+	+	+	Y

[1] Other trees of cen. and s. Fla. that produce substances irritating to the skin of some people include the Brazil Peppertree (Pl. F-21A), Lime (p. 263), Cajeput-tree (Pl. F-46A), Mango (Pl. F-46B), and Manchineel (Pl. F-46C). All have alternate leaves; those of Brazil Peppertree and Lime are compound.

[2] W = white, Y = yellowish.

POISON-SUMAC

POISON-IVY

FLORIDA POISONWOOD

Fig. 4

TREE SILHOUETTES
(BY R.T.P.)

An expert bird-watcher can often identify a bird by its silhouette alone. Birds are dependable: a grackle always is shaped precisely like a grackle, and one starling invariably resembles another starling. Trees, on the other hand, are not so consistent. The beginner, learning his trees, yearns for a book that will give him shapes and field marks by which he can make snap identifications from a moving car. But it isn't that easy. True, an American Elm (where it survives) somehow always looks like an elm, but many trees assume a variety of shapes. A young tree might look entirely unlike a grizzled veteran of the same species. And a forest-grown tree, reaching for the light, might be tall, slender, and restricted in its branching compared to a field-grown example where plenty of sun, soil, and moisture have enabled it to develop a maximum crown.

But within limits one can, with a little practice, recognize by shape and manner of growth quite a few of the trees and also some of the shrubs. On the following pages are presented some silhouettes of a selection of trees (and one or two shrubs). Not all examples will look like these, but they are, on the whole, typical. They represent open-grown specimens, not those of crowded woodland situations. If in doubt check the leaf and twig characters in the text.

WHITE PINE
Tall dark trunk; spreading horizontal limbs; delicate spraylike foliage

LOBLOLLY PINE
Tall, clean cinnamon trunk; open crown, drooping lower limbs

RED PINE
Tall, erect trunk; stout right-angle branches, symmetrical crown; long dark green foliage, ascending tips

PITCH PINE
Usually low, irregular, scraggly; many dead branches; coarse foliage in rigid tufts

WHITE SPRUCE
Pyramidal; upper branches ascending, lower nearly horizontal; foliage bluish green

RED SPRUCE
Rather open-branched, tips upcurved; foliage yellowish green

BLACK SPRUCE
Slender; short branches; foliage bluish green

NORWAY SPRUCE
Usually near houses; pyramidal; strongly drooping lateral branchlets

BALSAM FIR
Conical; branches ascending;
erect cones; flat needles

HEMLOCK
Loose, irregular, feathery;
short flat needles

EASTERN REDCEDAR
Conical head (wider with age);
short stem

NORTHERN WHITE-CEDAR
Dense conical head clothed almost
to base; flat sprays

COTTONWOOD
Wide-spreading open crown
(shaggier than Elm)

TAMARACK
Pyramidal (when young); short
needles in tufts (shed in winter)

WHITE OAK
Short trunk; crown often
much wider than high

BALD   CYPRESS
Flat-topped; irregular, feathery; buttressed; "knees"
often protrude from water

LOMBARDY POPLAR
Tall, slender; trunk continuous; many hugging branches

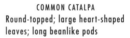

COMMON CATALPA
Round-topped; large heart-shaped
leaves; long beanlike pods

SUGAR MAPLE
Short stem; full egg-shaped head

AMERICAN ELM
Vase-shaped; trunk divided into
large outspreading limbs

SUGAR MAPLE
Short trunk; many ascending branches; symmetrical oval head; dark flaky bark

RED MAPLE
Short trunk; broad oval head (sometimes broader at top); gray beechlike upper branches

WHITE ASH
Trunk often divided low down; oval head; cross-shaped branching; diamond-ridged bark

TULIP TREE
Upright trunk; branches often angle upward; erect dry seed cones

BLACK WALNUT
Sharply divided trunk; heavy alternate branches; open spreading head

SHAGBARK HICKORY
Oblong; very shaggy bark (may be less twiggy, longer trunked)

BUTTERNUT
Round-topped or like inverted triangle; Y-like branches

PIGNUT HICKORY
Narrow oblong head; tight bark; contorted branches

AMERICAN ELM
Vase-shaped; trunk divided into
large outspreading branches

WHITE OAK
Broader than tall; short trunk;
branches gnarled

BUR OAK
Broad round top; spreading; lower
limbs often drooping

PIN OAK
Upper branches ascending; lower
branches drooping

EASTERN SYCAMORE
Large, open, irregular; bark in
patches revealing whitish under bark

QUAKING ASPEN
Upper bark whitish with dark
blotches; reddish-brown twigs

BEECH
Smooth light gray bark; dense ovate head;
often a few persistent leaves

GRAY BIRCH
Often clumped; chalky bark (not peeling)
with dark triangular patches; slender twigs

FLOWERING DOGWOOD
Spreading bushy head; conspicuous
erect flower buds at ends of twigs

BLACK WILLOW
Disheveled-looking; much branched,
often many shoots and suckers

WEEPING WILLOW
Drooping twigs and branches

PUSSY WILLOW
Clumped; catkins evident in early spring

BLACK LOCUST
Trunk usually divided; oblong head,
scraggly branches

HONEY LOCUST
Short trunk, broad rounded or flat-
topped head; thorny at bases of branches

STAGHORN SUMAC
Small, straggling, forked, flat-topped;
erect red fruit clusters

TREE-OF-HEAVEN
Flat-topped; branches without sprays;
clusters of winged seeds

SASSAFRAS
Oblong or flat-topped head; side branches at right angles, contorted, ending in bushy spray

SWEETGUM
Symmetrical; conical or flat-topped; twigs with corky wings; hanging seedballs

OSAGE-ORANGE
Low ragged crown; gnarled, thorny; often in hedges

BLACK CHERRY
Oblong head; branches irregular spreading, often zigzag

PLATES

PLATE 1

CONIFERS WITH NEEDLES IN CLUSTERS: LARCHES AND PINES I

Larches *(Larix)*: Needles numerous at ends of warty spur branches; dropping in autumn, leaving tree bare. Pines *(Pinus)*: Needles 2–5 in bundles, evergreen. Five- and three-leaved pines on this plate; two-leaved on following plate. Also see charts, pp. 165 and 168.

SPECIES AND REMARKS	Geographic distribution[1]	Needles per cluster[2]	Needle length (inches)	Trunk sprouts after fire	Many old cones on tree	Cones more than 3" long	Cones longer than wide[3]	Cone prickle type[4]	Text page
TAMARACK *Larix laricina* Trunk dark, scaly.	N	M	¾–1	–	–	–	±	0	157
(EUROPEAN LARCH *Larix decidua*) Trunk bark yellowish plates.	N	M	1–1½	–	–	–	+	0	157
EASTERN WHITE PINE *Pinus strobus* Needles thin, cones slim, branches parallel.	N/M	5	2–4	–	–	+	+	0	159
PITCH PINE *P. rigida* ½" branches tough to break, trunk sprouts tufted.	N/M	3	3–6	+	+	–	±	S	160
POND PINE *P. serotina* Trunk sprouts long, needles slender.	S	3	4–8	+	+	–	±	T/0	160
(SHORTLEAF PINE *P. echinata*)[5] Needles slender, see Pl. 2.	M/S	2(3)	3–5	–	+	–	+	T	169
LOBLOLLY PINE *P. taeda* Twigs ¼" thick, end buds brown.	S	3	6–9	–	+	+	+	S	161
(SLASH PINE *P. elliottii*)[5] Twigs ¼"–½" thick, end buds rusty-silver.	S	2–3	5–11	–	–	+	+	T	171
LONGLEAF PINE *P. palustris* Twigs ½"–1" thick, end buds white.	S	3	8–18	–	–	+	+	T	162

NOTE: In peninsular Fla., for tree called Australian-pine, see Pl. 2 and p. 172.
[1] N = northern, M = middle states, S = southern.
[2] M = many.
[3] Cone shape: ± = more or less ball-shaped.
[4] Cone prickles: O = lacking, S = stout, T = thin.
[5] Two- and three-needle clusters usually present; see Pl. 2.

PLATE 1

TAMARACK

WHITE PINE

PITCH PINE

POND PINE

LOBLOLLY PINE

LONGLEAF PINE

PLATE 2

CONIFERS WITH NEEDLES IN CLUSTERS: PINES II

These pines typically have 2 needles per bundle. Five- and three-leaved pines on preceding plate. Also see charts pp. 165, 168. None of these species sprouts after fires.

SPECIES AND REMARKS	Geographic distribution[2]	Needle length (inches)	Twigs rough near needles[3]	Many old cones on tree	Cones more than 3" long	Cones longer than wide[4]	Cone prickle type[5]	Text page
JACK PINE *Pinus banksiana* — Cones sharply curved.	N	1–1½	+	+	–	+	T/O	163
SCOTCH PINE *Pinus sylvestris* — Upper branches bright orange.	N	2–3	–	–	–	±	O	164
(AUSTRIAN PINE *P. nigra*) — Escapes cultivation; see text.	N	3–6	+	–	±	+	S	166
RED PINE *P. resinosa* — Bent needles break crisply.	N	4–6	±	–	–	+	O	166
MOUNTAIN PINE *P. pungens* — Needles prickly; cone thorns stout.	M	2–3	+	+	±	±	S	167
VIRGINIA PINE *P. virginiana* — ½" branches fibrous, tough to break.	M	2–3	–	+	–	±	T	169
SHORTLEAF PINE *Pinus echinata*[1] — ½" branches snap cleanly.	M/S	3–5	+	+	–	+	T	169
SPRUCE PINE *Pinus glabra*[6] — Scattered in broadleaf forests.	S	2–4	–	+	–	+	T/O	170
SAND PINE *Pinus clausa*[7] — Fla./se. Ala. only.	S	2–4	–	+	–	±	S	170
SLASH PINE *Pinus elliottii*[1] — Winter buds rusty-silver.	S	5–11	+	–	+	+	S	171
(AUSTRALIAN-PINE *Casuarina equisetifolia*) — "Needles" jointed. Fla.[8]	S	10–12	O	±	–	±	O	172

[1] Three-needle clusters may also be present in Shortleaf and Slash pines.
[2] N = northern, M = middle states, S = southern.
[3] On portions of the twig immediately adjacent to the needles; "smooth" twigs are reasonably smooth.
[4] Cone shape: ± = more or less ball-shaped.
[5] Cone prickles: O = lacking, S = stout, T = thin.
[6] Spruce Pine; not a spruce species.
[7] Inside tips of cone scales black.
[8] Not a true pine, see text p. 172.

PLATE 2

MOUNTAIN PINE

JACK PINE

RED PINE

SCOTCH PINE

SHORTLEAF PINE

VIRGINIA PINE

SAND PINE

SPRUCE PINE

SLASH PINE

PLATE 3

CONIFERS WITH NEEDLES SHORT ON WOODY PEGS: SPRUCES

Evergreen trees with needles square in cross section, stiff, sharp, attached singly. Twigs rough when needles removed. Cones pendent; brown, woody, with scales mostly smooth-edged. Mostly northern.

SPECIES AND REMARKS

SPECIES AND REMARKS	Twigs hairy[1]	Needle length (inches)	Branches drooping	Grows on boggy sites	Cone length (inches)	Text page
BLACK SPRUCE *Picea mariana* Cone scales with ragged edges. Old cones remain. Canada, n. U.S.	+	¼–⁷⁄₁₆	−	+	¾–1¼	174
RED SPRUCE *Picea rubens* E. Canada to Smokies.	±	½–⅝	−	−	1¼–1⅝	175
WHITE SPRUCE *Picea glauca* Canada and northern U.S.	−	⅜–¾	−	−	1–2	175
NORWAY SPRUCE *Picea abies* European; mostly planted.	−	½–1	+	−	4–6	175

[1] Remove needles and use hand lens.

PLATE 3

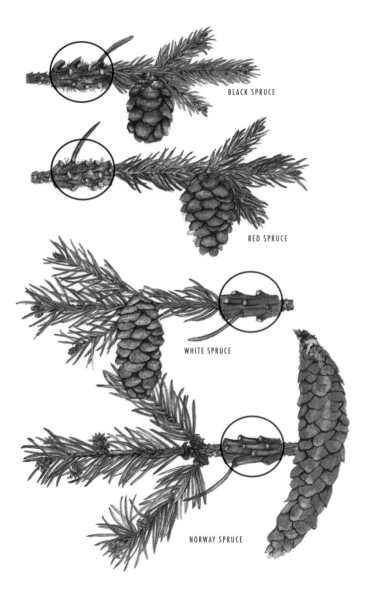

BLACK SPRUCE

RED SPRUCE

WHITE SPRUCE

NORWAY SPRUCE

PLATE 4

CONIFERS WITH FLAT NEEDLES

Evergreen[1] trees with needles flat and attached singly; needles and twigs mostly in flat sprays.

SPECIES AND REMARKS	Needles with slender stalks	Needles white-striped beneath	Needles sharp-pointed	Twigs rough	Major distribution[2]	Text page
BALSAM FIR *Abies balsamea* Bracts hidden by cone scales.	–	+	–	–	N	176
FRASER FIR *Abies fraseri* Bract tips visible between cone scales.	–	+	–	–	A	176
EASTERN HEMLOCK *Tsuga canadensis* Needles to $\frac{9}{16}$"; cones $\frac{1}{2}$"–$\frac{3}{4}$" long.	+	+	–	+	N	177
CAROLINA HEMLOCK *Tsuga caroliniana* Needles not in flat sprays; cones $\frac{3}{4}$"–$1\frac{3}{8}$".	+	+	–	+	A	178
BALDCYPRESS *Taxodium distichum*[1] Southern swamps. Foliage fernlike.	+	–	+	+	S	178
FLORIDA YEW *Taxus floridana* Fruits red, berrylike.	+	–	+	–	F	179
FLORIDA TORREYA *Torreya taxifolia* Fruits green/purple, olive-like.	–	–	+	–	F	180

[1] Baldcypress leaves (and most twigs) drop in winter and are not evergreen; branchlets rough; leaf scars lacking. **Pondcypress** (*T. distichum* var. *nutans*) needles three-sided, pressing close to drooping twigs rather than lying in flat sprays; not evergreen.

[2] N = northern states and Appalachian Mts.; A = Appalachians, mainly in the w. Carolinas (Smoky Mts.); S = South; F = nw. Fla. and sw. Ga. Rare.

PLATE 4

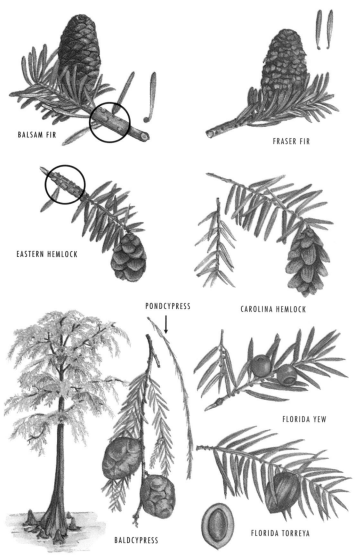

BALSAM FIR

FRASER FIR

EASTERN HEMLOCK

CAROLINA HEMLOCK

PONDCYPRESS

BALDCYPRESS

FLORIDA YEW

FLORIDA TORREYA

PLATE 5

CONIFERS WITH SCALELIKE OR THREE-SIDED HOLLOW LEAVES

Evergreen trees with leaves in pairs or whorls and often of two types, either or both of which may be present. Juniper fruits are fleshy but solid. See also Pondcypress (Pl. 4) and French Tamarisk (Fig. 7, p. 185), with pointed leaves.

SPECIES AND REMARKS	Tiny scalelike leaves present	Pointed, sharp leaves present	Leaf sprays flattened	Major distribution[1]	Text page
NORTHERN WHITE-CEDAR *Thuja occidentalis* Cones slim, ½" long.	+	−	+	N	181
ATLANTIC WHITE-CEDAR *Chamaecyparis thyoides* Fruits round, ¼" diameter.	+	−	±	C	182
COMMON JUNIPER[2] *Juniperus communis* Old fields, dry soils.	−	+	−	N	182
ASHE JUNIPER[3] *Juniperus ashei* Small round-topped tree. Ozarks, etc.	+	−	−	O	184
EASTERN REDCEDAR[4] *J. virginiana* Pointed tree; dry sites. Fruits ¼".	±	±	−	w	184
(SOUTHERN REDCEDAR[4] *J. silicicola***)** Similar to Eastern Redcedar; wet sites. Fruits ⅜". Branches ± droop.	±	±	−	SC	185

[1] N = North, C = Coastal Plain, O = Ozarks region, S = South, w = widespread.
[2] Needles in whorls of 3, 1 side white.
[3] The only species in this group with scalelike leaves that are not gland-dotted.
[4] Both scalelike and longer, sharp-pointed leaves may be present; either type may occur alone. Scalelike leaves less than 1.5mm (¹⁄₁₆") in Eastern Redcedar and more than 2mm (¹⁄₁₂") in Southern Redcedar. Eastern Redcedar is widespread but occurs on coastal Plain only from Va. northward.

PLATE 5

NORTHERN WHITE-CEDAR

ATLANTIC WHITE-CEDAR

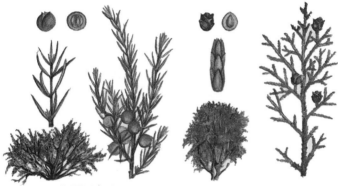

COMMON JUNIPER

ASHE JUNIPER

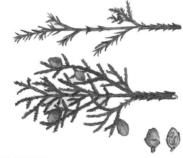

EASTERN REDCEDAR

PLATE 6

TREES WITH OPPOSITE FAN-COMPOUND LEAVES: BUCKEYES AND CHASTETREE

The only trees with opposite compound leaves whose leaflets are arranged like the spokes of a wheel. Buckeyes have toothed leaflets, large end buds, and 3 or more bundle scars.

SPECIES AND REMARKS	Trees growing to large size	Leaflets per leaf	End buds more than ½" long	Color of pith[1]	Trunk bark scaly[2]	Floer cluster length (inches)	Flower color[3]	Stamens longer than petals[4]	Fruit husks prickly[4]	Major distribution[5]	Text page
HORSECHESTNUT *Aesculus hippocastanum* European, planted; buds gummy.	+	7–9	+	W	+	6–12	W	+	+	w	189
YELLOW BUCKEYE *A. octandra* Broken twigs with sweet odor.	+	5	+	B	±	4–7	Y	–	–	A	189
OHIO BUCKEYE *A. glabra*[7] Broken twigs with foul odor.	+	5	+	W	+	4–6	Y	+	+	M	190
BOTTLEBRUSH BUCKEYE *A. parviflora* Native Ga. and Ala.; planted elsewhere.	–	5–7	–	W	–	8–20	W	+	–	S	190
RED BUCKEYE *A. pavia*[7] Calyx long-tubular (½" or more).[6]	–	5	±	B	–	4–8	R	–	–	S	190
PAINTED BUCKEYE *A. sylvatica* Flowers often particolored.	–	5	–	B	–	4–6	Y/R	–	–	P	191
(CHASTETREE *Vitex agnus-castus*) Leaflets not toothed; twigs four-angled.[8]	–	5	–	W	–	2–4	B	+	–	C	191

[1] Pith: B = brown, W = white.
[2] Rather than smooth.
[3] B = pale blue, R = dark red, Y = yellowish, W = white.
[4] Stamens are slender filaments ending in pollen-bearing anthers.
[5] A = Appalachians, C = Coastal Plain, M = Midwest, P = Piedmont plateau, S = South, w = widespread.
[6] Calyx = circle of sepals (here fused and colored like the petals) surrounding the base of the petals.
[7] Bud scales with a central ridge; use lens.
[8] Crushed foliage and twigs spicy, bundle scar one.

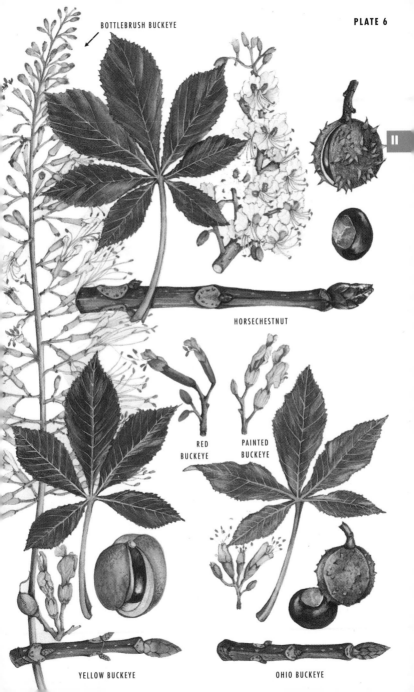

PLATE 6

BOTTLEBRUSH BUCKEYE

HORSECHESTNUT

RED
BUCKEYE

PAINTED
BUCKEYE

YELLOW BUCKEYE

OHIO BUCKEYE

PLATE 7

SMALL TREES WITH OPPOSITE COMPOUND LEAVES: BLADDERNUT AND ELDERBERRY

Leaves three-parted or feather-compound. Leaflets pointed, flowers white. Central end bud lacking. Both species are distributed widely. In Fla., see also Pl. F-7.

SPECIES AND REMARKS	Leaflets per leaf	Leaflets toothed	End leaflet present	Twigs stout[1]	Fruit color[2]	Text page
BLADDERNUT *Staphylea trifolia* Fruits inflated, balloonlike.	3–5	+	+	−	D	192
COMMON ELDERBERRY *Sambucus canadensis* Flat-topped flower/berry clusters.	5–11	+	+	+	P	193

[1] Also leaf scars large and connected by lines.
[2] D = dry, brownish; P = purplish.

PLATE 7

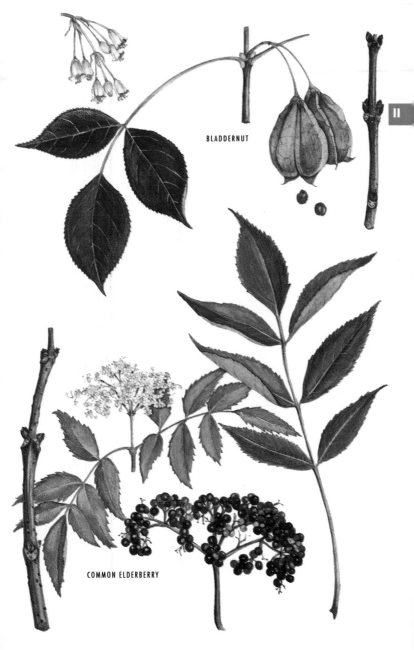

BLADDERNUT

COMMON ELDERBERRY

PLATE 8

TREES WITH OPPOSITE FEATHER-COMPOUND LEAVES: ASHES I

Leaflets mostly stalked. Twigs fine-hairy or smooth. Fruits dry, one-seeded, single-winged. None occurs primarily in southern swamps.

SPECIES AND REMARKS	Leaflets per leaf	Leaflets toothed	Twigs hairy	Seeds plump[1]	Fruits winged to base	Trunk[2]	Habitat[3]	Major distribution[4]	Text page
BLUE ASH *Fraxinus quadrangulata* Twigs four-lined or square in cross section.	7–11	+	–	–	+	S	U	C	194
WHITE ASH[5] *F. americana* Leaf scars notched; seed stout.	5–9	±	±	+	–	F	U	w	195
BLACK ASH *F. nigra* No leaflet stalks. Buds blackish.[6]	7–11	+	–	–	+	F/S	L	N	195
GREEN ASH[7] *F. pennsylvanica* Leaflet stalks narrowly winged; seed very slim.	7–9	±	±	+	–	F	L	w	196

[1] Seeds raised above the flat wing.
[2] F = furrowed, S = scaly.
[3] Habitat: L = lowland, U = upland.
[4] C = North-central states, N = northern U.S. and s. Canada, w = widespread.
[5] Including the velvet-twig form sometimes called Biltmore Ash.
[6] Brown in other species.
[7] Red and Green ashes (once separated) have been combined as 1 species.

PLATE 8

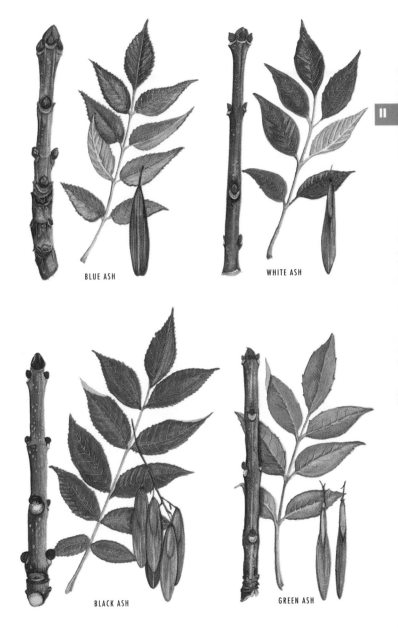

BLUE ASH

WHITE ASH

BLACK ASH

GREEN ASH

PLATE 9

TREES WITH OPPOSITE FEATHER-COMPOUND LEAVES: ASHES II AND ASHLEAF MAPLE

Leaflets stalked.
Twigs hairy or not.
Fruits winged.

SPECIES AND REMARKS	Leaflets per leaf	Leaflets toothed	Twigs hairy	Seeds plump[1]	Fruits winged to base	Mostly southern swamps[2]	Trunk[3]	Major distribution[4]	Text page
PUMPKIN ASH *Fraxinus profunda* Leaf scars U-shaped, seed plump.	7–9	–	+	+	–[5]	+	F/S	S	196
CAROLINA ASH *F. caroliniana* Leaf scars shield-shaped, seed flat.	5–7	+	+	–	+[6]	+	S	S	197
ASHLEAF MAPLE *Acer negundo* Twigs green or purplish, hairless.	3–5	+	–	+	–[7]	–	F	w	197

[1] Raised above the flat wing.
[2] Trunk bases of swamp trees often swollen.
[3] F = furrowed, S = scaly.
[4] S = southern, w = widespread.
[5] Seeds not extending to midlength of fruit.
[6] Seeds extending beyond midlength of fruit; fruits often three-winged.
[7] Fruits are double maple "keys" rather than single-winged ash fruits.

PLATE 9

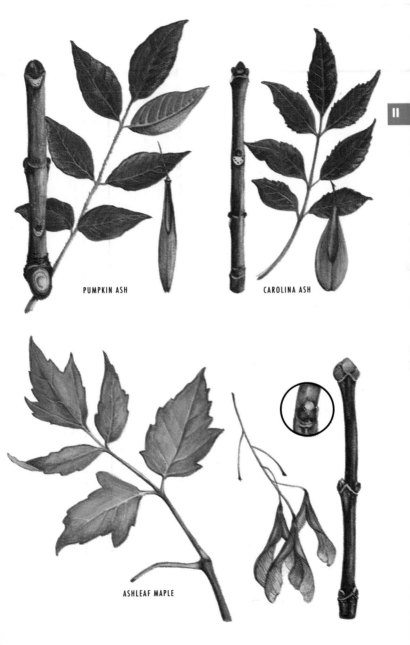

PUMPKIN ASH

CAROLINA ASH

ASHLEAF MAPLE

PLATE 10

TREES WITH OPPOSITE OR WHORLED HEART-SHAPED LEAVES: PRINCESS-TREE AND CATALPAS

Trees with large, opposite or whorled heart-shaped leaves. Twigs stout; central end buds lacking; leaf scars large and circular, bundle scars in ellipse. Flowers showy; fruits woody, hollow, many-seeded. Widespread from distribution centers.

SPECIES AND REMARKS	Leaves per node	Leaves long-pointed	Buds per leaf scar	Pith[1]	Flowers[2]	Fruits[3]	Major distribution[4]	Text page
PRINCESS-TREE *Paulownia tomentosa* Trunk with shiny ridges.	2	–	1+	C	PC	P	S	200
NORTHERN CATALPA *Catalpa speciosa* Trunk bark scaly; blossoms 2¼" across.	2–3	+	1	S	WO[5]	C	C	201
SOUTHERN CATALPA *Catalpa bignonioides* Trunk bark scaly; blossoms 1"–2" across.	2–3	–	1	S	WC	C	S	201

[1] C = chambered or hollow; S = solid, white.
[2] P = purple; W = white; C = in crowded cluster; O = in open clusters.
[3] C = cigar-shaped, 8"–18" long; P = pecan-shaped, 1¼" long.
[4] C = north-central states, S = South.
[5] Illustrated.

PLATE 10

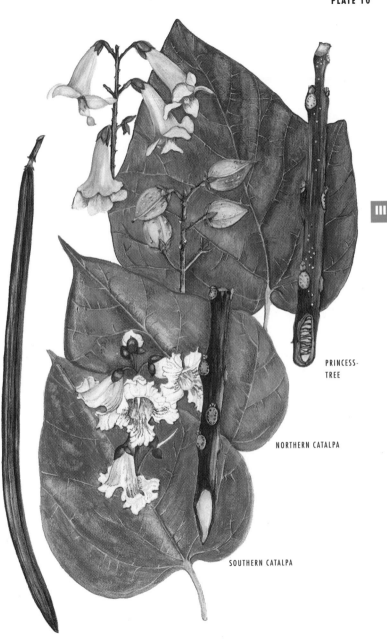

PRINCESS-
TREE

NORTHERN CATALPA

SOUTHERN CATALPA

PLATE 11

TREES WITH OPPOSITE LOBED LEAVES: MAPLES

Our only trees with opposite, three- to five-lobed leaves.[1] Foliage mostly sharp-toothed. Sycamore and Norway Maples may spread from plantings.

SPECIES AND REMARKS	Number of leaf lobes	Leaves whitened beneath	Leaves mostly less than 4" long	Buds with only 2 scales[2]	Extra buds often clustered	Fruit length (inches)[3]	Trunk bark whitish	Major distribution[4]	Text page
STRIPED MAPLE *Acer pensylvanicum* Bark green; thin white stripes.	3	–	–	+	–	¾–1	–	N	202
EASTERN MOUNTAIN MAPLE *A. spicatum* Bark brown; twigs velvety-hairy.	3	–	–	+	–	½–¾	–	N	203
RED MAPLE *A. rubrum* Shallow V leaf sinuses.	3(–5)	+	–	–	+	½–1	±	w	203
SILVER MAPLE *A. saccharinum* Deep U leaf sinuses.	5	+	–	–	+	1½–3	–	w	204
(SYCAMORE MAPLE *A. pseudoplatanus*) Leaf teeth blunt.	5	+	–	–	–	1–2	–	w	205
SUGAR MAPLE *A. saccharum* Leaf edges firm, sharply toothed.	5	–	–	–	–	¾–1¼	–	N	206
BLACK MAPLE *A. nigrum* Leaf edges droop; more wavy.	5	–	–	–	–	¾–1¼	–	N	207
(NORWAY MAPLE *A. platanoides*) Milky leafstalk sap.	5(–7)	–	–	–	–	1–2	–	w	205
FLORIDA MAPLE *A. barbatum*[5] Center leaf lobe narrowed at base.	3(–5)	+	+	–	–	½–¾	+	S	208
CHALK MAPLE *A. leucoderme*[5] Center leaf lobe wide at the base.	3(–5)	–	+	–	–	¾–1¼	+	S	208

[1] Cranberry Viburnum (*Viburnum trilobum*), a shrub, has three-lobed maplelike leaves, but these are hairy beneath and have leafstalk glands.
[2] And buds stalked. Also fruits in narrow clusters at the twig ends; in other species fruit clusters arise from points along the twig.
[3] A fruit is half of the winged pair of "keys."
[4] N = North, S = South, w = widespread.
[5] Low southern trees with small, few-toothed leaves.

PLATE 11

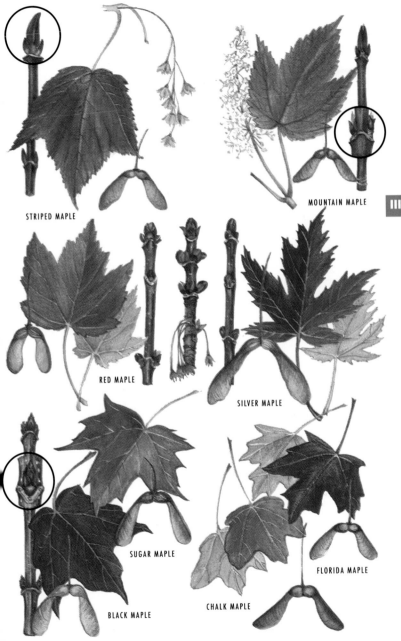

STRIPED MAPLE

MOUNTAIN MAPLE

III

RED MAPLE

SILVER MAPLE

SUGAR MAPLE

BLACK MAPLE

CHALK MAPLE

FLORIDA MAPLE

PLATE 12

TREES WITH OPPOSITE SIMPLE FINE-TOOTHED LEAVES

SPECIES AND REMARKS	Twig tips spiny	Leaves long-pointed	Leafstalks often winged	Leaves shiny above	Buds with only 2 scales	Bundle scars per leaf scar	Major distribution[1]	Text page
COMMON BUCKTHORN *Rhamnus cathartica* Veins follow leaf edges, inner bark yellow, spur branches common.	+	–	–	–	–	3	W	208
BURNINGBUSH *Euonymus atropurpureus* Twigs green, four-lined.	–	–	–	–	–	1	M	209
SWAMP FORESTIERA *Forestiera acuminata* Buds globular, often double.	±	+	–	–	–	1	S	209
RUSTY BLACKHAW *Viburnum rufidulum* Buds and midrib red-hairy, leaves shiny.	–	–	+	+	+	3	S	211
SMOOTH BLACKHAW *V. prunifolium* Buds brown, short, not hairy; leaves dull.	–	–	–	–	+	3	M	211
NANNYBERRY *B. lentago* Buds long, slender, brown or gray.	–	+	+	–	+	3	N	212
(BASKET WILLOW *Salix purpurea***)** Most leaves alternate; see Pl. 39.	–	–	–	–	–	3	N	213

[1] M = midlatitudes, N = North, S = South, w= widespread.

PLATE 12

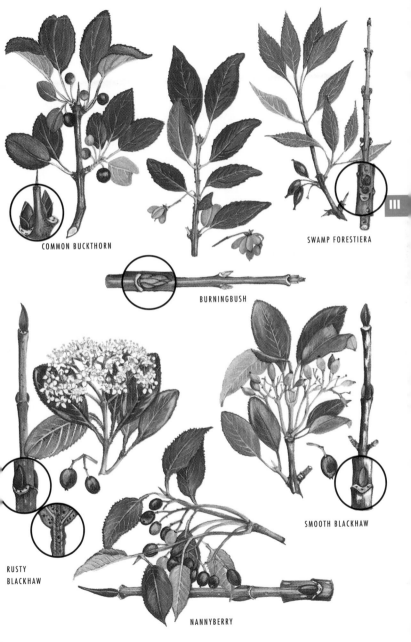

COMMON BUCKTHORN

SWAMP FORESTIERA

III

BURNINGBUSH

RUSTY
BLACKHAW

SMOOTH BLACKHAW

NANNYBERRY

PLATE 13

TREES WITH OPPOSITE SIMPLE LEAVES, NOT TOOTHED AND MOSTLY LEATHERY

Species of the southern Coastal Plain and seacoasts. Most have evergreen leaves with edges rolled under. See also Pl. 14. In Fla., see also Pls. F-13A and F-13B.

SPECIES AND REMARKS	Leaves leathery, evergreen	Leaves blunt	Leaves wedge-based	Leafstalks with glands	Leaf length (inches)	Twigs ringed	Bud scales per bud	Bundle scars	Seacoasts only	Mature fruit color[1]	Text page
SMALL-LEAF VIBURNUM *Viburnum obovatum*[2] Leaves short-stalked, fine-dotted; buds short.	±	+	+	−	1–2	−	2	3	−	BK	213
POSSUMHAW VIBURNUM *V. nudum*[2] Buds slender; see Pl. 14.	−	−	±	−	3–5	−	2	3	−	BU	213
DEVILWOOD *Osmanthus americanus* Buds small, twigs whitish.	+	−	+	−	2–6	−	2	1	−	BU	214
FLORIDA FORESTIERA *Forestiera segregata* Flowers in leaf angles.	±	+	+	−	1–2	−	4+	1	±	BK	214
RED MANGROVE *Rhizophora mangle*[4] Deep shallows; arching prop roots; see Fig. 10.	+	±	±	−	2–6	+	2	3	+	BR	215
BLACK MANGROVE *Avicennia germinans* Tidal shallows; breather roots erect; see Fig. 11.	+	+	+	−	2–6	+	2	1	+	G	216
WHITE MANGROVE *Laguncularia racemosa*[4] Shorelines; erect breather roots few.	+	+	−	+	2–3	−	0	1	+	R	216
(CAMPHOR-TREE *Cinnamomum camphora*) Crushed leaves with camphor odor; see Pl. 46.	+	−	±	−	3–7	−	0	2	−	D	217

Note: Leaf length includes stalk. Names in parentheses are of similar trees not illustrated here; see text.

1 BK = black, BR = brown, BU = blue, D =dark, G = green, R = red.
2 Buds 2-scaled; leaves fine-toothed or wavy-edged.
3 Use lens.
4 Fla. only.

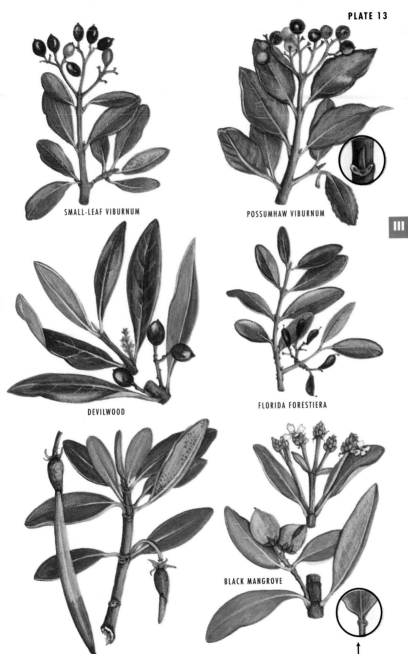

PLATE 13

SMALL-LEAF VIBURNUM

POSSUMHAW VIBURNUM

III

DEVILWOOD

FLORIDA FORESTIERA

BLACK MANGROVE

RED MANGROVE

WHITE MANGROVE

PLATE 14

TREES WITH OPPOSITE SIMPLE LEAVES NEITHER TOOTHED NOR LEATHERY

Pith mostly white. In the South, Crapemyrtle (Pl. 44) also may have some opposite leaves.

SPECIES AND REMARKS	Veins follow leaf edges	Leaves often in 3's, 4's	Leaves more than 2½" long	Bud scales, more than 2	Bundle scars	Aquatic habitat	Major distribution[1]	Text page
ROUGHLEAF DOGWOOD *Cornus frummondii* Pith brown; twigs red-brown; leaves rough.	+	–	±	–	3	–	E	218
FLOWERING DOGWOOD *Cornus florida* Pith white; twigs purple.	+	–	+	–	3	–	E	218
(STIFF DOGWOOD *Cornus stricta*) End buds in pairs; pith white.	+	–	±	–	3	±	S	219
(POSSUMHAW VIBURNUM *Viburnum nudum*)[2] End buds single, slender.	–	–	+	–	3	–	S	213
BUTTONBUSH *Cephalanthus occidentalis* Flowers/fruits ball-shaped.[5]	–	+	+	±[3]	1	+	E	220
(PINCKNEYA *Pinckneya pubens*) Leaves hairy; twigs ringed.	–	+	+	±	1	±	S	220
FRINGETREE *Chionanthus virginicus* Leaves hairless; twigs not ringed.	–	–	+	+	1	–	S	221
CALIFORNIA PRIVET *Ligustrum ovalifolium* Twigs hairless; buds many-scaled.	–	–	–	+	1	–	S	222
(JAPANESE PRIVET *Ligustrum japonicum*) Twigs hairless; buds few-scaled.	–	–	–	+	1	–	S	222
(CHINESE PRIVET *Ligustrum sinense*) Twigs fine-hairy.	–	–	–	+	1	–	S	222
SILVER BUFFALOBERRY *Shepherdia argentea* Leaves and twigs silver-scaly.[4, 5]	–	–	–	–	1	–	W	223

Note: Leaf length includes stalk. Names in parentheses indicate that the trees are not shown here but are similar; see text.
[1] E = East, widespread; S = South; W = West.
[2] See Pl. 13 and text.
[3] Buds often embedded in bark; bud scales indistinct; flowers/fruits replace central end bud.
[4] Side twigs often spine-tipped.
[5] Pith brown.

❧

PLATE 14

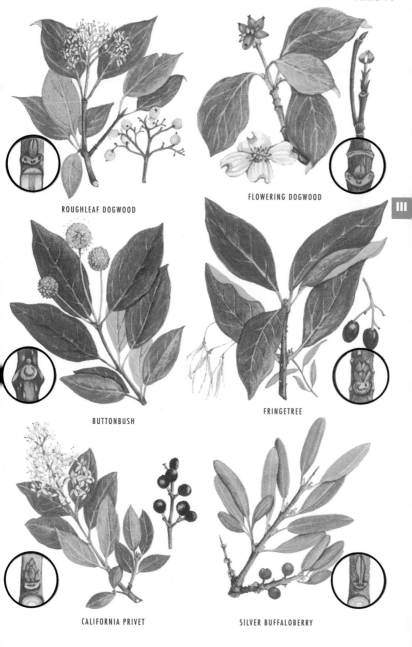

ROUGHLEAF DOGWOOD

FLOWERING DOGWOOD

III

BUTTONBUSH

FRINGETREE

CALIFORNIA PRIVET

SILVER BUFFALOBERRY

PLATE 15

THORNY TREES WITH ALTERNATE FEATHER-COMPOUND LEAVES

See also drawings in text (Fig. 14, p. 228); in Fla. see Pl. F-15.

SPECIES AND REMARKS	Thorns paired	Leaves twice-compound	Leaflets toothed	Crushed leaves aromatic	Bundle scars	Flower color[1]	Bean pods (inches)[2]	Major distribution[3]	Text page
HONEYLOCUST *Gleditsia triacanthos[4]* Uplands. Thorns 2"–10", often branched.	–	±	±	–	3	W	8–18	M	226
WATER LOCUST *G. aquatica* Lowlands. Thorns 3" ±, mostly unbranched.	–	±	±	–	3	G	1–2	C	227
NORTHERN PRICKLY-ASH *Zanthoxylum americanum* Trunk not knobby; buds red-hairy.	+	–	+	+	3	G	–	N	229
(SOUTHERN PRICKLY-ASH *Z. clava-herculis[5]*) Trunk with thorny knobs; buds dark, hairless.	±	–	+	+	3	G	–	S	229
BLACK LOCUST *Robinia pseudoacacia* Twigs/pods hairless; buds hidden.	+	–	–	–	3	W	2–6	W	230
CLAMMY LOCUST *R. viscosa* Twigs and pods sticky-hairy.	+	–	–	–	3	P	2–3	A	231
HERCULES-CLUB *Aralia spinosa[5]* Leaves huge (2'–4'long), leafstalks and trunk thorny.	–	+	+	–	20+	w	–	S	233

Note: Leaf length includes stalk.
[1] G = greenish, P = pink, W = white.
[2] Minus means species not in the bean family.
[3] A = Appalachians; C = Coastal Plain; M = Midwest; N = North; S = South; w = widespread.
[4] A thornless variety widely planted.
[5] Both of these species are known as Hercules-club. *A. spinosa* is also called Devil's Walking-stick.

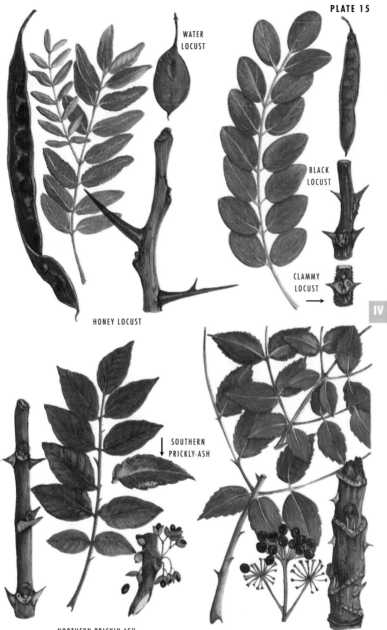

PLATE 15

WATER
LOCUST

BLACK
LOCUST

CLAMMY
LOCUST

IV

HONEY LOCUST

SOUTHERN
PRICKLY-ASH

NORTHERN PRICKLY-ASH

HERCULES-CLUB

PLATE 16

WALNUTS AND SIMILAR TREES

Leaves alternate and feather-compound, with 7–14 toothed or glandular leaflets. Most are plants of Canada, the northern states, and the high Appalachians. Walnuts and Tree-of-heaven are widespread in distribution.

SPECIES AND REMARKS	Leaves toothed, no glands	Mature pith chambered	Leaf scars narrow	Bundle scars	Bud type[1]	End bud true	Fruit type[2]	Fruit length (inches)	Text page
BLACK WALNUT *Juglans nigra* Upper edge of leaf scar not hairy.	+	+	−	3	WW	+	BN	2	233
BUTTERNUT *J. cinerea* Upper edge of leaf scar hairy.	+	+	−	3	WW	+	ON	2	235
TREE-OF-HEAVEN *Ailanthus altissima* Basal leaf glands. Widespread weed tree.	−	−	−	9±	BW	−	WS	1½	236
AMERICAN MOUNTAIN-ASH *Sorbus americana* Leaflets narrow, long-pointed.	+	−	+	5	RG	+	OB	¼	237
SHOWY MOUNTAIN-ASH *Sorbus decora* Leaflets broad, short-pointed.	+	−	+	5	RG	+	RB	⅜	238
EUROPEAN MOUNTAIN-ASH *Sorbus aucuparia* Leaflets small, white-hairy.	+	−	+	5	WW	+	RB	⅜	238

1 BW = brown-woolly; RG = red-gummy; WW = white-woolly.
2 BN = ball-shaped nut; ON = oblong nut; OB = orange, berrylike; RB = red, berrylike; WS = dry winged seed.

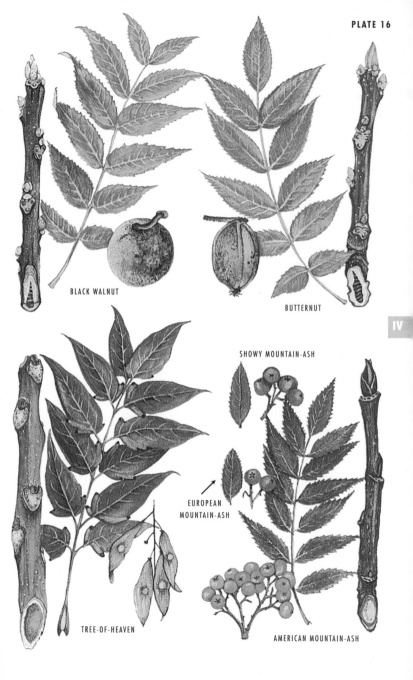

PLATE 16

BLACK WALNUT

BUTTERNUT

IV

SHOWY MOUNTAIN-ASH

EUROPEAN
MOUNTAIN-ASH

TREE-OF-HEAVEN

AMERICAN MOUNTAIN-ASH

PLATE 17

HICKORIES I: PECANS

Trees with alternate, toothed, feather-compound leaves. Husks of nuts four-parted. These species have somewhat hairy twigs and buds with 4–6 scales, paired and mostly yellow.

SPECIES AND REMARKS	Leaflets per leaf	End buds more than ½" long	Outer bud scales fall early[1]	Mature bark shaggy	Major distribution[2]	Text page
PECAN *Carya illinoensis* Buds yellow, hairy.	9–17	–	–	–	M	239
BITTERNUT HICKORY *C. cordiformis* Buds yellow, powdery.	7–11	+	–	–	w	240
WATER HICKORY *C. aquatica* Buds brown with yellow glands.	9–17	–	–	+	S	240
NUTMEG HICKORY *C. myristiciformis* Buds yellow- or brown-hairy.	5–9	–	–	±	S	241

[1] Buds look quite smooth after scales drop.
[2] M = Midwest, S = South, w = widespread.

PLATE 17

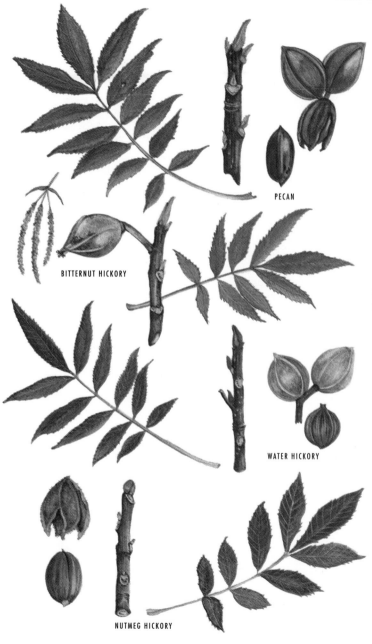

PECAN

BITTERNUT HICKORY

IV

WATER HICKORY

NUTMEG HICKORY

PLATE 18

HICKORIES II: SHAGBARKS

Trees with alternate, toothed, feather-compound leaves. Husks of nuts four-parted. These species have end buds more than ½" long with scales overlapping plus twigs and nut husks (not shells) both more than ⅛" thick.

SPECIES AND REMARKS	Leaflets per leaf	Leaflets hairy	Outer bud scales fall early[1]	Twigs hairy	Mature bark shaggy	Major distribution[2]	Text page
SHAGBARK HICKORY *Carya ovata* Twigs red-brown, end bud ½"–¾" long.	5–(7)	−	−	±	+	N	241
SHELLBARK HICKORY *C. laciniosa* Twigs pale orange, end bud ¾"–⅞" long.	7–(9)	±	−	−	+	C	242
MOCKERNUT HICKORY *C. tomentosa* Twigs red-brown, woolly; end bud ⅝"–1 " long.	7–(9)	+	+	+	±	S	243

[1] Buds look quite smooth after scales drop in autumn.
[2] C = central, N = northern and central states, S = southern (but north to s. New England).

PLATE 18

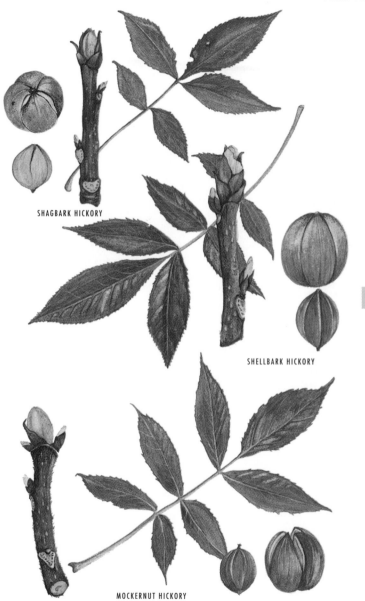

SHAGBARK HICKORY

SHELLBARK HICKORY

IV

MOCKERNUT HICKORY

PLATE 19

HICKORIES III: PIGNUTS

Trees with alternate, toothed, feather-compound leaves. Husks of nuts four-parted. These species have end buds less than ¼" long with scales overlapping, slender twigs, and thin nut husks.

SPECIES AND REMARKS	Leaflets per leaf	Outer bud scales fall early[1]	Twigs hairy	Mature bark shaggy	Major distribution[2]	Text page
SAND HICKORY *Carya pallida* End buds less than ¼" long, yellowish.	7–(9)	−	±	±	M	243
PIGNUT HICKORY *C. glabra* End buds ⅜"–½" long; silky.	5–(7)	+	−	−	W	244
BLACK HICKORY *C. texana* Buds rusty-hairy. Not in Fla.	(5)–7	+	+	−	O	245
SCRUB HICKORY *C. floridana* Buds rusty-hairy. Cen. Fla.	5–(7)	−	+	−	F	245

[1] Buds look quite smooth after scales drop in autumn.
[2] F = Fla. only, M = midlatitude states, O = Ozark region, w = widespread.

PLATE 19

SAND HICKORY

PIGNUT HICKORY

IV

BLACK HICKORY

SCRUB HICKORY

PLATE 20

SUMACS AND RELATIVES

Leaves alternate, feather-compound with 7–31 leaflets, toothed or not. Four red-fruited *Rhus* species have leaf scars U-shaped enclosing buds, buds hairy and mostly hidden when leaves present. Fruits red-hairy in dense, upright clusters. Two somewhat similar and related **poisonous**[1] species with 3–7 leaflets are also compared here (see Fig. 4, p. 17).[2]

SPECIES AND REMARKS	Midrib winged	Leaflets toothed	Leaves leathery, evergreen	Twigs densely hairy	Twigs flat-sided	Fruit type[3]	Major distribution[4]	Text page
WINGED SUMAC *Rhus copallina* Leaflets ¾" wide, short-pointed.	+	–	–	+	–	R	W	245
PRAIRIE SUMAC *R. lanceolata* Leaflets less than ¼" wide.	+	–	–	+	–	R	T	246
STAGHORN SUMAC *R. typhina*	–	+	–	+	–	R	N	246
SMOOTH SUMAC *R. glabra*	–	+	–	–	+	R	W	247
(POISON-SUMAC *Toxicodendron vernix*[1]**)** See Fig. 4, p. 17.	–	–	–	–	–	W	W	247
(FLORIDA POISONWOOD *Metopium toxiferum*[1]**)** Leaves triangular; black spots.	–	–	+	–	–	Y	F	248

[1] Two species contain chemicals that irritate the skin and eyes (see p. 247–248).

[2] All on this plate are members of the cashew family.

[3] R = red-hairy in dense upright clusters; W = white, small, smooth, spherical; Y = yellow-orange, ¼" long, smooth, oval.

[4] F = Fla. only; N = northern states and nearby Canada; T = Texas or nearby (see p. 245); w = widespread. All species occur mainly in old fields and forest openings.

PLATE 20

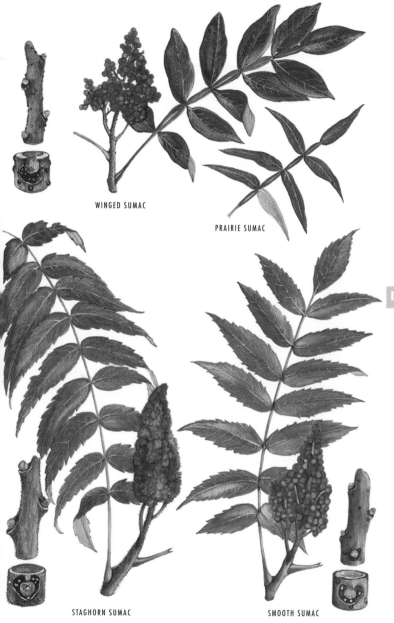

WINGED SUMAC

PRAIRIE SUMAC

IV

STAGHORN SUMAC

SMOOTH SUMAC

PLATE 21

TREES WITH ALTERNATE ONCE-COMPOUND LEAVES NOT TOOTHED

Twigs hairless; buds often several at a leaf scar; end bud false. Flowers white or greenish white. Trunks mostly grooved or scaly. See also Poison -sumac (Fig. 4, p. 17), Pl. 20, and thornless form of Honey Locust, Pl. 15. In Fla., see Pls. F-21A and F-21B.

SPECIES AND REMARKS

	Leaflets per leaf	Leaf scars U-shaped[1]	Buds hairy	Bundle scars	Fruit type[2]	Major distribution[3]	Text page
HOPTREE *Ptelea trifoliata* Buds silvery.	3	+	+	3	C	w	249
YELLOWWOOD *Cladrastis kentukea* Leaflets alternate; wood yellow; trunk bark smooth, gray.	5–11	+	+	5	P	M	249
WINGLEAF SOAPBERRY *Sapindus saponaria* Midrib usually winged, but see p. 250.	6–12	–	–	3	B	F	250
WESTERN SOAPBERRY *Sapindus drummondii* Midrib not winged.	8–18	–	±	3	B	O	251
TEXAS SOPHORA *Sophora affinia* Fruits "bearded."	13–15	±	+	3	P	T	251

[1] Buds mostly hidden when leaves present.
[2] C = circular, papery; P = peapod; B = berrylike.
[3] F = Fla. and se. Ga.; M = Midwestern states; O = Ozark region; T = Tex., etc.; w = widespread.

PLATE 21

HOPTREE

YELLOWWOOD

IV

WESTERN SOAPBERRY

WINGLEAF SOAPBERRY

TEXAS SOPHORA

PLATE 22

THORNLESS TREES WITH TWICE-COMPOUND LEAVES

Mostly southern species with leaves large, twigs hairless, and end bud false. See also thornless form of Honey Locust, Pl. 15. In Fla., see also Pl. F-22.

SPECIES AND REMARKS	Leaflets toothed	Leaves more than 12" long	Minor leaflets more than ¾" long	Minor leaflets blunt	Pairs of major leaflets	Twigs stout[1]	Flower color[2]	Major distribution[3]	Text page
CHINABERRY *Melia azedarach* Buds fuzzy, not sunken.	+	+	+	−	4–6	+	L	S	252
COFFEETREE *Gymnocladus dioica* Buds silky, sunk in bark.	−	+	+	−	5–9	+	W	M	252
LEBBEK *Albizia lebbeck* Pods more than 1" wide, seeds 8–10.	−	±	+	+	2–4	−	Y	F	253
SILKTREE *Albizia julibrissin* Pods slender, more than 15 seeds.	−	−	−	−	9–12	−	P	S	254

[1] Also leaf scars large, buds hairy, and trunk dark and rough.
[2] L = lavender, P = pink, W = white, Y = yellow.
[3] F = s. Fla. including Keys; M = midwestern states and s. Ontario; S = southern states.

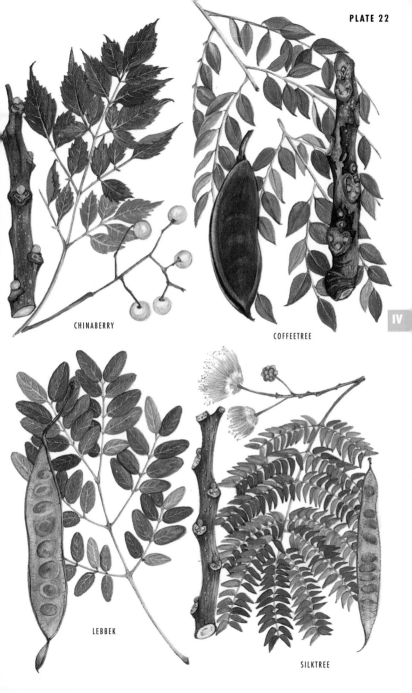

PLATE 22

CHINABERRY

COFFEETREE

IV

LEBBEK

SILKTREE

PLATE 23

THORNY TREES WITH ALTERNATE TOOTHED LEAVES

Long slender spines in hawthorns; spine-tipped short branches in crabapples and plums; thorns paired in Jujube. Spur branches present. Bundle scars 3 (1 in Jujube). Flowers white to pink. In Fla., see also Lime (Fig. 16, p. 263) and Governor's-plum (Pl. F-46C). For thornless relatives see Pls. 37 and 43.

SPECIES AND REMARKS	Bark with horizontal lines[1]	Broken twigs with sour odor[2]	Leafstalks with glands	Leaf teeth sharp	Leaf bases wedge-shaped	Twigs hairy	Major distribution[3]	Text page
HAWTHORNS[4] *Crataegus* species Spines long, mostly without buds.	−	−	−	+	±	−	w	256
AMERICAN CRABAPPLE *Malus coronaria* Fruits 1¼"–2". North-central.	−	−	−	+	−	−	M	257
NARROWLEAF CRABAPPLE *Malus angustifolia* Fruits less than 1". Southeast.	−	−	−	+	+	±	S	258
(PRAIRIE CRABAPPLE *Malus ioensis*) Twigs, leaves woolly. Midwest.	−	−	−	+	−	+	M	258
AMERICAN PLUM *Prunus americana* Bud red-brown, ⅛".	+	+	−	+	±	±	M	259
(BULLACE PLUM *Prunus institia*) See Garden Plum, Pl. 37.	+	+	+	−	±	+	N	260
(CANADA PLUM *Prunus nigra*) Buds gray-black, ³⁄₁₆".	+	+	+	−	+	−	S	260
CHICKASAW PLUM *Prunus angustifolia* Leaf scars raised; twigs reddish.	+	+	+	−	+	−	S	260
(JUJUBE *Ziziphus jujuba*) Thorns paired, one larger; leaves fan-veined.	−	−	−	−	−	+	S	260

Note: Names in parentheses indicate that the trees are not shown here but are similar; see text.
[1] These species also have false end buds and fruits with single seeds.
[2] The sour (almond) odor is weak in plums. It is difficult to describe but once learned is helpful in identifying cherries and (sometimes) plums.
[3] M = Midwest, N = North, S = South, w = widespread.
[4] A complex and difficult group whose species are poorly defined; see p. 256.

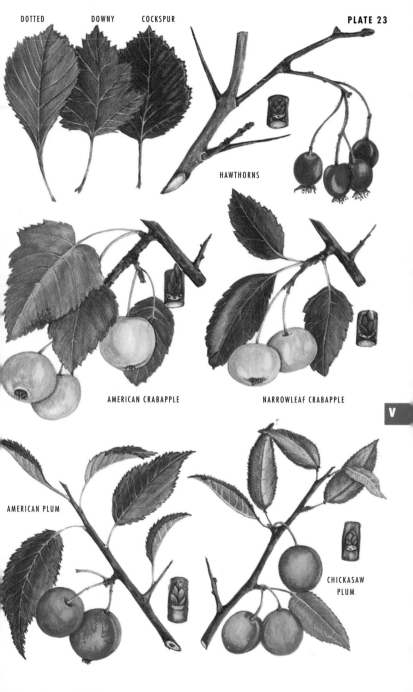

DOTTED   DOWNY   COCKSPUR

PLATE 23

HAWTHORNS

AMERICAN CRABAPPLE

NARROWLEAF CRABAPPLE

AMERICAN PLUM

CHICKASAW PLUM

V

PLATE 24

THORNY TREES WITH ALTERNATE LEAVES NOT TOOTHED

Thorns single. Spur branches with clustered leaves often present. Southern species.

SPECIES AND REMARKS	Sap milky[1]	Leaves wedge-based	Leaves blunt-tipped	Leaves velvety-hairy	Leafstalks winged[2]	Bundle scars per leaf scar	Flowers[3]	Fruits[4]	Fla. only,[5] evergreen	Text page
GUM (WOOLLY) BUMELIA *Bumelia lanuginosa* Leaves red- or gray-woolly.	+	+	+	+	−	3	C	B	−	261
(TOUGH BUMELIA *Bumelia tenax*) Leaves yellow- or white-silky.[6]	+	+	+	+	−	3	C	B	−	261
BUCKTHORN BUMELIA *Bumelia lycioides* Leaves 3"–6" long.	+	+	−	−	−	3	C	G	−	262
(SAFFRON-PLUM BUMELIA *Bumelia celastrina*) Leaves ½"–1½". Cen. & s. Fla., s. Tex. Twigs thorn-tipped.	+	+	+	−	−	3	C	B	C	262
OSAGE-ORANGE *Maclura pomifera* Leaves long-pointed.	+	−	−	−	−	1–5	B	GW	−	262
TALLOWWOOD *Ximenia americana* Parasitic on tree roots, evergreen.	−	±	±	−	−	1	C	YP	S	263
(LIME OR KEY LIME *Citrus aurantifolia*)[7] Fruit pulp green. See Fig. 16.	−	−	−	−	N	1	S	GO	S	264
(SOUR ORANGE *Citrus aurantium*)[7] Fruit sweet, core hollow; thorns few.	−	−	−	−	B	1	S	YO	C	264
(SWEET ORANGE *Citrus sinensis*)[7] Fruit acidic, core solid.	−	−	−	−	N	1	S	YO	G	264

[1] Try broken leafstalks or twigs.
[2] Leaves evergreen, gland-dotted (use lens), aromatic when crushed, leafstalks winged, twigs green; B = wings ¼" broad, N = wings narrow.
[3] B = ball-shaped, green; C = clustered, white; S = single or paired, white.
[4] B = berrylike, black; G = green; GO = green, orangelike; GW = green, coarse, much wrinkled; YO = yellow or green, orangelike; YP = yellow, plumlike.
[5] Fla. only = species not found in other states (but G = also Ga.); C = cen. Fla. and southward; S = southern three counties and/or Keys.
[6] Russian-olive (p. 33), seldom growing wild in the East, has silver-scaled leaves and twigs and is sometimes spiny.
[7] Asian origin, cultivated, escaped to wild; leaves may be wavy-edged.

PLATE 24

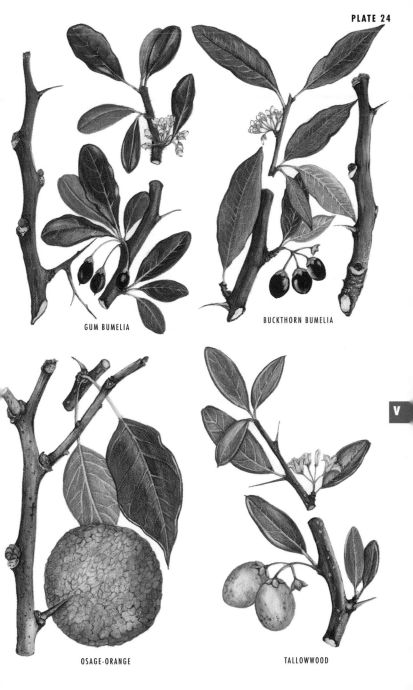

GUM BUMELIA

BUCKTHORN BUMELIA

V

OSAGE-ORANGE

TALLOWWOOD

PLATE 25

TREES WITH ALTERNATE FAN-LOBED LEAVES

Some or all leaves lobed.[1] Even unlobed leaves have 3–5 main veins meeting near their bases. Leaf bases mostly heart-shaped or broad. See also Chinese Parasoltree (p. 267)[7], White Poplar (Pl. 27), plus Papaya and Castorbean (p. 269); the latter two occur as trees only in tropical Florida. See also White Poplar, Pl. 27.

SPECIES AND REMARKS	Leaf lobes per leaf[1]	Sap milky[2]	Leaves toothed	Leaves sandpapery	Leaf undersides[3]	Leaf bases uneven	Crushed leaves/buds spicy	Twigs ringed[4]	Bud scales per bud	Major distribution[5]	Text page
TULIPTREE *Liriodendron tulipifera* Leaves notched; pith chambered.	4	–	–	–	N	–	+	+	2	E	265
SASSAFRAS *Sassafras albidum* Twigs green, forked.	1–3	–	–	–	N/V	–	+	–	4	E	265
EASTERN SYCAMORE *Platanus occidentalis* Leafstalks cover buds; trunk flaking.	3–5	–	+	–	N	–	–	+	1	E	266
SWEETGUM *Liquidambar styraciflua* Branchlets often corky-winged.	5	–	+	–	N	–	+	–	5–6	S	267
PAPER-MULBERRY *Broussonetia papyrifera* Twigs rough-hairy.[6]	1–5	+	+	+	V	+	–	–	2–3	w	268
WHITE MULBERRY *Morus alba* Buds reddish, pressed against twig; leaf lobes rounded; fruits cylindrical.	1–5	+	+	–	N	±	–	–	5–6	w	269
RED MULBERRY *M. rubra* Buds greenish, spreading, scales dark-edged; leaf lobes pointed; fruits elongate.	1–3	+	+	+	H	–	–	–	5–6	E	269

[1] In Sassafras, Parasoltree, and mulberries, some (rarely all) leaves not lobed.
[2] Try breaking leafstalks or twigs.
[3] H = hairy, N = not hairy, V = velvety.
[4] Stipule scars encircle twigs beneath each bud.
[5] E = widespread, eastern U.S.; F = tree-sized only in Fla.; N = North, principally northeastern states; S = South; w = widespread.
[6] Thin woody pith partitions near each bud (cut twig lengthwise); fruits round.
[7] Leaves with 3–5 lobes, narrow sinuses, no teeth; twigs green; buds brown-hairy.

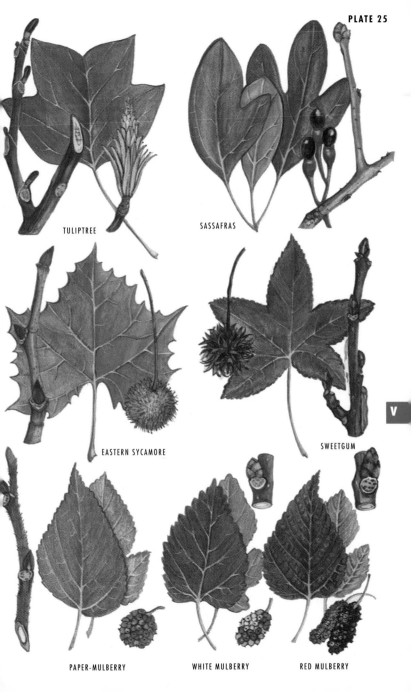

PLATE 25

TULIPTREE

SASSAFRAS

EASTERN SYCAMORE

SWEETGUM

V

PAPER-MULBERRY

WHITE MULBERRY

RED MULBERRY

PLATE 26

TREES WITH ALTERNATE FAN-VEINED AND TRIANGULAR OR HEART-SHAPED LEAVES

Leaves mostly heart-shaped or triangular with 3–5 main veins meeting at their bases. Leaf bases heart-shaped or uneven. End bud false.
Two species are evergreen and occur only in Fla.; see also poplars (Pl. 27) and Camphortree (Pl. 46).

SPECIES AND REMARKS	Leaf length (inches)	Leaves toothed	Leaf-tip shape[1]	Leaves sandpapery above	Leaves hairy beneath	Visible bud scales[2]	Bundle scars[2]	Inner bark fibrous	Pith chambered	Major distribution[3]	Text page
FLORIDA TREMA *Trema micrantha* Flowers greenish; fruits orange.	2–5	+	L	+	+	E	E	−	−	F	270
EASTERN REDBUD *Cercis canadensis* Leaf scars hairy-fringed at top.	2–6	−	S	−	−	5–6	3	−	−	w	270
NORTHERN HACKBERRY *Celtis occidentalis* Fruits dry wrinkled.	3–5	+	L	±	−	4–5	3	−	+	N	271
DWARF HACKBERRY *Celtis tenuifolia* Fruits dry smooth; leaf veins few.	2–3	±	S	±	−	4–5	3	−	+	S	272
SOUTHERN HACKBERRY *Celtis laevigata* Fruits dry smooth.	2–4	±	L	±	−	4–5	3	−	+	S	272
SEA HIBISCUS *Hibiscus tiliaceus* 9–11 main veins, glands on veins.[4,5]	5–10	−	S/L	−	+	E	E	+	−	F	273
AMERICAN BASSWOOD *Tilia americana* Inner bark fibrous.[5] Related species on p. 273.	5–10	+	S	−	−	2–3	3+	+	−	N	273

[1] L = long-pointed, S = short-pointed.
[2] E = evergreen; no need for bud scale or bundle scar counts.
[3] F = Fla. only, N = North, S = South, w = widespread.
[4] Portiatree, p. 273, is similar but is hairless and without glands.
[5] Inner bark can be pulled away in fibrous strips when cut.

PLATE 26

FLORIDA TREMA

REDBUD

NORTHERN HACKBERRY

DWARF HACKBERRY

SOUTHERN HACKBERRY

V

SEA HIBISCUS

AMERICAN BASSWOOD

PLATE 27

POPLARS AND TALLOWTREE

Poplars mostly with triangular single-toothed leaves with 3–5 main veins meeting near the leaf base. Leafstalks quite long. Lowermost bud scale exactly above the leaf scar. Flowers and fruits in catkins. Bundle scars 3. Young bark often smooth, greenish white. Tallowtree foliage aspenlike but without leaf teeth.

SPECIES AND REMARKS

	Leafstalks flattened[1]	Leaf bases with glands	Leaf length in inches[2]	Leaf teeth large, coarse	Twigs yellowish[3]	End bud characteristics[4]	Major distribution[5]	Text page
QUAKING ASPEN *Populus tremuloides* Buds to ⅜" long, shiny. Leaves rounded.	+	–	2–6	–	–	–	N	275
(TALLOWTREE *Sapium sebiferum*) Twigs green, sap milky[6]; see Fig. 17, p. 277.	–	+	2–6	0	–	–	S	276
BIGTOOTH ASPEN *P. grandidentata* Buds more than ⅜" long, dull.	+	–	2–6	+	–	H	N	277
EASTERN COTTONWOOD *P. deltoides* Branches large; tree spreading.	+	+	2–8	+	+	G	N	277
LOMBARDY POPLAR *P. nigra* var. *italica* Branches slender; tree column-shaped.	+	–	2–8	–	+	–	w	278
BALSAM POPLAR *P. balsamifera* Leaves narrowly heart-shaped.	–	±	6–10	–	–	S	N	279
SWAMP COTTONWOOD *P. heterophylla* Leaves broadly heart-shaped.	–	–	6–10	–	–	G	S	279
WHITE POPLAR *P. alba* Leaves and twigs white-woolly.	±	–	2–6	–	–	H	w	280

[1] At least at the leaf base.
[2] As always, including leafstalk.
[3] Not dark brown or red-brown (green in Tallowtree).
[4] Especially end buds may be: G = gummy, H = hairy, S = spicy-gummy; a minus sign means "none of these."
[5] N = North, S = South, w = widespread.
[6] Milky sap poisonous internally and to eyes; fruits white ("Popcorn-tree").

PLATE 27

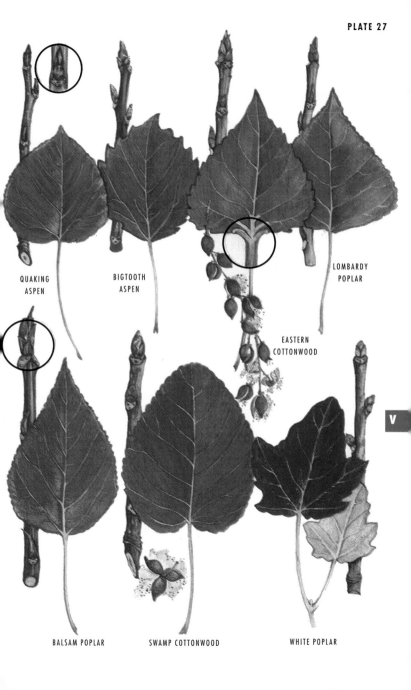

QUAKING
ASPEN

BIGTOOTH
ASPEN

LOMBARDY
POPLAR

EASTERN
COTTONWOOD

BALSAM POPLAR

SWAMP COTTONWOOD

WHITE POPLAR

V

PLATE 28

OAKS I: LEAVES FEATHER-LOBED WITH BRISTLE TIPS

End buds clustered; bundle scars more than 3. All species on this plate are "red oaks": leaves bristly, two-year acorn development, inside of acorn shell (not cup) hairy. Trunks dark. In winter see also chart, pp. 282–283.

SPECIES AND REMARKS	Leaf sinus depth[1]	Leaves thick/leathery	Leaves glossy above	Leaves hairy beneath[2]	End buds exceed ¼"	End buds sharp	End buds hairy	End buds angled	Twigs hairy	Acorn cup shape[3]	Major distribution[4]	Text page
SCARLET OAK *Quercus coccinea* Buds often white-tipped.	D	–	+	–	±	±	+	–	–	B	A	284
(PIN OAK *Quercus palustris*) Low branches slope down.	D	–	+	–	–	+	–	–	–	S	N	284
(JACK OAK *Quercus ellipsoidalis*) Northern; acorn cup conical.	D	–	+	–	–	+	–	–	–	B	N	285
(NUTTALL OAK *Quercus texana*) Southern Miss. R. valley.	D	–	+	–	–	+	+	–	–	B	S	286
(SHUMARD OAK *Quercus shumardii*) Widespread, esp. in South.	D	–	+	–	+	+	–	+	–	S	S	287
NORTHERN RED OAK *Q. rubra* Trunk dark with shiny ridges.	M	–	–	–	±	±	–	–	–	S	w	288
EASTERN BLACK OAK *Q. velutina* Twigs angled; trunk dark.	M	+	+	–	+	+	+	+	–	B	w	288
SOUTHERN RED OAK *Q. falcata* 3 main lobes, base rounded.	D	±	+	+	±	+	+	–	+	S	S	289
(CHERRYBARK OAK *Q. pagoda*)[5] Bark like Black Cherry.	D	–	+	+	±	±	+	+	+	C	S	289
(TURKEY OAK *Quercus laevis*) Leaf lobes narrow, like track.	D	+	+	–	+	+	±	–	±	B	S	290
BEAR OAK *Q. ilcifolia* Leaves small. Northeastern.	M	–	–	+	–	–	–	–	+	B	E	291
(GEORGIA OAK *Quercus georgiana*) N. Georgia/s. S. Carolina.	M	–	+	–	–	–	–	–	–	S	S	291
BLACKJACK OAK *Q. marilandica* Twigs angled; bark dark, blocky.	S	+	+	+	+	+	+	+	+	B	S	291

[1] D = deep, M = medium, S = shallow.
[2] Plus tufted vein angles.
[3] B = bowl, S = saucer.
[4] A = Appalachians, E = Northeast, N = North, S = South, w = widespread.
[5] Leaf lobes 7–11.

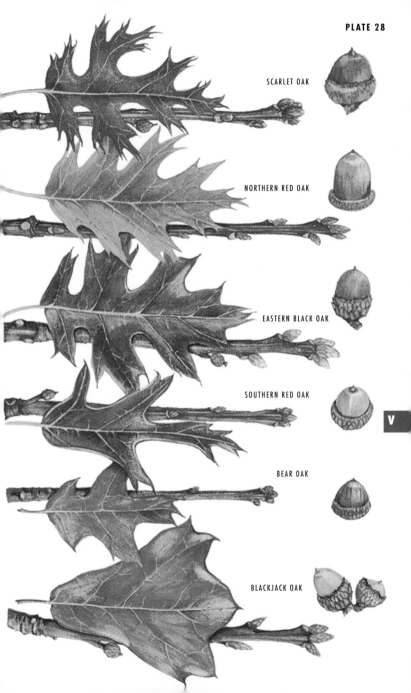

PLATE 28

SCARLET OAK

NORTHERN RED OAK

EASTERN BLACK OAK

SOUTHERN RED OAK

BEAR OAK

V

BLACKJACK OAK

PLATE 29

OAKS II: LEAVES FEATHER-LOBED WITHOUT BRISTLE TIPS

End buds clustered; bundle scars more than 3. Part of the "white oak group": These oaks lack bristle tips on the leaves and have acorns which mature in 1 summer with hairless inner acorn-shell (not cup) surfaces (see Pl. 28). Trunk bark mostly light gray. Other white oaks are on Pls. 30 and 31. In winter, also see chart, pp. 282–283.

SPECIES AND REMARKS	Depth of leaf sinus[1]	Leaves thick, leathery	Leaves whitened beneath	Leaves hairy beneath[2]	End buds more than ¼" long	End buds sharp	End buds hairy	End buds angled	Twigs hairy	Acorn cup shape[3]	Major distribution[4]	Text page
EASTERN WHITE OAK *Quercus alba* Leaves with 7–11 lobes.	M	−	+	−	−	−	−	−	−	B	E	292
POST OAK *Q. stellata* Leaves resemble a cross.	D	+	−	+	−	−	+	−	+	B	S	293
OVERCUP OAK *Q. lyrata* Cup nearly encloses nut.	M	−	+	+	−	−	−	−	−	U	S	294
BUR OAK *Q. macrocarpa* Leaves with a slender "waist," stipules among end buds.[5]	D	±	+	+	−	−	+	−	±	U	M	294
ENGLISH OAK *Q. robur* Leaves small; acorn stalks 1"–3" long; trunk dark.	M	−	−	−	+	−	−	±	−	B	P	294

1 D = deep, M = medium.
2 In addition to tufts in vein angles.
3 B = bowl shape; U = unique (see plate).
4 E = East, M = Midwest, P = spreading from plantings in North, S = South.
5 Corky wings often present on some branchlets.

PLATE 29

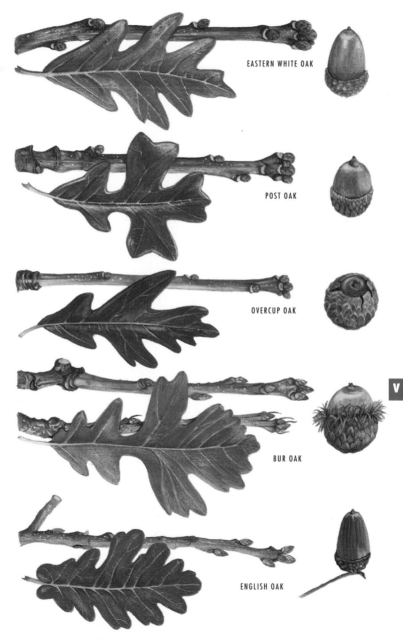

EASTERN WHITE OAK

POST OAK

OVERCUP OAK

BUR OAK

V

ENGLISH OAK

PLATE 30

OAKS III: LEAVES WAVY-EDGED OR TOOTHED

Recognized as oaks by clustered end buds and acorns. None has bristle-tipped leaves; all are in the "white oak group" (see Pl. 28). Only Durand Oak may have hairy twigs; only Chapman Oak has leaf bases mostly U-shaped. None of these species has hairy or angled end buds. End buds mostly under ¼" long. Trunk bark light gray (except Chestnut Oak). (Specimens of species on Pl. 31 may have some wavy-edged or toothed leaves.) In winter also see chart, pp. 282–283.

SPECIES AND REMARKS	Leaf edges¹	Leaves thick, leathery	Leaves whitened beneath	Leaves hairy beneath	End buds more than ¼" long	End buds sharp	Acorn cup more than 1" across	Acorn cup shape²	Moist-soil habitat	Major distribution³	Text page
DURAND OAK *Quercus sinuata* — Variable foliage; often ± lobed; buds rounded.	L/W	+	+	−	−	−	−	S	±	S	295
(BLUFF OAK *Q. austrina***)** — Leaf shape like Water Oak (Pl. 31)	L/W	±	±	+	−	+	−	B	+	SE	296
CHAPMAN OAK *Q. chapmanii* — Leaves shiny above, tips often notched.	W	+	−	−	−	−	−	B	−	SE	296
CHINKAPIN OAK *Q. muehlenbergii* — Teeth sharp, 8–13 pairs; uplands.	S	−	−	+	−	+	−	B	−	M	296
BASKET OAK *Q. michauxii* — Teeth ± blunt, 7–16 pairs; lowlands.	R	−	±	+	±	+	+	B	+	S	297
SWAMP OAK *Q. bicolor* — Acorn stalks 1"–3" long; 4–6 pairs teeth.	R	−	+	±	−	−	±	B	+	M	297
CHESTNUT OAK *Q. montana* — Trunk dark, deep ridges; leaf teeth 7–16 pairs.	R/W	±	−	±	±	+	−	B	−	A	298

¹ L = lobed, R = teeth rounded, S = teeth sharp, W = wavy.
² B = bowl-shaped, deep; S = saucerlike, shallow.
³ A = Appalachians, M = Midwest, S = South, SE = Southeast.

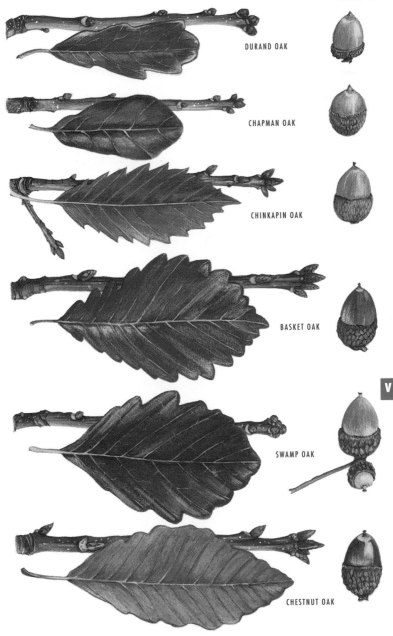

PLATE 30

DURAND OAK

CHAPMAN OAK

CHINKAPIN OAK

BASKET OAK

V

SWAMP OAK

CHESTNUT OAK

PLATE 31

OAKS IV: LEAVES TYPICALLY SMOOTH-EDGED

Clustered end buds and acorns identify these mostly southern trees as oaks. Most are red oak species. The two white oak species have leaves which lack terminal bristle tips.[1] End buds small, mostly less than ³⁄₁₆" long (see Bluejack Oak). See also Pl. 30. In winter, also see chart, pp. 282–283.

SPECIES AND REMARKS	Leaves thick, leathery	Leaves glossy above	Leaves hairy beneath	End buds sharp	End buds hairy	End buds angled	Twigs hairy	Acorn cup shape[2]	Red (R) White (W) oak[3]	Text page
ARKANSAS OAK *Quercus arkansana* Leaves wide.	–	–	–	+	–	–	+	S	R	298
WATER OAK *Q. nigra* Leaves wide near tip.	–	–	–	+	+	+	–	S	R	299
SHINGLE OAK *Q. imbricaria* Leaves 4"–10" long. North-central.	–	+	+	+	+	+	–	B	R	299
BLUEJACK OAK *Q. incana* End buds ³⁄₁₆"–⁵⁄₁₆" long; leaves white beneath. Southern.	+	+	+	+	+	–	±	S	R	300
OGLETHORPE OAK *Q. oglethorpensis* W. S.C., ne. Ga. Leaves yellow beneath.	–	–	+	±	–	–	–	B	W	300
WILLOW OAK *Q. phellos* Leaves narrow, dull beneath.	–	+	±	+	–	+	–	S	R	300
LAUREL OAK *Q. laurifolia* Leaves wider, shiny beneath, thin, bases ± V-shaped.	–	+	–	+	–	+	±	S	R	301
(DARLINGTON OAK *Q. hemisphaerica***)** Leaves thick, bases ± U-shaped.	+	±	–	+	–	–	–	S	R	302
MYRTLE OAK *Q. myrtifolia* Leaves 1"–2" long; acorn stalks short.	+	+	–	+	–	–	±	S	R	302
VIRGINIA LIVE OAK *Q. virginiana* Leaves 2"–4" long; acorn stalks ¾"–1" long. A white oak.[3]	+	+	±	–	–	–	–	B	W	302
(SAND LIVE OAK *Q. geminata***)** Leaves arched, edges rolled; veins deep above.	+	+	±	–	–	–	±	B	W	302

[1] Bristle tips are occasionally absent from some leathery-leaved red oaks.
[2] B = bowl-shaped, deep; S = saucerlike, shallow.
[3] For major oak categories, see charts for Pls. 29, 30.

PLATE 31

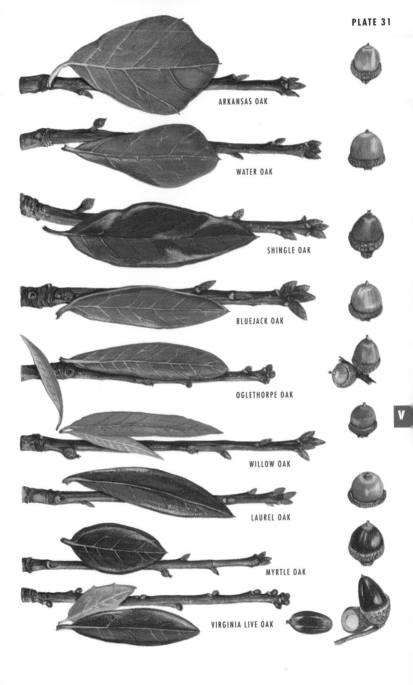

ARKANSAS OAK

WATER OAK

SHINGLE OAK

BLUEJACK OAK

OGLETHORPE OAK

WILLOW OAK

LAUREL OAK

MYRTLE OAK

VIRGINIA LIVE OAK

V

PLATE 32

TREES WITH ALTERNATE COARSE-EDGED LEAVES

Trees with large, sharp leaf teeth or deeply wavy-edged leaves. Bundle scars usually 3; sometimes more in American Chestnut.

SPECIES AND REMARKS	Leaf length (inches)	Leaves long, 3–4 times width	Leaves sharply toothed	Leaf bases uneven	Leaves hairy beneath	Twigs hairy	Buds hairy	End bud false	Major distribution[1]	Text page
AMERICAN CHESTNUT *Castanea dentata* Large specimens now rare.	5–8	+	+	–	–	–	–	+	A	303
OZARK CHINKAPIN *C. ozarkensis* Leaves white-downy beneath.	5–8	+	+	–	+	±	±	+	O	305
ALLEGHENY CHINKAPIN *C. pumila* Leaves white-woolly beneath.	3–5	±	+	–	+	+	+	+	S	305
FLORIDA CHINKAPIN *C. alnifolia* Leaves beechlike, buds short.	2–4	±	+	–	–	–	±	+	S	305
BEECH *Fagus grandifolia* Buds long, slender; bark smooth gray.	3–6	–	+	–	–	±	–	–	w	306
COMMON WITCH-HAZEL *Hamamelis virginiana* Buds without scales, stalked.	3–6	–	–	+	±	±	+	–	w	306
GROUNDSEL-TREE *Baccharis halimifolia* Twigs ridged; top leaves not toothed.	1–3	–	±	–	–	–	–	+	C	307
STRAWBERRY-TREE[2] *Muntingia calabura* Main leaf veins 3. Cen. and s. Fla.	2–4	–	+	+	+	+	+	+	F	307

[1] A = Appalachians, F = Fla., O = Ozarks, C = Coastal Plain, S = southeastern states, w = widespread.
[2] Leaf outline is similar to that of elms (Pl. 33).

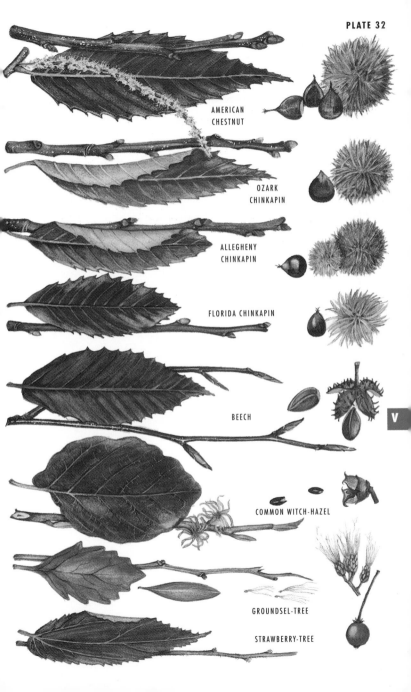

PLATE 32

AMERICAN CHESTNUT

OZARK CHINKAPIN

ALLEGHENY CHINKAPIN

FLORIDA CHINKAPIN

BEECH

V

COMMON WITCH-HAZEL

GROUNDSEL-TREE

STRAWBERRY-TREE

PLATE 33

ELMS AND WATER-ELM

Trees mostly with double-toothed[1] and uneven-based leaves. Buds many-scaled, the scales in 2 regular rows; end buds false. Bundle scars 3. Inner bark tough, fibrous. In Florida, see Strawberry-tree (Pl. 32).

SPECIES AND REMARKS	Leaf length (inches)	Leaves sandpapery above	Branchlet "wings" common[2]	Twigs hairy	Bud scales dark-edged	Fruits more than 3/8" long	Fruit tip deeply notched[3]	Fruit hairiness pattern[4]	Fruiting season[5]	Major distribution[6]	Text page
AMERICAN ELM *Ulmus americana* Disease has killed many.	4–6	±	−	−	+	±	+	−	S	w	308
SLIPPERY ELM *U. rubra* Buds red-hairy; leaves hairy-edged.	4–8	+	−	+	−	+	−	*	S	w	309
(ENGLISH ELM *U. procera*) Buds brown, leaf edges hairless.	3–6	±	+	±	−	+	−	−	S	E	309
WINGED ELM *U. alata* Leafstalks less than ¼" long; "wings" wide.	1–3	±	+	−	+	−	+	±	S	S	309
ROCK ELM *U. thomasii* Leafstalks more than ¼" long; low branches droop.	2–4	−	+	+	+	+	−	−	S	N	310
CEDAR ELM *U. crassifolia* Corky "wings" not prominent.	1–2	+	+	−	−	±	+	+	F	M	311
(SEPTEMBER ELM *U. serotina*) Mainly Tenn.; uncommon.	2–4	−	+	−	−	±	+	−	F	C	311
(SIBERIAN ELM *U. pumila*)[1] Buds dark and blunt; fruits circular.	1–3	−	−	−	−	+	+	o	S	W	311
WATER-ELM *Planera aquatica*[1] Fruits fleshy, without wings.	2–4	+	−	−	−	−	o	o	S	S	311

[1] Siberian Elm and Water-elm have single-toothed leaves.
[2] But not always present.
[3] Deep (+), slight (−), and none (o).
[4] All surfaces hairy (+), centers only (*), edges only (−), not hairy (o).
[5] S = spring, March–May; F = fall, Sept.–Oct.
[6] C = central states, M = lower Mississippi Valley, N = north-central states, S = South, W = West, w = widespread.

PLATE 33

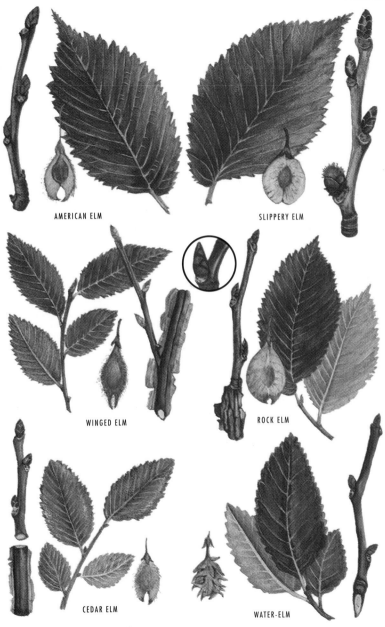

AMERICAN ELM

SLIPPERY ELM

WINGED ELM

ROCK ELM

V

CEDAR ELM

WATER-ELM

PLATE 34

BIRCHES

Leaves double-toothed with bases even, mostly wide or heart-shaped. Bark with many narrow cross-stripes. Buds with 2–3 scales. Bundle scars 3. Fruiting catkins on short spur branches.

SPECIES AND REMARKS

	Trunk bark color[1]	Trunk bark peeling	Leaves long-pointed	Wintergreen odor[2]	Twigs rough-warty	Buds hairy	Fruit catkins erect[3]	Major distribution[4]	Text page
PAPER BIRCH *Betula papyrifera* Trunk chevrons[5] few.	W	+	–	–	–	–	–	N	313
GRAY BIRCH *B. populifolia* Trunk chevrons[5] large, black.	W	–	+	–	+	–	–	E	315
SWEET BIRCH *B. lenta* Broken twigs sharply aromatic.[2]	D	–	–	+	–	–	+	A	315
YELLOW BIRCH *B. alleghaniensis* Broken-twig aroma reduced.[2]	Y	+	–	+	–	+	+	N	317
RIVER BIRCH *B. nigra* Leaf bases often broadly V-shaped.	O	+	–	–	+	±	+	S	317
(VIRGINIA BIRCH) *B. uber*)[6] Smyth Co., sw. Va.; rare.	D	–	–	+	–			S	316

[1] D = dark, O = orange, W = white, Y = yellowish or silver-gray.
[2] Broken twigs yield a wintergreen or peppermint odor and taste.
[3] Fruiting catkins either (+) short-stalked and rather upright or (–) long-stalked and pendent.
[4] A = Appalachians, E = New England and Maritime Provinces, N = North, S = South.
[5] Chevron-shaped (shallow inverted Vs) dark trunk markings at bases of branches.
[6] Virginia Birch is little known. It may be a variety of Sweet Birch.

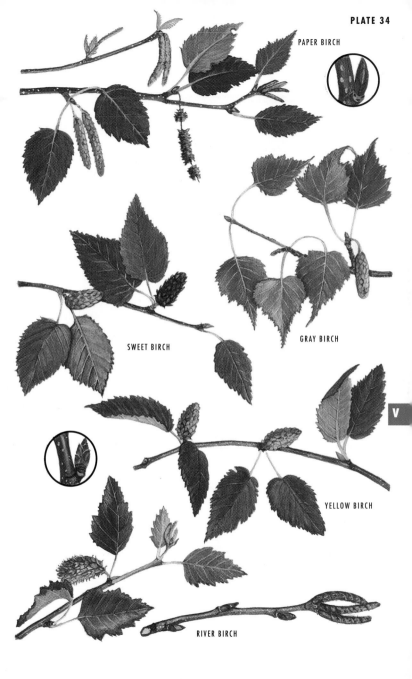

PLATE 34

PAPER BIRCH

GRAY BIRCH

SWEET BIRCH

YELLOW BIRCH

V

RIVER BIRCH

PLATE 35

OTHER TREES WITH MOSTLY DOUBLE-TOOTHED LEAVES AND/OR SMALL WOODY CONES

Leaves broad, 2"–5" long (including stalks), bases even. Twigs variably hairy or hairless. Bundle scars 3. Flowers/fruits in catkins. Alder cones are distinctive.

SPECIES AND REMARKS	Buds stalked, reddish, blunt[1]	Bud scales per bud	Leaves double-toothed	Leaf base U- or V-shaped	Trunk bark[2]	Fruit type[3]	Site[4]	Major distribution[5]	Text page
IRONWOOD *Carpinus caroliniana* Trunk "sinewy"; leaf veins not forked; buds angled.	–	10+	+	U	G	N	M	E	318
EASTERN HORNBEAM *Ostrya virginiana* Some side leaf veins forked, buds not angled.	–	6–8	+	U	B	S	M	E	319
SMOOTH ALDER *Alnus serrulata* Few white trunk speckles; cones erect.	+	2–3	±	V	D	C	W	E	321
SPECKLED ALDER *Alnus rugosa* Trunk speckles many; cones droop.	+	2–3	+	U	D	C	W	N	321
EUROPEAN ALDER *Alnus glutinosa* Leaves blunt; twigs gummy.	+	2–3	+	U	D	C	W	N	322
SEASIDE ALDER *Alnus maritima* Leaves pointed; bud scales separated.	+	2–3	–	V	D	C	W	–[6]	322

[1] And end bud true.
[2] B = brown, rough, shreddy; D = dark, smoothish, with short white, horizontal stripes; G = gray, smooth, "muscular."
[3] C = small, woody, pine-cone-like catkins; N = tiny nuts attached to three-pointed leafy bracts; S = clustered sacs containing flat nuts.
[4] W = wet, M = moist.
[5] E = East, widespread; N = northern states and Canada.
[6] Eastern Md., Del., and again in Okla.

PLATE 35

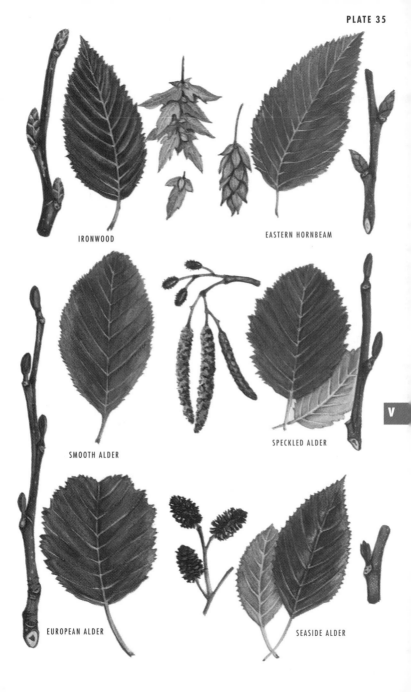

IRONWOOD

EASTERN HORNBEAM

SMOOTH ALDER

SPECKLED ALDER

EUROPEAN ALDER

SEASIDE ALDER

V

PLATE 36

CHERRIES AND PEACH

Leaves mostly single-toothed[1] and leafstalks bearing glands (use lens). Trunk bark with narrow cross-stripes. Broken twigs with characteristic sour odor. End bud true. Bundle scars 3. Flowers white; fruits fleshy; seed large, mostly globular. Carolina Laurelcherry (Pl. 43) and West Indies Laurelcherry (Pl. F-46C) are evergreen.

SPECIES AND REMARKS	Leaves narrow[2]	Leaf teeth sharp	Buds more than ½" long	Bud scales pointed	Spur branches present[3]	Flowers/fruits in slender clusters	Fruit with persistent calyx[4]	Fruit color[5]	Major distribution[6]	Text page
CHOKE CHERRY *Prunus virginiana* — Midrib bare, vein pairs 8–11.	−	+	+	−	−	+	−	P	N	323
BLACK CHERRY *Prunus serotina* — Midrib often hairy-fringed beneath, vein pairs 13+.	+	−	−	+	−	+	+	B	E	323
(EUROPEAN BIRD CHERRY *P. padus*) — Fruits bitter; seeds grooved.	±	+	−	+	−	+	−	B	N	324
DOMESTIC PEACH *Prunus persica* — Buds/fruits velvety; seeds pitted.	+	+	+	−	+	−	−	Y	w	324
FIRE CHERRY *Prunus pensylvanica* — Leafstalks reddish, leaves/buds crowded at twig tips.[7]	+	+	−	+	+	−	−	R	N	325
SWEET CHERRY *Prunus avium*[1] — Leaves dull, 10–14 vein pairs.	−	±	+	±	+	−	+	R/B	w	325
SOUR CHERRY *Prunus cerasus*[1] — Leaves shiny, 6–8 vein pairs.[8]	−	−	+	±	+	−	+	R	w	326
(MAHALEB CHERRY *Prunus mahaleb*) — Leaves aromatic, rounded; twigs hairy.	−	−	−	+	+	−	−	B	N	326

Note: The 2 cherries in parentheses are similar to others in this group; see text.

[1] Only sweet and sour cherries have double-toothed leaves.

[2] Narrow leaves (including leafstalks) are four or more times as long as broad.

[3] Spur branches are short with crowded leaf scars and grow from older growth (not twigs); see illustration, p. 6.

[4] The calyx is the circle of sepals located just beneath the flower petals and, usually dried, at the stem of the cherry fruit.

[5] B = black, P = purple, R = red, Y = yellow.

[6] E = East, widespread; N = North; w = widespread, spreading from plantings.

[7] On all twigs, not just spur branches.

[8] Also, unlike Sweet Cherry, central main trunk lacking.

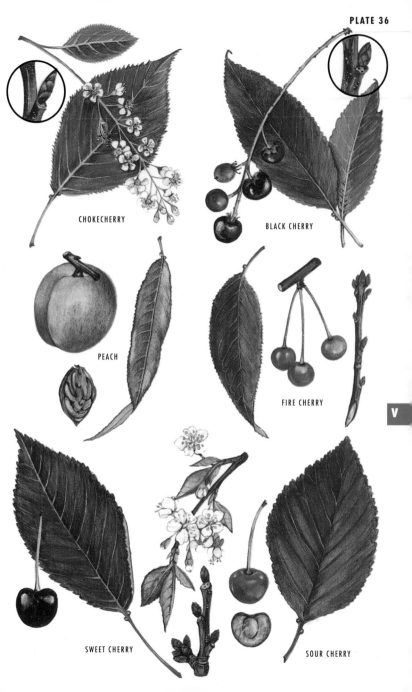

PLATE 36

CHOKECHERRY

BLACK CHERRY

PEACH

FIRE CHERRY

SWEET CHERRY

SOUR CHERRY

V

PLATE 37

THORNLESS PLUMS

Leaves mostly single-toothed and usually with leafstalk or leaf-base glands; end bud false. Bundle scars 3. Fruiting spurs present on branchlets (except in Hortulan Plum). Flowers white, mostly in rounded or flat-topped clusters. Fruits fleshy, single-seeded, stone mostly flattened and with opposite lengthwise ridges. Broken twigs often with weak sour odor. Plants sometimes with thorns. See also thorny plums on Pl. 23.

SPECIES[1] AND REMARKS	Leaf teeth sharp	Leafstalk glands present[2]	Twigs hairy	Fruit color[3]	Seeds pointed both ends	Text page
ALLEGHENY PLUM *Prunus alleghaniensis* Mountains. Leaves long-pointed.	+	±	+	P	+	327
FLATWOODS PLUM *Prunus umbellata* Coastal Plain. Leaves short-pointed.	+	±	+	B	+	327
MEXICAN PLUM *Prunus mexicana* Leaves double-toothed, base broad. Mississippi Valley.	+	+	−	P	−	327
HORTULAN PLUM *Prunus hortulana* Spur branches lacking. Upper Midwest.	−	+	−	R/Y	+	328
WILDGOOSE PLUM *Prunus munsoniana* Spur branches short, Midwest.	−	+	−	R/Y	−	328
GARDEN PLUM *Prunus domestica* Perhaps a variety of Bullace Plum (p. 260).	−	+	−	P	−	328

1 Some Florida species also called plums are unrelated; see Pls. F-46A, F-46B, F-46C.
2 On upper leafstalk or nearby leaf base, use lens.
3 B = black, P = purple, R = red, Y = yellow.

PLATE 37

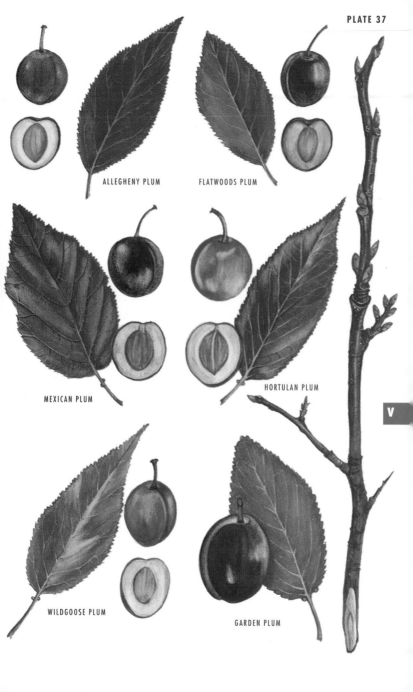

ALLEGHENY PLUM

FLATWOODS PLUM

MEXICAN PLUM

HORTULAN PLUM

V

WILDGOOSE PLUM

GARDEN PLUM

PLATE 38

WILLOWS I: LEAVES VERY NARROW TO MEDIUM IN WIDTH

Catkin-bearing trees with a single hoodlike bud scale. Bundle scars 3; end buds false. Leaves mostly narrow and usually fine-toothed. Also narrow-leaved: Willow Oak (Pl. 31), Domestic Peach (Pl. 36), bayberries (Pl. 43), and Russian-olive[6].

SPECIES AND REMARKS

	Leaf width[1]	Leaves toothed	Leaves long-pointed	Leaves whitened beneath	Leaves hairy at least beneath	Leafstalk glands present[2]	Leaf teeth mainly above middle	Buds blunt	Stipules usually present[3]	Leaf bases mostly U- or V-shaped	Major distribution[4]	Text page
BLACK WILLOW *Salix nigra* Leafstalks less than 5/16" long.	N	+	+	−	−	−	±	−	+	V	W	331
MEADOW WILLOW[5] *S. petiolaris* Leafstalks ¼"–½" long.	N	+	+	+	−	−	−	−	−	V	N	332
SANDBAR WILLOW *S. exigua* Leafstalks nearly lacking.	N	±	+	±	±	−	+	+	−	V	N	332
OSIER WILLOW *S. viminalis* Leaves dense white beneath.	N	−	±	+	+	−	−	−	±	V	N	333
WEEPING WILLOW *S. babylonica* Twigs long, hang vertically.	I	+	+	+	±	±	−	+	−	V	w	333
COASTAL PLAIN WILLOW *S. caroliniana* Twigs do not hang.	I	+	+	+	−	−	−	−	±	U	S	334
CRACK WILLOW *S. fragilis* Teeth ± coarse, buds ± sticky..	I	+	+	+	−	+	−	+	−	V	w	334
WHITE WILLOW *S. alba* Leaves white-hairy.	I	+	±	+	+	±	−	+	−	V	w	334
SILKY WILLOW[5] *S. sericea* Leaves mostly silky beneath.	I	+	−	+	+	−	−	+	+	V	N	335
ONTARIO (SATINY) WILLOW *S. pellita* Subarctic and N. Eng. Leaves often leathery.	I	−	−	+	+	−	−	−	−	V	N	335

[1] N = narrow, 8–15 times longer than width; I = intermediate, 5–7 times longer than width.

[2] At apex of stalk near leaf base.

[3] Stipules often tiny but sometimes large, conspicuous, paired leafy structures at each side of buds or leafstalk bases, dropping early and lacking in some species.

[4] E = eastern states, N = North, S = South, w = widespread.

[5] Young leaves become black upon drying.

[6] Russian-olive (p. 331) has silvery leaves and twigs.

PLATE 38

BLACK WILLOW

MEADOW WILLOW

SANDBAR WILLOW

OSIER WILLOW

WEEPING WILLOW

COASTAL PLAIN WILLOW

CRACK WILLOW

WHITE WILLOW

SILKY WILLOW

ONTARIO (SATINY) WILLOW

V

PLATE 39

WILLOWS II: LEAVES RELATIVELY WIDE

Catkin-bearing trees with a single hoodlike bud scale. The leaves of these willow are somewhat wider than those of the preceding plate.[1] They are mostly toothed. Bundle scars 3; end buds false. Mostly northern species. See also Domestic Peach (Pl. 36), bayberries (Pl. 43), and Russian-olive (p. 331). For winter identification, see text identification chart, p. 330.

SPECIES AND REMARKS	Leaves toothed	Leaves long-pointed	Leaves whitened beneath	Leaves hairy at least beneath	Leafstalk glands present[2]	Leaf teeth mainly above middle	Buds blunt	Stipules usually present[3]	Leaf bases mostly U- or V-shaped	Text page
SHINING WILLOW *Salix lucida* Leaves shiny; twigs dark.	+	+	−	−	+	−	+	+	U	335
PEACHLEAF WILLOW *S. amygdaloides* Leaves dull; twigs light.	+	+	+	−	−	−	−	−	U	336
PUSSY WILLOW *S. discolor* Teeth above the middle, V-based.	+	−	+	−	−	+	+	+	V	336
BROADLEAF WILLOW[4] *S. glaucophylloides* Leaf bases often heart-shaped.	+	−	+	−	−	−	±	+	U	336
BEBB WILLOW *S. bebbiana* Leaves gray-woolly, veiny.	±	−	±	+	−	−	+	−	V	337
BASKET WILLOW *S. purpurea* Leaves nearly opposite, teeth above the middle, U-based. See Pl. 12	±	−	+	−	−	+	+	−	U	337
BALSAM WILLOW *S. pyrifolia* Crushed leaves spicy.	+	−	+	±	−	−	−	−	U	337
FLORIDA WILLOW *S. floridana* Local; s. Ga. to cen. Fla. only.	+	−	+	+	−	−	−	−	U	338

1 Leaves 2–4 times longer than wide.
2 At apex of stalk, near leaf base.
3 Stipules often tiny but sometimes large, conspicuous, paired leafy structures at each side of buds or leafstalk bases, dropping early or lacking in some species.
4 Young leaves become black upon drying.

PLATE 39

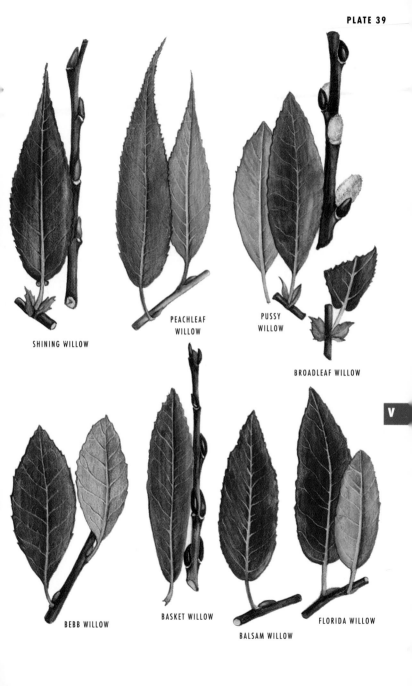

SHINING WILLOW

PEACHLEAF WILLOW

PUSSY WILLOW

BROADLEAF WILLOW

V

BEBB WILLOW

BASKET WILLOW

BALSAM WILLOW

FLORIDA WILLOW

PLATE 40

DECIDUOUS HOLLIES

As a group, hollies lack obvious distinctive vegetative characteristics. They are our only trees, however, with spur branches common and a single bundle scar. Leaves are thin, mostly toothed, 2"–4" long, pointed, and V-based. They are alternate along fast-grown twigs and clustered on spurs. Twigs are hairless, two or more buds may be present at a leaf scar, and the end bud is true. Small greenish flowers or red/orange fruits are often crowded among the leaves. Species on this plate have red or orange fruits. Evergreen hollies are shown on Pl. 41.

SPECIES AND REMARKS	Leaf edges scalloped[1]	Leaf bases narrowly V-shaped	Leaves hairy beneath	Leaves fine-toothed	Side buds pointed	Flower/fruit stalks more than ½" long	Seeds ridged[2]	Wet sites	Major distribution[3]	Text page
POSSUMHAW HOLLY *Ilex decidua* Leaves wavy-edged[1], tips blunt.	+	+	−	−	+	−	+	+	S	339
LARGELEAF HOLLY *Ilex montana* Leaves 4"–6½" long, teeth sharp.	−	±	−	+	+	−	+	−	A	339
COMMON WINTERBERRY HOLLY *Ilex verticillata* Leaves dull, teeth ± coarse.	−	+	+	−	−	−	−	+	E	340
SMOOTH WINTERBERRY HOLLY *Ilex laevigata* Leaves shiny, teeth ± fine.	−	+	−	+	−	−	−	+	C	341
CAROLINA HOLLY *Ilex ambigua*	−	±	±	−	+	−	+	−	S	341
GEORGIA HOLLY *Ilex longipes*	−	+	−	+	+	+	+	+	S	341
(JUNEBERRY HOLLY *Ilex amelanchier***)** Leaf bases U-shaped; species uncommon.	−	−	+	+	+	±	+	+	S	341

[1] Larger wavy teeth may alternate with small sharp teeth.
[2] On curved surfaces.
[3] A = Appalachians; C = mostly coastal states, Maine to W. Penn. to S.C.; S = South; w = widespread.

PLATE 40

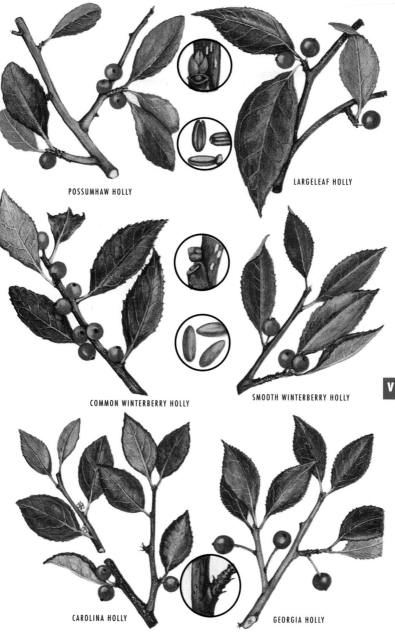

POSSUMHAW HOLLY

LARGELEAF HOLLY

COMMON WINTERBERRY HOLLY

SMOOTH WINTERBERRY HOLLY

V

CAROLINA HOLLY

GEORGIA HOLLY

PLATE 41

EVERGREEN HOLLIES

Except for the American Holly, the holly group is difficult to identify (details on Pl. 40). The species on this plate have leaves leathery, usually with edges rolled under, and mostly with a few sharp teeth or none. Fruits mostly red or black. These trees occur principally on the Coastal Plain in the southeastern states.

SPECIES AND REMARKS	Leaves small, less than 1½" long	Leaf bases V-shaped	Leaf edges spiny or wavy	Leaf teeth mainly above middle	Color of fruits[1]	Seeds ridged[2]	Text page
YAUPON HOLLY *Ilex vomitoria* Leaf edges wavy, tips blunt.	+	±	+	−	R	+	342
MYRTLE HOLLY *I. myrtifolia* Leaves ⅛"–¼" wide.	+	+	−	+	R	+	342
DAHOON HOLLY *I. cassine* Leaves ½"–1¼" wide.	−	+	−	+	R	+	343
TALL GALLBERRY HOLLY *I. coriacea* Leaves few-toothed, black-dotted beneath (use lens); fruits blue.	−	+	−	+	U	−	343
AMERICAN HOLLY *I. opaca* Only native holly with thorny leaves.	−	−	+	−	R	+	343
TAWNYBERRY HOLLY *I. krugiana* Mainland — Dade Co., Fla. Leaf edges toothed or not. Leaves/fruits dry black.	−	−	+	−	B	−	344

[1] B = black, R = red, U = blue.
[2] On curved surface; see illustrations on Pl. 40.

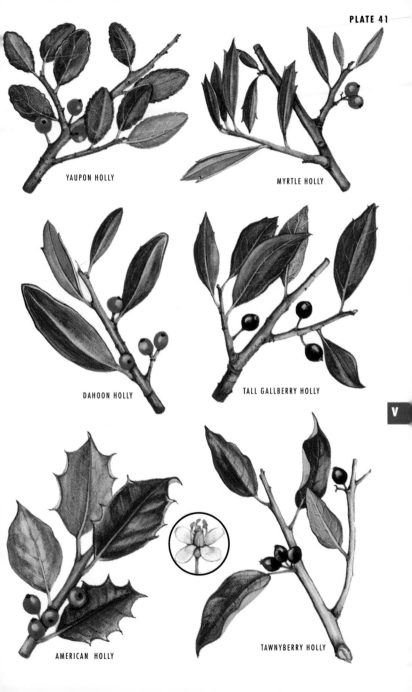

PLATE 41

YAUPON HOLLY

MYRTLE HOLLY

DAHOON HOLLY

TALL GALLBERRY HOLLY

V

AMERICAN HOLLY

TAWNYBERRY HOLLY

PLATE 42

MISCELLANEOUS TREES WITH ALTERNATE TOOTHED LEAVES

These species lack the characteristics of other trees with alternate toothed leaves (Pls. 32–39). Except for Sourwood, the end bud is true. Only Loblolly-bay has thick, leathery leaves. In cen. and s. Fla., see also Pl. F-42.

SPECIES AND REMARKS	Buds slim, pink, black-tipped	Pith chambered	Flower/fruit clusters long, slender	Flowers showy, more than 2" wide	Leafstalks winged	Buds hairy	Bundle scars per leaf scar	Major distribution[1]	Text page
DOWNY JUNEBERRY *Amelanchier arborea* Leaves short- to medium-pointed, fine teeth 14–30/inch[3].	+	−	±	−	−	−	3	E	346
ROUNDLEAF JUNEBERRY *A. sanguinea* Leaves blunt, teeth 6–12/inch[4].	+	−	±	−	−	−	3	N	347
MOUNTAIN PEPPERBUSH *Clethra acuminata* End bud larger than side buds, hairy; fruits 3-parted.	−	−	+	−	−	+	1	M	347
SOURWOOD *Oxydendrum arboreum* End bud small, hairless; bundle scar U-shaped; fruits 5-parted.	−	−	+	−	−	−	1	E	348
CAROLINA SILVERBELL *Halesia carolina*[5] Fruits broadly 4-winged; leaves 2"–7" long.	−	+	−	−	−	−	1	S	348
LOBLOLLY-BAY *Gordonia lasianthus*[2] Leaves evergreen, bases V-shaped.	−	−	−	+	±	+	1	C	349
VIRGINIA STEWARTIA *S. malachodendron* Leaf bases U-shaped; trunk mottled.	−	−	−	+	+	+	1	M	350
MOUNTAIN STEWARTIA *Stewartia ovata* Leaf bases U-shaped; trunk smooth.	−	−	−	+	+	+	1	C	351

[1] E = East, widespread, M = mountains, southern; N = northern states, etc.; C = Coastal Plain, southern; S = South, widespread.

[2] See *Franklinia* text, p. 350; extinct in wild.

[3] Bartram and Oblongleaf juneberries (p. 346) are fine-toothed, the former with foliage pointed at both ends and the latter with blunt leaves.

[4] Alderleaf Juneberry (p. 347) has leaves ± square-tipped.

[5] Little Silverbell has 2"–4" leaves and fruits narrowly 4-winged; Two-wing Silverbell has 3"–5" leaves and fruits 2-winged; see p. 349.

PLATE 42

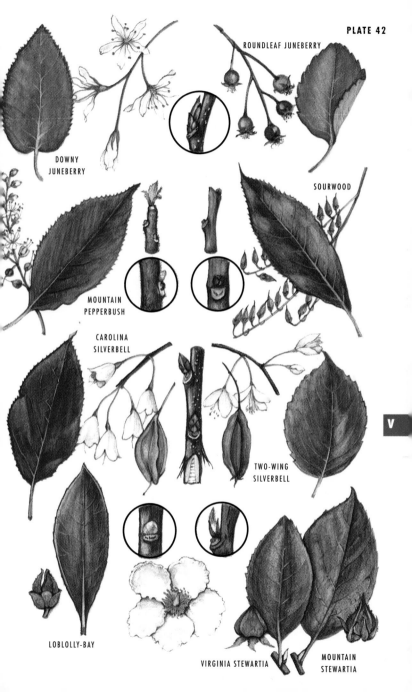

DOWNY JUNEBERRY

ROUNDLEAF JUNEBERRY

SOURWOOD

MOUNTAIN PEPPERBUSH

CAROLINA SILVERBELL

TWO-WING SILVERBELL

V

LOBLOLLY-BAY

VIRGINIA STEWARTIA

MOUNTAIN STEWARTIA

PLATE 43

MISCELLANEOUS TREES WITH ALTERNATE LEAVES SOMETIMES TOOTHED

See text for other distinctive features of these species. Foliage of these bayberries[1] is yellow-dotted beneath (use lens) and aromatic when crushed. Groundsel-tree (Pl. 32) also may have some leaves not toothed. In s. Fla., see also Geiger-tree, p. 357.

SPECIES	Buds without scales	Pith chambered	Spur branches usually present	Leaves evergreen, leathery[2]	Leaves hairy beneath	Twigs hairy	Bundle scars per leaf scar	Major distribution[3]	Text page
SOUTHERN BAYBERRY *Myrica cerifera* Leaf dots both sides.	−	−	−	+	−	±	3	S	351
EVERGREEN BAYBERRY *M. heterophylla* Leaf dots beneath.	−	−	−	+	−	+	3	S	352
NORTHERN BAYBERRY *M. pensylvanica* Leaf dots beneath.	−	−	−	−	−	+	3	N	352
CAROLINA BUCKTHORN *Rhamnus caroliniana*[4]	+	−	−	−	±	+	3	S	353
BIGLEAF SNOWBELL *Styrax grandifolius*	+	−	−	−	+	+	1	S	353
(AMERICAN SNOWBELL *Styrax grandifolius*)	+	−	−	−	−	−	1	S	354
SWEETLEAF *Symplocos tinctoria*	−	+	−	±	±	−	1	S	354
WATER TUPELO *Nyssa aquatica* Leafstalks 1″−3″.	−	+	−	−	±	−	3	S	354
(OGEECHEE TUPELO *Nyssa ogeche*) Leafstalks ½″−1″.	−	+	−	−	±	+	3	S	355
DOMESTIC APPLE *Malus sylvestris* Tree spreading.	−	−	+	−	+	+	3	w	355
DOMESTIC PEAR *Pyrus communis* Tree narrow.	−	−	+	−	−	−	3	w	356
CAROLINA LAURELCHERRY *Prunus caroliniana*	−	−	−	+	−	−	3	S	356

[1] Male flower clusters elongated; female plants produce small, gray, waxy nutlets. Odorless Bayberry (Pl. 46) lacks resin dots and is not aromatic.
[2] See also Pls. 46−48 and in Fla., F-46A−D.
[3] N = Northeast, S = South, w = widespread.
[4] European Buckthorn (p. 353) has unbranched flower/fruit stalks.

PLATE 43

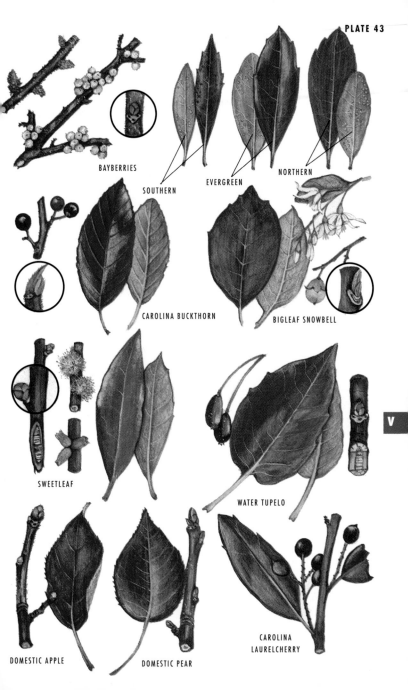

BAYBERRIES

SOUTHERN

EVERGREEN

NORTHERN

CAROLINA BUCKTHORN

BIGLEAF SNOWBELL

SWEETLEAF

WATER TUPELO

V

DOMESTIC APPLE

DOMESTIC PEAR

CAROLINA
LAURELCHERRY

PLATE 44

TREES WITH LEAVES NEITHER TOOTHED NOR EVERGREEN

These species and many of those on Pls. 43 and 45 comprise the rather small group of trees with foliage of this type. The leaves of Persimmon and Sourgum may be somewhat leathery but not evergreen[1]. Except for Persimmon, all on this plate have a true end bud.

SPECIES AND REMARKS	Leaves mostly more than 6" long	Leaf tips blunt	Twigs hairy	Pith partitioned	Bundle scars per leaf scar	Bud scales per bud	Major distribution[2]	Text page
COMMON PAWPAW *Asimina triloba* — End bud long, brown-hairy, no scales; leaves 6"–12"; flowers more than 1" across.	+	−	±	±	3	0	M	357
(SMALLFLOWER PAWPAW *A. parviflora***)** — Similar but leaves under 7", and blossoms less than 1" across.	±	−	±	±	3	0	S	358
AMERICAN SMOKETREE *Cotinus obovatus* — Rare. Leaves blunt, fruits feathery.	−	+	−	−	3	2–4	M	358
ALTERNATE-LEAF DOGWOOD *Cornus alternifolia* — Veins follow leaf edges.	−	−	−	−	3	2	N	358
CORKWOOD *Leitneria floridana* — End buds large, clustered.	−	−	+	−	3	3+	S	359
COMMON PERSIMMON *Diospyros virginiana*[1] — Bark deeply checkered; buds blackish.	−	−	−	±	1	2	S	359
SOURGUM *Nyssa sylvatica*[1] — Bark deeply checkered; buds brown.	−	−	−	+	3	3+	S	360
CRAPEMYRTLE *Lagerstroemia indica* — Some leaves opposite; flowers showy. Twigs 4-lined or 4-winged.	−	±	−	−	1	2	S	361
ELLIOTTIA *Elliottia racemosa* — Rare; Ga. only. Fruits dry; end clusters.	−	−	−	−	1	2–3	S	362

1 Leaves thin relative to those of evergreen trees (Pls. 45–46).
2 M = midlatitudes; N = North; S = South.

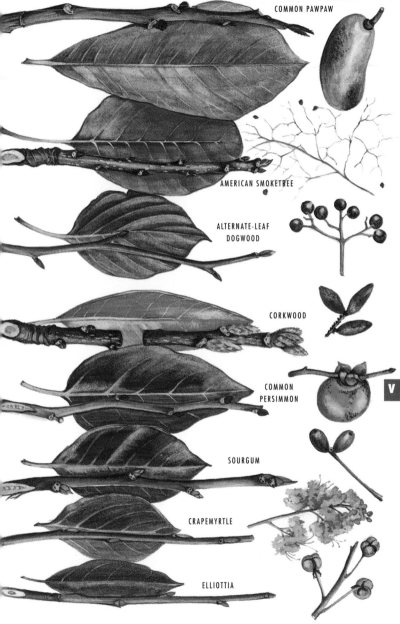

PLATE 44

COMMON PAWPAW

AMERICAN SMOKETREE

ALTERNATE-LEAF
DOGWOOD

CORKWOOD

COMMON
PERSIMMON

V

SOURGUM

CRAPEMYRTLE

ELLIOTTIA

PLATE 45

MAGNOLIAS

Leaves not toothed. Twigs ringed, buds mostly hairy, with a single bud scale; bundle scars many. Flowers large and white (green in Cucumber Magnolia); fruit "cones" woody with fleshy seeds. In cen. and s. Fla., see Pls. 46A–D.

SPECIES AND REMARKS

	Leaf length (inches)	Leaf base shape[1]	Leaves crowded near twig tips[2]	Leaf underside hairy[3]	Leaf underside and bud color[4]	Twigs stout	End bud color[4]	Pith chambered	Cone shape[5]	Major distribution[6]	Text page
EVERGREEN MAGNOLIA *Magnolia grandiflora* — Leaves leathery, evergreen.	6–8	U	−	+	B	+	B	+	E	S	363
SWEETBAY MAGNOLIA *M. virginiana* — Crushed leaves/buds spicy.[7]	4–6	V	−	+	W	−	G	+	E	S	363
CUCUMBER MAGNOLIA *M. acuminata* — Leaf scars U-shaped.[8]	4–10	U	−	±	G	−	W	−	C	A	364
UMBRELLA MAGNOLIA *M. tripetala* — End bud hairless[9].	10–24	V	+	−	G	+	P	−	C	A	365
EARLEAF MAGNOLIA *M. fraseri* — Ear lobes deep, leafstalks ± 3″ long.	8–12	E	+	−	G	+	P	±	C	A	365
(PYRAMID MAGNOLIA *M. pyramidata*)	5–9	E	+	−	G	+	P	±	C	S	366
BIGLEAF MAGNOLIA *M. macrophylla* — Southeast, north of Fla.	20–30	E	+	+	W	+	W	−	E	A	366
(ASHE MAGNOLIA *M. ashei*)	14–22	E	+	+	W	+	W	−	C	F	366

[1] E = ear-lobed, U = U-shaped, V = V-shaped.
[2] And at twig swellings; also end buds more than 1″ long.
[3] Buds and twigs also hairy (twigs hairless in Cucumber Magnolia).
[4] B = brown, G = pale green, P = purplish, W = white- or silvery-hairy.
[5] C = candle-shaped (upper right corner of plate), E = egglike (center left of plate).
[6] A = Appalachians; F = nw. Florida; S = South.
[7] Leaves may be evergreen and somewhat leathery in South.
[8] Leaf scars not crescent-shaped or circular, as in other magnolias.
[9]   Flower odor unpleasant.

PLATE 45

EVERGREEN MAGNOLIA

SWEETBAY
MAGNOLIA

CUCUMBER
MAGNOLIA

V

UMBRELLA
MAGNOLIA

EARLEAF
MAGNOLIA

BIGLEAF
MAGNOLIA

PLATE 46

TREES WITH LEATHERY EVERGREEN LEAVES MOSTLY NOT TOOTHED

Except for the rhododendrons and Mountain Laurel, these species are mainly restricted to the South. See also Pls. 31, 41, 43, and 45. In Fla., also see F-46A–D.

SPECIES AND REMARKS	Leaf length in inches	Flower clusters finger-shaped	Leafstalks short or lacking	Crushed leaves odorous	Leaf edges rolled under	Leaves clustered near twig tips	Leaf tips rounded	Some leaves wavy or toothed	Fruits[1]	Southernmost Fla. range[2]	Major distribution[3]	Text page
SPARKLEBERRY *Vacciunium arboreum* Tiny leaf tips.	1–2	−	±	−	−	−	±	+	F	C	S	367
TREE LYONIA *Lyonia ferruginea* Leaves rusty-hairy.	1–3	−	−	−	+	−	±	+	C	N	C	367
BUCKWHEAT-TREE *Cliftonia monophylla* Fruits 4-winged.	1–2	+	+	−	±	+	−	−	L	N	S	367
CYRILLA *Cyrilla racemiflora* Leaves narrow.	2–4	+	+	−	±	+	±	−	L	C	S	368
ODORLESS BAYBERRY *Myrica inodora* Leaves wide.	2–4	+	±	−	+	−	±	−	W	N	G	368
MOUNTAIN LAUREL *Kalmia latifolia*	2–5	−	−	−	−	±	±	−	C	N	A	368
FLORIDA ANISE-TREE *Illicium floridanum*	3–6	−	−	+	−	+	−	±	S	N	G	370
REDBAY *Persea borbonia*	3–8	−	−	+	+	−	±	−	F	S	S	370
CATAWBA RHODODENDRON *Rhododendron catawbiense*[4]	3–9	−	−	−	+	±	−	−	C	−	A	370
GREAT RHODODENDRON *Rhododendron maximum*[4]	3–11	−	−	−	+	±	−	−	C	−	A	371
CAMPHOR-TREE *Cinnamomum camphora*	2–6	−	−	+	−	−	−	±	F	S	S	371

[1] C = capsules dry; F = fleshy, black or blue; L = long fingerlike clusters of tiny dry fruits; S = star-shaped with many points; W = waxy spheres, small.

[2] Southernmost distribution in Fla. (see also Pls. F-46A–D); C = central counties, N = northern (northwestern, except Mountain Laurel), S = southern; minus sign means "absent from Florida."

[3] A = Appalachians, G = Gulf Coastal Plain, C = southeastern Coastal Plain, S = southeastern states.

[4] Spring flower clusters large and showy. Compare width of leaf base.

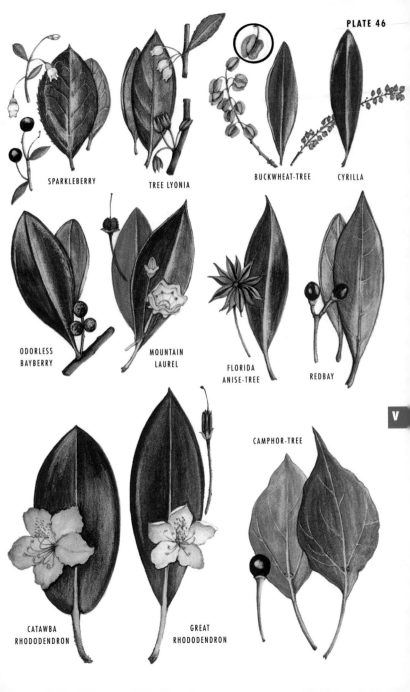

PLATE 46

SPARKLEBERRY

TREE LYONIA

BUCKWHEAT-TREE

CYRILLA

ODORLESS
BAYBERRY

MOUNTAIN
LAUREL

FLORIDA
ANISE-TREE

REDBAY

V

CAMPHOR-TREE

CATAWBA
RHODODENDRON

GREAT
RHODODENDRON

PLATE 47

FAN-LEAVED PALMS

Evergreen leaves 1'–4' in diameter and fan-shaped; segments with parallel veins. Trunks single, unbranched.[1] Southern plants.

SPECIES AND REMARKS	Trunks several, clumped[1]	Old leafstalks cover trunk	Fiber matting covers trunk[2]	Leafstalk bases forked[3]	Flower color[4]	Fruit color[4]	Occurs in s. Fla. only[5]	Text page
CABBAGE PALM *Sabal palmetto* Leafstalk extends through leaf blade, loose fibers at edge.	–	±	–	+	W	D	–	373
DWARF PALMETTO[6] *Sabal minor* Leafstalk enters leaf blade about 2", no loose fibers.	–	±	–	–	W	D	–	374
SAW-PALMETTO[6] *Serenoa repens* Leafstalk sawtoothed with ⅒" spines.	+	+	–	–	W	D	–	374
PAUROTIS PALM *Acoelorrhaphe wrightii* Leafstalk thorns ³/₁₆"–¼"; ± curved.	+	+	+	–	G	D	+	375
FLORIDA THATCHPALM *Thrinax radiata* Leaves 3'–4'; yellow-green, pale beneath; fruits ¼", stalks ¼".	–	–	±	+	W	W	+	375
KEY THATCHPALM *Thrinax morrisii* Leaves 2'–3'; pale green, silvery beneath; fruits ⅛", stalkless.	–	–	±	+	W	W	+	375
FLORIDA SILVERPALM *Coccothrinax argentata* Leaves 1'–2'; dark green, silvery beneath, divided ± to leaf base.	–	–	±	–	W	D	+	375

[1] Trunk branched in some Saw-palmetto specimens.
[2] Trunks wrapped with sheets of woven fibers, but these may fall away on old trees, leaving the trunks ring-scarred.
[3] Split at attachment to the trunk.
[4] D = dark (blue to black), G = green, W = whitish.
[5] Species not restricted to Fla. may occur north to the Carolinas; Fla. species also range into the Caribbean.
[6] Trunks sometimes sprawling rather than upright.

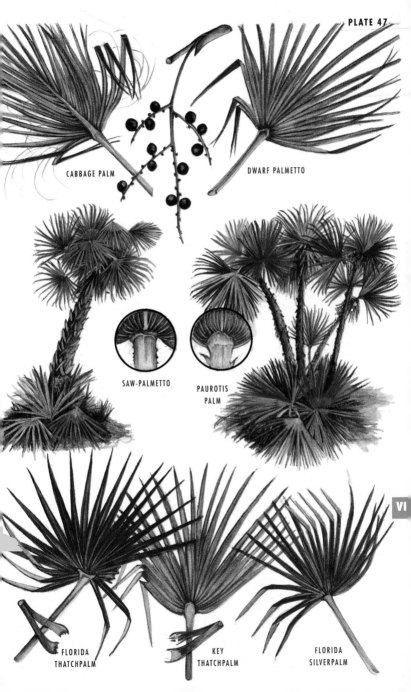

PLATE 47

CABBAGE PALM

DWARF PALMETTO

SAW-PALMETTO

PAUROTIS
PALM

FLORIDA
THATCHPALM

KEY
THATCHPALM

FLORIDA
SILVERPALM

VI

PLATE 48

FEATHER-LEAVED PALMS, TREE-CACTI, AND YUCCAS

Evergreen leaves large and feather-shaped, bristly, or swordlike. The palms of this plate are native to Florida, the leaves featherlike without thorny leafstalks. Trunks single, un-branched, ring-scarred, and free of old leafstalk bases. Cacti and yuccas distinctive.

SPECIES AND REMARKS

	Leaves feather-compound[1]	Flat thorny pads present[2]	Leaves simple, swordlike[3]	Flower color[4]	Fruit color[4]	Occurs in s. Fla. only[5]	Text page
FLORIDA ROYALPALM *Roystonea elata* Trunk cement gray; crownshaft[6] 5'–6'; leaflets irregular.	+	–	–	Y	D	+	376
COCONUT PALM *Cocos nucifera* Trunk ± leaning, no crownshaft[6]; leaflets in flat plane.	+	–	–	Y	G/B	+	376
BUCCANEER PALM *Pseudophoenix sargentii* Rare on Keys. Crownshaft[6] 1'–3'; leaflets form Vs.	+	–	–	G	R	+	377
BRAZIL PRICKLYPEAR *Opuntia brasiliensis* Cactus; some branches cylindrical.	–	+	–	Y	Y	+	377
(INDIAN-FIG PRICKLYPEAR *O. ficus-indica)* Cactus; only flat pads present.	–	+	–	Y	R	+	377
(KEY GIANT-CACTUS *Cereus robinii)* Trunk a spiny, grooved pole. Rare; Florida Keys only.	–	–	–	G	R	+	378
SPANISH BAYONET *Yucca aloifolia* Leaves 1'–3' long; edges fine-toothed.	–	–	+	W	G/D	–	378
MOUNDLILY YUCCA *Y. gloriosa* Leaves 1'–2' long; edges smooth.	–	–	+	W	G/D	–	378

[1] In contrast to the fan-compound leaves of palms on Pl. 48.
[2] Technically the fleshy pads are modified stems, and the leaves are evolved bristles.
[3] And spine tipped; yucca flower clusters are upright, showy.
[4] Flower/fruit clusters: B = brown, D = dark (blue to black), G = green, R = orange-red, W = white, Y = yellow.
[5] Fla. species range into the Caribbean. Yuccas may occur north to the Carolinas. Key Giant-cactus rare.
[6] A smooth, green cylinder of tightly rolled leaf bases topping the trunk of some palms; trunk bulges in these species.

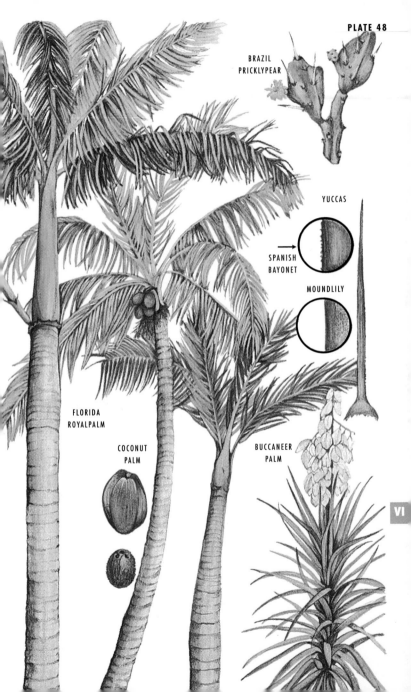

PLATE 48

BRAZIL
PRICKLYPEAR

YUCCAS

SPANISH
BAYONET

MOUNDLILY

FLORIDA
ROYALPALM

COCONUT
PALM

BUCCANEER
PALM

VI

SMALL TREES OF FLORIDA WITH OPPOSITE COMPOUND LEAVES

Leaves evergreen, three-parted or feather-compound; leaflets pointed. See also Pl. 7.

SPECIES AND REMARKS	Leaflets per leaf	Leaflets toothed	End leaflet present	Crushed leaves aromatic[1]	Flower color[2]	Fruit color[2]	Fla. distribution[3]
SMALL TORCHWOOD *Amyris elemifera* Leaflets 1"–3"; fruits round, ¼".	3–5	±	+	+	W	B	E/S
BALSAM TORCHWOOD *A. balsamifera*[4] Leaflets 2"–4"; fruits elliptic, ⅜".	(3–)5	–	+	+	W	B	S
ROUGHBARK LIGNUMVITAE *Guaiacum sanctum* Leaflets 1/2"–1", stalkless, with tiny tips. Keys only.	6–8	–	–	–	U	Y	S
YELLOW-ELDER *Tecoma stans*[5] Flowers showy; fruits cigarlike; escapes cultivation.	5–13	+	+	–	Y	D	S

1 Leaves with gland dots; wood also fragrant.
2 B = black; D = dry, brownish; U = blue; W = white, Y = yellow.
3 E = eastern coastal counties; S = s. or tropical Fla. (Collier, Dade, and Monroe counties).
4 Probably extirpated (R. Hammer, Goulds, Fla.).
5 Native in Fla. and possibly spreading in southern states; rarely tree size.

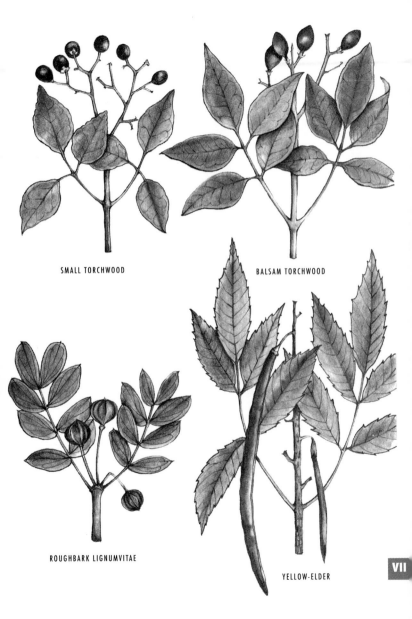

SMALL TORCHWOOD

BALSAM TORCHWOOD

ROUGHBARK LIGNUMVITAE

YELLOW-ELDER

VII

TREES OF LOWER FLORIDA WITH OPPOSITE SIMPLE LEAVES

Caribbean species not found north of cen. Fla.[1] Leaves somewhat leathery and sometimes in whorls. See also Pls. 13 and F-13B.

SPECIES AND REMARKS	Leaf length in inches	Leaf tips blunt	Leaf tips may be notched	Leaf bases wedge-shaped	Leafstalks under ¼"	Leaves with tiny dots[2]	Leaf edges rolled under	Color of flowers[3]	Color of fruits[3]
LONGLEAF BLOLLY *Guapira discolor* Flower clusters at twig ends.	1–2	+	+	+	–	–	–	G	R
LEADWOOD *Krugiodendron ferreum* Flower clusters in leaf angles.	1–2	±	+	–	+	–	–	G	D
RED STOPPER *Eugenia rhombea* Leaf edge yellow; menthol odor. Keys only.	1–2	–	–	±	±	+	–	W	D
BOXLEAF STOPPER *Eugenia foetida* No odor near plant.	1–3	+	–	+	+	+	+	W	D
WHITE STOPPER *Eugenia axillaris* Skunk odor near plant.	1–3	–	–	–	–	+	+	W	D
SURINAM-CHERRY *Eugenia uniflora*[4] Fruits edible, to 1".	1–3	–	–	–	+	+	+	W	O
JOEWOOD *Jacquinia keyensis* Flowers showy, fragrant.	1–3	+	+	+	±	+	+	Y	O
TWINBERRY STOPPER *Myrcianthes fragrans* Crushed leaves aromatic.	1–3	±	+	+	±	+	±	W	R
DOWNY-MYRTLE *Rhodomyrtus tomentosa* Leaves with 3 main veins, velvety.	1–3	+	+	+	–	±	±	P	D
GUAVA *Psidium guajava*[4] Leaf veins parallel; twigs lined.	2–4	±	–	–	±	–	–	W	Y
SEVEN-YEAR-APPLE *Casasia clusiifolia* Twigs ringed; leaves wide.	3–6	+	–	+	–	–	±	W	G
SCARLETBUSH *Hamelia patens* Leaves often in 3's; twigs ridged.	2–9	–	–	±	–	–	–	R	D
FLORIDA FIDDLEWOOD *Citharexylum fruticosum* Twigs ridged, ringed.	3–6	±	+	+	–	–	–	W	O

[1] Not reported occurring north of Citrus, Sumpter, Lake, and Volusia counties.
[2] Use lens; very fine gland dots on one or both surfaces.
[3] D = dark, G = green, O = orange-red, P = pink, R = red, W = white, Y = yellow.
[4] Escapes cultivation.

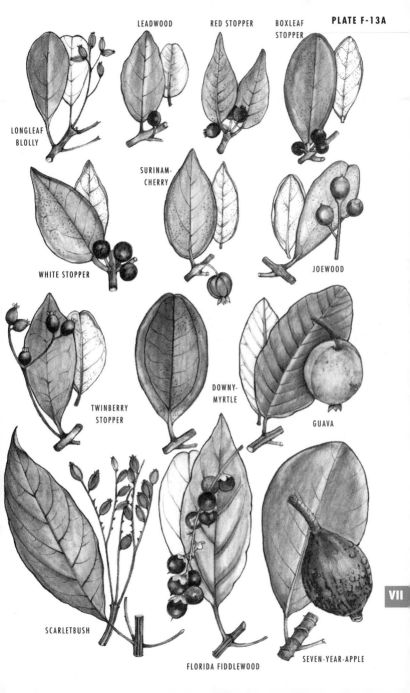

LONGLEAF
BLOLLY

LEADWOOD

RED STOPPER

BOXLEAF
STOPPER

SURINAM-
CHERRY

WHITE STOPPER

JOEWOOD

TWINBERRY
STOPPER

DOWNY-
MYRTLE

GUAVA

SCARLETBUSH

FLORIDA FIDDLEWOOD

SEVEN-YEAR-APPLE

VII

TREES OF SOUTHERN FLORIDA WITH OPPOSITE SIMPLE LEAVES

Caribbean plants reported in extreme s. Fla. only from Collier, Dade, and Monroe counties. Five species occur only in the Fla. Keys.[1] Leaves mostly leathery. See also Pls. 13 and F-13A.

SPECIES	Leaf length in inches, including stalk	Leaf tips blunt	Leaf tips may be notched	Leaf bases wedge-shaped	Leafstalks less than ¼" long	Leaf edges rolled under	Leaves with tiny dots[2]	Color of flowers[3]	Color of ripe fruits[3]
LONGSTALK STOPPER *Psidium longipes*	1–2	±	+	±	±	−	±	W	D
FLORIDA CROSSOPETALUM *Crossopetalum rhacoma*	1–2	±	+	+	+	−	−	R	R
LOCUSTBERRY *Byrsonima lucida*	1–2	±	−	+	+	±	−	W/P	O
ELLIPTIC-LEAF VELVETSEED *Guettarda elliptica*	1–2	±	−	−	−	−	−	W	D
REDBERRY STOPPER *Eugenia confusa*	1–3	−	−	±	−	+	±	W	R
MYRTLE-OF-THE-RIVER *Calyptranthes zuzygium*	2–3	−	−	+	+	−	+	W	O
PALE LIDFLOWER *Calyptranthes pallens*	2–3	−	−	+	−	±	±	W	R
ROUGHLEAF VELVETSEED *Guettarda scabra*	3–4	±	−	−	−	+	−	W	R
FLORIDA TETRAZYGIA *Tetrazygia bicolor*	3–5	−	−	−	−	−	−	W	D
FALSE-BOXWOOD[1] *Gyminda latifolia*	1–2	+	+	+	+	±	−	W	D
DARLING-PLUM[1] *Reynosia septentrionalis*	1–2	+	+	±	+	+	−	G	D
PRINCEWOOD[1] *Exostema caribaeum*	1–2	−	−	±	−	+	−	W/O	D
PISONIA[1] *Pisonia rotundata*	1–3	+	+	±	−	−	−	G	T
FLORIDA CLUSIA[1] *Clusia rosea*	4–7	+	+	±	−	+	−	W	G

1 Absent from mainland.
2 Use lens; very fine gland dots on one or both surfaces of some specimens.
3 D = dark, G = greenish, O = orange, P = pink, R = red, T = tan, W = white.

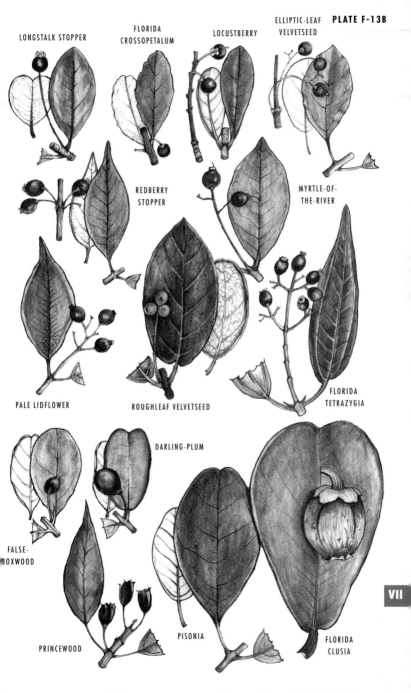

LONGSTALK STOPPER

FLORIDA CROSSOPETALUM

LOCUSTBERRY

ELLIPTIC-LEAF VELVETSEED

REDBERRY STOPPER

MYRTLE-OF-THE-RIVER

PALE LIDFLOWER

ROUGHLEAF VELVETSEED

FLORIDA TETRAZYGIA

FALSE-BOXWOOD

DARLING-PLUM

PRINCEWOOD

PISONIA

FLORIDA CLUSIA

VII

THORNY FLORIDA TREES WITH ALTERNATE COMPOUND LEAVES

Thorns mostly paired at leaf-stalk bases.[1] Leaflets blunt-tipped. Species of s. Fla. with some in central counties[2] but none northward. See also Pl. 15 and Cinnecord (Pl. F-22).

SPECIES AND REMARKS	Leaves twice-compound	Minor leaflets per leaf	Minor leaflet length (inches)	Minor leaflet bases V-shaped	Crushed leaves aromatic	Minor leaflets toothed[3]	Flower color[4]	Bean pod length (inches)[5]	Also cen. Florida[2]
BISCAYNE PRICKLY-ASH *Zanthoxylum coriaceum* Flowers/fruits at twig ends.	−	4–14	1–3	±	+	−	G	0	+
WILD-LIME PRICKLY-ASH *Z. fagara*[6] Flowers/fruits in leaf angles.	−	5–11	1–2	+	+	+	G	0	+
CATCLAW BLACKBEAD *Pithecellobium unguis-cati* Leaves thin, not leathery; pods coiled; thorns ± ¼".	+	(2)4	1–2	±	−	−	P	2–6	+
GUADELOUPE BLACKBEAD *P. guadalupense*[6] Leaves leathery; pods coiled. Thorns tiny. See Pl. F-22.	+	(2)4	1–3	−	−	−	P	2–6	+
FLOWERFENCE POINCIANA *Caesalpinia pulcherrima*[1] Rare escape from gardens.	+	120–400	1	−	−	−	R/Y	3–5	−
HUISACHILLO[7] *Acacia tortuosa* Major leaflets 2–5 pairs.	+	200–650	¼	−	−	−	Y	3–4	+
LONGSPINE ACACIA *Acacia macracantha* Major leaflets 8–20 pairs. Keys only. Fruits flat.	+	400–1800	¼	−	−	−	Y	3–5	+

[1] Thorns may be elsewhere or lacking in Flowerfence Poinciana. Fruits flat.
[2] S. Fla. counties are Collier, Monroe, and Dade; cen. Fla. counties extend north to include Citrus, Sumpter, Lake, and Volusia.
[3] And leafstalks winged.
[4] G = green, P = pink, Y = yellow, R/Y = red/yellow.
[5] O = fruits not bean pods but small round follicles.
[6] Thorns may be few or none.
[7] Pronounced weesatchEEyo.

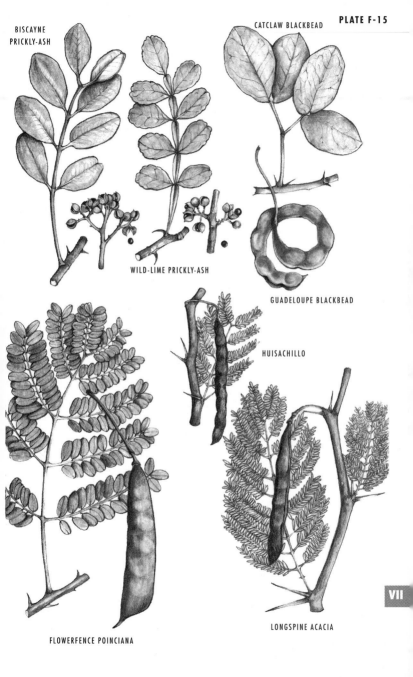

BISCAYNE PRICKLY-ASH

CATCLAW BLACKBEAD

WILD-LIME PRICKLY-ASH

GUADELOUPE BLACKBEAD

HUISACHILLO

FLOWERFENCE POINCIANA

LONGSPINE ACACIA

THORNLESS FLORIDA TREES WITH ALTERNATE ONCE-COMPOUND LEAVES

Most of these trees have leathery evergreen foliage. They are tropical species that occur in Collier, Dade, and Monroe counties. Some range north into cen. Fla. See also Wingless Soapberry (Pl. 21) and Pl. F-21B. Note: Florida Poisonwood and Brazilian Peppertree may cause skin irritations or other medical difficulties.

SPECIES AND REMARKS

	Leaflets per leaf[1]	Leaflets opposite	Leaflets blunt-tipped[2]	Leaflet bases V-shaped	Leaflet length (inches)	Flower color[3]	Fruit color[3]	North to cen. Fla.[4]
WHITE IRONWOOD *Hypelate trifoliata* Leaflets not stalked.	3		+	+	1–2	G	B	–
INKWOOD *Exothea paniculata*[1] Leaflets 4 (often 2); sap dries black.	2–6	+	±	+	3–5	W	B	+
GUMBO-LIMBO *Bursera simaruba* Leaflet bases uneven; bark red, peels.	3–9	+	–	–	2–3	G	R	–
FLORIDA POISONWOOD *Metopium toxiferum* Avoid: see p. 16. Brown bark flakes, shows orange. Leaf blotches present.	3–7	+	±	–	1–3	Y	O	+
JAMAICA-DOGWOOD *Piscidia piscipula* Shredded bark stuns fish (illegal!)	5–9	+	±	±	2–10	W	Br	+
BITTERBUSH *Picramnia pentandra* Not on Fla. Keys. Inner bark bitter.	5–9	±	–	±	3–5	G	R	–
BRAZILIAN PEPPERTREE *Schinus terebinthifolius* Leafstalks red, winged; foliage aromatic.[5]	3–11	+	±	+	2–3	W	R	+

[1] Leaves with even pairs of leaflets may lack an end leaflet, but sometimes a single end leaflet occurs although the total number of leaflets is even.

[2] And sometimes notched.

[3] B = black, Br = brown, G = green, R = red, W = white, Y = yellow-green, O = orange.

[4] Including Citrus, Sumpter, Lake, and Volusia counties.

[5] Crushed leaves with turpentine odor.

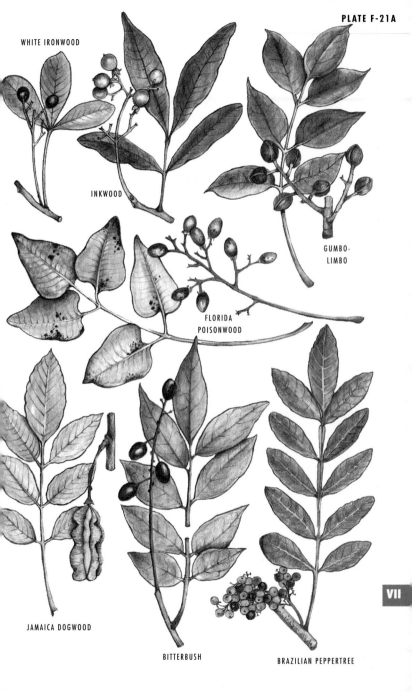

WHITE IRONWOOD

INKWOOD

GUMBO-
LIMBO

FLORIDA
POISONWOOD

JAMAICA DOGWOOD

BITTERBUSH

BRAZILIAN PEPPERTREE

VII

THORNLESS FLORIDA TREES WITH ALTERNATE ONCE-COMPOUND LEAVES

Thornless species, mostly with leathery evergreen foliage. Tropical species with restricted ranges in cen. and s. Fla. See also Pls. 21 and F-21 A.

SPECIES AND REMARKS	Leaflets per leaf[1]	Leaflets opposite	Leaflets blunt-tipped[2]	Leaflet bases V-shaped	Leaflet length (inches)	Flower color[3]	Fruit color[3]	Northernmost Fla. distribution[4]
SATINWOOD *Zanthoxylum flavum* Small teeth or none. Tiny gland dots (use lens).	5–11	+	±	±	1–3	W	D	K
FLORIDA CUPANIA *Cupania glabra* Fla. Keys only; rare. Leaflets toothed.	6–10	−	+	±	3–4	W	D	K
WEST INDIES MAHOGANY *Swietenia mahagoni* Leaflet bases uneven; fruits 3"–5".	8–16	+	−	±	1–3	G	Br	C
PARADISE-TREE *Simarouba glauca* Leaflet bases often uneven; fruits ¾".	8–16	±	+	±	2–4	G	R/D	S
TAMARIND *Tamarindus indica* Leaflets not stalked.	20–30	+	+	−	½–1	Y	Br	S
MEXICAN ALVARADOA *Alvaradoa amorphoides* Fingerlike fruit. Rare.	21–41	−	+	±	½–1	G	D	C

[1] Leaves with even pairs of leaflets may lack an end leaflet, but sometimes a single end leaflet occurs although the total number of leaflets is even.
[2] Sometimes notched.
[3] Br = brown, D = dark, G = green, P = pink, R = red, W = white, Y = yellow.
[4] C = central Fla. n. to include Citrus, Sumpter, Lake, and Volusia counties; K = Fla. Keys; S = southern Fla.: Collier, Dade, and Monroe counties.

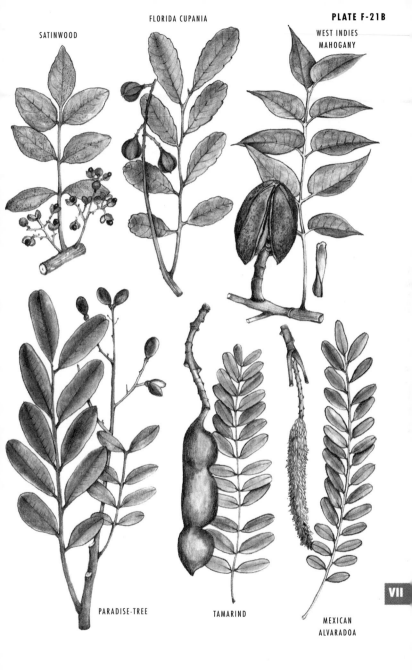

SATINWOOD

FLORIDA CUPANIA

WEST INDIES
MAHOGANY

PARADISE-TREE

TAMARIND

MEXICAN
ALVARADOA

VII

THORNLESS TREES OF SOUTHERN FLORIDA WITH TWICE-COMPOUND LEAVES

Plants of the Florida Keys; some also occur on the mainland in s. Fla.[2] Leaves large; minor leaflets blunt, not toothed. Twigs hairless, leaf scars large; buds hairy; end bud false. Fruits bean pods. See also Lebbek (Pl. 22) and F-15.

SPECIES AND REMARKS	Leaflets more than ¾" long	Leaflets blunt-tipped	Major leaflet pairs	Flower color[1]	S. Fla. mainland[2]
LEADTREE *Leucaena leucocephala* Pods 4"–6" × ¾". Native of Mexico.	–	–	4–8	W	+
BAHAMA LYSILOMA *Lysiloma latisiliquum* Pods 4"–8" × 1"–2".	–	±	3–5	W	+
CINNECORD *Acacia choriophylla*[3] Pods 2"–3" × 1". Rare. Occasional small thorns.	–	+	1–3	Y	–
(GUADELOUPE BLACKBEAD *Pithecellobium guadalupense*)[4] Pods 2"–6" × 1". See Pl. F-15.	+	+	2–4	P	+
(FLOWERFENCE POINCIANA *Caesalpinia pulcherrima*)[5] Pods 3"–5" × 1". See Pl. F-15.	±	+	5–10	R/Y	+

[1] P = pink, W = white, Y = yellow, R/Y = red/yellow.
[2] Collier, Dade, and Monroe counties.
[3] Tiny paired stipules at some leaf scars may be found upon careful examination (use lens). Perhaps these represent spines, but they are not usually noticed, and the species is listed here as thornless.
[4] May have weak thorns.
[5] Prickly or not.

LEADTREE

BAHAMA LYSILOMA

CINNECORD

VII

TREES OF PENINSULAR AND SOUTHERN FLORIDA WITH ALTERNATE EVERGREEN LEAVES NOT TOOTHED

Plants of the semitropics and tropics, occurring north to Marion and Levy counties. Leaves mostly leathery. See also Pls. 46 and F-46B, F-46C, and F-46D.

SPECIES	Leaf length (inches)	Twigs ringed	Sap milky[1]	Leaves crowded at twig tips	Leafstalks essentially lacking	Leaf tips blunt[2]	Leaf bases wedge-shaped	Leaves thick, leathery	Flowers/fruits at twig tips	Flower color[3]	Fruit color[3]
BAY-CEDAR *Suriana maritima*	1	−	−	+	+	±	+	−	+	Y	D
FLORIDA MAYTEN *Maytenus phyllanthoides*	1–2	−	−	−	−	±	+	+	−	W	R
COCOPLUM *Chrysobalanus icaco*	1–3	−	−	±	±	±	+	±	±	W/D	W/D
GRAYTWIG *Schoepfia chrysophylloides*	1–3	−	−	−	−	±	+	+	−	R	R
MYRSINE *Myrsine floridana*	2–4	−	−	+	−	±	+	+	−	G	D
BUTTONWOOD *Conocarpus erectus*	2–4	−	−	±	−	±	+	+	±	G	D
LIMBER CAPER *Capparis flexuosa*	2–4	+	−	−	−	+	−	+	+	W	D
BIGFLOWER PAWPAW *Asimina obovata*	2–4	−	−	−	−	+	±	−	−	G/D	G
CAJEPUT-TREE *Melaleuca quinquenervia*	2–4	−	−	−	−	−	+	−	−	W	D
SATINLEAF *Chrysophyllum oliviforme*	3–4	−	+	−	−	±	−	−	−	W	D
YELLOW ANISE-TREE *Illicium parviflorum*[4]	3–5	−	−	+	−	±	+	+	+	Y	D
SEAGRAPE *Coccoloba uvifera*	3–5	+	−	−	−	+	−	+	+	W	D

1 Try broken leafstalk or twig, but avoid contact with milky sap.
2 Often notched.
3 D = dark, G = greenish, R = red, W = white, Y = yellow.
4 Reported by Lakela and Wunderlin (1980) as occurring north to Ga.

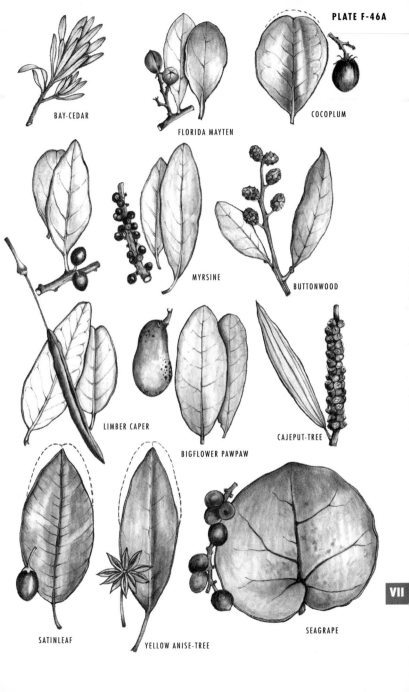

BAY-CEDAR

FLORIDA MAYTEN

COCOPLUM

MYRSINE

BUTTONWOOD

LIMBER CAPER

BIGFLOWER PAWPAW

CAJEPUT-TREE

SATINLEAF

YELLOW ANISE-TREE

SEAGRAPE

VII

TREES OF PENINSULAR AND SOUTHERN FLORIDA WITH ALTERNATE EVERGREEN LEAVES NOT TOOTHED

Plants of the semitropics and tropics, occurring north to Marion and Levy counties. Leaves mostly leathery, with distinct stalks. See also Pls. 46, F-46A, F-46C, and F-46D. For additional recently naturalized figs, see p. 384.

SPECIES	Leaf length (inches)	Twigs ringed	Sap milky[1]	Leaves crowded at twig tips	Leaf tips blunt[2]	Leaf bases wedge-shaped	Leaves thick, leathery	Flowers/fruits at twig ends	Flower color[3]	Fruit color[3]
STRANGLER FIG *Ficus aurea*	3–5	+	+	–	–	±	–	–	–[4]	R
SHORTLEAF FIG *F. citrifolia*	3–5	+	+	–	–	–	–	–	–[4]	R
VARNISHLEAF *Dodonaea viscosa*	3–6	–	–	+	±	+	–	±	Y	G/B
JAMAICA CAPER *Capparis cynophallophora*	3–6	–	–	±	±	±	+	+	W	G
SUGAR-APPLE *Annona squamosa*	3–6	–	–	–	±	±	–	–	W	G
POND-APPLE *A. glabra*	3–6	–	–	–	±	–	–	+	W	Y
LANCEWOOD *Nectandra coriacea*	3–6	–	–	–	–	–	+	±	W	D
GUIANA-PLUM *Drypetes lateriflora*	3–6	–	–	–	–	±	–	–	G	R
MARLBERRY *Ardisia escallonioides*	3–6	–	–	–	–	+	+	+	W	D
MASTIC *Mastichodendron foetidissimum*	3–7	–	+	+	±	±	–	–	Y	Y
SAPODILLA *Manilkara zapota*	4–7	–	+	+	±	±	–	±	W	D
PIGEON-PLUM *Coccoloba diversifolia*	5–7	+	–	–	+	±	–	±	W	D
MANGO *Mangifera indica*	6–11	–	–	+	–	±	–	+	Y	G/P

[1] Try broken leafstalk or twig but avoid contact with milky sap.
[2] Often notched.
[3] B = brown (dry), D = dark, G = greenish, P = pink, R= red, W = white, Y = yellow.
[4] Fig flowers hidden within developing walls of fruits; aerial roots drop from tree branches; gray-barked fig tissues envelop host trees.

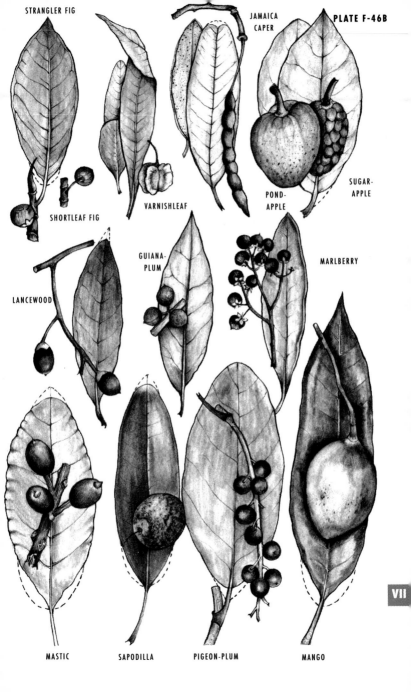

STRANGLER FIG

JAMAICA CAPER

PLATE F-46B

SHORTLEAF FIG

VARNISHLEAF

POND-APPLE

SUGAR-APPLE

LANCEWOOD

GUIANA-PLUM

MARLBERRY

MASTIC

SAPODILLA

PIGEON-PLUM

MANGO

VII

TREES OF EXTREME SOUTHERN FLORIDA WITH ALTERNATE EVERGREEN LEAVES, MOSTLY NOT TOOTHED

Tropical species recorded only from Collier, Dade, and Monroe counties. No species has leafstalks lacking or twigs ringed. Sour Orange (Pl. 24) may lack thorns; it has winged leafstalks half an inch wide. See also Tawnyberry Holly (Pl. 41).

SPECIES	Leaf length (inches)	Sap milky[1]	Leaves crowded at twig tips	Leaf tips blunt[2]	Leaf bases wedge-shaped	Leaves thick, leathery	Leaf edges wavy	Flowers/fruits at twig tips	Flower color[3]	Fruit color[3]
CINNAMON-BARK *Cannella winterana*	2–4	−	−	+	+	+	−	+	R	D
FLORIDA LICARIA *Licaria triandra*[4]	2–4	−	−	−	−	+	+	−	W	D/R
BAHAMA STRONGBARK *Bourreria ovata*	2–5	−	−	±	+	−	−	+	W	O
WILD-DILLY *Manilkara bahamensis*	2–5	+	+	+	±	+	−	+	Y	D
SOLDIERWOOD *Colubrina cubensis*	3–4	−	−	+	±	−	+	−	GW	D
CRABWOOD *Gyminanthes lucida*	3–5	−	−	±	±	±	±	−	G	D
MANCHINEEL *Hippomane mancinella* AVOID; poisonous![5]	3–5	+	+	−	−	±	±	−	G	Y/R
WILLOW BUSTIC *Dipholis salicifolia*	3–5	−	−	−	+	+	+	−	W	D
WEST INDIES LAURELCHERRY *Prunus myrtifolia*	3–5	−	−	−	−	+	+	−	W	D
(GOVERNOR'S-PLUM *Flacourtia indica*)	2–4	−	−	±	±	+	+	−	Y	D

[1] Try broken leafstalks or twigs, but avoid contact with milky sap.
[2] Often notched.
[3] D = dark, G = green, O = orange, R = red, W = white, Y = yellow.
[4] Possibly extirpated (Roger Hammer, Goulds, Fla.).
[5] It is said (Morton 1971) that Manchineel smoke and even rainwater dripping from the leaves can cause skin irritations, that native Americans once used the sap as arrow poison, and that they poisoned the spring water of enemies with the leaves.

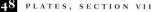

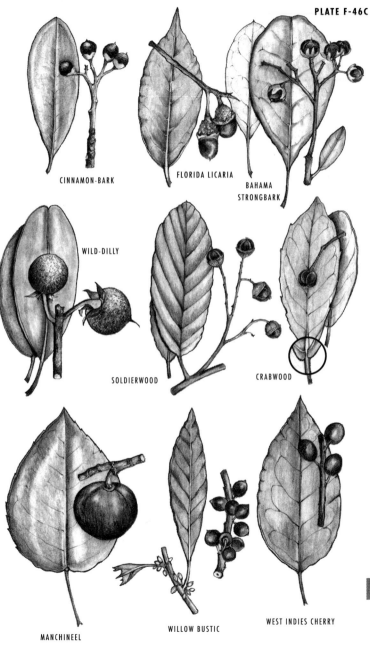

CINNAMON-BARK

FLORIDA LICARIA

BAHAMA
STRONGBARK

WILD-DILLY

SOLDIERWOOD

CRABWOOD

MANCHINEEL

WILLOW BUSTIC

WEST INDIES CHERRY

VII

TREES OF EXTREME SOUTHERN FLORIDA WITH ALTERNATE EVERGREEN LEAVES MOSTLY NOT TOOTHED

Tropical species recorded only from Collier, Dade, and Monroe counties. No species has sap milky, leaf-stalks lacking, or twigs ringed.

SPECIES AND REMARKS	Total length (inches)	Leaves crowded at twig tips	Leaf tips blunt[1]	Leaf bases wedge-shaped	Veins follow leaf edges	Flowers/fruits at twig tips	Flower color[2]	Fruit color[2]
COFFEE COLUBRINA *Colubrina arborescens* New growth rusty-hairy.	3–8	–	–	–	+	–	G	D
POTATO-TREE *Solanum erianthum* Leaves woolly, with tar odor; stalks 1"–2".	3–8	–	–	±	–	+	W	Y
BLACK-CALABASH *Amphitecna latifolia* Leaves shiny; flowers malodorous. Rare.	5–8	–	±	+	–	+	W	G
INDIA-ALMOND *Terminalia catappa* Beaches, cultivation. Edible.	4–12	±	±	+	–	±	W	D
FLA. KEYS (NOT ON MAINLAND).[3]								
MAIDENBUSH *Savia bahamensis* Clusters of flower buds ball-like.	1–2	–	+	±	–	–	G	D
FLORIDA-BOXWOOD *Schaefferia frutescens* Twigs green, lined (use lens).	1–2	–	+	±	–	–	G	R
ROUGH STRONGBARK *Bourreria radula* Leaves sandpapery.	1–3	–	±	+	–	+	W	O
NAKEDWOOD *Colubrina elliptica* Leaves long-pointed, basal glands.[4]	3–4	–	–	–	+	–	Y	O
MILKBARK *Drypetes diversifolia* Bark white; toothed leaves few.	3–5	–	±	±	–	–	G	W

1 Sometimes notched.
2 D = dark, G = greenish, O = orange, R = red, W = white, Y = yellow.
3 According to Little (1979), but Long and Lakela (1971) state that the range of some includes s. Fla.
4 Small glands present on base of leaf blades; use lens.

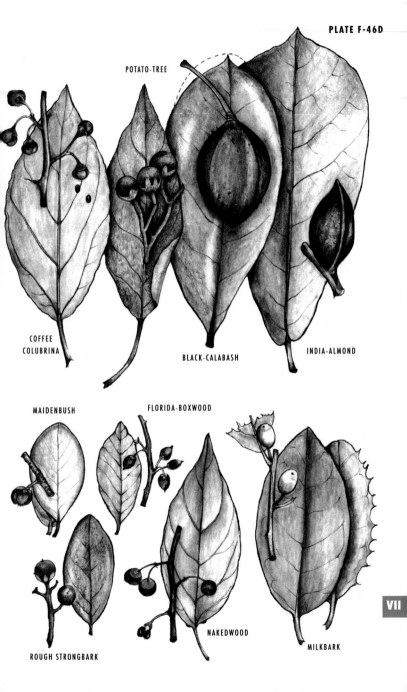

POTATO-TREE

COFFEE
COLUBRINA

BLACK-CALABASH

INDIA-ALMOND

MAIDENBUSH

FLORIDA-BOXWOOD

ROUGH STRONGBARK

NAKEDWOOD

MILKBARK

VII

SPECIES
ACCOUNTS

TREES WITH NEEDLELIKE OR SCALELIKE LEAVES MOSTLY EVERGREEN

(PLATES 1–5)

The cone-bearing trees and a few non-coniferous plants with tiny evergreen leaves compose this well-defined group. The leaves are either long and slender (needlelike) or small and overlapping (scalelike). Though individual needles and needle clusters may drop throughout the year, most conifers are green the year around. The larches and Baldcypress, however, are exceptions. They drop all of their foliage in autumn; their branches remain bare until spring. Conifers are not the only evergreen trees; many broad-leaved trees (such as American Holly) and tropical trees, such as palms, also hold green leaves throughout the year, but they are not described in this section.

The female fruits of conifers are usually woody cones with seeds developed at the bases of the cone scales. They may take more than one year to mature. If none is present on the tree, old ones can often be found on the ground nearby. Male cones are small pollen-producing organs that are obvious only during the early flowering period.

Florida Yew, Torreya, and junipers (Pls. 4, 5) have fleshy, somewhat berrylike fruits. While these bear little resemblance to the usual cones of members of the pine family, all of them develop from naked ovules. Higher flowering plants have ovules enclosed in ovaries.

Identify unknown plants in this section by looking through Pls. 1–5, or trace the proper plate number by means of the key below:

1. Leaves ¾"–18" long, needle-shaped. **2**
   2. Needles in groups along the twigs. **3**
   2. Needles attached singly to twigs. **5**
3. Needles many, clumped on short spurs.   **Larches, Pl. 1**
3. Needles bound at the base in bundles. **4**

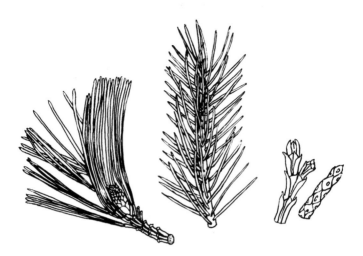

Fig. 5. Needlelike or scalelike leaves.

    4. Needles 3–5 per bundle.   **Pines I, Pl. 1.**
    4. Needles 2 per bundle.   **Pines II, Pl. 2.**
 5. Needles on woody pegs, 4-sided, not in flat sprays..
                                         Spruces, Pl. 3.
 5. Needles not on woody pegs, flat, in flattened sprays.
                                         Firs, etc., Pl. 4.
 1. Leaves small and hugging the twigs, either blunt and scalelike
    or hollowed and sharp-pointed, or both kinds present.
                      White-cedars, junipers, etc., Pl. 5.

CONIFERS WITH NEEDLES IN CLUSTERS: LARCHES AND PINES I (PLATE 1)

The larches and Baldcypress (Pl. 4) are our only conifers that *drop their leaves* in autumn. In larches, there are conspicuous warty *branches* on the twigs. In season, numerous needles are clustered at the ends of these spurs. Leaf scars have 1 bundle scar. Larch cones lack prickles and have relatively few thin scales. Larch cones stand erect; pine cones are pendent.

Tamarack

TAMARACK (AMERICAN LARCH) PL. 1
Larix laricina (Du Roi) K. Koch.

A medium-sized to large pointed-top tree (see silhouette p. 23) with many slender needles ¾"–1" long, on *short spurs*. On longer shoots, needles are single. Branchlets do *not* droop. Cones ½"–¹³⁄₁₆" long and nearly as wide. Trunk bark dark, flaking off in small scales. Height 40'–80' (90'); diameter 1'–2' (3'). Northern wet soils. **SIMILAR SPECIES:** (1) European Larch has longer needles and cones, drooping branchlets, and bark with large plates. (2) Baldcypresses (Pl. 4) are trees of southern swamps. **REMARKS:** An important northern timber tree (used for poles, posts, railroad ties). Seeds, needles, or inner bark eaten by ruffed and sharptail grouse, snowshoe hare, red squirrel, porcupine, and deer.

EUROPEAN LARCH *Larix decidua* Mill. NOT ILLUS.

A European tree sometimes spreading from northern plantings. Needles 1"–1½" long; branchlets may *droop*. Cones ¹³⁄₁₆"–1⅜" in length. Red-brown trunk bark divided into large plates. Mostly an upland species.

The pines are probably the world's most important timber trees. Growing principally on dry, sandy soils of little value, they yield not only lumber but also turpentine, tar, pitch, and a medicinal oil.

The pines are cone-bearing evergreen trees with slender needles occurring in groups of 2 to 5 along the twigs. The needle groups are bound in bundles at the base. Only White Pine has 5 needles per cluster. All of our remaining species, generally known as yellow pines, have 2 or 3 needles per bundle. Winter buds of most pines are reddish brown.

The mature bark of the White, Scotch, Austrian, Spruce, and Sand pines is dark and furrowed, but that of other pines is usually divided into more or less rectangular plates. Pine branches usually occur in whorls around the trunks; normally the tree is topped by a new whorl each year. Only a few pine species occur in any one state; they are more numerous to the south and east. The distribution maps will often assist in identification.

Seeds are sometimes useful in species identification. When the paired seeds cannot be seen easily between cone scales, cones can be allowed to dry in a paper bag and the seeds shaken loose.

White Pine

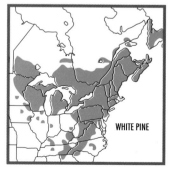

WHITE PINE

Several western pines produce edible seeds: those of the pinyon pines of the Great Basin region (*Pinus edulis* and *P. monophylla*) are especially delicious. Seeds of many species rank high among the foods of nearly all game birds, rabbits, hares, squirrels, and chipmunks, and are also eaten by coyotes and black bears. The twigs and needles serve as food for deer, moose, and other browsing animals but mostly when preferred foods are lacking.

EASTERN WHITE PINE *Pinus strobus* L.   PL. 1

A tall upland tree with relatively few large limbs in horizontal whorls. Needles 2"–4" long, slender, flexible, and occurring 5 *to the bundle* and with remnants of deciduous sheaths only about 1/32" long. Cones slender, tapering, thornless, long-stalked, 3"–6" long. Seed 1/4", wing 1/2" × 3/16". Bark not scaly, as in many other pines, but dark with deep furrows. A dwarf matted form occurs in windswept northern areas. Height 80'–110'; diameter 2'–3' (6'). **SIMILAR SPECIES:** The only native five-needle pine in the eastern U.S. and Canada. **REMARKS:** One of the most important and tallest timber trees in the Northeast. So extensively lumbered that few virgin trees, which once grew to heights of 200' to 220', remain. In some areas reforestation is considerable. Wood light, soft, straight-grained, and generally not as resinous as in other pines; of great value in woodworking. Plagued by white pine blister rust, a fungus attacking the inner bark, and white pine weevil, an insect that kills the topmost shoot, deforming the tree and limiting its value. The rust can be controlled by removal of currant and gooseberry shrubs — upon which the fungus spends a portion of its life cycle — from within a quarter mile of the pines. Called Weymouth Pine in England. Though only one 5-needle pine occurs in the e. U.S., there are several important white (or soft) pines in the West.

YELLOW PINES

Pines with either 2 or 3 needles per cluster are known collectively as yellow (or hard) pines. One to three whorls of new branches may top these trees each year. There are 14 yellow pine species in our area. Those shown on Plate 1 have 3 needles, while those of Plate 2 mainly have only 2 per cluster. Shortleaf and Slash pines of Plate 2 may both have 2- and 3-needle clusters present. The half-inch-thick branches of most pines will snap cleanly in two when bent sharply. Those of a few species, however, are fibrous and cannot readily be broken. Winter end buds are mostly brown.

Several yellow pines once were tapped for their sap but synthetic materials have largely replaced these natural resins in industry. Pitch-filled chips of yellow pine wood are useful in start-

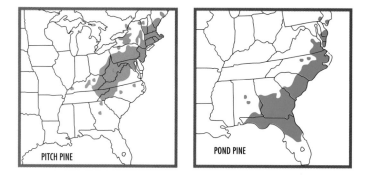

PITCH PINE

POND PINE

ing fires. Yellow pine lumber, stronger than that of white pines, is
widely used in house construction.

PITCH PINE *Pinus rigida* Mill.   **PL. 1**

The only 3-needle pine with half-inch branches that are fibrous
and *tough*; they do *not* snap cleanly when bent sharply. A medium-sized tree of the Northeast and Appalachians with needles
3"–5" long. Trunk sprouts, usually *short* and tufted, sometimes
present, especially after fires. Cones stout, 1"–3" long, often
remaining long on the tree. The inner cone scale tips are either
dark or plain. The outer scales are mostly tipped with thorns
1/32"–1/8" long, but the cones are not always prickly when handled.
Seed 3/16", wing 5/8" × 3/16". Height 40'–60' (70'); diameter 1'–2' (3').
Mainly dry sites. **SIMILAR SPECIES:** (1) Pond Pine has more frequent
and lengthy trunk sprouts plus branches that break cleanly. (2)
Virginia and (3) Mountain pines (both Pl. 2) also have tough,
fibrous branches but are 2-needle species whose foliage is more
flat-sided. (4) Shortleaf Pine (Pl. 2) has mostly paired needles and
easily snapped branches. See also (5) Loblolly Pine. **REMARKS:** The
common pine of se. New Jersey pine barrens.

POND (SWAMP) PINE   **PL. 1**
Pinus serotina Michx.

Similar to Pitch Pine but more *southern*, with *brittle* half-inch
branches and needles 4"–8" long. Trunk sprouts are *common* and
often *10" or more* long. Cones rather *globular*, 2"–3" across, opening late and remaining attached. Cone scale tips plain or narrowly
brown; prickles only 1/32" long, weak, or absent. Crown branches
tend to be tangled. Seed 3/16", wing 11/16" × 3/16". Height to 80'; diameter to 2'. A lowland species. **REMARKS:** Hybrids with Pitch, Shortleaf, and Loblolly pines have been found.

Loblolly Pine

LOBLOLLY PINE *Pinus taeda* L.   PL. 1

A common *southern* tree with needles 6"–9" long and 3 per cluster. Basal needle sheaths are ⁷⁄₁₆"–1¹⁄₁₆" long. Half-inch branches snap cleanly when bent. Twigs are about ¼" in diameter. Trunk sprouts *lacking*. Cones more or less cylindrical, 3"–6" long; many old cones remain on the tree. Cone scales mostly ⅜"–½" wide, brown-tipped or plain inside, with ¹⁄₁₆"–⅛" thorns outside. Cones mostly *prickly* when handled. Trunk bark blackish, forming plates with a dark orange tinge. Seed ¼", wing ¾" × ⁵⁄₁₆". Height 80'–100' (115'); diameter 1'–2' (5'). Old fields, dry and wet sites. Coastal Plain and Piedmont Plateau. **SIMILAR SPECIES:** (1) Shortleaf Pine (Pl. 2) has needles about half as long, mostly in 2's, and with short (⅛"–¼") sheaths. Its cones also are half-size, with prickles tiny or absent. In addition, the bark plates may show tiny pitch-pocket holes. (2) Pitch and (3) Pond pines have shorter needles, needle sheaths, hardly prickly cones, and also may have trunk sprouts. Pond Pine has cones more or less ball shaped. (4) Slash Pine (Pl. 2) typically has both 2- and 3-needle clusters present with longer needles and needle sheaths, stouter twigs, and larger cones with wider scales (photo, p. 163). (5) Longleaf Pine has very long needles and thumb-wide twigs with white winter end buds. It also has longer, less-prickly cones with much wider scales. **REMARKS:** An

Longleaf Pine

important lumber tree. Invades old fields. Reported to hybridize with several other pines.

LONGLEAF PINE
PL. 1

Pinus palustris Mill. (*P. australis* Michx. f.)

A handsome straight southern tree with *very long needles* grouped in 3's. Needles 8"–18" (mostly more than 11") long and clustered toward the ends of twigs, giving a *tufted* appearance. Needle sheaths mostly ⅝"–1" long. Twigs *very stout,* appearing to be thumb-wide (always ½" or more), brittle when bent, and ending in one or more *white-silvery buds* each 1"–2" long. Cones conical, 6"–10" long; scales *more than* ¾" wide, brown-tipped inside, and with tiny, thin prickles. The large cones are often conspicuous beneath mature trees. Seed ⅜", wing 1⅜" × ⅜". Height 60'–70' (85'); diameter 1'–2' (3.5'). Coastal Plain soils. **REMARKS:** The long

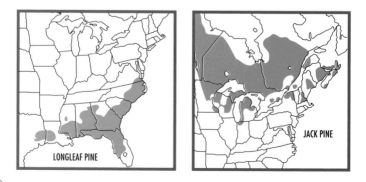

LONGLEAF PINE

JACK PINE

Pine cones clockwise from upper left: Slash Pine, Longleaf Pine, Loblolly Pine, and Shortleaf Pine

grasslike needles of seedlings protect them against fires for several years. Once an important source of turpentine and a valuable timber tree in South. Nevertheless, cut-over stands are being widely replaced by plantations of Slash Pine. Hybrids with Loblolly Pine have been recorded.

CONIFERS WITH NEEDLES IN CLUSTERS: PINES II (PLATE 2)

The following are two-needle pines. Shortleaf Pine, nevertheless, *often* carries some 3-needle clusters, while Slash Pine *regularly* has a mixture of 2- and 3-needle groups. If green foliage is out of reach, see dead needles under the tree. Only Mountain and Virginia pines have *fibrous* half-inch branches that do not snap cleanly when bent.

JACK PINE *Pinus banksiana* Lamb.   **PL. 2**
A scrubby, small or medium-sized *northern* tree with needles *very short,* only 1"–1½" long, with a somewhat flattened surface, and sheaths ¼6"–⅛" (³⁄₁₆") long. Cones usually curved or *bulging* on one side. 1½"–2½" long; persistent. Cone scales with inside edges black in older cones and either thornless or with tiny weak prickles. Seed ⅛", wing ¼" × ¼6". Height 15'–40'; diameter 9"–15". **SIMILAR SPECIES:** No other pine in our area has such short needles or curved cones. **REMARKS:** Produces poor timber but widespread in some northern areas of dry, infertile soils that would otherwise support no tree growth. Fires cause cones to open and release seeds.

Jack Pine

SCOTCH PINE *Pinus sylvestris* L.

A medium-sized to tall northern tree with yellow-green needles 2"–3" long and sheaths ⅟₁₆"–⅛" in length. Cones 1½"–2½" long, seldom remaining long on the tree; scales without shaded inside edges but with a raised, more or less sharp but actually thornless point. Higher trunk and large branches a rather smooth *bright orange*. Seed ¼", wing ⅟₁₆" × ³⁄₁₆". Height usually under 50' and diameter under 1'. **SIMILAR SPECIES:** No other eastern pine has bright, non-checkered, orange upper bark. (1) Jack Pine has shorter needles and curved cones. (2) Austrian and (3) Red pines both have longer foliage and more or less brown-edged cone scales. The former also has white winter end buds,

Scotch Pine

SPECIES AND REMARKS	Average needle length (inches)	Average cone length (inches)	Open cones longer than wide[1]	Many old cones on tree	Needles per bundle[2]
JACK PINE *Pinus banksiana* Cones narrow, curved. **Pl. 2**	1	2	+	+	2
VIRGINIA PINE *P. virginiana* Needles gray-green, stiff.[3] **Pl. 2**	2	2	−	+	2
SCOTCH PINE *P. sylvestris* Upper bark smooth, orange. **Pl. 2**	2	2	−	−	2
MOUNTAIN PINE *P. pungens* Cones wide, very thorny. **Pl. 2**	2	2	−	+	2
RED PINE *P. resinosa* Trunk straight, bark ± reddish. **Pl. 2**	5	2	+	−	2
PITCH PINE *P. rigida* Needles yellow-green, stiff.[3, 4] **Pl. 1**	5	2	−	+	3
(AUSTRIAN PINE *P. nigra*) Bark plates grayish yellow; buds white.[5]	5	2	+	−	2
WHITE PINE *P. strobus* Branches in horizontal whorls. **Pl. 1**	4	5	+	−	5

[1] ± = more or less ball-shaped; + = elongated.
[2] Not a "roadside" characteristic but useful if close scrutiny is undertaken.
[3] Branches usually more tangled and trunk more twisted than other pines.
[4] May show trunk sprouts after fire; see also Pond Pine, p. 160.
[5] Mostly planted specimens.

and the latter has brittle, clean-breaking needles. Both (4) Virginia and (5) Mountain pines have branches mostly difficult to break, the former with slender cone prickles and the latter with coarse, prickly needles and long-thorny cones. REMARKS: Imported from Europe and spreading locally from forest and Christmas tree plantings.

AUSTRIAN PINE *Pinus nigra* Arnott   **NOT ILLUS.**

Needles dark green, *stiff,* and 3"–6" long with sheaths ¼"–½" (¾") in length. Fresh winter end buds whitish or scales white-edged, slightly resinous. Cones 2"–3", somewhat pointed, without stalks, soon dropping; scales with a faint brown border and usually with a tiny prickle. Seed ¼", wing ⁷⁄₁₆" × ³⁄₁₆". Mature trunks have rather distinctive vertical grayish yellow bark plates (see photo below). Height 50'–100' (165'); diameter 1'–2' (3'). **SIMILAR SPECIES:** The needles of (1) Scotch Pine are shorter and not as dark, while those of (2) Red Pine are brittle, snapping crisply when bent. Both species have brown winter end buds and lack cone prickles. (3) Longleaf Pine (Pl. 1) also has white end buds, but it is a southern tree with 3 needles per cluster, each 8"–18" long. **REMARKS:** Mostly in northern landscaped parks and occasionally spreading from cultivation there.

RED PINE *Pinus resinosa* Ait.   **PL. 2**

A typically straight-trunked *northern* tree with 4"–6" needles bound by sheaths ³⁄₁₆"–⅜" long. Unlike other pines in its range, the fresh needles *break crisply* when bent. Winter buds are *resinous.* Cones 1½"–2½" long; scales *thornless,* sometimes with brown inside tips. Old cones do not accumulate on the tree. Seed ¼", wing ½" × ³⁄₁₆". Bark plates dark with a reddish tinge. Height

50'–80' (85'); diameter 1'–2' (3'). Upland sites. **SIMILAR SPECIES:** See (1) Scotch, (2) Austrian, and (3) Japanese Black pines. **REMARKS:** A beautiful tree widely used in reforestation. Often called Norway Pine but native only to North America. The distinctive crispness with which the needles snap may have to be learned on a tree of known identity.

Bark of Austrian Pine

RED PINE

Bark of Red Pine

JAPANESE BLACK PINE *Pinus thunbergii* Parl. **NOT ILLUS.**
An Asiatic import much like Red Pine. Needles, however, do *not* snap crisply when bent, and their sheaths may display threadlike filaments. Winter end buds *white,* not resinous. Cones are stalked, the scales with tiny prickles. Seed ¼"; wing ⁹⁄₁₆" × ¼". **REMARKS:** An important timber tree in Japan. Naturalized in Massachusetts.

MOUNTAIN PINE *Pinus pungens* Lamb. **PL. 2**
A small to medium-sized tree with paired, *flat-sided*, and *prickly* needles 2"–3" long. Sheaths ⅛"–⁵⁄₁₆" in length. Half-inch-thick branches are fibrous and usually do *not* break with a clean snap. Cones 2"–4" long, often equally wide, the base generally off-center, with short stalks or none, mostly *clinging tightly* to the branches and remaining long on the tree. Cone thorns are rather stout, out-curved, and ³⁄₁₆"–⁵⁄₁₆" long. Seed ¼", wing ¹³⁄₁₆" × ¼". Height to 60'; diameter to 2'. Scattered, mainly dry Appalachian locations. **SIMILAR SPECIES:** No other eastern pine has such sharp-tipped needles and long-thorned cones. Limited distribution also helpful. See (1) Virginia and (2) Pitch pines. **REMARKS:** The basis of an alternate common name, Table Mountain Pine, is unclear.

SOUTHERN PINES,
WITH CLUES FOR ROADSIDE IDENTIFICATION

SPECIES AND REMARKS	Average needle length (inches)	Average cone length (inches)	Open cones longer than wide[1]	Many old cones on tree	Needles per bundle[2]
SAND PINE *Pinus clausa* Sandhills, Fla., and se. Ala. **Pl. 2**	3	2	−	+	2
SPRUCE PINE[3] *P. glabra* Bark dark, fine cracks. **Pl. 2**	3	2	+	+	2
SHORTLEAF PINE *P. echinata* Twigs ¼" thick, no cone prickles. **Pl. 2**	4	2	+	+	2−(3)
POND PINE *P. serotina* Trunk sprouts common.[4] **Pl. 1**	6	2	−	+	3
LOBLOLLY PINE *P. taeda* Twigs ¼" thick; cones prickly. **Pl. 1**	7	4	+	+	3
SLASH PINE *P. elliottii* Twigs ¼"−½" thick; end bud rusty-silver. **Pl. 2**	9	5	+	−	2−3
LONGLEAF PINE *P. palustris* Twigs ½"−1 "; end bud white. **Pl. 1**	13	8	+	−	3

[1] ± = more or less ball-shaped; + = elongated.
[2] Not a "roadside" characteristic but useful if close scrutiny is undertaken.
[3] Usually scattered in broadleaf forests.
[4] Needles yellow-green, dull. See also Pitch Pine, p. 160.

MOUNTAIN PINE

VIRGINIA PINE

VIRGINIA (SCRUB) PINE *Pinus virginiana* Mill.   **PL. 2**
   A somewhat shrubby, scraggly, small or medium-sized tree of the
   south-central states with sturdy, slightly flat-sided, and somewhat
   spiraled 2"–3" needles. Needle sheaths ¹⁄₁₆"–³⁄₁₆" long. Half-inch
   branches tough, fibrous, and *difficult to break*. Cones broad or
   somewhat egg-shaped, 2"–3" long, numerous, remaining on the
   tree for a long time. Cone scales with inside borders dark brown
   and tips with straight thorns ¹⁄₁₆"–¹⁄₈" long. Seeds ¼", wing ⁵⁄₁₆" × ³⁄₁₆".
   Height 30'–40' (60'); diameter 1'–2' (3'). Poor soils and old fields.
   SIMILAR SPECIES: (1) Mountain and (2) Pitch (Pl. 1) pines also have
   tough, fibrous branches, but the first has spiny-tipped needles
   and strong, out-curved cone thorns, while the second has longer
   needles 3 per cluster. (3) Scotch Pine spreads from plantings
   mostly north of Virginia Pine range. Its upper bark is bright
   orange, cones are thornless, and half-inch branches snap easily.
   See also (4) Shortleaf Pine.

SHORTLEAF PINE *Pinus echinata* Mill.   **PL. 2**
   A tall, mostly southern tree with 2- and usually *also* with 3-needle
   clusters. Needles 3"–5" with sheaths ¹⁄₈"–¼" long. Twigs are about
   ¼" thick. Half-inch branches break cleanly. Cones egg-shaped and
   1½"–3" long; scales with or without shaded inside borders. The

Bark of Shortleaf Pine

SHORTLEAF PINE

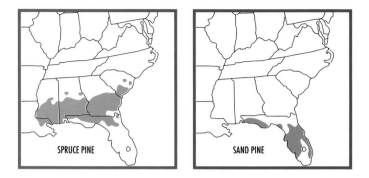

cone scales are ⅜"–½" wide and have a straight but weak prickle; thorns do not hurt when handled. Many old cones usually present on the tree. Seed ³⁄₁₆", wing ½" × ³⁄₁₆". Trunk bark similar to that of Loblolly Pine but the plates often with small scattered resin pockets (pitch-filled or empty holes). Height 90'–100' (150'); diameter 3'–4'. Old fields and uplands. **SIMILAR SPECIES:** (1) Virginia Pine has shorter, 2-needle clusters, branches difficult to snap, and cone scales distinctly brown-edged. See also (2) Loblolly and (3) Pitch pines. **REMARKS:** Small trees are reported to produce root sprouts after fires. An important timber tree. Hybrids with several pines have been identified.

SPRUCE PINE *Pinus glabra* Walt.   **PL. 2**

Scattered in southern hardwood (broad-leaved) forests, this is a mostly small to medium-sized and uncommon pine with twigs (remove needles) *very smooth*. Needles slender and 2"–4" long with sheaths ¹⁄₁₆"–³⁄₁₆" in length. Cones 1"–2", with old cones remaining on the tree. Inside tips of cone scales are either brown-bordered or plain; scale prickles tiny or lacking. Trunk bark dark and ridged. Seeds ³⁄₁₆", wing ¾" × ³⁄₁₆". Height 80'–100' (120'); diameter 1'–2' (3'). Fertile soils. **SIMILAR SPECIES:** Only (1) Sand Pine also has distinctively smooth twigs, but it is confined to Florida and se. Alabama and has black inner cone scale margins. (2) Virginia and (3) Mountain pines are more northern with branches fibrous and difficult to break. Mature cones of Mountain Pine have long thorns. **REMARKS:** A more or less shade-tolerant pine. Hybrids with Shortleaf Pine have been found.

SAND PINE *Pinus clausa* (Chapm. ex Engelm.) Sarg.   **PL. 2**

Occurring in cen. to ne. Florida and again in nw. Florida and se. Alabama, this small to medium-sized pine has twigs that are

Slash Pine

remarkably smooth (remove needles). The 2"–3" cones have scale tips with *black* inside edges and prickles short or absent yet sometimes stout. Cones persist on the tree. The slender needles are 2"–4" long with sheaths ⅛"–¼". Seed ¼", wing ½" × ³/₁₆". Height 15'–20' (25'); diameter to 1'. On poor sandy soils. SIMILAR SPECIES: See Spruce Pine, also with smooth twigs. REMARKS: Capable of rapid recolonization after fires.

SLASH PINE *Pinus elliottii* Engelm. var *elliottii*   PL. 2
Resembles Loblolly and Longleaf pines (Pl. 1) in southern distribution but needles are 7"–11" long, and *both* 2- and 3-needle clusters are usually present (but see under Remarks). The twigs are ¼"–½" in diameter with the winter end buds *rusty-silver*. Needle sheaths are ⅜"–⅝" long. Cones are 3"–6" long, the old ones in most areas *not* accumulating on the tree. Cone scales are ½"–¾" wide, tipped with small, thin thorns, and sometimes brown-edged. Seeds ¼", wing ¹⁵/₁₆" × ⁵/₁₆". Height 80'–115'; diameter 1'–3'. Moist to dry soils. SIMILAR SPECIES: (1) Longleaf Pine has longer needles in 3's, thumb-wide twigs, and pure white winter end buds. It also has wider cone scales, longer needle sheaths, and larger seed wings. See (2) Loblolly Pine (Pl. 1). REMARKS: A fast-growing tree much planted for timber, especially where Longleaf Pine stands

have been harvested. Formerly tapped for turpentine. Reported to hybridize with Loblolly Pine. In s. and cen. Fla., a 2-needle form (var. *densa* Little and Dorman) predominates. It has a grasslike seedling stage like Longleaf Pine and is the only pine in the Everglades.

NOT PINES BUT RESEMBLING THEM

AUSTRALIAN-PINE (HORSETAIL CASUARINA)   **FIG. 6**
Casuarina equisitifolia L.

Drooping "needles" are up to 1' long and attached *singly*. Each "needle" comprises a series of *jointed*, fine-grooved green sections, which are technically twigs; the true leaves form whorls of 6–8 tiny gray scales or leaf teeth fringing each joint. Branchlets *hairy*. The ⅛"–1" fruits are brown and conelike but ball-shaped. Height 60'–90' (100'); diameter 10"–15" (18"). Seashores and other sandy soils. **SIMILAR SPECIES:** No native tree has jointed "needles." **REMARKS:** The casuarinas, or beefwoods, represent a large group of tropical species. Unlike the pines, the casuarinas are true flowering plants. The blossoms are minute. The needles resemble those of the herbaceous horsetails (*Equisetum*). They are also similar to the drooping feathers of the flightless cassowary bird from which the casuarina name derives. Australian-pine is used in windbreaks and hedges. Though it has value in erosion control, this fast-growing species has become naturalized and is spreading in s. Florida.

Fig. 6. Australian-pine.

CUNNINGHAM BEEFWOOD   **NOT ILLUS.**
Casuarina cunninghamiana Miquel

Another Australian casuarina with 8–10 scale leaves per whorl and branchlets nearly *hairless*. To 100' tall. Spreading in Florida.

BRAZILIAN BEEFWOOD   **NOT ILLUS.**
Casuarina glauca Sieber ex Sprengel

This casuarina has also been introduced into tropical Florida. It may be distinguished by its having 12–17 scale leaves per joint-whorl.

CONIFERS WITH NEEDLES SHORT ON WOODY PEGS: SPRUCES (Plate 3)

Spruces are ornamental, sharply steeple-shaped (silhouette, p. 21) evergreen trees of cold climates. The needles of eastern spruces are somewhat four-angled, short, stiff, and sharp. They tend to grow all around the twigs. When needles fall, twigs and branchlets remain *very rough* from persistent needle bases. To determine the hairiness of spruce twigs and the shape of buds, remove the needles and use a lens. Like firs and yews, spruce branchlets are tipped with twigs arranged in the shape of Christian crosses. Spruce cones are brown and woody when mature. Unlike the firs, they are not erect and do not fall apart on the tree. Their scales are thin, not heavy or thorny as in the pines. The bark is rough and dark.

Spruces grow north to the limit of trees; forests thin down to dwarf specimens extending far into the tundra. Red Spruce persists on mountaintops as far south as Georgia.

Spruces are often used as Christmas trees, but their needles fall quickly upon drying. The wood is soft, light, resinous, and

BLACK SPRUCE

RED SPRUCE

WHITE SPRUCE

White Spruce

straight-grained. It provides a principal source of pulp for paper and is valuable for sounding boards in pianos and for construction, interior finishing, and boatbuilding. Tannin and "burgundy pitch," used in varnishes and medicinal compounds, come from the bark of certain species. In Europe some spruces are tapped for turpentine, and in times of food shortage the inner bark has been ground and added to flour. Spruce beer is reportedly made from the fermented leaves and twigs after being boiled with honey. Several spruces are of value in landscaping.

BLACK SPRUCE *Picea mariana* (Mill.) BSP.   **PL. 3**

Twigs and buds *hairy*; winter buds *acutely* pointed. Needles *short*, mostly ¼"–⁷⁄₁₆" long, and green (sometimes blue-green with a white powder). Cones only ¾"–1¼" long, somewhat gray-brown, with scale edges finely ragged (use lens). Cones usually remain on tree for several years. Low, matlike forms are known from northern mountains, especially where exposed to severe winds and cold. Narrow silhouette common (p. 21). Height 25'–30'; diameter 1'–2'. Bogs and wet soils. **SIMILAR SPECIES:** (1) Red and (2) White spruces have longer needles and cones (the latter with smooth-edged scales) and occur mostly on uplands. White Spruce also has hairless twigs and broadly pointed winter buds.

RED SPRUCE *Picea rubens* Sarg.   **PL. 3**

Like Black Spruce, but twigs sometimes hairless and cones 1¼"–1⅝" long, more or less reddish brown, with scale edges *smooth*. Cones fall soon after maturity. Needles ½"–⅝" long and often curved upward. Height 60'–70' (75'); diameter 1'–2' (3'). Well-drained soils. **SIMILAR SPECIES:** See Black Spruce.

WHITE SPRUCE *Picea glauca* (Moench) Voss   **PL. 3**

Twigs and buds *hairless;* winter buds *obtusely* pointed. Needles *blue-green,* ⅜"–¾" long. Branchlets do *not* droop. Cones *cylindrical,* 1"–2" long, dropping soon after they mature; scales *smooth-edged* (use lens). In Far North and on high mountains, a low, mat-like form occurs in exposed locations. Height 50'–60'; diameter 1'–2'. Uplands. See silhouette, p. 21. **SIMILAR SPECIES:** See (1) Black Spruce and (2) Norway Spruce. **REMARKS:** The pliable rootlets were once used by Native Americans in making canoes and baskets.

NORWAY SPRUCE *Picea abies* (L.) Karst   **PL. 3**

Twigs *hairless* or nearly so. Needles *dark green,* mostly ½"–1" long. The twigs and *branchlets hang downward* (silhouette, p. 21). Cones 4"–6" *long,* falling soon after they mature. Height 60'–90'; diameter 1'–3'. European; occasionally spreads from plantings on uplands. **SIMILAR SPECIES:** Our only spruce with drooping twigs and branchlets and the only one in our area with large cones.

CONIFERS WITH FLAT NEEDLES (PLATE 4)

Mostly unrelated cone-bearing species that are alike in having flat needles.

BALSAM FIR

FRASER FIR

BALSAM FIR *Abies balsamea* (L.) Mill.   **PL. 4**

A steeple-shaped evergreen tree (silhouette, p. 22) with needles
⅜"–1½" long and *whitened beneath*. Needles occur mostly in flattened sprays. Each needle has a *broad circular base*. Twigs rather
smooth, with round, flat scars after needles are removed. Cones
1"–3" long, *upright and fleshy*, purplish to green, *no bracts visible
between scales*. Fir cones fall apart upon ripening in late autumn,
leaving erect, slender central cores. The plant may grow as a low
matlike shrub at timberline. Bark rather smooth, with resin blisters. Height 40'–60' (75'); diameter 1'–2' (3'). Moist woods. **SIMI-
LAR SPECIES:** When present, the upright cones are distinctive. See
(1) Fraser Fir. (2) Hemlocks have stalked needles and rough
twigs. **REMARKS:** A good Christmas tree that holds its needles. Soft,
perishable wood of less value than spruce as lumber or pulp. Firs,
like spruces (Pl. 3), are evergreen trees of cold climates. Canada
balsam obtained from bark blisters, a gum used by woodsmen as a
wound plaster and waterproof cement; sold in stores as a confec-
tion before the advent of chicle chewing gum. Formerly used in
cementing lenses and in mounting specimens on microscope
slides. Fire-by-friction sets are often made of this wood; resinous
fir knots were once used as torches. Seeds eaten by ruffed,
spruce, and sharptail grouse; twigs browsed by snowshoe hares,
whitetail deer, and moose; bark gnawed by porcupines.

FRASER FIR *Abies fraseri* (Pursh) Poir.   **PL. 4**

Differs from Balsam Fir in distribution and cone scale structure.
Cones adorned with bracts whose three-parted tips *project obviously* from between the scales. Foliage occurs less frequently in
flattened sprays. Appalachians, mostly above 4000' altitude. The
only fir in the Great Smoky Mountains National Park, N.C.-Tenn.

Eastern Hemlock

EASTERN HEMLOCK *Tsuga canadensis* (L.) Carr.   **PL. 4**
Frequently a more round-topped tree than the firs or spruces.
Unlike those trees, the topmost (leader) shoot of hemlocks *droops*
markedly, often allowing them to be identified at a distance. Needles mostly ⅝"–⅞" long, in *flat sprays*, *whitened* beneath, attached
to the twigs *by slender stalks*. Twigs *somewhat rough* after leaves
fall. Cones only ⅝"–1 " long, brown, few-scaled, pendent. A mat-
like form occurs in exposed places in n. New England and e.
Canada. Bark dark and rough. Height 60'–70' (100'); diameter
2'–3' (6'). Mature forests and wooded ravines. **SIMILAR SPECIES:** (1)
Firs have circular needle bases, smooth twigs, and, when present,
upright cones. (2) See Carolina Hemlock. **REMARKS:** The delicate
silvery foliage and small, pendent, perfectly formed brown cones
of the hemlock make this one of our most beautiful forest trees. It
makes a poor Christmas tree because its leaves fall upon drying.
Formerly spared the ax because of the poor quality of its wood
and the stonelike hardness of the knots, which will chip steel
blades. Even so, the increased value of timber has doomed most
virgin stands. Lumber is taken for pulp but is, or at least was, particularly useful for railroad ties, since it holds spikes exceptionally
well. Bark rich in tannin; a tea was once made from leaves and
twigs by woodsmen and Native Americans. As fuel, the wood

throws sparks. Seeds and needles eaten by ruffed and sharptail grouse and red squirrels, twigs browsed by deer, snowshoe hares, and cottontail rabbits.

CAROLINA HEMLOCK *Tsuga caroliniana* Engelm. **PL. 4**

Like Eastern Hemlock but with needles ½"–⅞" long and *not* in flat sprays. Cones 1"–1⅝" long. Occurs in mountains from w. Virginia to w. South Carolina, n. Georgia, and e.Tennessee.

BALDCYPRESS **PL. 4**
Taxodium distichum (L.) Richard. var. *distichum*

A handsome *non*-evergreen tall tree of *southern swamps.* Needles ¼"–⅞" long, green on both sides, mostly flat, but sometimes somewhat three-sided; arranged *alternately* along slender greenish twigs. Needles and most twigs *fall in winter,* leaving branchlets roughened by small, few-scaled buds. Leaf scars lacking; areas similar to leaf scars present but without bundle scars. Bark brown, rather smooth but fibrous. Trunk base often deeply ridged. In deep water, *peculiar root growths* called "cypress knees" grow upward to the surface (silhouette, p. 23). Cones *ball-shaped,* about 1" in diameter, with thick scales. Height 80'–120' (140'); diameter 3'–4' (20'). Swamps and streambanks. **SIMILAR SPECIES:** (1) Larches, our only other non-evergreen conifers, are northern, with needles in clusters and thin cone scales. (2) Dawn-redwood (*Metasequoia glyptostroboides* Hu & Cheng), found in China in 1941 and regarded as a living fossil, is often planted. It, too, is deciduous, but the needles, buds, shoots, and cone scales are in opposite pairs. **REMARKS:** Once seen, a mature stand of this majestic relative of the California Redwood is not soon forgotten. A large

Baldcypress

tree in Florida is estimated to be 3000–3500 years old. A valuable lumber tree used for construction, railroad ties, posts, shingles. Wood is soft, light, straight-grained, and durable and does not warp easily. Only distantly related to true cypresses, such as the famed Monterey Cypress of California. Seeds eaten by cranes and some songbirds. Grows on uplands if planted. The *evergreen* Montezuma

BALDCYPRESS

Baldcypress (*T. mucronatum* Ten.) of Mexico and the lower Rio Grande Valley of Texas is no longer separated.

PONDCYPRESS

PL. 4

Taxodium distichum (L.) Rich. var. *imbricarium* (Nutt.) Croom

A distinctive form of Baldcypress with three-sided, *sharp,* needle-shaped leaves *pressed against* the twigs. Growth habits and habitat of the Pondcypress are identical with those of the parent species. The general appearance of the appressed and often drooping foliage, however, is much different from the fernlike sprays of the typical form. Some botanists regard Pondcypress as a distinct species. Common as stunted forests in Everglades National Park, Fla.

FLORIDA YEW *Taxus floridana* Nutt. ex. Chapm.

PL. 4

A rare evergreen shrub or small tree with needles ¾"–1" long, pointed, *green on both sides.* Needles *stalked,* stalks following

FLORIDA YEW

FLORIDA TORREYA

along the twig for a distance below needle. Crushed foliage with a mild odor. Twigs *smooth*. On female plants, fruits juicy, red, *berry-like,* about ¼" in diameter; open-ended, single brown seed visible. Height to 25'. Local along the Apalachicola River and near Bristol, Liberty County, nw. Florida. **SIMILAR SPECIES:** Florida Torreya is also rare and occurs in the same area. Its pointed needles are more stiff and decidedly sharp to the touch, its crushed foliage has a stronger and more pungent odor, and its fruits are larger and green. **REMARKS:** Fruits possibly poisonous.

FLORIDA TORREYA *Torreya taxifolia* Arn.　　　　**PL. 4**
Sometimes called Stinking-cedar, this rare species is a relative of Florida Yew and occurs with it in the vicinity of the Apalachicola River and also in adjacent Decatur County, sw. Georgia. The crushed foliage yields a foul odor. See Florida Yew.

CONIFERS WITH SCALELIKE OR THREE-SIDED HOLLOW LEAVES (Plate 5)

Most of these related species differ from all other cone-bearing trees. They possess very small, peculiarly flattened leaves that form scaly coverings for at least some twigs. *Juniperus* fruits, though technically similar to cones, are fleshy and berrylike.

The white-cedars possess only scalelike, flattened needles; the junipers (especially the redcedars) may bear either scaly or hollowed and whitened three-sided needles, or both. All needles of Pondcypress and occasionally some leaves of the Baldcypress (see Pl. 4) are three-sided rather than flat, but they are not whitened.

The three-sided type of leaf is only approximately triangular in cross section. It is easily recognized, however, by the concave, whitish inside surface. The needles may occur in pairs or 3's but unlike pine needles are never bound at the base in bundles.

It may be necessary to use a hand lens to determine how the scaly leaves are arranged, but usually more readily determined characteristics are available. Seedlings may be impossible to identify. The fruiting structures are quite diverse.

Although several of these species are popularly known as cedars, only members of the Old World genus *Cedrus,* including the cedars of Lebanon, N. Africa, and the Himalayas, are true cedars. They may be seen in this country only where they have been planted for decorative purposes. True cedars have larchlike clusters of needles that remain evergreen.

Northern White-cedar

NORTHERN WHITE-CEDAR (ARBOR VITAE)   PL. 5
Thuja occidentalis L.

A medium-sized tree with leaves scalelike and ¹⁄₁₆"–⅛" long. They occur in 4 rows around the twigs but are flattened from the sides. Central leaves show tiny glands. Twigs and leaves occur in *flattened sprays* that are typically aligned vertically. Heartwood light-colored. Cones slender, more or less bell-shaped, about ½" long. A prostrate, carpetlike form occurs in Quebec. Bark is fibrous with numerous cross-thatched ridges. Height 40'–50' (125'); diameter 2'–3' (5'). Swamps and limestone soils. **SIMILAR SPECIES:** (1) Atlantic White-cedar has a different range, leaves and leaf sprays less flattened, and cones globular. (2) See French Tamarisk (Fig. 7). **REMARKS:** An earlier, widely used name is Arbor Vitae, a latinized French name meaning "tree of life." The tree was so named after it cured the men of Jacques Cartier's Canadian expedition of a disease, probably scurvy. As a result of the incident, this became the first tree to be imported from America into Europe. Over 50 varieties are now in cultivation. It was once used by the native Americans and is known also as Canoe-wood. Thin slabs of the wood were prepared by pounding the ends of short logs until they

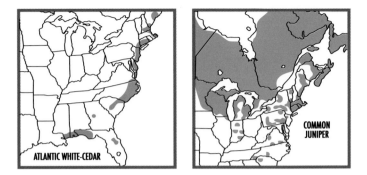

ATLANTIC WHITE-CEDAR

COMMON JUNIPER

separated along the annual rings. Wood is soft, light-colored, and durable. It is used for shingles and fire-by-friction sets. Outer bark supplies tinder. Cedar swamps provide favorite winter quarters and food for deer. Moose, snowshoe hares, and cottontail rabbits also eat the twigs and foliage; red squirrels and many songbirds consume the seeds.

ATLANTIC WHITE-CEDAR   PL. 5
Chamaecyparis thyoides (L.) B.S.P.

Similar to Northern White-cedar but the leaves *narrower less flattened* on the twigs. Foliage sprays somewhat flattened. Cones *globular*, ³⁄₁₆"–¼" in diameter. Height 40'–60'; diameter 1'–2' (3'). Swamps near coast. **SIMILAR SPECIES:** See (1) Northern White-cedar and (2) French Tamarisk (Fig. 7). **REMARKS:** Both the lumber and the crushed foliage are aromatic. Wood is soft, durable, very light. The lumber, used in shipbuilding and construction work and as shingles, is of such value that large logs buried in prehistoric times have been mined in New Jersey bogs. Organ pipes used to be made of this resonant wood. White-cedar charcoal was used in making gunpowder during the American Revolution. A number of horticultural varieties of this tree and its oriental relatives are used in landscaping because of their beauty and their resistance to insects and disease. Like Northern White-cedar, this species is sometimes known as Arbor Vitae. It is browsed by deer.

COMMON (DWARF) JUNIPER *Juniperus communis* L.   PL. 5

A widespread species rarely seen as a tree, more commonly a shrub, with sharp, hollowed, three-sided needles that occur in *whorls of 3, whitened above* and ¼"–⅞" long. Twigs, or at least branchlets, are *three-sided*. Fruits are berries, rather hard, blue-

Common Juniper

black, ball-shaped, and with a white powder. Height 1'–4' (35');
diameter 1"–6" (1'). Pastures and infertile soils. **SIMILAR SPECIES:** Our
only species with needles in 3's and strongly whitened. (1) Pondcypress is southern and aquatic (see Plate 4). (2) French
Tamarisk (Fig. 7) is taller, with flowers and fruit capsules. **REMARKS:**
Oil from leaves and wood is used in perfumery, and the aromatic
foliage is burned as an incense in India. The plant supplies food
for ruffed and sharptail grouse, bobwhite, European partridge,
pheasant, whitetail deer, moose, and smaller birds and mammals.
Grows also throughout Europe and all of northern Asia.

ASHE JUNIPER *Juniperus ashei* J. Buchholz   **PL. 5**
A round-topped shrub or tree of *south-central* distribution. The

ASHE JUNIPER

SOUTHERN REDCEDAR

EASTERN REDCEDAR

Bark of Eastern Redcedar

tiny leaves are nearly *all* scalelike and tightly *pressed* against the twigs. Trunks often *several*. Height to 20'. Fruits about 5/16" across, dark blue with a whitish bloom, and usually 1–2 seeds per fruit, each seed more than 3/16" long. Ozarks area to w. Texas. Limestone soils.

EASTERN REDCEDAR *Juniperus virginiana* L.   **PL. 5**

A narrow (see silhouette, p. 22), medium-sized tree, usually with both scalelike and longer, sharply three-sided, needlelike leaves. Leaves 1/16"–1/4", entirely green, in pairs along *four-sided twigs* and branchlets. Heartwood reddish. Fruits more or less *globular,* hard whitish to blackish green berries about 1/4" in diameter. Bark dry, shreddy; trunk *single*, often fluted. Rarely (in severely windswept locations) shrubby and creeping. Height 40'–50' (62'); diameter 1'–2' (4'). Old fields and dry soils. **SIMILAR SPECIES:** (1) Ashe Juniper seldom has needlelike leaves and barely enters our area. (2) French Tamarisk (Fig. 7) has tiny, alternate needles, colorful small flowers, and capsular fruits. (3) See Southern Redcedar. **REMARKS:** Birds pass the seeds through their digestive tracts undamaged, dropping them particularly along fences. Redcedar acts as alternate host to apple rust. During half its life cycle, this fungus spots apples and their leaves; during the other half, it forms ball-shaped brown galls on Eastern Redcedar twigs. After heavy rains these galls extrude numerous hanging brown gelatinous threads. Do not confuse galls with fruits, which are hard but berrylike. Heartwood is aromatic and of rose-brown color. It is light, strong, durable, and widely used for cedar chests, cabinets, lead pencils, fuel, and fence posts. The outer bark, when stripped, dried, and rubbed between the hands, provides excellent tinder and is used in flint-and-steel and sunglass fire sets. A volatile oil derived from juniper leaves is used in perfumes, and a flavoring may be derived from the berries. The dried berries are used as a cooking spice. In the wild the fruits are consumed by well over 50 species of birds, including bobwhite, sharptail grouse, pheasant, and mourning dove, and also by opossums.

SOUTHERN REDCEDAR PL. 5
J. virginiana L. var. *silicicola* (Small) E. Murray

Like Eastern Redcedar but with twigs more slender (about ¹⁄₃₂") and slightly *drooping*. Fruits are only ⅛"–³⁄₁₆" in diameter. Moist sites in the South.

NEEDLE-BEARING NON-CONIFERS

In addition to the cone-bearers, a few flowering plants also have scalelike leaves. French Tamarisk is the only such tree species in our area. It has colorful blossoms and is becoming widely established. (See also Australian-pine and Brazilian Beefwood, p. 172 and 173).

Fig. 7. French Tamarisk.

FRENCH TAMARISK *Tamarix gallica* L. FIG. 7

An importation from southern Europe, this tree is becoming established widely. Often called Salt-cedar. Alternate pale green leaves less than ⅟₁₆" long, *scalelike,* on long, slender, often drooping twigs. Numerous slender spikes of pink, or sometimes whitish, flowers usually present from May to Sept. Fruits small dry capsules. Roadsides and thickets; Massachusetts, Indiana, and Kansas to Florida, s. Texas, and s. California.

II

BROAD-LEAVED TREES WITH OPPOSITE COMPOUND LEAVES

(PLATES 6–9)

Only a few plants bear leaves of this type. Their identification is therefore comparatively simple when foliage is present. In southern Florida, the several tropical species with opposite compound leaves (Pl. F-7) are evergreen.

In winter in more northern areas, unless dead leaves are attached to the twigs, there is no indication of whether a plant once bore compound or simple leaves. This section must then be considered in conjunction with the next, whose twigs also bear opposite (or occasionally whorled) leaf scars and buds. The twigs of a leafless unknown plant with opposite leaf scars may be compared with the illustrations in Sections II and III, or see Appendix A (winter key).

Some alternate-leaved plants bear stubby, scarred, leaf-crowded spur branches. Take care not to assume that their leaves

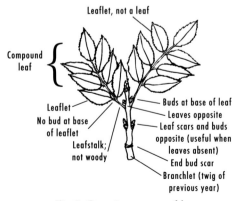

Fig. 8. *Opposite compound leaves.*

and leaf scars are opposite or whorled because of this crowding. None of the plants in our area with true opposite or whorled leaf scars ever develops spur branches. Twigs with uncrowded leaves or leaf scars should be selected for identification.

1. Leaves fan-compound, the leaflets arranged like the spokes of a wheel. **Buckeyes, etc., Pl. 6**
1. Leaves feather-compound. **2**
   2. Leaflets 3. **3**
   2. Leaflets 5–11. **4**
3. Not evergreen, northern. **Bladdernut, Pl. 7**
3. Evergreen trees of Florida. **Torchwoods, Pl. F-7**
   4. Evergreen trees of s. Florida. **Miscellaneous, Pl. F-7**
   4. Not evergreen. **5**
5. Fruits fleshy; flowers/fruits in upright, flat-topped clusters. **Elderberry, Pl. 7**
5. Fruits dry, winged; flower/fruit clusters drooping, not flat-topped. **Ashes I and II and Ashleaf Maple, Pls. 8, 9**

TREES WITH OPPOSITE FAN-COMPOUND LEAVES: BUCKEYES AND CHASTETREE (PLATE 6)

Buckeyes (and the Chastetree, which is usually shrubby) are our only trees with opposite compound leaves whose leaflets are arranged like the spokes of a wheel. Buckeyes have toothed leaflets; Chastetree has smooth-edged foliage. In winter, a combination of characteristics will identify the buckeye group: leaf scars have 5 or more bundle scars, twigs and end buds are large, and side buds have 4 or more pairs of scales. Chastetree twigs are usually four-angled.

If flowers or fruits are present, they can be of considerable help in identifying buckeyes. The stamens (threadlike filaments tipped by pollen-bearing anthers) are shorter than the petals in some species and longer in others. In this group, too, the calyx (the circle of sepals immediately exterior to the petals) is colored like the petals and tubular. The calyx tube is short (¼"–⅜") in most species but longer (⅜"–1 ") in the Red Buckeye. The flowers are mostly in large showy upright spikes at twig ends, and the fruits have three-parted husks that contain 1–3 large shiny brown nuts. Chastetree flower spikes are erect but shorter, and the fruits are small and fleshy.

The native Ohio and Sweet buckeyes may be large and important trees in forests west of the Appalachian Mountains. There

they are sometimes dominant with White Oak in the few areas of virgin timber remaining. Hybrids are known. An imported relative, the Horsechestnut, common in shade-tree plantings, occasionally escapes to grow wild.

The seeds, young twigs, and leaves of buckeyes can be toxic to livestock. Crushed fruits and branches have been used to kill fish for food, but this practice is now illegal.

HORSECHESTNUT *Aesculus hippocastanum* L.   PL. 6

A large imported tree with 7–9 wedge-shaped leaflets. End bud more than ¼" long, very *sticky*. Broken twigs do not have a disagreeable odor. Pith *white*. Trunk bark somewhat scaly. Leaves 4"–15". Height 60'–75' (80'); diameter 1'–2' (3'). Flowers white, clusters 6"–12", stamens long, May. Fruits with *strongly thorny* husks, Sept.–Oct. European, rarely spreading from northern plantings. **SIMILAR SPECIES:** The only buckeye with sticky end buds and strongly thorny fruit husks. The true chestnuts (Plate 32) have large brown nuts but are unrelated and otherwise dissimilar.

YELLOW (SWEET) BUCKEYE *Aesculus octandra* Marsh.   PL. 6

Similar to Horsechestnut but usually with 5 (4–7) leaflets and *non-sticky* buds. End bud large, with bud scales *not* ridged. Broken twigs without foul odor. Pith *brown*. Trunk bark fairly smooth or broken with large plates. Leaves 4"–15". Height to 90'; diameter to 3'. Flowers yellow, clusters 4"–7", stamens short, May–June. Fruits with *smooth* husks, Sept.–Oct. Mature woods. **SIMILAR SPECIES:** Ohio Buckeye has ridged end-bud scales and foul-smelling broken twigs. **REMARKS:** Fruits, unlike those of other buck-

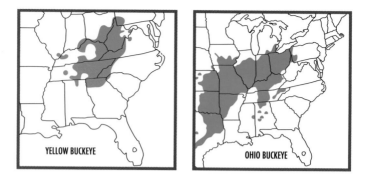

YELLOW BUCKEYE

OHIO BUCKEYE

eyes, are sometimes eaten by cattle and hogs. They are also said to make an excellent paste when powdered and mixed with water. Wood is light and tough.

OHIO BUCKEYE *Aesculus glabra* Willd.   **PL. 6**

A smaller tree than Yellow Buckeye and with *weakly* ridged scales more than ¼" long. Twigs emit a *foul odor* when broken. Bundle scars in 3 groups. Pith *white*. Trunk bark scaly. Leaves 4"–15" long, with 5 leaflets. Height to 40'; diameter to 2'. Flowers yellow, clusters 4"–6", stamens long, April–May. Fruit husks with *weak thorns,* fruits Sept.–Oct. Moist forests. **SIMILAR SPECIES:** No other native buckeye has prickly fruit husks. (1) Yellow and (2) Painted buckeyes have end bud scales not ridged and pith brown. (3) Red Buckeye has smooth brown bark, brown pith, and tubular red blossoms.

BOTTLEBRUSH BUCKEYE *Aesculus parviflora* Walt.   **PL. 6**

Rarely growing to tree size, this buckeye has a restricted native range, 5–7 leaflets, and striking blooms. Mature end bud not ridged and *less than* ¼" long. Pith *white*. The many-flowered cylindrical stalks of white blossoms are *up to* 20" long, with stamens ½"–1½" in length and longer than the petals. Trunk and fruit husks smooth. Height to 20'. Local in Alabama and sw. Georgia. **SIMILAR SPECIES:** No other buckeye has such long flower spikes. **REMARKS:** Twigs and fruits said to be poisonous. An attractive species cultivated even in the northern U.S.

RED BUCKEYE *Aesculus pavia* L.   **PL. 6**

A shrub or small tree with 5 leaflets that are narrow to elliptic and hairless when mature. Mature flowers and buds are about ½"

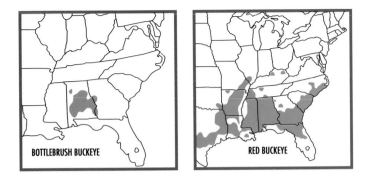

BOTTLEBRUSH BUCKEYE

RED BUCKEYE

long. Bud scales *ridged*. Pith *brown, wide*. Flowers bright *red*, long-tubular, and stamens about equal to petals in length. Clusters 4"–8". Fruits *not* prickly. Trunk smooth, gray. Height to 25'. The Particolored Buckeye (*A. discolor* Pursh.) is now considered part of this species. Coastal Plain woods.

PAINTED (DWARF) BUCKEYE *Aesculus sylvatica* Bartr.   **PL. 6**
A thicket-forming shrub or small tree of southern areas. Leaves 4"–15" long, with 5 leaflets. End bud *less than* ½" long and *not* keeled. Flowers yellow, cream-colored, or pink, clusters 4"–6", stamens short. Pith brown, narrow. Fruits *not* prickly. Mostly Coastal Plain and Piedmont plateau bottom lands.

CHASTETREE *Vitex agnus-castus* L.   **NOT ILLUS.**
A small tree but usually shrubby, with opposite fan-compound leaves whose leaflets are long-stalked, long-pointed, and *not*

PAINTED BUCKEYE

toothed. They are dark green above, gray beneath, and *spicy-scented* when crushed. The twigs also have a spicy odor when rubbed; they are gray-hairy, often four-angled, and with more than 1 bud above each leaf scar. Pith *white.* Bundle scar *single.* The flowers are small, *bluish,* and fragrant, occurring in 2"–4" erect spikes at the twig ends. The ⅛" fleshy fruits contain a single seed. SIMILAR SPECIES: Buckeyes are not spicy-scented and have toothed leaves, rounded twigs, and larger flowers and fruits. REMARKS: Native to southern Europe and Asia but spreading from plantings over much of the Coastal Plain, especially in the southern states.

SMALL TREES WITH OPPOSITE COMPOUND LEAVES: BLADDERNUT AND ELDERBERRY (PLATE 7)

Bladdernut and Common Elderberry are *non-evergreen* small trees which occur widely in the eastern United States. Winter twigs lack central end bud. In Florida see Pl. F-7.

BLADDERNUT *Staphylea trifolia* L.   **PL. 7**
A shrub or small tree whose leaves have 3 (rarely 5) fine-toothed, elliptic leaflets. Twigs *slender* with few small wartlike lenticels or none. Pith white, *narrow.* Buds brown, with 2–4 scales, small. Leaf scars small, without connecting lines between. Bundle scars 4–7, often obscure. Bark of older branches greenish or gray *streaked* with white. Leaves 2"–6". Height 5'–15' (25'); diameter 1"–2" (6"). Flowers whitish, clustered at twig ends, drooping, April–June. Fruits inflated papery capsules. 1"–2", Aug.–Oct. SIMILAR SPECIES: No other woody species in our area has such fruits.

COMMON ELDERBERRY

BLADDERNUT

Ashleaf Maple (Pl. 9) may have some three-parted leaves, but normally leaves with 5–11 leaflets are also present.

COMMON ELDERBERRY *Sambucus canadensis* L. PL. 7

A shrub or small tree with large leaves composed of 5–11 coarse-toothed, elliptic leaflets. Twigs *stout* with *large white pith.* Small wartlike lenticels common. Leaf scars large, with connecting lines between; 5–7 bundle scars. Buds small, green or brown. Bark brownish. Leaves 4"–11". Height 3'–20'; diameter ¾"–3" (10"). Flowers small, white, in dense terminal *flat-topped* clusters, June–July. Fruits small (mostly less than ¾₆" in diameter), juicy, *purple-black,* rarely bright red, yellow, or orange, Aug.–Oct. **SIMILAR SPECIES:** The pithy twigs and lack of central end bud will separate it from the ashes. In s. Florida, Yellow-elder (Pl. F-7) has more slender twigs and distinctive flowers and fruits. **REMARKS:** All parts of the plant are reported to yield hydrocyanic acid. Regardless, fruits are used in making jam, jelly, wine, pies. Ripe fruits are eaten by 43 species of birds, including pheasant, mourning dove, and wild turkey.

FLORIDA-ONLY TREES PL. F-7

Four other small-tree species with opposite compound leaves are *evergreen* and are not found north of Collier, Dade, and Monroe counties in tropical s. Florida.

TREES WITH OPPOSITE FEATHER-COMPOUND LEAVES: ASHES AND ASHLEAF MAPLE (Plates 8 and 9)

Over most of our area, the ashes and Ashleaf Maple (Box-elder) are the only native trees with opposite feather-compound leaves. All are tall trees. Only in southern Florida could several distinctively marked evergreen tropical species (see Pl. F-7) possibly be confused with the Carolina Ash, the only ash to occur so far south. Young trees may be distinguished from shrubs with similar leaves by the presence of true end bud. In winter, ashes have moderately stout, mostly gray twigs; central end bud present (but not exceptionally large); and opposing leaf scars that do not meet. Leaf scars are large and shield-shaped, with 4 or more bundle scars; buds are mostly brown and have a somewhat granular surface texture. Ashleaf Maple has green or purplish, smooth, hairless, often white-powdered twigs whose opposite leaf scars meet at raised points.

Identification of ash species is never simple except in the case of a few well-marked forms. If the winged fruits, which look like the blades of canoe paddles, are present, they can be quite useful evidence. Except as noted (Pls. 8–9), the leaflets may be variably toothed or not. Though the leaflets are found most frequently as illustrated, slight variations are common. The flowers are small, dark, and densely clustered in the leaf angles. They are without petals.

The ashes yield quality lumber for furniture, tool handles, baseball bats, baskets, and many special purposes. The twigs serve as deer food; the flowers provide pollen for bees. Native Americans once made a dark bitter sugar from the sap.

TREES WITH OPPOSITE FEATHER-COM-POUND LEAVES: ASHES I (PLATE 8)

BLUE ASH *Fraxinus quadrangulata* Michx.   **PL. 8**

A mainly Midwestern tree of high ground with vigorous twigs often *square* in cross section. Twigs grayish and hairless, with *long lines* leading from leaf scars. Leaflets 7–11, green beneath, stalked, and *always* toothed. Upper edges of leaf scars only shallowly or occasionally deeply concave. Trunk bark whitish and somewhat scaly. Leaves 8"–12". Height 60'–70' (115'); diameter 2'–3' (3½'). Flowers April–May. Fruits with seed *not* plump; wing extending to the seed base and tip *broad, squared*, June–Oct. **SIMILAR SPECIES:** Where twigs are not sharply angled, the long lines along them are distinctive. Few other opposite-leaved trees have four-lined or squarish twigs. (1) Burningbush (Pl. 12) has four-lined twigs, but they are green, and bundle scars are single. (2) The winter twigs of Chastetree (p. 191) are four-lined but slender and the bundle scar is single. **REMARKS:** Inner bark yields a blue dye.

BLUE ASH

WHITE ASH

White Ash

WHITE ASH *Fraxinus americana* L.

An *upland* tree with twigs that have the brown side buds usually set in deep *U-* or *V-shaped notches* in upper edges of leaf scars. Twigs round and either hairless or velvety. Leaflets 5–9, toothed or not, stalked (sometimes short-stalked), usually *white* or pale beneath. Trunk bark rather dark and tight, with rigid interwoven pattern of shallow ridges and furrows. Leaves 8"–12". Height 70'–80' (100'); diameter 2'–3' (7'). Flowers April–June. Fruits not winged to the seed base; seed blunt, plump, raised above the flat wing, Oct.–Nov. **SIMILAR SPECIES:** When present, the deeply notched leaf scars are a good field mark among ashes with hairless twigs. Unfortunately, there is some variation in depth of notch. (1) Black Ash is a bottomland tree with no leaflet stalks. It has black buds and fruits blunt at both ends. (2) Green Ash, also on damp soils, has leaflet stalks narrowly winged and seeds slim but plump. See (3) Pumpkin Ash. **REMARKS:** The most valuable and largest native ash, providing hard, strong timber for furniture, interior millwork, agricultural implements, tool handles, oars, tennis rackets, musical instruments, baseball bats, snowshoes, and skis. As a campfire fuel, it ranks with oak and hickory. Biltmore Ash was formerly separated as a variety with velvety-hairy twigs.

BLACK ASH *Fraxinus nigra* Marsh. PL. 8

A tree of swamps and bottomlands whose leaflets are *not stalked.* The 7–11 leaflets are *always* toothed. Twigs round, hairless, rather dull. Leaf scars not deeply notched. Buds *very dark,* nearly black. Trunk bark generally rather tight and furrowed but may be somewhat scaly. Leaves 12"–16". Height 40'–80'; diameter 1'–2'.

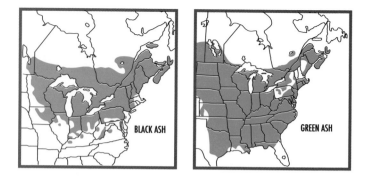

BLACK ASH   GREEN ASH

Flowers April–May. Fruits *blunt at both ends,* winged to the base, seed *not* plump, June–Sept. SIMILAR SPECIES: Both (1) White and (2) Green ashes may have short-stalked leaflets, but they lack the blackish buds and blunt fruits of this species. REMARKS: Known also as Hoop or Basket Ash. Short logs or planks when hammered repeatedly on the ends split along the annual growth rings into thin sheets that can be cut into strips for weaving pack baskets, chair seats, barrel hoops, etc. Knotty burls of the trunk are made into veneers and furniture.

GREEN (RED) ASH *Fraxinus pennsylvanica* Marsh.   PL. 8
A lowland tree whose leaflets are stalked (mostly short-stalked) and *narrowly* winged (use lens). Leaflets 5–9, green on both sides, toothed or not. Twigs hairless or velvety; buds *brownish.* Trunk bark tight and closely furrowed. Leaves 10"–12". Height 60'–70' (85'); diameter 2'–3' (4'). Flowers April–May. Fruits narrow, wedge-shaped, not winged to the base; seed plump but very slender, narrowly pointed at *both* ends, often nearly *needlelike* at the base, Sept.–Oct. SIMILAR SPECIES: (1) White Ash is an upland species with leaves pale beneath, leaf scars notched, leaflet stalks not winged, and fruits with shorter, wider seeds, blunt at one or both ends. See (2) Black Ash. REMARKS: Green Ash was formerly classified as a hairless variety of Red Ash. Now the two have been combined.

TREES WITH OPPOSITE FEATHER-COMPOUND LEAVES: ASHES II AND ASHLEAF MAPLE (PLATE 9)

PUMPKIN ASH *Fraxinus profunda* (Bush) Bush   PL. 9
A small to large tree of swamps and bottomlands, mostly with *vel-*

vety-hairy twigs, U-shaped leaf scars, and large fruits. The leaves are *large, shiny above,* and sometimes leathery. The 7–9 *long-pointed* leaflets are *not toothed* but are sometimes wavy-edged; they vary from red-brown hairy to nearly hairless beneath. Trunk bark is tight (with shallow furrows) to somewhat scaly. Trunk base usually *swollen* on wet sites. Leaves 4"–18". Height to 125'. Flowers April–May. Fruits, 1¼"–3" long, quite broad, not winged to the base, seed *plump,* not extending to midlength of the fruit. Sept.–Oct. SIMILAR SPECIES: (1) Carolina Ash is strictly southern, and its leaves are neither leathery nor rusty-hairy and are more likely to be toothed. (2) Green Ash (Pl. 8) has shield-shaped leaf scars, narrowly winged leafstalks, and very slender seeds. (3) White Ash (Pl. 8) is an upland species with twigs less velvety, leaves usually whitened beneath, and fruits smaller.

CAROLINA (WATER) ASH *Fraxinus caroliniana* Mill.   PL. 9

A small tree of *southern swamps* with leaflets mostly toothed and twigs usually hairless but sometimes *velvety-hairy.* Leaflets may also be hairy or hairless. Trunk bark tight and somewhat scaly. Trunk base usually *swollen* when growing in water. Leaves 7"–12". Height to 35'; diameter 10"–12". Flowers April–May. Fruits to 2"; broadly winged to the narrow seed base, seed *not* plump and extending beyond the mid-length of the fruit, May–Oct. SIMILAR SPECIES: See Pumpkin Ash.

ASHLEAF MAPLE (BOX-ELDER) *Acer negundo* L.   PL. 9

A medium-sized tree of moist, fertile soils, with *hairless,* green or purplish, glossy, frequently white-powdered twigs. Leaflets 3–5 (uncommonly 7) with few *coarse* teeth or none. End leaflets often three-pointed and somewhat *lobed.* Narrow leaf scars *meet in*

PUMPKIN ASH

CAROLINA ASH

ASHLEAF MAPLE

Ashleaf Maple

raised points on opposite sides of twigs. Bundle scars 3 (or 5); buds white-hairy. Trunk bark furrowed. Leaves 4"–10". Height 50'–75'; diameter 2'–4'. Flowers in hanging clusters, April–May. Fruits paired "keys," Sept.–Oct. **SIMILAR SPECIES:** Only ashlike tree with leaf scars meeting in raised points. (1) When only 3 leaflets are present, the foliage often resembles that of Poison-ivy (see Fig. 4), whose leaves are alternate. (2) Other maples (Pl. 11) have simple leaves and dissimilar winter characteristics. **REMARKS:** The name Box-elder, widely used, fails to indicate proper taxonomic relationships. Soft white wood is used for boxes, etc. Syrup can be made from the sap. Squirrels and songbirds eat the seeds. Introduced into Europe and elsewhere.

BROAD-LEAVED TREES WITH
OPPOSITE SIMPLE LEAVES

(PLATES 10–14)

Though the trees with opposite simple leaves are more numerous than those of Section II, they are still so few as to be rather easily identified. In winter, plants with opposite leaf scars may be members of either Section II or Section III, and the illustrations for both sections must be reviewed (see also Appendix A). Care should be taken that the leaves or leaf scars on the stubby, scar-crowded spur branches (see Fig. 3) of some alternate-leaved plants are not interpreted as opposite or whorled.

When opposite simple leaves are present, the plants bearing them may be identified using the key on the next page.

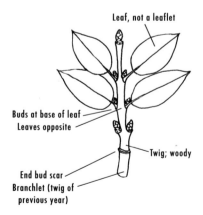

Leaf, not a leaflet

Buds at base of leaf
Leaves opposite

Twig; woody

End bud scar
Branchlet (twig of
previous year)

Fig. 9. Opposite simple leaves.

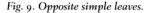

1. Leaves large (5"–18" long), heart-shaped.   **Princess-tree and Catalpas, Pl. 10.**
1. Leaves smaller, not heart-shaped. **2**
    2. Leaves with 3–5 lobes.   **Maples, Pl. 11.**
    2. Leaves not lobed. **3**
3. Leaf edges fine-toothed.   **Buckthorn, etc., Pl. 12.**
3. Leaf edges not toothed. **4**
    4. Leaves leathery, mostly evergreen. **Viburnums, etc., Pl. 13.**
    4. Leaves not leathery, deciduous.   **Dogwoods, etc., Pl. 14.**

TREES WITH OPPOSITE OR WHORLED HEART-SHAPED LEAVES: PRINCESS-TREE AND CATALPAS (Plate 10)

Princess-tree and the catalpas are the only trees in our range that have opposite or whorled heart-shaped leaves. In winter they are differentiated from other species with opposite leaf scars by their stout twigs and *elliptical* series of tiny bundle scars within each circular leaf scar. The twigs lack central end buds.

PRINCESS-TREE (PAULOWNIA)   PL. 10
Paulownia tomentosa (Thunb.) Sieb. & Zucc. ex Steud.

A medium-sized oriental tree with *large, paired heart-shaped* leaves, *chambered* or hollow pith, and clusters of *persistent* large nutlike fruits or husks. Naturalized in the South. Leaves velvety-hairy beneath, usually short-pointed and *not whorled.* Sometimes only with shallowly heart-shaped bases and frequently with 1 or more large teeth. Twigs stout, leaf scars circular, bundle scars numerous. Buds sometimes more than 1 above each leaf scar. Trunk bark rough, with interlaced smooth, often *shiny* areas. Leaves 6"–13". Height 30'–60'; diameter 1'–2'. Flowers about 2",

NORTHERN CATALPA

SOUTHERN CATALPA

Princess-tree

purplish with yellow stripes inside, in large terminal clusters, April–May; buffy spikes of next year's flowers present after autumn. Fruits 1¼"–1¾", somewhat *pecanlike woody capsules* containing many small, winged seeds; husks present all winter. **SIMILAR SPECIES:** Catalpas have solid white pith, sometimes whorled leaves, and long slender fruit capsules. **REMARKS:** Called Foxglovetree in England, where it is grown for ornament.

NORTHERN CATALPA (CATAWBA-TREE)   PL. 10
Catalpa speciosa Warder ex Engelm.

Similar to Princess-tree but with *solid* whitish pith and slender *cigar-shaped* fruits. Leaves paired or in whorls of 3, *long-pointed* and sometimes hairy beneath. Trunk bark scaly. Leaves 6"–13". Height 50'–70' (120'); diameter 2'–4' (5'). Flowers *many,* in twig-end clusters, each 2½"–3" across, white with yellow and purple spots, May–June. Fruits slender pods *less than* ⁷⁄₁₆" thick and 10"–24" long, containing many small seeds (seed about 2" long, including end fibers), Sept.–winter. Wet woods. **SIMILAR SPECIES:** (1) Princess-tree has chambered or hollow pith. (2) Southern Catalpa has short-pointed leaves and smaller flowers and fruits. **REMARKS:** Once planted for fence posts, but its rapid growth may be counteracted by insect, storm, and frost damage. Often highly productive of "catawba worms" for fish bait. Native to Mississippi Valley but planted elsewhere.

SOUTHERN (COMMON) CATALPA   PL. 10
Catalpa bignonioides Walt.

Resembles Northern Catalpa but smaller and with somewhat *short-pointed,* non-odorous leaves. Height 40'–50'; diameter

Northern Catalpa

1'–4'. Flowers *few* per cluster, each 1"–2" across, with *numerous* purple spots, May–July. Fruits 8"–15" long and *more than* 7⁄16" thick. **REMARKS:** Native to southeastern states but widely planted.

TREES WITH OPPOSITE LOBED LEAVES: MAPLES (Plate 11)

Maples are our only trees with opposite, lobed leaves. Some shrubby viburnums, however, also bear opposite, fan-lobed, maplelike leaves. One of these, Cranberry Viburnum (American Cranberry-bush, *Viburnum trilobum* Marsh.), is reported to attain small-tree size only rarely and only in Michigan. It is not given full treatment here, but the three-lobed leaves are hairy beneath and carry tiny dome-shaped leafstalk *glands* near the leaf base (use lens). Unlike maples, Cranberry Viburnum has fleshy red fruits with a single flat seed.

A related species, Ashleaf Maple, bears opposite compound leaves and is pictured with the ashes (Pl. 9). Maple flowers are mostly small and greenish. The dry, double, winged fruits, known as "keys," are eaten by many birds and by squirrels.

The native maples are of great value for shade, ornament, and lumber. Some species yield the delicious maple syrup and maple sugar sold commercially. Porcupines sometimes eat the inner bark of maples, and the twigs are a staple food of the cottontail rabbit, snowshoe hare, whitetail deer, and moose.

STRIPED MAPLE (MOOSEWOOD)   PL. 11
Acer pensylvanicum L.

A small, slender, mostly northern tree with *green* bark vertically marked with thin *white stripes.* Leaves *three-lobed,* sometimes with 2 additional small lobes near base, lobes somewhat long-pointed. Foliage *finely* double-toothed, hairless, green on both

Bark of Striped Maple

sides, paler beneath. Twigs hairless, mostly greenish. Winter buds stalked, with only 2 scales, and ⅜"–½" long. Leaves 2"–10". Height 5'–15' (35'); diameter 1"–2" (9"). Flowers at *twig ends* in long *hanging* clusters, May–June. Single fruits ¾"–1", June–Sept. **SIMILAR SPECIES:** Mountain Maple has darker, unstriped bark, hairy twigs, smaller buds, and erect flower clusters.

EASTERN MOUNTAIN MAPLE *Acer spicatum* Lam.　　**PL. 11**
　Also a small, mostly northern tree but with bark dark or some-what greenish and *not* white-striped. Leaves three- to five-lobed, coarsely toothed, hairless or slightly hairy beneath. Twigs *velvety-hairy*, mostly greenish. Winter buds stalked, with 2 scales, and ⅛"–¼" long. Leaves 2"–10". Height mostly under 20'. Flowers in long *upright* twig-end clusters. May–Aug. Single fruits ½"–¾", July–Oct. **SIMILAR SPECIES:** See Striped Maple.

RED MAPLE *Acer rubrum* L.　　**PL. 11**
　A medium-sized tree with *smooth gray* young bark, at least on the upper trunk (almost white in some localities), and broken darker older bark. Leaves 3 (–5) lobed, *whitened* and hairless or hairy beneath. Notches (sinuses) between leaf lobes relatively *shallow* and *V-shaped* base of terminal leaf lobe *wide*. Twigs and buds *red-*

Red Maple

dish, the latter *blunt* and *several-scaled*. Extra buds may be present above some side buds. Broken twigs do *not* have unpleasant odor. Leaves 2"–8". Height 20'–40' (100'); diameter 1'–2' (4'). Flowers red, rarely yellow, in short, umbrella-like clusters along the twigs, March–May. Single fruit ¼"–1", reddish, May–July. **SIMILAR SPECIES:** (1) Silver Maple has deep U-shaped leaf sinuses, a narrow base of the end leaf lobe, reportedly malodorous twigs, and rough trunk bark. (2) Sugar Maples that have whitened leaf undersides can be recognized by slender, pointed brown buds. (3) Sycamore Maple is mostly cultivated and has blunt-toothed leaves and green buds. **REMARKS:** Though Red and Silver maples are often called soft maples, the wood is sometimes used for furniture.

SILVER MAPLE *Acer saccharinum* L.   **PL. 11**
A tall tree with grayish older bark that tends to *flake,* leaving brown spots. Leaves *deeply five-lobed,* with U-shaped sinuses and the base of the terminal leaf lobe *narrowed*. Foliage *whitened* beneath, sometimes hairy. Twigs, buds, and flowers/fruit as in

EASTERN
MOUNTAIN
MAPLE

RED MAPLE

SILVER MAPLE

Red Maple, but broken twigs may have an *unpleasant odor.* Leaves 2"–10". Height 40'–60' (120'); diameter 1'–3' (5'). Flowers greenish or reddish, short-clustered, Feb.–May. Single fruit 1½"–3", greenish or reddish, April–June. **SIMILAR SPECIES:** See (1) Red and (2) Sycamore maples. **REMARKS:** Sap sweet but less sugary than that of Sugar Maple.

SYCAMORE MAPLE *Acer pseudoplatanus* L.   NOT ILLUS.

A European maple that resembles the preceding two species in having leaves 5-lobed and somewhat *whitened beneath.* The foliage has many small, rather *blunt* teeth and deep V-based sinuses. The buds are large (³⁄₁₆"–⁷⁄₁₆" long), *green,* and blunt. Edges of opposing leaf scars do *not* meet. Flowers are in *slender,* hanging clusters, April–May; fruits each 1"–2" long, in *wide-angled* pairs. Height to 100'. Sometimes escaping from cultivation. **SIMILAR SPECIES:** Both (1) Silver and (2) Norway maples have leaf teeth sharp and U-shaped spaces between the leaf lobes. The former additionally shows silvery leaf undersides, while the latter also has milky leafstalk juice, opposing leaf scars whose edges meet, umbrella-like flower/fruit clusters, and fruit pairs in a horizontal line. (3) Red Maple has pointed leaf teeth and red twigs and buds. **REMARKS:** Known only as sycamore in much of Europe. Our sycamores (*Platanus,* Pl. 35) are known there as planetrees.

NORWAY MAPLE *Acer platanoides* L.   NOT ILLUS.

Mostly seen as a street tree, this European species sometimes spreads from plantings. Its foliage resembles that of Sugar and Black maples but the 5(–7)-lobed leaves have mostly shallow sinuses and relatively few *long-pointed* teeth often with hairlike tips. The broken leafstalks display a *milky sap.* Twigs brown; buds large (over ³⁄₁₆"), hairless, green or reddish, blunt, and single. Opposing leaf scars have *edges meeting* in a point. Flowers in *rounded,* upright clusters, March–April; fruits each 1"–2" long, in

nearly *horizontal* pairs, May–June. Leaves 4"–8". Height 40'–70'; diameter 1'–2'. **SIMILAR SPECIES:** See (1) Sycamore Maple. In winter, (2) Ashleaf Maple (Pl. 9) also shows leaf scars that meet. Its twigs, however, are green or purple with buds white-hairy. **REMARKS:** A useful street tree that resists urban smoke and grime.

SUGAR MAPLE   PL. 11
Acer saccharum Marsh.

A large tree with gray-brown trunk bark marked with rough vertical grooves and loose-edged plates when old. Leaves mostly *five-lobed*, with moderately deep U-shaped notches between lobes. Foliage *pale green* and usually hairless *beneath*, occasionally somewhat whitened. Leaf edges firm, *not* drooping. Leafstalk bases not much enlarged; stipules absent or small and not covering buds. Buds slender, *pointed*, brown. Side buds occur singly. Twigs glossy and reddish brown. Leaves 2"–10". Height 40'–60' (80'); diameter 1'–2' (3'). Flowers yellowish, long-stemmed, in loose, drooping clusters along twigs and at twig ends, April–June. Single fruit 1"–1¼", June–Sept. **SIMILAR SPECIES:** (1) Black Maple has shallowly lobed leaves with drooping edges, fewer teeth, larger stipules, swollen leafstalk bases, and dull twigs. (2) Florida Maple has whitish gray bark, smaller, mostly three-lobed leaves, and whitened leaf undersides. **REMARKS:** One of our most valuable hardwood trees. Neither sap nor wood is differentiated commercially from those of Black Maple; both species supply maple syrup as well as birdseye, curly, tiger, blister, and plain lumber. Wood much used for furniture. Sugar and Black maples are categorized as hard maples. Declining vigor of Sugar Maples in some areas is attributed to acid rain.

SUGAR MAPLE

Sugar Maple

BLACK MAPLE *Acer nigrum* Michx. f. PL. 11

Similar to Sugar Maple but with darker older bark and mostly *shallowly lobed* leaves that are darker green and more hairy, and have fewer teeth. Leaf edges tend to *droop*. Leafstalks enlarged at the base and, along with stipules, often tend to enclose buds. Twigs duller, somewhat orange-brown.

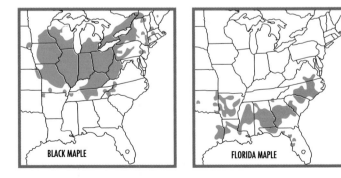

BLACK MAPLE

FLORIDA MAPLE

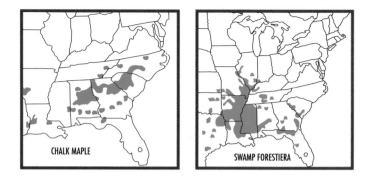

CHALK MAPLE

SWAMP FORESTIERA

FLORIDA MAPLE *Acer barbatum* Michx.   **PL. 11**

Much like Sugar Maple but with smooth *light gray* bark on young trunk resembling that of Red Maple or Beech. Leaves small, few-toothed, *whitened* and somewhat hairy beneath, and mostly three-lobed. The lobes, especially the central one, are *narrowed* at the base. Leaves 2"–5". Height 20'–60'; diameter 1'–2'. Bottomlands and slopes of Coastal Plain and Piedmont.

CHALK MAPLE *Acer leucoderme* Small.   **PL. 11**

Also related to Sugar Maple, with small leaves and light-colored bark like Florida Maple. The leaves are *green* beneath, however, and the leaf lobes are mostly *not narrowed* at the base. Height to 40'. Widespread in South but uncommon; bottomlands.

TREES WITH OPPOSITE SIMPLE FINE-TOOTHED LEAVES (PLATE 12)

Surprisingly few woody plants have unlobed leaves of this type. Maples (Pl. 11) have toothed opposite leaves, but these are also deeply lobed.

COMMON BUCKTHORN *Rhamnus cathartica* L.   **PL. 12**

A European shrub or tree with twigs ending in *sharp spines.* Leaves elliptical, hairless, fine-toothed. Leaf veins *depressed* from upper surface; main veins *sweep toward* leaf tip. A few leaves may be alternate rather than opposite. Twigs dark and unlined, buds with several scales and *spur branches common.* Bundle scars 3, occasionally fused and single. Inner bark *yellow.* Leaves 1½"–2". Height to 16' (26'). Flowers small, greenish, clustered at leaf angles and on spurs. May–June. Fruits dark, fleshy, and several-seeded. Hedgerows and thickets, Nova Scotia and N. Dakota to

N. Carolina and Kansas. **SIMILAR SPECIES:** The combination of thorn-tipped twigs and yellow inner bark is distinctive. The pattern of leaf veins is similar to that of dogwoods (Pl. 14), but buckthorn leaves are toothed. The only other regularly thorny tree with opposite leaves is the silver-scaly Silver Buffaloberry (Pl. 14).

SWAMP FORESTIERA **PL. 12**
Forestiera acuminata (Michx.) Poir.

An occasionally thorny shrub or small tree. Buds small, straw-colored, and *globular,* often more than 1 above each leaf scar. Leaves *long-pointed at both ends,* fine-toothed mainly above the middle, long-stalked, usually attached in 2 planes but often clustered. Twigs hairless or slightly hairy, sometimes with small spur branches; buds *globose,* often multiple; bundle scars single. Leaves 1¼"–3". Height to 12' (25'). Flowers small, along the twigs, March–May. Fruits small, single-seeded, fleshy, May–Oct. Coastal Plain swamps and riverbanks. **SIMILAR SPECIES:** Leaf shape of this species unique among trees and shrubs with opposite toothed leaves. When thorny, it is one of the few prickly species with opposite leaves. (1) See Common Buckthorn. The only other plant with globose buds and single bundle scars is (2) Buttonbush (Pl. 14), which has leaves often whorled, leaf scars connected by lines, and buds single above leaf scars. **REMARKS:** Fruits eaten by wood ducks, mallards, other waterfowl. Also called Swamp-privet.

BURNINGBUSH *Euonymus atropurpureus* Jacq. **PL. 12**
A shrub or small tree with *green, four-lined* twigs. Leaves egg-shaped or elliptic, short-pointed, fine-toothed, somewhat hairy beneath. Buds scaly, bundle scar single, leaf scars not connected by lines. Leaves 2"–6". Height 6'–12' (25'). Flowers purple, clustered in leaf angles, June–July. Fruits *reddish,* beneath *purplish woody* bracts, Aug.–Nov. Damp woods. **SIMILAR SPECIES:** Other opposite-leaved species with four-lined twigs have compound leaves: (1) Chaste-tree (p. 191) has spicy-scented twigs and fan-compound foliage. (2) Blue Ash (Pl. 8) has feather-compound leaves, gray twigs, and 4 or more bundle scars. **REMARKS:** Fruits reported to be poisonous to children. Recorded as eaten by only a few birds.

BURNINGBUSH

Though widespread and common in the eastern U.S., viburnums are difficult to identify as a group. Few of the common names ordinarily include the word "viburnum," and no single vegetative characteristic defines the group. Most are shrubs. All viburnums, however, have 3 bundle scars and small, fleshy fruits containing a single somewhat flattened seed. Usually the flowers are small and white. They and the fruits occur in mostly flat-topped clusters 3"–5" across growing at the twig tips.

The viburnums that grow to tree size have buds with only 2 scales. Unlike the maples with 2 bud scales, viburnum buds are *not* stalked. And unlike dogwoods, the leaf scars on twigs are *not* raised. The three species on Pl. 12 have thin foliage that is always fine-toothed. The two species on Pl. 13 have somewhat leathery leaves with no teeth.

VIBURNUMS

Leaves with fine teeth or none; white flowers and dark fleshy fruits in flat-topped clusters 2½"–5" across; leaf scars narrow, with 3 bundle scars, buds with 2 scales; fruits mostly egg-shaped.

SPECIES AND REMARKS	Distribution	Leaves with fine teeth	Leaf length (inches)	Leaves shiny above	Leaves long-pointed	Leaf bases wedge-shaped	Side twigs short, stiff
SMOOTH BLACKHAW *Viburnum prunifolium* Buds brown, short. **See Pl. 12**	N	+	1–3	–	–	–	+
NANNYBERRY *V. lentago* Scales cover flower buds. **See Pl. 12**	N	+	2–5	–	+	–	–
RUSTY BLACKHAW *V. rufidulum* Leaves/buds red-hairy. **See Pl. 12**	S	+	1–4	+	–	±	±
SMALL-LEAF VIBURNUM[1] *V. obovatum* Leaves evergreen, short-stalked, blunt, dotted.[2] **See Pl. 13**	S	–	1–2	+	–	+	+
POSSUMHAW VIBURNUM[1] *V. nudum* Scales partly cover flower buds. Leafstalks moderately long; fruits globular. **See Pl. 13**	S	–	3–5	+	–	±	–

[1] Occasionally leaves may bear some teeth.
[2] Use lens.

Bark of Rusty Blackhaw

RUSTY BLACKHAW *Viburnum rufidulum* Raf.   **PL. 12**

A southern shrub or small tree with short, somewhat flexible side twigs. Leaves elliptic to egg-shaped, blunt or somewhat pointed (but not long-pointed), sharply fine-toothed, and *shiny-surfaced*. Leaf undersides (at least midribs), leafstalks, buds, and sometimes twigs, *densely red-hairy*. Leafstalks *winged*. Foliage may become somewhat leathery. Buds short. Leaf scars narrow. Trunk bark dark, divided into many small, squarish blocks. Leaves 1"– 4". Height 6'–18' (40'); diameter 2"–10" (18"). Flowers April– May. Fruits blackish, Sept.–Oct. Woods and thickets. **SIMILAR SPECIES:** (1) Smooth Blackhaw has leaves and buds not hairy; Nannyberry has long-pointed leaves and large flower buds. In trunk bark, (2) Flowering Dogwood (Pl. 14), (3) Persimmon, and (4) Sourgum (Pl. 44) are similar. **REMARKS:** Fruits eaten by foxes, bobwhites, and several songbirds. Some people also like them.

SMOOTH BLACKHAW *Viburnum prunifolium* L.   **PL. 12**

Like Rusty Blackhaw but more northern and with *dull,* nearly hairless leaves. Buds are brown and powder-covered or somewhat brown-hairy. Leafstalks *not winged* or with very narrow wings. Twigs mostly stiff and short; buds short-pointed. Leaves 1"–3". Height 6'–15' (30'); diameter 2"–6" (10"). Woods and old fields.

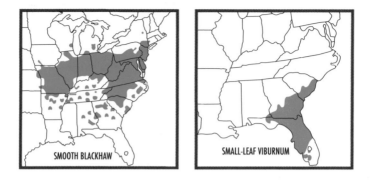

SMOOTH BLACKHAW

SMALL-LEAF VIBURNUM

NANNYBERRY *Viburnum lentago* L.

PL. 12

A northern shrub or small tree with sharply fine-toothed and short- to rather *long-pointed* leaves. Leaves hairless or nearly so and somewhat egg-shaped to narrowly elliptic. Leafstalks *winged*. Twigs long and flexible. The brown or gray buds are *long, slender,* and have rough-granular scales. They are of 2 sizes, the larger flower buds being *completely* covered by the 2 scales. Twigs rough-granular and side twigs flexible. Leaves 2"–5". Height 9'–

Nannyberry

NANNYBERRY

18' (30'); diameter 1"–3" (10"). Flowers, May–June. Fruits blue-black, Aug.–Sept. Woods. **SIMILAR SPECIES:** The only tree viburnum whose leaves and buds are regularly long and slender. Possumhaw Viburnum (Pl. 13) has the large flower buds *not* completely covered by scales.

BASKET WILLOW *Salix purpurea* L.   **PL. 39**
Many or even most leaves may be opposite. See Pl. 39 and p. 337.

TREES WITH OPPOSITE SIMPLE LEAVES, NOT TOOTHED AND MOSTLY LEATHERY (PLATE 13)

Trees with opposite, *leathery evergreen* leaves are few north of Florida, and those few typically range on the southern Coastal Plain. Among these, Possumhaw Viburnum extends north on the Coastal Plain to s. Connecticut and has leaves that are *not* always leathery, especially in northern areas. Yet this species is reviewed here as being in association with the viburnums on Pl. 12. The two viburnums on this plate may carry some leaves that are wavy-edged or have only a few teeth. In Florida, see Pls. F-13A and F-13B. Mangroves are restricted to s. Florida except for Black Mangrove, whose range extends locally around the Gulf of Mexico.

SMALL-LEAF VIBURNUM *Viburnum obovatum* Walt.   **PL. 13**
A common *evergreen* shrub or small tree of the southeastern states. Leaves 1"–2½" long, *short-stalked, wedge-based,* widest and sometimes slightly toothed near the *blunt* tip. Foliage also *finely dotted* beneath (use lens). Twigs mostly short and stiff, sometimes with spur branches; buds *two-scaled,* brown, and under ¼" long. Flowers small, white, in flat-topped and short-stalked *end* clusters, March–April; fruits fleshy, black, about ¼" long, egg-shaped, Sept.–Oct. Wet sites. **SIMILAR SPECIES:** (1) Possumhaw Viburnum has larger pointed foliage with differences also in twigs, flowers, and fruits. (2) Florida Forestiera has 4 or more bud scales, only 1 bundle scar, and slender fruits growing in the leaf angles.

POSSUMHAW VIBURNUM *Viburnum nudum* L.   **PL. 13**
A small Coastal Plain tree whose principal range is in the South. Leaves are glossy and somewhat leathery (but non-evergreen) and moderately stalked. They are pointed, often wavy-edged, but rarely fine-toothed. Twigs long and flexible, glossy or fine-grooved, and with slender brown leaf buds. Flower buds over ½" long, terminal, and only partly covered by the 2 scales. The single slender end bud usually leans to 1 side. Leaves 3"–5". Height to

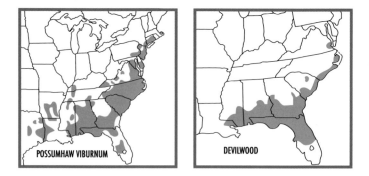

POSSUMHAW VIBURNUM

DEVILWOOD

20'. Flower/fruit clusters on *1"–3"* stalks; flowers small, white, May–July. Fruits fleshy, blue, *globular,* July–Oct. or later. Bottomland forests. **SIMILAR SPECIES:** (1) Devilwood has evergreen leaves, short blunt side buds, and leaf scars with a single bundle scar. See also (2) Small-leaf Viburnum and (3) chart opposite Pl. 14.

DEVILWOOD *Osmanthus americanus* (L.) Gray   PL. 13

Leaves evergreen, shiny, thick, narrow, green or pale beneath, and with edges rolled under. Twigs hairless, stout, *whitish.* End bud 2-scaled and 1/2" long; lateral buds *small,* sometimes one above the other. Bundle scar 1. Leaves 2"–6". Height to 50'. Flowers small, white, fragrant clusters in leaf angles. April–May. Fruits blue, fleshy, one-seeded, about ½" long, June. Bottomlands and other fertile soils. **SIMILAR SPECIES:** (1) The foliage somewhat resembles that of Mountain Laurel (Pl. 46), whose wider leaves are occasionally opposite. (2) Possumhaw Viburnum has non-evergreen leaves, longer buds, 3 bundle scars, and flat seeds. **REMARKS:** Wood is difficult to split, perhaps giving rise to the name.

FLORIDA FORESTIERA   PL. 13

Forestiera segregata (Jacq.) Krug & Urban

A southern shrub or small tree of coastal Georgia and Florida with small leathery, privetlike, evergreen leaves and tiny buds. Bud scales are 4 or more and buds sometimes above each other. Bundle scars 1. Leaves 1"–2¼". Height to 15'. The small flowers lack petals; clusters are produced in the leaf angles of the branchlets; spring. Fruits small, fleshy, *slender, black,* and one-seeded. Leaves 1"–2¼". Height to 15'. Swamps. **SIMILAR SPECIES:** (1) Swamp Forestiera (Pl. 12) has toothed leaves. (2) See Small-leaf Viburnum. **REMARKS:** Like Devilwood, forestieras are members of the olive family.

FLORIDA FORESTIERA

MANGROVES

Mangroves are small to large trees that grow in shallows along tropical and subtropical coasts. Their root systems slow water movements and cause deposits of sand, silt, and debris to extend the shoreline seaward. Their leathery, dark green, evergreen leaves are mostly blunt-tipped with the leaf edges rolled under. The single seed often germinates within the fruit, either on the tree or while the fruit is floating on the water.

RED MANGROVE *Rhizophora mangle* L. PL. 13

This s. Florida species usually occurs in the deeper shallows and is marked by *arching prop roots* (see Fig. 10). Leaves more or less wedge-based, clustered near the twig tips, yellow-green beneath, and sometimes with *black dots.* End bud *enclosed* by a pair of slender stipules 1"–3" long. These fall as the leaves grow, leaving scars that *encircle* the twigs. Bud scales 2; bundle scars 3. Trunk smooth, gray, mottled; inner bark reddish. Wood reddish brown, heavy. Leaves 2"–6". Height to 80'.

Red Mangrove

Flowers pale yellow, in leaf angles, all year. Fruits 1"–1½", leathery, brown. **SIMILAR SPECIES:** (1) Black and (2) White mangroves have erect breather roots and grow in more shallow water. White Mangrove has rounded leaf bases and bears leafstalk glands. It lacks stipule-enclosed end buds, and the foliage is not black-dotted. **REMARKS:** Bark is remarkably high in tannic acid.

BLACK MANGROVE *Avicennia germinans* (L.) L.   PL. 13

Ranges widely along Florida coasts and also west to s. Louisiana and s. Texas. Occupies shallower embayments than the last species and lives also in brackish and fresh waters near the coast. The numerous *erect breather roots* (see Fig. 11) are a useful first field mark. The thick, blunt-tipped and wedge-based leaves are *whitish hairy* beneath and often display salt grains on the surface. The leaves arise from squarish *ringed* twigs; leaf scars bear a *single* bundle scar. Bud scales 2. Outer bark dark with narrow furrows; inner bark bright orange or yellow. Wood dark brown to black. Leaves 2"–6". Height to 65'. Flowers white, fragrant, at twig ends, May–July or over a longer period in tropical countries. Fruits 1", yellow-green, irregularly egg-shaped but pointed, Sept.–Oct. or later. **SIMILAR SPECIES:** See Red and White mangroves. **REMARKS:** Bees produce an excellent honey from the blossoms.

WHITE MANGROVE   NOT ILLUS.
Laguncularia racemosa (L.) Gaertn. f.

Resembles Black Mangrove in having erect breather roots, but these are fewer, wider, and more often branched than in that species. Breather roots sometimes absent. The 2"–3" leaves,

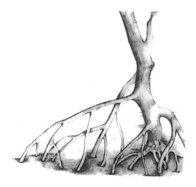

Fig. 10. Red Mangrove with prop roots.

approximately the same color on both sides, are marked by *paired leafstalk glands*. Twigs *not* ringed and buds *without* scales. Outer bark gray-brown, inner bark light brown. Wood yellow-brown, heavy. Height to 65'. Flowers white, fragrant, in loose clusters, at the leaf angles or twig ends, April–June. Fruits fleshy, reddish, ¾" long, Aug.–Sept. S. Florida coasts. **SIMILAR SPECIES:** White Mangrove grows landward of (1) Red and (2) Black mangroves. It often occurs onshore with (3) Buttonwood, a related but alternate-leaved plant (Pl. F-46A) with twigs ridged and leafstalk glands not as prominent as those of the White Mangrove. **REMARKS:** Distributed in tropical America and Africa.

CAMPHOR-TREE *Cinnamomum camphora* (L.) J. S. Presl. **PL. 46**
Some leaves may be opposite. Glands on leaf veins beneath.

FLORIDA-ONLY TREES   **PLS. F-13A AND F-13B**
There are 13 species with opposite, mostly leathery, non-toothed leaves, plus Red and White mangroves (above), that do not occur north of *peninsular* Florida. Most extend throughout s. Florida. See Pl. F-13A. Fourteen species do not occur north of the three southernmost (tropical) counties of Collier, Dade, and Monroe. Five of these trees have been observed only on the Florida Keys, south of the mainland. See Pl. F-13B.

Fig. 11. Black Mangrove with breather roots.

TREES WITH OPPOSITE SIMPLE LEAVES NEITHER TOOTHED NOR LEATHERY
(PLATE 14)

The remaining trees with opposite simple leaves without teeth have thin and membranous leaves as in most plants. Of the several dogwood species in the eastern United States, 3 reach tree size. Only the Flowering Dogwood has large blossoms; the other 2 species have small flowers in clusters at the twig ends. All dogwoods, however, have leaf veins which tend to *follow* the outer edge of the leaf. Dogwoods have 2 bud scales and 3 bundle scars per leaf scar. In contrast to viburnums, the leaf scars on dogwood twigs are *raised*. Also, the fleshy fruits contain 1–2 somewhat *rounded* seeds. The origin of the name dogwood is obscure, but may relate to *dag* (dagger), a goad, rather than to the animal. Possumhaw Viburnum (Pl. 13 and p. 213), with leaves usually leathery, may sometimes have thin, nonleathery foliage like the plants shown on this plate. See also Basket Willow, p. 337 and Pl. 39.

ROUGHLEAF DOGWOOD   PL. 14
Cornus drummondii C. A. Meyer

A midwestern shrub or, in the South, a medium-sized tree. Leaves *sandpapery above, woolly beneath*, egg-shaped or elliptic with 3–5 pairs of side veins. Twigs *red-brown* or brownish; branchlets brown or gray. Buds slender, somewhat hairy, pointed. Pith *brown*, rarely white. Leaves 2"–5". Height 1'–15' (50'); diameter 2"–8" (10"). Flowers small, whitish, in round-topped clusters, May–June. Fruits white to light blue, 3/16"–1/4", Aug.–Oct. SIMILAR SPECIES: No other dogwood has sandpapery leaves. Both the (1) Flowering and (2) Stiff dogwoods have white pith. REMARKS: Fruits eaten by many songbirds and by prairie chicken, sharptail and ruffed grouse, bobwhite, wild turkey, pheasant.

FLOWERING DOGWOOD *Cornus florida* L.   PL. 14

A small to medium-sized tree with hidden side buds and *stalked* flower buds. Leaves hairless or nearly so, elliptic to egg- or wedge-shaped, 5–6 *pairs* of lateral veins. Twigs and branchlets sometimes green, *mostly dark purple,* often swollen from insect attacks. Flower buds globular, *stalked.* Pith *white.* Trunk bark dark, *deeply checkered* like an alligator hide. Leaves 2"–5". Height 10'–40'; diameter 12"–18". Flowers small, clustered, each cluster with 4 (rarely 6–8) *large white* (seldom pink) *bracts* (not true petals). March–June. Fruits *red* or rarely yellow. Aug.–Nov. SIMILAR SPECIES: The only eastern dogwood with showy white bracts, hid-

FLOWERING DOGWOOD

Flowering Dogwood

den side buds, and stalked flower buds. Checkered bark less corky than similar bark of (1) blackhaw viburnums (Pl. 12), (2) Persimmon, and (3) Sourgum (Pl. 44). **REMARKS:** Powdered bark is reported to have been made into a toothpaste, a black ink (when mixed with iron sulphate), and a quinine substitute. Bark of the roots yields a scarlet dye. Shuttles, bobbins, tool handles, mallets, and the heads of golf clubs are manufactured from the hard, close-grained wood. Humans find the bitter red fruits inedible, but with twigs, they are important foods for numerous song and game birds, skunks, deer, rabbits, and squirrels.

STIFF DOGWOOD   **NOT ILLUS.**
Cornus stricta Lam. (*C. foemina* Mill.)
A stiff-branched shrub or small tree with leaves green on both sides, slightly paler beneath, somewhat long-tipped, 4–5 pairs of side veins. Twigs and branchlets *reddish* or brown; pith white. End bud often absent, leaving *paired lateral buds* at the twig end and resulting in forked branching. Leaves 2"–5". Height to 15'. Flowers small, whitish, in somewhat *round-topped clusters*, May–June. Fruits *blue*. Aug.–Oct. Wet places.

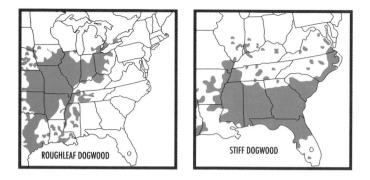

ROUGHLEAF DOGWOOD

STIFF DOGWOOD

BUTTONBUSH *Cephalanthus occidentalis* L. PL. 14

An *aquatic* shrub or small tree with leaves over 2½" long, often occurring in 3's and 4's, elliptic and short-pointed. Leafstalks often red. Side buds embedded in bark. Twigs round, hairless, not ringed, with single bundle scar. Pith pale *brown*. Leaves 3"–6". Height 3'–8' (18'). Flowers small, white, tubular, densely clustered in *ball-like heads* at twig ends. May–Aug. Fruits small, dry, brown balls, Sept.–Dec. or later. **SIMILAR SPECIES:** Pinckneya is a southern tree and has larger leaves, ringed twigs, and bell-shaped flowers. **REMARKS:** Honey plant. Wilted leaves may poison stock.

PINCKNEYA *Pinckneya pubens* Michx. FIG. 12

Uncommon small tree of the se. Coastal Plain. Leaves *large* (3"–8"), sometimes in 3's or 4's, *hairy*, tapering at both ends. Twigs are round, mostly hairy, and *ringed*. Buds have centrally ridged scales,

Buttonbush

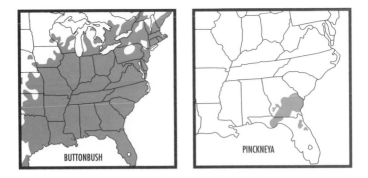

BUTTONBUSH

PINCKNEYA

sometimes occur one above the other. Leaf scars are raised, with 1 bundle scar. Pith white. Height to 25'. Large, pinkish, petal-like sepals form *conspicuous, bell-shaped blossom clusters* at the twig ends, May. Fruits dry, 1" long, or two-parted capsules, Aug.–Sept. Damp soils. **REMARKS:** A relative of *Chincona*, which produces quinine, this species was once thought to be a useful substitute for treating malaria and gained the alternate name Fevertree.

Fig. 1 2. Pinckneya.

FRINGETREE *Chionanthus virginicus* L.   PL. 14

A shrub or small tree with leaves moderately large, non-evergreen, non-aromatic, and *hairless* or nearly so, narrowly egg-shaped to elliptic. Twigs moderately stout, more than ⅟₁₆" thick, slightly hairy or hairless, *not* ringed. Pith white. Buds with 6–8 ridged scales, sometimes several together; leaf scars raised, bundle scar 1. Leaves 3"–8". Height 8'–18' (35'); diameter 1"–4" (8"). Flowers white, in drooping clusters from side buds, petals very slender, May–June. Fruits purple, ball-shaped, 1-seeded, fleshy, Sept.–Oct. Floodplains. **SIMILAR SPECIES:** (1) The privets have twigs less than ¹⁄₁₆" thick. (2) Viburnums (Pls. 12, 13) have only 2 bud scales. (3) Ashes (Pls. 8, 9) have larger leaf scars and more bundle scars. **REMARKS:** The showy flower clusters give rise to the alternate common name of Old-Man's-Beard.

CALIFORNIA PRIVET *Ligustrum ovalifolium* Hassk.   PL. 14

A Japanese shrub or small tree planted widely and escaping from cultivation in the southeastern states. Leaves firm, shiny, sometimes evergreen, slightly less than 2½" long, elliptic, and hairless. Leafstalks *less than* ¼" long. Twigs slender (¹⁄₁₆" or less thick) and *hairless.* The buds have 8–12 or more *long-pointed* scales. Leaf scars are much raised and contain only a single bundle scar. Leaves 1"–2¼". Height to 15'. Flowers small, white, in cone-shaped clusters at twig ends, June–July. Fruits small, black, fleshy, several-seeded, Sept.–Oct. or longer. **SIMILAR SPECIES:** (1) The next 2 privets have either fewer and less pointed bud scales or hairy twigs. (2) In winter, Fringetree has stouter twigs.

JAPANESE PRIVET *Ligustrum japonicum* Thumb.   NOT ILLUS.

Similar to the California Privet in having hairless twigs, but the leafstalks are *more than* ¼" long and the buds are tighter, darker, and have *fewer* pointed (and *not long-pointed*) scales. The leaves are sometimes longer, 2"–4", possibly evergreen. This Asian species is planted in the Southeast and has become naturalized in some localities.

CHINESE PRIVET *Ligustrum sinense* Lour.   NOT ILLUS.

Similar to the California Privet but with twigs fine-hairy. Widely escaped in the southeastern region.

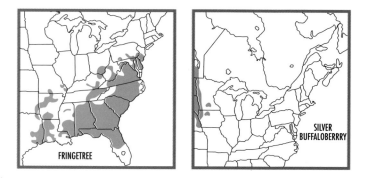

FRINGETREE

SILVER BUFFALOBERRRY

Shepherdia argentea (Pursh) Nutt.

A *western* shrub or small tree with twigs and somewhat leathery, wedge-shaped leaves covered with *silver scales*. Small leaves may be present at bases of leafstalks. Twigs *silvery* and often thorn-tipped; pith dark *brown*. Buds two-scaled, with narrowed bases. Leaves 1½"–2½". Height to 15'. Flowers small, greenish yellow, bell-shaped, along the twigs. April–June. Fruits bright red, berry-like, July–Sept. Streambanks. **SIMILAR SPECIES:** The only opposite-leaved plant with all-silver scales. (1) Russian-olive (p. 331) also has all-silver scales but has narrow alternate leaves. It is widely planted on the prairies as a windbreak and in the East for orna-ment. (2) The opposite-leaved Canada Buffaloberry [*S. canaden-sis* (L.) Nutt.] and (3) the alternate-leaved American Silverberry (*Elaeagnus commutata* Bernh.) have brown as well as silver scales, but both are shrubs. **REMARKS:** Fruits contain a bitter sub-stance that foams in water. Sometimes known as soapberries (but see *Sapindus* species, p. 250–251).

BROAD-LEAVED TREES WITH ALTERNATE COMPOUND LEAVES

(PLATES 15–22)

Relatively few trees have compound leaves. Those with opposite leaves were presented in Section II (Pls. 6–9). The rest are in this section. In winter, the alternate leaf scars may sometimes indicate by their large size the former presence of compound leaves. Where there is doubt, however, the twigs of a leafless unknown plant with alternate leaf scars will have to be compared with the illustrations of *both* Sections IV and V or will have to be identified by means of the Winter Key in Appendix A. *Warning:* Poison-ivy, Poison-sumac, and several tropical trees, including Florida Poisonwood (see Fig. 4), have leaves of this type. Do not handle them. Be careful of unknown plants of this type.

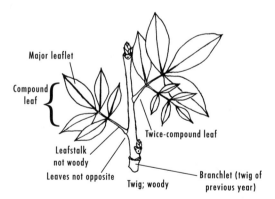

Fig. 13. Alternate compound leaves.

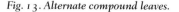

1. Plants thorny. **2**
1. Plants without thorns. **3**
  2. Specimens growing north of Florida. **Locusts, etc., Pl. 15.**
  2. Specimens found growing in Florida. **See Pls. 15, F-15.**
3. Buds hidden by leafstalk bases. **Honey Locust, Pl. 15.**
3. Buds visible. **4**
  4. Leaves only once-compound. **5**
  4. Leaves twice- or thrice-compound (major leaflets divided into minor leaflets). **12**
5. Leaflets toothed (though in Tree-of-heaven with only 1 basal pair of glandular teeth). **6**
5. Leaflets not toothed (sometimes wavy-edged). **10**
  6. Buds easily visible (somewhat hidden in Tree-of-heaven). **7**
  6. Buds nearly hidden beneath the leafstalk bases.
    Sumacs, Pl. 20.
7. Leaflets mostly 11–14 (rarely 7–10). **8**
7. Leaflets 5–9. **9**
  8. Buds white-woolly, brown-woolly, or red-gummy.
    Walnuts, etc., Pl. 16.
  8. Buds yellow, yellow-brown, or brown-hairy.
    Hickories I, Pl. 17.
9. End buds more than ¼" long; twigs stout.
    Hickories II, Pl. 18.
9. End buds less than ¼" long; twigs slender.
    Hickories III, Pl. 19.
  10. Bundle scars more than 5. **Sumacs, Pl. 20.**
  10. Bundle scars 1–5. **11**
11. Leaves thin, deciduous. **Hoptree, etc., Pl. 21.**
11. Leaves leathery, evergreen.
    Florida species, Pls. F-21A and B.
  12. Trees of cen. and s. Florida. **Lebbek, etc., Pls. 22, F-22.**
  12. Trees of the Midwest and South.
    Chinaberry, etc., Pl. 22.

THORNY TREES WITH ALTERNATE FEATHER-COMPOUND LEAVES
(PLATE 15 AND FIGURE 14, P. 228)

The following few species are the only thorny trees with compound leaves, whether alternate or opposite. Most of these species (the bean-producing legumes and the Trifoliate Orange) have smooth-edged or fine-toothed leaflets whose leafstalks never bear thorns. The prickly-ashes have more coarsely toothed leaflets and often thorny leafstalks. The upright thorny plants with

alternate simple leaves appear on Pls. 23–24. For the few opposite-leaved thorny trees, see Pls. 12 and 14. In Florida see also Pl.
F-15.

HONEY LOCUST *Gleditsia triacanthos* L. PL. 15

A tall tree with *feather-compound* leaves, often some *twice-compound* leaves. Bark dark, somewhat scaly, in the wild uncultivated
form. Trunk with numerous stout thorns, often *several inches* long
and frequently branched. A thornless cultivated variety is widely
planted. Leaves divided into numerous narrow leaflets, which
may be slightly toothed. The leaflets, in turn, are frequently subdivided. Hairless buds, *hidden* by the leafstalk bases in summer,
are nearly *surrounded* by leaf scars when twigs are leafless. They
may be supplemented by smaller buds located just above them.
End bud false. Twigs stout; bundle scars 3. Spur branches present. Leaves 6"–15". Height 70'–80' (140'); diameter 2'–3' (6').
Flowers small, greenish, clustered May–July. Fruits 8"–18", flattened twisted pods with sweet pulp between numerous oval
seeds, Sept.–Feb. SIMILAR SPECIES: (1) Only Water Locust has e-
qually long thorns. (2) Black Locust has small paired thorns.
REMARKS: Honey Locust, believed originally to have been restricted
to Mississippi Valley, is now common eastward. The long thorns

Bark of Honey Locust

HONEY LOCUST

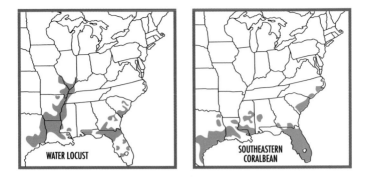

WATER LOCUST

SOUTHEASTERN
CORALBEAN

have been used by woodsmen for pins, spear points, and animal traps. Heavy, durable wood used for railroad ties, fence posts, and agricultural implements. Unlike most legumes, the tree does not harbor root bacteria capable of fixing nitrogen. Fruits eaten by cattle, deer, rabbits, squirrels, and bobwhite.

WATER LOCUST *Gleditsia aquatica* Marsh.　　　**FRUIT, PL. 15**
Similar to Honey Locust but smaller, with leaflets somewhat shorter, thorns mostly *unbranched*, and fruit pods 1"–2", *without* pulp and containing only 1–3 seeds. Coastal Plain and Mississippi floodplain swamps. **SIMILAR SPECIES:** A hybrid Water/Honey Locust is reported from the lower Mississippi Valley.

TRIFOLIATE ORANGE *Poncirus trifoliata* (L.) Raf.　　**FIG. 14**
A shrub or small tree imported from Asia and often planted as a hedge in the South. Easily identified by stiff *green* twigs that bear many stout *green* thorns. Leaves divided into 3 small, blunt, wavy-edged leaflets. Crushed leaves aromatic and leafstalks *winged.* Buds bright red, ball-like; leaf scars very small, with 1 scarcely visible bundle scar; end bud false. Small citrus fruits are bitter. Height rarely to 20'. Flowers white, April–May. Fruits Sept.–Oct. Thickets.

SOUTHEASTERN CORALBEAN　　　　　　　　　　**FIG. 14**
Erythrina herbacea L.
A shrub in most of the southeastern U.S., this species attains tree size in s. Florida. The leaves are three-parted, with the leaflets rather triangular or *nearly three-lobed,* long-pointed, and smooth-edged. The midrib may be prickly beneath. The stout green twigs often bear curved thorns. Bundle scars indefinite. Bark smooth to ridged, gray, with some thorns. Leaves 6"–8". Flowers red, tubu-

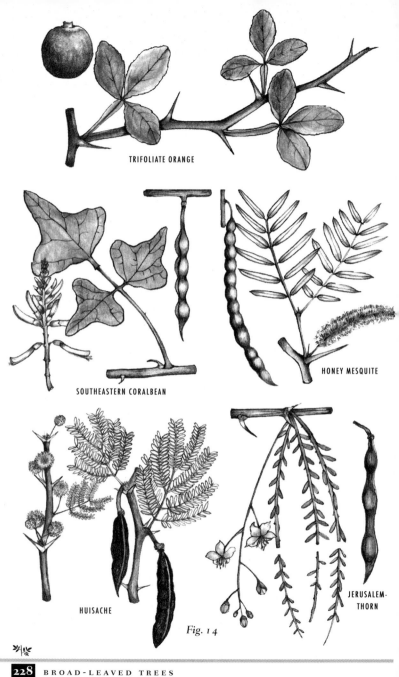

TRIFOLIATE ORANGE

SOUTHEASTERN CORALBEAN

HONEY MESQUITE

HUISACHE

JERUSALEM-THORN

Fig. 14

lar, in showy upright clusters, April–June. Fruits are slim, *beaded* pods, 3"–6" long, containing poisonous *red* seeds.

NORTHERN PRICKLY-ASH   PL. 15
Zanthoxylum americanum Mill.

A shrub or small tree, often thicket-forming, with *paired prickles* flanking leaf scars and buds. Leaves once-compound, with 5–11 egg-shaped, hairless leaflets that are quite finely toothed, and often with *prickly* leafstalks. Foliage has *lemonlike odor* when crushed and is *hairy* when young. Buds small, blunt, *red-hairy*, located above leaf scars. Bundle scars 3. True end bud present. Specimens without prickles are encountered rarely. Leaves 3"–10". Height 4'–10' (25'). Flowers small, greenish, clustered, at the leaf angles, April–May. Fruits small, dry, reddish brown, one- to two-seeded (not bean-type) pods, Aug.–Oct. **SIMILAR SPECIES:** (1) Among once-compound thorny trees with many leaflets, the locusts have hidden buds, leafstalks that are not prickly, and beanpod fruits. (2) See Southern Prickly-ash. **REMARKS:** A member of the citrus family. Leaves, fruits, or bark were once chewed to cure toothache. Known as Toothache-tree in some places. The genus is sometimes incorrectly spelled *Xanthoxylum*.

SOUTHERN PRICKLY-ASH   LEAF, PL. 15
Zanthoxylum clava-herculis L.

This southern shrub or tree is similar to but larger than the north- ern species. Has a peculiar smooth gray trunk bark decorated with scattered *large corky knobs*, often prickle-tipped. Leaflets mostly toothed, somewhat curved and *uneven-based*. Buds small, blunt, dark, *hairless*. Flowers and fruits clustered at twig ends. Leaves 4"–16". Height 10'–20' (50'); diameter 4"–8" (18"). Poor

Coastal Plain soils. **REMARKS:** This species and *Aralia spinosa,* also in this group, are both known alternatively as Hercules-club.

BLACK LOCUST *Robinia pseudoacacia* L. PL. 15

A medium-sized tree with *once-compound* leaves. Leaflets 6–20, blunt, egg-shaped. Strong ½"–1" *paired thorns* flank nearly circular leaf scars. *Hidden* white-hairy buds burst through leaf scars upon enlargement. Tiny additional buds may be present above the leaf scars. Twigs moderately stout, hairless; bundle scars 3. End bud false. Bark on old trunks dark, deeply ridged, and cross-hatched. Leaves 6"–12". Height 70'–80' (100'); diameter 2'–3' (6'). Flowers medium-sized, *white,* clustered, fragrant, May–June. Fruits 2"–6" long, flat pods, Sept.–April. **SIMILAR SPECIES:** Among other once-compound species, (1) other *Robinia* locusts have bristly, glandular, or hairy twigs and mostly hidden buds. (2) Prickly-ashes are smaller trees and have exposed buds, toothed leaflets, and usually thorny leafstalks. (3) Honey and Water locusts have large unpaired thorns. (4) Southeastern Coralbean has only 3 leaflets. **REMARKS:** Black Locusts are often planted for fence posts. Wood strong, hard, and durable in the soil. Young shoots and bark sometimes poisonous to livestock, but the seeds are eaten by bobwhite, pheasant, mourning dove, cottontail rabbit, snowshoe hare, and deer. Spreading around the world in temperate zones.

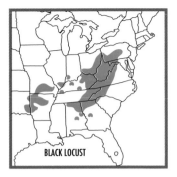

Black Locust

CLAMMY LOCUST *Robinia viscosa* Vent.   **TWIG, PL. 15**
A shrub or small tree; leaves similar to those of Black Locust.
Thorns paired, *weak,* usually no more than ¼" long; twigs covered
with *sticky glands.* Bark smooth, light brown, marked with short
horizontal streaks. Leaves 6"–12". Height 5'–20' (40'); diameter
1"–3" (6"). Flowers *pink,* not fragrant, May. Fruits sticky pods,
2"–3", Aug.–Sept. Mountain woods.

KELSEY LOCUST *Robinia kelseyi* Hutch.   **NOT ILLUS.**
Localized in the mountains of western N. Carolina, this shrub or
small tree resembles the other *Robinias,* but the leaflets are *narrow* and pointed, the leaves and twigs are *hairless,* and the 2"–3"
fruit pods are *sticky-hairy.* Leaves 4"–6" with 9–16 leaflets. Flowers *pink,* spring. Woods.

HONEY MESQUITE *Prosopis glandulosa* Torr.   **FIG. 14**
A thorny *southwestern* shrub or small tree whose drooping, twice-
compound leaves have 2(–3) major leaflets, each bearing 12–20
narrow 1"–2" minor leaflets. Usually paired (less commonly single) 1"–2" spines and short but obvious knobby *spurs* occur at the
leafstalk bases. Occasionally thornless. Leaves 6"–8". Height to

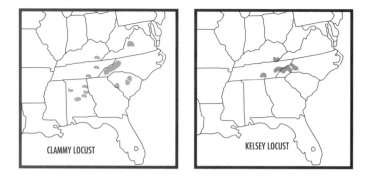

CLAMMY LOCUST

KELSEY LOCUST

30'. Flowers small, greenish yellow, in elongate spikes. May–Sept. Fruits 4"–10" beans, somewhat beaded and flattened. **SIMILAR SPECIES:** (1) Huisache has tiny minor leaflets, thorns invariably paired, ball-shaped flower clusters, and shorter fruit pods. (2) Jerusalem-thorn has long, slender, grasslike leaves with tiny (less than ¼" long), early-falling minor leaflets. Grasslands and pastures. **REMARKS:** A plant of western rangelands whose seeds are spread by livestock and whitetail deer and possibly also by javelinas, raccoons, and other wildlife. Foliage is consumed by hoofed animals; fruits and seeds are eaten by many mammals and birds. Mesquite beans have been pounded into a nutritious flour by native Americans and others; reported also to have been fermented and made into a beverage. A gum exuded from the branches is said to have been chewed as candy and used to mend pottery.

HUISACHE *Acacia farnesiana* (L.) Willd.   **FIG. 14**
This shrub or small tree has finely divided twice-compound foliage. There are 4–8 pairs of major leaflets, each of which is subdivided into *numerous* ¼"-long minor leaflets. A pair of 1"–3" thorns occurs at the leafstalk bases. Buds small; end bud false. Bundle scar single. Leaves 2"–4". Height to 30'. Flowers in fragrant, ball-shaped, yellow, long-stalked clusters. Fruits stout, brownish pods, 2"–3" long. **SIMILAR SPECIES:** Silktree (Pl. 22), also with many minor leaflets, is thornless and has larger leaves and minor leaflets plus pink flowers. **REMARKS:** Southwestern in its original distribution but now becoming widespread in the Gulf states. Cultivated in Europe for perfume. Sap has been used as a glue. Pronounced weesah-chay.

JERUSALEM-THORN *Parkinsonia aculeata* L.   **FIG. 14**
Thorny green-barked shrub or small tree whose 40–60 tiny (⅛"–

³⁄₁₆") minor leaflets drop early, leaving 2–4 evergreen *grasslike* mid-ribs, 10"–15" long, on the plant to represent the major leaflets of the twice-compound leaf. One or more thorns occur at the leafstalk bases, one usually being larger (to 1"). The green, drooping twigs tend to have fine lengthwise grooves. Bundle scars 3. Flowers yellow, pealike, spring and summer. Fruits 2"–4" bean pods. Dry soils, Gulf states. Also called Paloverde, though this name is better reserved for species of *Cercidium,* a group of western desert plants.

HERCULES-CLUB

HERCULES-CLUB *Aralia spinosa* L.   PL. 15

A very *spiny* shrub or small tree with *very large twice- or even thrice-compound* leaves. Trunk and twigs stout, with numerous coarse prickles. Leaflets toothed, pointed; leafstalks *thorny.* Long, narrow leaf scars have about 20 bundle scars. End bud may be false. Leaves 24"–48". Height 5'–15' (35'); diameter 1"–4" (9"). Flowers white, in flat-topped clusters, July–Sept. Fruits black, fleshy, one-seeded, Aug.–Nov. **SIMILAR SPECIES:** Prickly stout stems and V-shaped leaf scars with numerous bundle scars are distinctive at all seasons. **REMARKS:** This species is sometimes called Devil's Walking-stick. The name "Hercules-club" is also an alternate name for the Southern Prickly-ash (p. 229).

FLORIDA-ONLY TREES   PL. F-15

Seven species of thorny trees with compound leaves occur only in s. and cen. Florida.

WALNUTS AND SIMILAR TREES (PLATE 16)

These are trees with alternate, feather-compound leaves. The leaflets are numerous and *toothed,* although Tree-of-heaven mostly has only one pair of gland-bearing teeth at the leaflet base.

BLACK WALNUT *Juglans nigra* L.   PL. 16

A tall tree whose large leaves have (9) 15–23 narrow, toothed leaf-

BLACK WALNUT

Bark of Black Walnut

lets slightly hairy beneath. Often the end leaflet is *lacking*. Crushed leaves are spicy-scented. Twigs more or less hairless, stout; pith *light* brown and chambered by woody partitions (pith of branchlets usually better developed than that of twigs). Buds *whitish-woolly;* leaf scars large, *without hairy fringe;* bundle scars in 3 groups. End bud true, *blunt*, and ⅛"–⅜" long. Bark dark and deeply grooved; ridges not shiny. Leaves 12"–24". Height 70'–100' (150'); diameter 2'–4' (6'). Flowers catkins, April–June. Fruits *large spherical nuts* with husks of 1 piece, Oct.–Nov. Fertile soils. SIMILAR SPECIES: Butternut is our only tree with compound leaves and chambered pith. There is a hairy ridge above the leaf scar, darker pith, end leaflet present, bark shiny-ridged, fruits oblong and four-lined. REMARKS: Black Walnut is one of the most valuable and beautiful native trees. Heavy, strong, durable heart-wood is easily worked and in great demand for veneers, cabinet-making, interior finishing, and gunstocks. Large trees have been almost exterminated in some regions. Bark is used in tanning; yel-low-brown dye can be made from nut husks. Nuts eaten by humans, squirrels, and mice; twigs by deer. The bruised nut husks were once used to stun fish for food, but this practice is now illegal. Tomatoes, apples, and other species may not survive near large walnut trees.

Bark of Butternut

BUTTERNUT *Juglans cinerea* PL. 16

Similar to Black Walnut but with a prominent *hairy fringe* above leaf scar. Pith *dark* brown; end leaflet normally *present*. The wider bark ridges are smooth-topped, making a *shiny,* interlaced gray network superimposed upon the black fissures. Leaflets (7) 11–17. Twigs and leafstalk bases somewhat hairy. End bud ½"–¾" long and *pointed*. Height 40'–80' (100'); diameter 1'–2' (3'). Fruits somewhat *oblong and sticky;* nuts with one-piece, 4–(8)-*lined* husks. Oct.–Nov. REMARKS: Also known as White Walnut; wood lighter in color than that of its more valuable relative. Lumber is light, soft, and weak but easily worked and polished; darkens upon exposure to air. Though not an important timber species, it is used for interiors, cabinetwork, furniture, and instrument cases. The early colonists are reported to have prepared a yellow-brown stain by boiling the soft, half-ripe fruits. They also pickled the boiled nuts and made a dark stain from the husks and inner bark to dye uniforms. Indians are said to have boiled the nuts to obtain oil for use as butter. The nutmeats were then collected and dried. In spring, sap was boiled down to make syrup. The crushed fruits were once also used to poison fish. Bark yields useful drugs. Nuts are eaten by many wild animals. The species reportedly is being destroyed by a canker.

Ailanthus altissima (Mill.) Swingle

A fast-growing, small to large tree with very large leaves having 11–41 leaflets. Leaflets *not toothed* except for pair of *gland-tipped teeth near bases*. Twigs hairless, yellow-brown, stout, with continuous yellowish pith. Buds small, brown-woolly; end bud false. Leaf scars *very large,* somewhat triangular, with numerous bundle scars. Bark gray-brown, smooth, or with narrow light-colored grooves. Leaves 12"–24" or more. Height 80'–100'; diameter 1'–2'. Flowers small, yellowish, clustered, male blossoms with foul odor, June–July. Fruits in large clusters, dry, narrow, one-seeded, winged, Sept.–winter. SIMILAR SPECIES: Our only tree with such gland-tipped leaflet teeth. In winter, stout twigs, false end buds, large leaf scars, and numerous bundle scars are distinctive. Coffeetree (Pl. 22) has large leaf scars but fewer bundle scars. It has twice-compound leaves and salmon-colored pith. REMARKS: An Asian species that has become the most rapidly growing woody plant in our area. Will thrive under extremely adverse conditions, growing as much as 8' in a year. Annual sprouts 12' long not uncommon where a tree has been cut down. Since it is adapted to disturbed sites, even a crack between bricks in an alleyway may provide a seedbed for this plant. Immune to dust and smoke and useful in polluted cities where other plants will not grow. The soft

wood has limited lumber and fuel values. The common name, supposed to be of Asiatic or Australian origin, refers to the tree's height.

Tree-of-heaven

Mountain-ashes are northern trees whose dense terminal clusters of small white blossoms, colorful autumn foliage, and bright fruit clusters are attractive both in the wild and when planted in ornamental landscaping. The small, fleshy, applelike fruits often remain until late winter. Eaten by some people and by many birds and mammals including ruffed and sharptail grouse, ptarmigan, fisher, and marten. Deer, elk, and moose browse the twigs. Spur branches present. Leaves 4"–9" long. Leaf scars crescent-shaped, narrow. Some species are hardy even in Labrador, Greenland, Iceland, and Scandinavia. Sometimes called Rowan-tree, an old Scandinavian name. True ashes (Pls. 8, 9) also have feather-compound leaves, but they are opposite.

AMERICAN MOUNTAIN-ASH   PL. 16
Sorbus americana Marsh.

A shrub or small tree. Compound leaves have 11–17 long, narrow, toothed, *long-pointed* leaflets; leaflets *more than 3 times as long as broad*. Leaves and twigs hairless. Buds *reddish, sticky, and hairless;* leaf scars narrow, with 3 or 5 bundle scars. End bud true. Spur branches may be present; bark rather smooth and gray-

American Mountain-ash

SHOWY MOUNTAIN-ASH

brown. Leaves 6"–9". Height to 40'; diameter to 12". Flowers small, about ¼", clustered, May–June. Fruits *small,* about ¼", *orange-red, clustered,* Aug.–March. Woods and openings. **SIMILAR SPECIES:** (1) Showy Mountain-ash has wider leaflets, flowers, and fruits. (2) European Mountain-ash has hairy leaves and woolly buds. **REMARKS:** One of the most ornamental northern trees. Colorful, fleshy fruits often remain on tree late in winter. Eaten by many birds and mammals, including ruffed and sharptail grouse, ptarmigan, fisher, and marten. Deer and moose browse the twigs.

SHOWY MOUNTAIN-ASH   **LEAFLET AND FRUIT, PL. 16**
Sorbus decora (Sarg.) Schneid.

    Like American Mountain-ash but leaflets *less than 3 times* as long as broad and somewhat whitened beneath. Flowers about ⅜" across and *fruits red, more than* ⁵⁄₁₆". Woods and rocky places. **REMARKS:** Also known as the Northern Mountain-ash.

EUROPEAN MOUNTAIN-ASH   **LEAFLET AND FRUIT, PL. 16**
Sorbus aucuparia L.

    Widely cultivated in northern states and Canada and established in the wild. Resembles previous 2 species except that leaflets and twigs are somewhat *white-hairy;* buds *white-woolly* and not sticky. Leaflets *short-pointed or blunt.* Flowers and fruits resemble those of Showy Mountain-ash. Called Quickbeam in Europe.

HICKORIES I–III (PLATES 17–19)

    The hickories are trees with feather-compound leaves whose leaflets are toothed and mostly long-pointed. Twigs are stout and tough yet flexible. Winter end buds are true, leaf scars are large and shield-shaped, bundle scars are many, and pith is continuous. Male flowers are in prominent catkins, occurring in spring. Husks of hickory nuts characteristically break into 4 rather separate parts upon ripening; those of walnuts (Pl. 16) remain whole.

    Most non-thorny plants with alternate compound leaves have a false end bud. Among those that resemble the hickories in having a true end bud, Black Walnut and Butternut (Pl. 16) have chambered piths, and mountain-ashes (Pl. 16) have narrow leaf scars.

    Fruits of several hickories, especially Pecan and Shagbark, are edible and have commercial value. They usually fall in September and October. Nuts of most species are eaten by domestic swine, squirrels, opossums, wild turkey, and occasionally ducks. Twigs are browsed by rabbits and deer. Crushed green nut husks were formerly used to stun fish for food, but this practice is now illegal.

Hickory wood is strong, heavy, tough, and elastic, but is subject to insect attacks and decays on contact with moisture. It is of value in the manufacture of skis, tool handles, agricultural implements, wagons, gunstocks, chair backs, and baskets. It was once important as the best American wood for barrel hoops. As fuel it is excellent, producing great heat and high-grade charcoal.

The hickories may be divided into 3 groups: *pecans*, with paired and usually yellow bud scales and four-ridged nuts mostly with winged sutures; *shagbarks*, with overlapping bud scales, large winter end buds (more than ½" long), stout twigs (more than ⅛" in diameter), thick nut husks (about ¼" thick), plus for 2 species, mature trunk bark that peels in strips; and *pignuts*, with overlapping bud scales, small winter end buds, slender twigs, thin nut husks, and tight bark.

HICKORIES I: PECANS (PLATE 17)

PECAN *Carya illinoenis* (Wang.) K. Koch   **PL. 17**
A tall tree with 9–17 leaflets per leaf. End bud ⅜"–⅝" long, with 2–3 *pairs* of non-overlapping *yellow-hairy* bud scales. Twigs hairless; bark closely ridged, *not peeling*. Nuts edible; considerably longer than wide. Husks *thin*, ridged along 4 joint lines and splitting more or less to the base. Bark medium dark, with numerous vertical ridges. Leaves 12"–20". Height 100'–120' (160'); diameter 3'–4' (6'). Floodplains. **SIMILAR SPECIES:** Three other hickories have bud scales in pairs with edges meeting: (1) Water Hickory has brownish buds with yellowish glands that soon fall off; (2) Bitternut has permanently yellow hairless bud scales and 7–9 leaflets; (3) Nutmeg Hickory has yellow-hairy buds, 5–9 leaflets, and thick nut husks. **REMARKS:** About 100 varieties of this tallest hickory are cultivated widely for their delicious nuts. The fruits of orchard trees have thinner husks than those of wild specimens. Although originally a species of Mississippi River bottoms, it

PECAN

BITTERNUT HICKORY

Pecan

will grow in sheltered places on uplands as far north as Massachusetts. Fruits rarely mature in North, where pecans are mostly planted for ornament. In South, opossums, wild turkeys, and squirrels feed on nuts.

BITTERNUT HICKORY PL. 17
Carya cordiformis (Wang.) K. Koch
A medium-sized to tall tree. Leaflets 5–11, somewhat hairy beneath. Buds *bright yellow-powdery,* with scales in *pairs,* not overlapping. End bud often more than ½" long and with 2 exposed scales. Twigs *slender,* mostly hairless. Bark *tight* with network of fine smooth ridges. Nuts cylindrical, smooth, and bitter; husks *thin,* ridged toward outer end and splitting to the middle. Hybrids with Pecan and Shagbark Hickory sometimes occur. Leaves 6"–12". Height 50'–60' (100'); diameter 18"–24" (36"). Woods. **SIMILAR SPECIES:** See Pecan.

WATER HICKORY (BITTER PECAN) PL. 17
Carya aquatica (Michx. f.) Nutt.
Similar to Pecan but more southern and smaller. Buds *red-brown* with yellowish gland spots that soon disappear. Bark shreddy. Nuts bitter, egg- or *ball-shaped.* Husks ridged, splitting nearly to

WATER HICKORY

NUTMEG HICKORY

base. Leaves 8"–18". Height 50'–70' (100'); diameter 12"–24" (30"). Coastal Plain rivers and swamps. SIMILAR SPECIES: (1) Shagbark and (2) Shellbark hickories (Pl. 18) have trunk bark peeling in wide strips and bud scales overlapping.

NUTMEG HICKORY   PL. 17
Carya myristiciformis (Michx. f.) Nutt.
A rare tree of scattered southern swamps, with 5–9 leaflets, often *shiny* beneath. Buds brown- to yellow-hairy or granular. Trunk bark smooth to scaly. Leaves 6"–15". Height to 110'; diameter 2'. Nut husk ⅛" thick, smooth, splitting *to the base*; kernel edible. Bottomlands. SIMILAR SPECIES: See Pecan.

HICKORIES II: SHAGBARKS (PLATE 18)

SHAGBARK HICKORY *Carya ovata* (Mill.) K. Koch   PL. 18
A tall tree whose leaves have 5–7 (usually 5) hairless leaflets, the end ones mostly larger. Buds covered by overlapping scales; end bud ½"–¾" long. Twigs *stout, red-brown,* slightly hairy to shiny. Bark light-colored, *very shaggy,* in long, loose strips. Nuts *egg-shaped,* 1⅜"–2¼", edible, four-angled, not ridged. Nut husk yellowish, thick, splitting to base. Leaves 8"–14". Height 60'–90' (120'); diameter 2'–3' (4'). Dry woods. SIMILAR SPECIES: This is the only one of the shagbark group with so few leaflets; the 3 other hickories mostly with 5–7 leaflets are in the pignut group (Pl. 19), and all have small end buds and tight bark. On this plate (1) Shellbark Hickory has (5) 7–9 leaflets that are more or less soft-hairy beneath, light tan or orange twigs, and sometimes shaggy mature bark. (2) Mockernut Hickory also has (5) 7–9 leaflets, but its hairy twigs and foliage, early-falling outer bud scales, and tight trunk bark distinguish it.

SHAGBARK HICKORY

Bark of Shagbark Hickory

SHELLBARK HICKORY *Carya laciniosa* (Michx. f.) Loud. **PL. 18**
A tall, uncommon tree. Leaflets 7–9 (usually 7), more or less
hairless, or short-hairy beneath. Buds have overlapping scales;
end bud ¾"–⅞" long and hairy, *outer scales present*. Twigs *stout,
orange-brown, hairless* or slightly hairy. Bark *very shaggy,* loosening
in *long strips.* Nuts egg-shaped 1⅛"–2⅜", edible, angled but not
ridged. Husks thick, splitting to base. Leaves 15"–22". Height

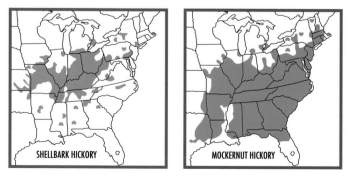

SHELLBARK HICKORY

MOCKERNUT HICKORY

80'–100' (120'); diameter 3'–4'. Rich soils, often bottomlands.
SIMILAR SPECIES: See (1) Shagbark, (2) Mockernut, and (3) Water
(Pl. 17) hickories.

MOCKERNUT HICKORY *Carya tomentosa* (Poir.) Nutt. **PL. 18**

A medium-sized to tall tree with 7–9 leaflets; leaf undersides and
twigs *matted-woolly*. Hairs curly and clustered. Leaves *extra-fra-grant* when crushed, pale or orange-brown beneath. Buds have
overlapping scales. End bud ⅝"–1"; *outer scales fall* in autumn.
Twigs stout. Bark *tight* and deeply furrowed. Nuts 1"–1½" long,
ball- to egg-shaped, edible, with thick husk *not* splitting to base.
Bark shaggy or tight with network of smooth ridges. Leaves
8"–15". Height 50'–80' (100'); diameter 18"–24" (36"). Hills and
dry soils. **SIMILAR SPECIES:** Three hickories have end buds more than
½" long. This is the only one with matted-woolly twigs and foliage
and the end bud dropping its outer scales in autumn.

HICKORIES III: PIGNUTS (PLATE 19)

SAND (PALE) HICKORY   **PL. 19**
Carya pallida (Ashe) Eng. & Graebn.

The only hickory with 7–9 leaflets and a *small* (less than ¼" long)
end bud. Leaflets usually 7 and often somewhat silver-scaly
beneath. Buds with overlapping scales and usually yellowish.
Leafstalks and midribs mostly long-hairy. Twigs slender, fine-hairy or not. Trunk pale to dark gray, smooth to furrowed, some-times shaggy. Fruit husks very *thin,* yellow-powdery, ridged, typi-cally splitting to the base. Nuts sweet. Height 40'–50' (110');
diameter 18"–20". Southeastern forests. **SIMILAR SPECIES:** The very
small end bud tends to be distinctive. See Pignut Hickory.

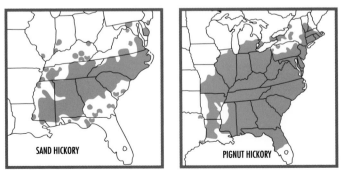

SAND HICKORY

PIGNUT HICKORY

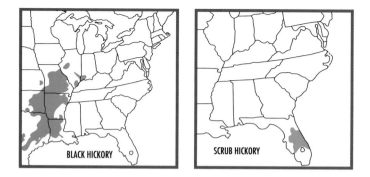

BLACK HICKORY

SCRUB HICKORY

PIGNUT HICKORY *Carya glabra* (Mill.) Sweet   PL. 19

A tall tree with leaves of 5 (less commonly 7) hairless leaflets. Buds have overlapping scales; end bud ⅜"–½", silky-hairy after outer scales drop in autumn. Twigs *slender* (to ⅛" thick), red-brown, and hairless. Bark dark, *tight,* and smooth-ridged. Nuts egg-shaped, ⅝"–1⅜", hard-shelled, sometimes sweet. Nut husks thin, brown, usually *not* splitting to the base. Leaves 6"–12". Height 80'–90' (120'); diameter 2'–3' (4'). Dry woods. **SIMILAR SPECIES:** (1) Shagbark Hickory, also with 5–7 leaflets, has loose bark plus a large end bud and end leaflets. (2) Sand Hickory has an end bud less than ¼" long. (3) Black Hickory has rusty-hairy twigs and leaves. (4) Mockernut Hickory has a large end bud, hairy twigs, and 7–9 woolly leaflets. **REMARKS:** Intergrades occur between these several species. Sweet Pignut Hickory (C. *ovalis*), with fully splitting nut husks, is no longer separated.

Pignut Hickory

BLACK HICKORY *Carya texana* Buckl. **PL. 19**
Like Pignut Hickory, a large, close-barked, small-budded tree
with 5–7 leaflets, usually 7. Twigs, buds, and leaf undersides are
rusty-hairy. The outer bud scales fall early. Fruits ball- to egg-
shaped, to 2". Nut edible, husk yellow-scaly. Does not range into
Florida (see Scrub Hickory). Dry woods.

SCRUB HICKORY *Carya floridana* Sarg. **PL. 19**
Like Black Hickory but known only as an uncommon species in
the sand-pine scrub country of cen. Florida. Twigs are *rusty-hairy*
but outer bud scales *do not* fall early. Leaflets 5–7, usually 5.
Height to 80'; diameter to 1½'. Fruit to 1½". **SIMILAR SPECIES:** Pignut
Hickory is not rusty-hairy, and its outer bud scales fall early.

SUMACS AND RELATIVES (Plate 20)

Warning: Two poisonous species occur among the non-thorny
plants with alternate compound leaves. See under Poison-sumac
and Florida Poisonwood in this group and also Pl. F-21A. Plants
of fields and forest openings, the sumacs and their relatives vary
by species; only some have toothed leaves. *Rhus* sumacs are red-
fruited, with dense, upright, cone-shaped clusters of small, dry,
hairy fruits present much of the year (silhouette, p. 30). They provide an apparently little-relished but available food supply for
wildlife. Twigs are stout with large brown pith. These sumacs
have hairy side buds, in summer mostly hidden by the leafstalk
bases and in winter nearly surrounded by the leaf scars. End buds
are false and sap in summer is often milky. Bundle scars are
numerous. Flowers are small, greenish, and clustered. Fruits of
Poison-sumac and Florida Poisonwood (p. 247 and 248) are
smooth and whitish or yellow-orange; the irritating sap is not milky.

WINGED SUMAC *Rhus copallina* L. **PL. 20**
A shrub or, especially in South, sometimes a small tree. Leaves
large, divided into 11–23 narrow, *smooth-edged, shiny, short-
pointed* leaflets, each about ¾" wide; the midrib bordered by thin
"wings." Twigs and leafstalks *velvety*, round, and marked with
obvious raised dots. Buds hairy, partly surrounded by *shallow* U-
shaped leaf scars. Trunk is dark and smooth, with numerous
raised cross-streaks (lenticels). Leaves 6"–14". Height 4'–10'
(30'); diameter 1"–3" (10"). Flowers small, yellow-green,
July–Sept. Fruits red, short-hairy. **SIMILAR SPECIES:** In Texas and
Oklahoma, see (1) Prairie Sumac. (2) In Florida, see Wingleaf
Soapberry (Pl. 21). See also (3) Poison-sumac. **REMARKS:** Bark and
leaves can be used in tanning leather. Twigs cropped by deer;
seeds eaten by many birds.

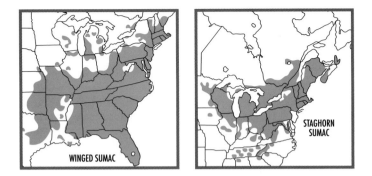

PRAIRIE SUMAC   *Rhus lanceolata* (Gray) Britton   LEAF, PL. 20

A western plant similar to and often considered a variety of Winged Sumac. The leaflets and midrib wings are quite *narrow*— leaflets less than ½" wide and *long-pointed.* Leaves 5"–10". Thickets, s. Oklahoma and e. Texas to New Mexico. **SIMILAR SPECIES:** (1) Western Soapberry (Pl. 21) lacks winged midribs; (2) Wingleaf Soapberry (Pl. 21) occurs in the U.S. only in Florida and se. Georgia. The soapberries have larger yellow, fleshy, single-seeded fruits. **REMARKS:** Fruits eaten by prairie chickens and other birds.

STAGHORN SUMAC   *Rhus typhina* L.   PL. 20

A shrub or small tree with *very hairy* twigs and leafstalks. Leaves large, made up of 11–31 *toothed* leaflets. Twigs round, no obvious dots. Sap milky in summer at fresh cuts. Buds hairy, without scales, surrounded by deep U-shaped leaf scars. Bark dark and

Staghorn Sumac

smooth, with numerous raised cross-streaks. Wood yellow. Leaves 12"–24". Height 4'–15' (50'); diameter 2"–4" (15"). Flowers June–July. Fruits red, long-hairy. **SIMILAR SPECIES:** (1) Lack of winged midribs and twig dots plus deeper leaf scars differentiates this species from Winged Sumac. (2) Hybridization with Smooth Sumac sometimes occurs, and intermediate characteristics result. **REMARKS:** Aptly named, branches bear a marked resemblance to the antlers of a deer "in velvet." Staghorn Sumac is cultivated in Europe and the West. Bark and leaves rich in tannin; it is reported that a black ink can be made by boiling leaves and fruit. The long-haired fruits have been found in stomachs of many songbirds, ruffed and sharptail grouse, bobwhite, pheasant, mourning dove, and skunk. Twigs cropped by browsing mammals.

SMOOTH SUMAC *Rhus glabra* L.   **PL. 20**
Much like Staghorn Sumac but with twigs and leafstalks *hairless.* Twigs somewhat flat-sided. Fruits red, short-hairy.

POISON-SUMAC *Toxicodendron vernix* (L.) Kuntze   **FIG. 4, P. 17**
Danger: Do not touch or burn any part of this plant. All parts contain a watery, dangerous skin irritant. Shrub or small tree with large leaves composed of 7–13 pointed leaflets *not toothed* and *opposite* along the midrib. Twigs and buds round, *hairless;* leaf scars crescent- or shield-shaped, do *not* surround buds. End bud true. Bark smooth and dark with numerous narrow cross-streaks often tending to encircle trunk. Sap clear, quickly turning black, and poisonous. Leaves 6"–12". Height 6'–20' (30'); diameter 3"–8" (10"). Flowers May–July. Fruits *white*, about 3/16" in diameter, Aug.–spring. Widespread but local. **SIMILAR SPECIES:** Over most

of our area the only tree or shrub with *hairless* buds and twigs and *once-compound* leaves that are *not toothed*. Its open, *swampy* habitat is a clue. Most similar are (1) Yellowwood, with leaflets alternate on the midrib, and (2) Western Soapberry, with greater height and the end leaflet usually lacking (see Pl. 21). (3) Winged Sumac has winged midribs. **REMARKS:** Though more virulent than Poison-ivy, this species is generally uncommon; largely confined to moist soils. Contact with the plant (or with smoke from burning it) usually results in itching and other symptoms within a few hours. Washing the exposed parts of the body with a thick lather of soap soon after exposure helps. Water alone, unless in large amounts, may only spread the oil. Mild irritations may be treated with astringent lotions, but cases involving the eyes or genitals and widespread irritations of other parts of the body should be treated promptly by a physician. The merits of taking injections for the prevention of sumac poisoning are a matter for medical opinion. Common names such as Poison-elder or Poison-dog-wood usually refer to Poison-sumac. The fruits are eaten by many birds, including bobwhite, pheasant, and ruffed grouse. Twigs browsed by cottontail rabbit. Foliage may turn yellow or red in autumn. Formerly named *Rhus vernix* L.

FLORIDA POISONWOOD   FIG. 4; PL. F-21A
Metopium toxiferum (L.) Krug & Urban
   Danger: Poisonous. Do not touch or burn. Like Poison-sumac, the sap of this species is caustic, and all parts should be avoided. A shrub or small tree of cen. and s. Florida with *mostly triangular, leathery, evergreen* leaves. The 3–7 alternate, smooth- or wavy-edged leaflets may be pointed or blunt, and squarish based or not. The clear sap turns *black* and may mark the foliage and outer bark. The latter is thin, brown, and *flaky* and shows the *orange* underbark. Leaves 6"–10". Height to 40'. Flowers yellowish green. Fruits yellow-orange, ¼" long, fleshy, shiny, one-seeded. **SIMILAR SPECIES:** See Pl. F-21A. **REMARKS:** Common within its tropical range south and east of Lake Okeechobee in s. Florida. An attractive plant but one whose undesirable characteristics should be learned. Contact with it should be avoided!

TREES WITH ALTERNATE ONCE-COMPOUND LEAVES NOT TOOTHED (Plate 21)

Except for some sumacs (Pl. 20) and many specimens of thorn-less Honey Locust (Pl. 15), only 17 species in our area have leaves of this type. Thirteen of these occur only in Florida (see Pls. F-21A, F-21B), and 2 others are mainly west of the Mississip-

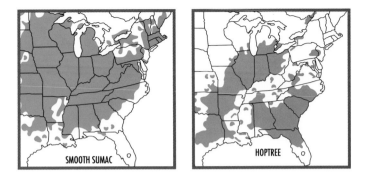

SMOOTH SUMAC

HOPTREE

pi River. Only the first 2 beyond occur widely in the eastern U.S., and they are common only locally. Twigs are generally hairless. Buds may be more than 1 above each leaf scar. End bud false.

HOPTREE   *Ptelea trifoliata* L.   PL. 21

An upright shrub or small tree with *three-parted leaves* that are usually hairless but may be hairy beneath. Leaflets usually without teeth; the end leaflet *short-stalked*. Crushed leaves may emit a musky odor. Twigs brownish and round; buds hairy and hidden in summer by leafstalks; leaf scars U-shaped; bundle scars 3. Trunk bark rather smooth, light-colored, shallowly grooved. On Lake Michigan sand dunes, a variety has velvety twigs and leaves. Leaves 4"–10". Height 10'–20' (25'); diameter 2"–10" (16"). Flowers greenish, small, clustered, May–July. Fruits flat, circular, papery, two-seeded, Sept.–spring. Fertile woods. SIMILAR SPECIES: Small specimens are often mistaken for Poison-ivy (see Fig. 4, p. 17), but the end leaflet of that irritating shrub or vine is long-stalked. REMARKS: Fruits reportedly have been used as a substitute for hops (*Humulus*) in flavoring beer.

YELLOWWOOD   *Cladrastis kentukea* (Dum.-Cours.) Rudd   PL. 21

A medium-sized tree with 7–11 *smooth-edged* and sometimes silky leaflets, each 2"–4" long, mostly in a distinctly *alternate* arrangement along the midrib. Buds hairy, brownish, often several above each other, mostly hidden beneath hollow leafstalk bases or, in winter, surrounded by U-shaped leaf scars. Twigs brownish, stout; bundle scars 5. Bark smooth, gray; wood *yellow*. Leaves 5"–8". Height to 60'; diameter to 3'. Flowers white, clustered, May–June. Fruits pealike pods, Sept.–Oct. Rich soils. SIMILAR SPECIES: In its range, the only other thornless species with alternate once-compound toothless leaves of more than 3 leaflets are: (1)

YELLOWWODD

Bark of Yellowwood

Poison-sumac (see Fig. 4, p. 17), which is usually shrubbier and has more or less visible buds; (2) Winged Sumac (Pl. 20), with winged midribs; and (3) Western Soapberry, with an even number of narrow leaflets, visible buds, and 3 bundle scars. These do not usually have leaflets arranged in a markedly alternate manner. (4) In winter, Beech (Pl. 32) has similar bark but buds are long.

WINGLEAF SOAPBERRY *Sapindus saponaria* L. **PL. 21**

Principally a tree of s. Florida, but reported north to coastal Georgia. Leaves feather-compound, with 6–12 pointed and usually opposite leaflets, each leaflet 3"–5" long, hairless to velvety beneath. Generally the end leaflet is lacking. Midribs are typically *winged* (though a non-winged form of Fla. and se. Ga. has been described as *S. marginatus* Willd. with the common name Florida Soapberry). Twigs hairless, leaf scars large, buds small, smooth, globular, with 2 visible scales. Bundle scars 3. Bark gray to reddish, scaly. Leaves 6"–9". Height to 50'. Flowers small, white, in loose 6"–10" end clusters, November. Fruits in spring; *yellow,* smooth, half-inch, rounded, single-seeded, *poisonous.* **SIMILAR SPECIES:** See Brazilian Peppertree (Pl. F-21 A). **REMARKS:** According to Little (1979), this species and Varnishleaf (Pl. F-46B) are the only trees native both to Hawaii and the continental U.S.

WINGLEAF SOAPBERRY

WESTERN SOAPBERRY

TEXAS SOPHORA

Wingleaf Soapberry also occurs on other Pacific islands
and southward to Argentina. In
water, the fruits produce a
soapy lather that is *poisonous*
when taken internally. Seeds
may be made into buttons,
beads, etc.

WESTERN SOAPBERRY PL. 21
Sapindus drummondii Hook. & Arn.
  Typically a tree of the Great Plains, this tree has leaves with 7–19
  narrow, sharply pointed, somewhat leathery leaflets that are not
  toothed. Leaflets usually opposite; end leaflet often lacking. Buds
  usually hairy, small. Bark light gray, scaly. Pulp of clustered fruits
  forms lather in water (see Wingleaf Soapberry) and is reportedly
  poisonous. Flowers white, clustered, May–June. Fruits ball-
  shaped, white, Sept.–Oct. or longer. Leaves 4"–15". Height
  20'–50' (75'); diameter 10"–18" (24"). Bottomlands.

TEXAS SOPHORA *Sophora affinis* Torr. & Gray PL. 21
  Barely penetrates Louisiana, Arkansas, and Oklahoma from its
  main range in cen. and e. Texas. The leaves are 6"–10" long and
  divided into 13–15 or more, nearly hairless, pointed or somewhat
  blunt leaflets. Twigs green to brown; buds woolly; bundle scars 3.
  Buds *surrounded* by the leafstalk base and leaf scars. Bark red-
  brown, scaly. Leaves 6"–10". Flowers white, ½" long, pealike, in

3"–5" clusters, April–June. Fruits black, 2"–3" long, non-splitting pods, beaded, summer. Height 18'–20'; diameter 8"–10". Limestone soils.

FLORIDA-ONLY TREES   PLS. F-21A, F-21B
Thirteen other trees with alternate compound leaves not toothed are mostly evergreen and occur only in tropical Florida.

THORNLESS TREES WITH TWICE-COMPOUND LEAVES (PLATE 22)

These, plus the several prickly species on Pl. 15 and Fig. 14 (p. 228), are the only trees in our area with foliage of this type (but do not overlook the thornless form of Honey Locust (Pl. 15). (In Florida, see also Pl. F-22.) In these plants, not only are the leaves divided into major leaflets, but these major leaflets are further divided into minor leaflets. In this group, except in Coffeetree, both major and minor leaflets are opposite. The leaves are large, the twigs hairless, and the end bud false. Except for Chinaberry, these species are all legumes and produce characteristic beanlike or pealike fruit pods.

CHINABERRY *Melia azedarach* L.   PL. 22
An Asian tree, widely planted in dooryards in the South, that often escapes to the wild. Leaves with many *toothed,* 1"–3", pointed minor leaflets. Twigs *stout.* Buds small, nearly spherical, fuzzy, not sunken as in Coffeetree. Leaf scars *large,* somewhat three-lobed, with 3 groups of scattered bundle scars. Pith white. Leaves 8"–16". Height to 40'. Flowers purplish with an unpleasant odor, clustered, May–June. Fruits usually present; *yellowish, ball-like,* internally *poisonous.* REMARKS: Fruits have been used to make flea powder. They are known, too, to have paralyzed livestock and birds. Their bad taste may account for the relatively few cases of human poisoning. The bark has been used to stun fish.

COFFEETREE *Gymnocladus dioica* (L.) K. Koch   PL. 22
A tall tree with *very large* leaves. Minor leaflets 1"–3", *very numerous,* pointed, *not toothed.* Both major and minor leaflets are mainly *alternate.* Twigs very stout, somewhat whitened; leaf scars large, shield-shaped, 3–5 bundle scars. Buds silky, sunk in bark, often one above the other. Pith pinkish. Bark dark and scaly. Leaves 17"–36". Height 40'–60' (100'); diameter 1'–2' (3'). Flowers whitish, clustered, May–June. Fruits 2"–10" brown pods, Sept.–winter. SIMILAR SPECIES: (1) Chinaberry has toothed leaflets; (2) Lebbek has blunt leaflets; and (3) Silktree has fernlike foliage.

Coffeetree

In winter, the sunken lateral buds of Coffee-tree are distinctive among species with large alternate leaf scars. **REMARKS:** Often planted as a shade tree in city parks along eastern seaboard; sometimes escapes. Native mostly west of Appalachians. One of few members of pea family which do not grow bacterial root nodules capable of fixing nitrogen. Seeds were roasted and used as coffee in some areas during Civil War. Native Americans are supposed to have roasted seeds, eating them as nuts. Pulp between seeds is nevertheless reported to be poisonous; cattle become sick when leaves or fruits drop into their drinking water. Reddish wood is strong and coarse but takes a good polish. Useful in cabinetwork and for fence posts and railroad ties. Often called Kentucky Coffeetree. A related species occurs in China; fossil members of the genus are found in Europe.

LEBBEK *Albizia lebbeck* (L.) Benth.   **PL. 22**

A deciduous tropical tree of s. Florida and the Keys. It has 6"–1 6" leaves and 2–4 pairs of major leaflets. The many minor leaflets are ¾"–1 ¾" long, opposite, smooth-edged, and *rounded* at both ends. Twigs slender; leaf scars small. Pith whitish. Leaves 8"–1 4". Height to 50'. Flowers whitish yellow, in round clusters, with numerous 1"–1 ½" threadlike (pollen-bearing) stamens protruding. Fruits 5"–8" dry pods *more than 1*" wide and containing loose seeds when ripe. **SIMILAR SPECIES:** The only other twice-compound species with blunt leaflets are found only on the Florida Keys and have smaller leaflets (see Pl. F-22). **REMARKS:** A native of tropical Asia naturalized in s. Florida and other tropical areas.

SILKTREE (ALBIZIA) *Albizia julibrissin* Durazzini   PL. 22

A small tree with feathery *fernlike foliage*. There are 6–16 pairs of major leaflets and numerous tiny, pointed, and very *uneven-sided* minor leaflets, each less than ¼" long. On being handled, leaflets *close like pages of a book*. Twigs hairless, slender, leaf scars small, with 3 bundle scars. Buds few-scaled, small, blunt, not sunk in bark, sometimes occur one above the other. Pith whitish. Bark smooth, light brown. Leaves 5"–8". Height 20'–40'; diameter 6"–12". Flowers powderpuff-like, pink, June–Aug. Fruits beanlike pods. 2"–3". **SIMILAR SPECIES:** Other trees with such feathery foliage occur only in lower Florida (see Pl. F-22). **REMARKS:** Native to S. Asia but widely planted and naturalized in the eastern U.S.

FLORIDA-ONLY TREES   PL. F-22

Trees of this type that are distributed only in peninsular Florida and the Keys include 3 other species, plus Lebbek (above).

Silktree

BROAD-LEAVED TREES WITH ALTERNATE SIMPLE LEAVES

(PLATES 23–46)

Over half of our trees fall in this category. Dividing the group into subdivisions, therefore, facilitates identification. The outline below may be used as a general guide to identification. A winter key to leafless plants with alternate leaf scars appears in Appendix A.

MAJOR SUBDIVISIONS OF BROAD-LEAVED PLANTS WITH ALTERNATE SIMPLE LEAVES

1. Trees with thorns.   Pls. 23–24.
1. Trees without thorns. **2**
    2. Leaves fan-lobed or fan-veined.   Pls. 25–27.
    2. Leaves feather-lobed or feather-veined. **3**
3. End buds clustered, fruits acorns.   Oaks. Pls. 28–31.
3. End buds not clustered or, if so, then fruits not acorns. **4**
    4. Leaves toothed.   Pls. 32–43.
    4. Leaves not toothed.   Pls. 44–46.

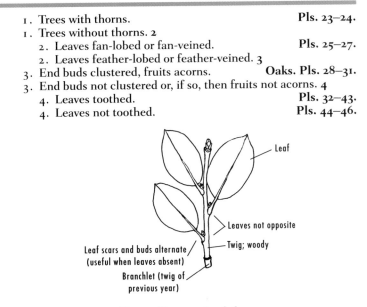

Fig. 15. Alternate simple leaves.

THORNY TREES WITH ALTERNATE TOOTHED LEAVES (Plate 23)

In addition to the species below, Common Buckthorn (Pl. 12) has spine-tipped twigs and may bear some alternate leaves. Sour Orange (Pl. 24) may occasionally be somewhat thorny.

HAWTHORNS *Crataegus* species **PL. 23**

These plants, though distinctive as a group, are virtually indistinguishable as species except by a few botanists. Frequent hybridization and great individual variation confound accurate identification. Even specialists vary greatly in their decisions regarding the validity of many forms. The number of species of *Crataegus* in the U.S. has been variously determined as more than 1,000 and as less than 100. In this volume, therefore, no attempt is made to differentiate between the many species. The drawings serve only to indicate major leaf types as an aid to identification of the genus. Thornless hawthorns are occasionally encountered.

In general, the hawthorns are a widespread group of very dense shrubs or small trees mostly with long thorns and smooth or scaly bark. Bundle scars are 3. Buds are nearly spherical, end bud true. Spur branches are usually present. Hawthorn spines are *long and slender,* seldom with buds or leaves. They may occur on twigs as well as on older wood.

The fruits are small, yellow to red, and applelike. They often remain on the plants all winter, providing food for numerous birds and mammals, including bobwhite, ringneck pheasant, ruffed and sharptail grouse, gray fox, cottontail rabbit, and whitetail deer. Apparently because of their density, hawthorns are much used for nesting by many songbirds. They are important honey plants but are pests in pastures. They were formerly widely used for fences in England. Many varieties are used in landscaping. The name "haw" comes from the same root as "hedge."

The hawthorns illustrated are **Dotted Hawthorn** (*C. punctata* Jacq.), **Downy Hawthorn** (*C. mollis* Schede), and **Cockspur Hawthorn** (*C. crus-galli* L.). SIMILAR SPECIES: (1) Some crabapples and plums may have long thorns, but some or all thorns usually carry buds or leaves on them. Plums have false end buds. (2) Possumhaw Holly (Pl. 40) is not a hawthorn. It is not thorny and has only 1 bundle scar. (3) Possumhaw Viburnum (Pl. 13), with opposite leaves and no thorns, is also not a hawthorn.

NATIVE CRABAPPLES *Malus* species **PL. 23**

Crabapples have sharp leaf teeth, scaly non-striped bark, true end buds, 3 bundle scars, several-seeded fruits, and no glands on leafstalks. In crabapples and plums, the thorns occur only on the older wood (not on the twigs) and usually bear buds or leaves. Some hawthorns have thorns, leaves, and fruits resembling those of apples, but their thorns seldom bear buds or leaves and may also occur on the twigs. Spur branches occur in all 3 groups. Some apple species are more regularly thorny than others. The following three are the only apples native to our area. The domesticated apple and pear (Pl. 43), introduced from the Old World, do escape to grow wild but are not likely to be thorny. Since they could be sharp-twigged, however, their text discussions (p. 355 and 356) should also be reviewed in identifying members of the group. Hybrids between species are frequent and usually have intermediate characteristics. Botanists may use either *Malus* or *Pyrus* (and sometimes *Sorbus*) as the name for the genus.

AMERICAN CRABAPPLE *Malus coronaria* L.   PL. 23

A thicket-forming shrub or small tree of north-central states with hairless twigs and leaves. Leaves have *round or heart-shaped bases.* Those on vigorous shoots are deeply toothed to somewhat lobed. Though usually heart-shaped to triangular, foliage may be narrowly long-pointed. Buds sharp-pointed. Bark gray, rough, cracked vertically. Leaves 1"–5". Height 15'–30'; diameter 6"–14". Flowers pink or white, highly fragrant, March–May. Fruits yellow-green, 1¼"–2", bitter, Sept.–Nov. Woods borders. **SIMILAR SPECIES:** (1) Narrowleaf Crabapple is more southern and has leaves more elliptic and wedge-based. (2) Prairie Crabapple is woolly. **REMARKS:** Widely planted for ornament. Fruits used in preserves and vinegar. Trunks used as stock on which to graft less hardy cultivated apples. Also called Sweet Crabapple.

AMERICAN CRABAPPLE

NARROWLEAF CRABAPPLE

NARROWLEAF CRABAPPLE *Malus angustifolia* Ait.   **PL. 23**
More southern than American Crabapple, with elliptic leaves, leaf bases more *wedge-shaped* and tapering, and leaf tips often more blunt. Leaves tend to be evergreen in some areas, but even where they are not, dead leaves can often be found and will assist in winter identification. Twigs hairy or not. Fruits less than 1 " and bitter but used for preserves and cider. Southern woods and thickets. See map, p. 257.

PRAIRIE CRABAPPLE *Malus ioensis* (Wood) Bailey   **NOT ILLUS.**
Midwestern. Similar to American Crabapple, but twigs and leaf undersurfaces densely *woolly.* Flowers April–May. Fruits bitter but make delicious jelly; eaten by many wildlife species. Thickets and open places.

WILD PLUMS *Prunus* species   **PLS. 23, 37**
Though the cherries, also in the genus *Prunus,* are never spiny, the plums are variously thorny or not. Allegheny Plum (p. 327), for example, sometimes has spine-tipped twigs. For cherries and such usually thornless plums, see Pls. 36 and 37.

Some thorns of plums may be simple spines, but most are short, stiff, bud-bearing spur branches with sharpened tips. Thorns are generally present on branchlets and absent from twigs. As in other species of *Prunus,* leafstalks of most plums bear small paired glands (usually lacking in American Plum). The distinctive "almond" odor of broken twigs is less prominent in plums than in cherries. Bundle scars 3. Bark often marked with horizontal linelike lenticels. Unlike the end bud on cherries, those on wild plums are mostly regarded as *false,* though their status is not always easily determined. Wild plum fruits are small and ball-shaped, with single large seeds.

AMERICAN PLUM

CANADA PLUM

The American Plum (Pl. 23) is the only regularly thorny plum that usually lacks leafstalk glands. The several other plums are not easy to identify as to species. Those that regularly bear thorns, however, may usually be separated by the following key. Also see species accounts.

1.   Twigs velvety or woolly. **2**
1. Twigs hairless or nearly so; fruits yellow or red. **3**
    2. Leaf teeth sharp; fruits yellow-red.   **American Plum.**
    2. Leaf teeth rounded; fruits blue-black.   **Bullace Plum.**
3. Leaf teeth sharp; buds red-brown, about ⅛" long; fruits ¾"–1".
                                             American Plum.
3. Leaf teeth rounded. **4**
    4. Leaves broad, length no more than twice width; buds gray to black, about ³⁄₁₆"; fruits 1–1¼".   **Canada Plum.**
    4. Leaves narrow, length more than twice width; buds reddish, about ⅛"; fruits ½".   **Chickasaw Plum.**

AMERICAN PLUM *Prunus americana* Marsh.   **PL. 23**

A shrub or small tree with leaves dull, bases heart- to wedge-shaped, hairless or nearly so, somewhat long-pointed, *sharply* and often doubly toothed. Usually *no glands* on leafstalks or leaf teeth. Twigs either hairy or hairless and reddish brown. Buds *red-brown,* mostly about ⅛", *narrow.* Leaves 1"–5". Height 15'–30' (35'); diameter 5"–10" (14"). Flowers about 1" across, white, 3–5 in clusters, April–June. Fruits red or yellow, ¾"–1", seed somewhat flattened, Aug.–Oct. Thickets. **SIMILAR SPECIES:** This is the only thorny plum that has sharp leaf teeth and usually lacks glands on leafstalks. **REMARKS:** Several hundred varieties have been named. Some are cultivated.

American Plum

BULLACE PLUM *Prunus institia* L.   NOT ILLUS.

Similar to American Plum but with rounded teeth plus *hairy* twigs and leaf undersides. It also has smaller leaves and dark fruits. Leaves 1½"–3", buds light brown, broad. Flowers mostly in pairs, white, 1" across. Height to 20'. Fruits blue to black. Eurasian; occasionally spreading from cultivation. **REMARKS:** Sometimes regarded as only a thorny variety—*P. domestica* var. *institia*—of the Garden Plum (Pl. 37).

CANADA PLUM *Prunus nigra* Ait.   NOT ILLUS.

Similar to American Plum, but leaf teeth *rounded* and *glands* usually present on leafstalks. Twigs hairless. Buds *gray* or blackish, about ³⁄₁₆". Leaves 1"–5". Height 6'–20' (25'); diameter 4"–10" (12"). Flowers white to pink, April–June. Fruits yellow to reddish, 1"–1¼", slightly elongate, Aug.–Oct. Thickets.

CHICKASAW PLUM *Prunus angustifolia* Marsh.   PL. 23

A southern shrub or small tree with *shiny,* hairless, *narrow* leaves with very fine, gland-tipped, *rounded* teeth. Leafstalks often bear small glands. Twigs *hairless, reddish;* buds about as long as wide; leaf scars raised. Leaves 1"–3". Height to 20'; diameter to 10". Flowers about ½" across, white, clustered, March–April. Fruits red to yellow, ½", seeds nearly spherical, July–Aug. Thickets.

JUJUBE *Ziziphus jujuba* Mill.   NOT ILLUS.

Shrub or small tree with ¼"–¾" *paired* thorns at the leafstalk base (one thorn usually longer). Leaves shiny, egg-shaped and pointed, with 3 *main veins* meeting at the leaf base. Twigs hairy, usually green; bundle scar 1; spur branches present. Leaves 1"–2½". Height to 50'. Flowers tiny, greenish, March–May. Fruits red-

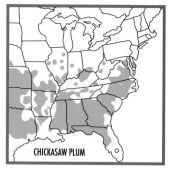

CHICKASAW PLUM

GUM BUMELIA

brown at maturity, edible, July–November. Thickets. **REMARKS:** Native of s. Asia and se. Europe, escaped in Gulf states. Not a plum. Sugared fruits are tasty; also known as Chinese Date.

THORNY TREES WITH ALTERNATE LEAVES NOT TOOTHED (PLATE 24)

Trees in this category are essentially southern in distribution. Only Osage-orange has been transplanted and naturalized in some northern areas. All species have single, mostly strong, thorns and spur branches. Sap is *milky* in all Bumelias and the Osage-orange. Five of these plants, including 3 *Citrus* species, occur mainly in Florida. Russian-olive (p. 33) sometimes has thorns present.

GUM (WOOLLY) BUMELIA   PL. 24
Bumelia lanuginosa (Michx.) Pers.

A shrub or small tree with sharp thorns at the leaf bases and at some twig ends. Leaves wedge-shaped or parallel-sided, tips *blunt* and *rusty- or gray-hairy* beneath, mostly clustered near twig tips. Spur branches present. Twigs and buds *woolly.* Buds ball-like. Bundle scars 3. Leaves 1"–4". Height to 50'. Flowers, small, white, bell-shaped, clustered in leaf angles, June–July. Fruits small, black, cherrylike; autumn. **SIMILAR SPECIES:** See other bumelias and Osage-orange. **REMARKS:** A clear gum can be collected from freshly cut wood or at trunk wounds.

TOUGH BUMELIA   *Bumelia tenax* (L.) Willd.   **NOT ILLUS.**
A small tree of the Atlantic Coastal Plain. Similar to Gum Bumelia, but the sometimes-evergreen leaves are densely *yellow-*

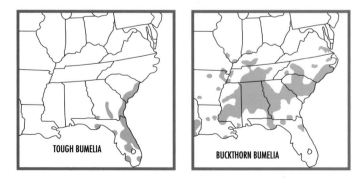

TOUGH BUMELIA

BUCKTHORN BUMELIA

or white-silky beneath. Branches are difficult to break. Leaves 1"–3". Height to 30'.

BUCKTHORN BUMELIA *Bumelia lycioides* (L.) Pers.   **PL. 24**
Similar to Gum Bumelia but with narrow to elliptic, egg-shaped, or even parallel-sided leaves that are larger, *pointed and hairless* to slightly silky beneath. Also, twigs and buds *hairless* to slightly silky. Leaves 3"–6". Height to 30'. Moist soils. **REMARKS:** Buckthorn Bumelia should not be confused with buckthorns of the genus *Rhamnus* (Pls. 12 and 43).

SAFFRON-PLUM BUMELIA   **NOT ILLUS.**
Bumelia celastrina H. B. K.
Mainly Caribbean in distribution with *small, blunt, hairless,* evergreen, leathery leaves. Thorns ½" long are supplemented by spine-tipped twigs. Leaves ¼"–1½". Height to 20'. Flowers late summer to early winter. Fruits black, somewhat edible, autumn or later. Bark dark. Cen. and s. Florida and s. Texas, mainly coastal ridges.

OSAGE-ORANGE *Maclura pomifera* (Raf.) Schneid.   **PL. 24**
A medium-sized tree. Leaves egg-shaped and somewhat *long-pointed.* Bare, unbranched thorns at the leaf scars. Sap *milky* (*caution:* sap causes a rash in some people). Wood *yellow.* Buds nearly ball-shaped; end one false. Bundle scars 1–5. Bark orange-brown, furrowed, tight, fibrous. Leaves 1"–8". Height 50'–60'; diameter 18"–36". Flowers May–June. Fruits green, *totally wrinkled, grapefruit-sized,* Oct. Thickets. **SIMILAR SPECIES:** Osage-orange and the bumelias are our only thorny plants with milky sap. This species differs from the bumelias in leaf shape and in having shorter, more rounded spur branches. **REMARKS:** Once native in n. Texas, se. Oklahoma, and nearby Arkansas, home of the Osage Indians, this species was widely planted for living fences before the invention of barbed wire. It is now widely distributed in our area. Sometimes called hedge-apple. Because of its use in making bows, the French name *bois d'arc* (colloquially Bodarc, Bodock) is still heard. It is sometimes said that the name of the Ozark Mountains is a corruption of Bodarc. Bark yields tannin; boiled wood chips yield yellow dye.

OSAGE-ORANGE

Osage-orange

TALLOWWOOD *Ximenia americana* L.   **PL. 24**
A shrub or twisted small tree of peninsular Florida and world tropics. The small, leathery *evergreen* leaves are variously sharp, blunt, or notched at the tip, mostly with a wedge base and tiny *bristle tip*. Stout straight thorns and spur branches are present. Bundle scar 1. Wood yellow. Leaves 1"–3". Height to 20'. Flowers yellowish, clustered, in leaf angles, April–May or later. Fruits yellow, plumlike, edible, oily, nearly all year. Often parasitic on the roots of other trees. Fragrant and fine-grained wood takes a fine polish. Bark useful in tanning.

FLORIDA-ONLY TREES
In addition to Saffron-plum Bumelia and Tallowwood (above),

Fig. 16. Key Lime.

which also do not occur in our area except in Florida, 3 commercially important citrus species of Asiatic origin have escaped from cultivation to grow also in the wild. They are evergreen with leathery or near-leathery leaves sometimes toothed. The fruits have the structure of the familiar oranges, lemons, and grapefruits of commerce. The gland-dotted leaves are *aromatic* when crushed, and the twigs are *green*. Trees are also marked by leaf-stalks with *winged* edges. See identification chart on Pl. 24 and Fig. 16 for Lime (Key Lime, *Citrus aurantifolia*), Sweet Orange (*C. sinensis*), and Sour Orange (*C. aurantium*). Sour Orange is reported also from Georgia.

TREES WITH ALTERNATE FAN-LOBED LEAVES (PLATE 25)

These are the only thornless, alternate-leaved trees with fan-lobed leaves. The mulberries and Sassafras have leaves that may be either lobed or not. In addition, White Poplar (Pl. 27) has white-woolly leaves that are often fan-lobed. The fan-lobed leaves of maples (Pl. 11) are opposite, not alternate.

Tuliptree

TULIPTREE

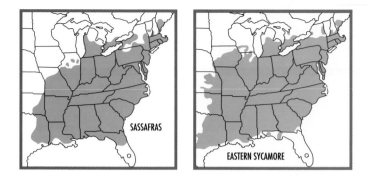

SASSAFRAS

EASTERN SYCAMORE

TULIPTREE *Liriodendron tulipifera* L.   **PL. 25**

A tall, straight tree with unique *notched-tip, four-pointed* hairless leaves. Pairs of large leafy stipules attach to twigs and enclose buds. Twigs hairless, with *completely encircling lines* (stipule scars) at leaf scars. Pith *chambered*. Only 2 bud scales cover each end bud; side buds small or indistinct. Crushed buds and leaves *spicy-aromatic*; bundle scars more than 3. Bark light gray, *often whitened* in grooves and in patches on younger bark. Leaves 6"–10". Height 50'–100' (190'); diameter 2'–6' (10'). Flowers large, *tuliplike,* orange and green, May–June. Fruits slim, dry, winged, whitish, 1"–2", clustered upright in conelike structure about 3" long, Sept.–Nov., or longer; often central stalks of cones remain throughout winter and are evident on higher limbs. **SIMILAR SPECIES:** None; distinctive at all seasons. **REMARKS:** Tallest and in many ways handsomest eastern forest tree. Second only to Sycamore in trunk diameter. Wood straight-grained, fine, soft, resistant to splitting, and easily worked. Used for furniture, interiors, shingles, boats, implements, boxes, toys, pulp, and fuel. Native Americans made trunks into dugout canoes. Seeds eaten by squirrels and songbirds. Though widely known as Yellow Poplar and Tulip Poplar, this relative of magnolias (Pl. 45) is not closely related to true poplars (Pl. 27).

SASSAFRAS *Sassafras albidum* (Nutt.) Nees   **PL. 25**

A medium-sized to large tree. Leaves not toothed; lobed or not, in 3 *patterns* (3 "fingers," a "thumb-and-mitten" outline, or smooth egg shape), usually all present. Leaves hairless to velvety-hairy beneath. Twigs *green,* often *branched,* sometimes hairy. Only 1 bundle scar per leaf scar; true end bud present. Crushed leaves,

Sassafras

twigs, and bark *spicy-fragrant.* Mature bark *red-brown* and furrowed. Leaves 2"–9". Height 10'–50' (90'); diameter 2"–12" (6'). Flowers greenish yellow, April–June. Fruits blue, fleshy, one-seeded, Aug.–Oct. **SIMILAR SPECIES:** Green forked twigs, peculiar leaf outlines, and aromatic odor distinctive. **REMARKS:** The durable coarse lumber was once used for barrels, buckets, posts, small boats, dugout canoes, and fuel. A tea may be made by boiling pieces of the outer bark of roots. This was once common, but medical restrictions may now apply. Sassafras oil used in some soaps; a bark extract can be used to dye wool orange. Fruits eaten by songbirds, bobwhite, wild turkey, and black bear. Twigs browsed by marsh and cottontail rabbits and by whitetail deer.

EASTERN SYCAMORE *Platanus occidentalis* L. **PL. 25**
A very large lowland tree with distinctive mottled brown bark that flakes off in puzzlelike pieces, exposing *yellowish and whitish underbark* (silhouette, p. 28). Leaves nearly hairless, *three- or five-lobed,* edged with *large* teeth. Leafstalk bases hollow, covering buds; leaf scars *surround* buds. Single saucerlike, leafy, toothed stipule clasps and encircles twig at points of leaf attachment; stipule scars *ring* winter twigs. Buds covered by a *single* scale; end bud false. Bundle scars many. Leaves 6"–10". Height 50'–130' (175'); diameter 3'–8' (14'). Flowers small, in *globose* heads, April–June. Fruits small and hairy, in tight, brown, long-stalked hanging *balls,* ¾"–1½" in diameter, Oct., often through winter. **SIMILAR SPECIES:** Old World sycamores, often planted in our cities, are called Plane-trees. They usually have 2 (London Plane, *P. acerifolia* Willd.) or more (Oriental Plane, *P. orientalis* L.) fruit balls per stalk rather than 1 and have more yellowish underbark.

Bark of Eastern Sycamore

REMARKS: Tuliptree may occasionally be taller, but Sycamore is generally conceded to be the most massive tree of eastern U.S. Attains greatest size in Ohio and Mississippi river basins but, unlike sequoias, redwoods, and bristlecone pines of California, is old at 500–600 years. Hard coarse-grained wood used for boxes, barrels, butcher blocks, cabinetwork, and furniture. Native Americans used trunks for dugouts. One such canoe reported to have been 65' long and to have weighed 9000 pounds. Twigs eaten by deer and muskrats. Cavities sought for nests and shelter by wood duck, opossum, and raccoon.

CHINESE PARASOLTREE   NOT ILLUS.
Firmiana simplex (L.) W. F. Wight

An Asian tree of the chocolate family, planted throughout the southern states and locally growing wild. Large, long-stalked leaves are sycamorelike, 3–5 lobed, with narrow sinuses and *without* teeth. Twigs *green* and *not* ringed. Buds brown-hairy, with 2–3 scales. Bundle scar *single* or indistinct. Bark smooth, *gray-green*. Height to 35'. Leaves 6"–12". Flowers small, in greenish yellow clusters mostly at twig ends. Fruits leathery capsules 2"–4", opening into 5 leaflike sections. Dark fluid released when capsule opens. Thickets and woods.

SWEETGUM   *Liquidambar styraciflua* L.   PL. 25

A tall tree with *star-shaped*, toothed, hairless leaves. Leaves may be *five-* or *seven-lobed*; pleasantly fragrant when crushed. Twigs not ringed; branchlets often *corky-winged*. Stubby spur branches densely covered by leaf scars or crowded leaves. Bud scales numerous, glossy and hairy-fringed; bundle scars 3; pith continuous. Mature bark grayish, regularly grooved. Leaves 5"–8". Height 50'–120' (140'); diameter 3'–4' (5'). Flowers in spherical heads, April–May. Fruits brown, dry, somewhat *prickly, long-stemmed, hanging balls,* Sept.–Nov. or longer. **SIMILAR SPECIES:** None in summer. In winter the twigs of some elms (Pl. 33) and Bur Oak (Pl. 29) may have corky wings. Elms have a false end bud, and their bud scales often have dark borders without a hairy fringe. Bur Oak has clustered end buds. **REMARKS:** Both common and scientific names allude to the sap that exudes from wounds. Hardened clumps of this gum are chewed by some people. Sweetgum veneer takes a high polish and is widely used for furniture. Lumber also used for interiors, woodenware, boats, toys, boxes, and fuel. Fruits often painted and used to decorate Christmas trees. Seeds eaten by songbirds, bobwhite, wild turkey, chipmunks, and gray squirrel.

MULBERRIES and PAPER-MULBERRY   **PL. 25**

These plants have toothed leaves either lobed or not and often both present at the same time. Unlobed leaves generally heart-shaped with 3–5 main veins meeting near the ends of leafstalks. Sap of twigs and leafstalks *milky* (not always evident in winter twigs): end bud false. Bundle scars more than 3, varying by species. Fibrous inner bark of both branches and roots can be twisted into ropes and cords and also serves as a field mark (along with basswoods, Pl. 26, and elms, Pl. 33).

PAPER-MULBERRY *Broussonetia papyrifera* (L.) Vent.   **PL. 25**

A medium-sized Asiatic tree with *sandpaper-textured* leaves and twigs. Leaves toothed (and sometimes opposite), varying from unlobed and heart-shaped to deeply and intricately *lobed.* Leaf

SWEETGUM

RED MULBERRY

lobes *pointed*. Leaves sandpapery above and velvety below, with *uneven* or more or less heart-shaped bases. Twigs *rough-hairy;* buds with only 2–3 visible scales. Bundle scars more than 3 per leaf scar. Pith blocked by a *woody partition* near each bud. Bark a *yellow-brown* smooth network of fine ridges. Leaves 4"–11". Height to 50'; diameter to 4'. Flowers April–May. Fruits red, *round,* fleshy, barely edible, Sept. Fencerows, widespread. **SIMILAR SPECIES:** North of Florida, no other plant has such rough leaves and twigs. In Florida, see (1) Geiger-tree (p. 357), (2) Florida Trema, etc. (Pl. 26). **REMARKS:** Inner bark once was used as paper. In some parts of the world, it is beaten into *tapa cloth*.

WHITE MULBERRY *Morus alba* L.   **PL. 25**

A Chinese tree whose toothed leaves are hairless and *not* sandpapery. Leaf bases often *uneven,* sometimes heart-shaped at the base. Foliage often lobed, the lobe tips *rounded*. Twigs *hairless* or slightly hairy. Buds *red-brown,* pressed *against* the twigs, with 5–6 visible scales mostly *lacking* darker scale borders. Bundle scars more than 3 per leaf scar. Pith continuous. Trunk bark *yellow-brown*. Leaves 3"–10". Height 30'–60' (80'); diameter 1'–3' (4'). Flowers April–June. Fruits *whitish* when mature but often purple or black, *cylindrical,* rather tasteless, June–July. Thickets, widespread. **SIMILAR SPECIES:** Red Mulberry is quite similar in winter but may be separated by its greenish brown *spreading* buds and red-brown bark. **REMARKS:** Introduced by the British before the Revolution in an unsuccessful attempt to establish a silkworm industry. Now widespread.

RED MULBERRY *Morus rubra* L.   **PL. 25**

The only native mulberry and widespread in our area. Similar to White Mulberry, but leaves *sandpapery* above and hairy beneath, lobes *pointed,* and bases *even*. Buds *greenish brown,* spreading *away* from the twigs, mostly with darker scale borders. Bark *red-brown*. Fruits red-black, blackberrylike, *elongate, long-stalked,* tasty. Lowlands. **REMARKS:** Fruits eaten by squirrels and many song and game birds as well as by humans.

BLACK MULBERRY *Morus nigra* L.   **NOT ILLUS.**

Mulberries with dark fruits once thought to be this species are now considered to be White Mulberries.

FLORIDA-ONLY TREES

Two species with alternate, fan-lobed leaves occur as trees only in tropical Florida: Papaya (*Carica papaya* L.) and Castorbean (*Ricinus communis* L.).

TREES WITH ALTERNATE FAN-VEINED AND TRIANGULAR OR HEART-SHAPED LEAVES (PLATE 26)

These trees have more or less triangular leaves with 3–5 main veins meeting at the leaf base. Leaf bases are either *heart-shaped or uneven.* End bud false. See also mulberries (Pl. 25), Strawberry-tree (Pl. 32), and Camphor-tree (Pl. 46).

FLORIDA TREMA   *Trema micrantha* (L.) Blume   **PL. 26**
Found only in Florida from Palm Beach and Pinellas counties southward, this *evergreen* species has toothed, long-pointed, short-stalked leaves *rough-hairy* above. Twigs mostly *rough-hairy;* buds tiny, spur branches present. Leaves 2"–5". Height to 80', usually smaller. Flowers *greenish,* inconspicuous, all year. Fruits small, one-seeded, orange-yellow. Pioneer species, open sites.

WEST INDIES TREMA   **NOT ILLUS.**
Trema lamarckiana (Roem. & Schult.) Blume
Similar to Florida Trema but smaller and with *short-pointed* leaves only ¼"–2" (5") long. Twigs densely hairy. Flowers *white;* fruits pink. Miami area and Upper Keys.

EASTERN REDBUD   *Cercis canadensis* L.   **PL. 26**
A small tree with *showy reddish* springtime flowers that appear before the leaves. Leaves smoothly *heart-shaped,* hairless or slightly hairy beneath. Twigs hairless. Leaf buds dark, mostly more than 1 per leaf scar, 2-scaled; flower buds stalked and with several scales. Bundle scars 3 per leaf scar. Most leaf scars *fringed* with hairs at top, with 2 or sometimes 3 lines descending from them on vigorous twigs. Bun-

dle scars 3. Bark dark with fine grooves. Leaves 2"–6". Height 20'–40' (50'); diameter 10"–12". Flowers *red-purple* (rarely white), in showy clusters, March–May. Fruits dry pods, July–Aug. or longer. **SIMILAR SPECIES:** Leaves distinctive. In winter, combination of 3 bun-

Eastern Redbud

dle scars, raised and fringed leaf scars, buds with many scales, and the false end bud differentiates it from other species. **REMARKS:** Blossoms, not buds, reddish. Flowers reported to be sometimes eaten in salads; red roots yield a dye. Wood of commercial value in some areas. Though a member of the pea family, Redbud is exceptional in *not* growing nitrogen-fixing root nodules. Only bobwhite and a few songbirds are known to eat the seeds.

EASTERN REDBUD

NORTHERN (AMERICAN) HACKBERRY PL. 26
Celtis occidentalis L.

A small to large tree with *long-pointed,* coarse-toothed leaves; bases mostly *uneven.* Typically, foliage is *rough-hairy* above and hairless beneath. Twigs hairless; *pith usually chambered* through-

Bark of Northern Hackberry

NORTHERN HACKBERRY

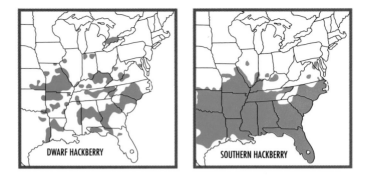

DWARF HACKBERRY

SOUTHERN HACKBERRY

out, sometimes only near the leaf scars. Side buds sometimes to
¼" long, triangular; bud scales 4–5, hairy. Bundle scars 3 (rarely
more). Bark basically light gray, rather smooth, but becoming covered with *dark warty knobs* and ridges (photo, p. 271). Leaves
3"–5". Height 20'–70' (100'); diameter 1'–3' (4'). Flowers greenish, April–May. Fruits spherical, ⅛"–⅜", one-seeded, becoming
wrinkled when dry, Oct.–Nov., or longer. Mostly floodplains. **SIMI-
LAR SPECIES:** All 3 hackberries are highly variable and furthermore
may hybridize. (1) Sourgum (Pl. 44) and (2) Tupelo (Pl. 43) are
similar in having chambered winter twigs but have true end
buds and fleshy fruits. **REMARKS:** Wood similar to ash; of commercial value. Fruits ("sugarberries") eaten by numerous birds,
including bobwhite, lesser prairie chicken, sharptail grouse,
pheasant, and wild turkey. W. H. Wagner, Jr., an authority on
Celtis, described (1974) some of the identification marks for the
3 species and suggested the preferred common names given here.

DWARF (UPLAND) HACKBERRY   PL. 26
Celtis tenuifolia Nutt.

Similar to the previous species but smaller and *upland.* Leaves
either toothed or not, short-pointed, with *few side veins* and larger
spaces (areoles) between them. Foliage may be sandpapery or not.
Buds ⅛"–⅛" long. Leaves 2"–3". Height to 25'. Fruits *smooth*
upon drying, ³⁄₁₆"–⅜", Sept.–Oct. Dry sites.

SOUTHERN (LOWLAND) HACKBERRY   PL. 26
Celtis laevigata Willd.

Like Northern Hackberry, but leaves mostly not toothed and
often with very long-pointed tips. Buds ⅛"–⅛" long. Leaves
2"–4". Fruits *smooth* upon drying, ³⁄₁₆"–⅜", Oct.–Nov. Mostly
southern Coastal Plain *bottomlands.*

SEA HIBISCUS   *Hibiscus tiliaceus* L.   PL. 26

An evergreen shrub or small tree native to Asia, reportedly escaped to the wild along Florida coasts. Leaves 5"–10", heart-shaped, 9–11 main leaf veins, *teeth absent* or few, slightly *hairy* to velvety beneath, with one or several lengthened dark *glands* on the bases of main leaf veins beneath. Twigs *ringed* by narrow stipule scars. Height to 20'. Flowers large, showy, yellow. Fruits dry capsule *splitting* into 5 valves. SIMILAR SPECIES: (1) Named after the basswoods (*Tilia*); the foliage is similar but lacks teeth. (2) See Portiatree. REMARKS: The fibrous inner bark can be twisted into cord to make fish nets, mats, and rope. Highly ornamental and a honey plant.

PORTIATREE   *Thespesia populnea* Soland. ex Correa   NOT ILLUS.

Similar to Sea Hibiscus in appearance, fibrous inner bark, distribution, and habitat. The leaves, however, are *hairless,* with only 5(–7) main veins and *vein glands lacking.* Leaves 5"–10". Height to 50'. Flowers yellow, with purple spreading from the petal bases. Fruits leathery capsules, nearly spherical, *not splitting* to base.

BASSWOODS   *Tilia* species   PL. 26

The basswoods, or lindens, make up a small but complex group of trees. As a genus, characterized by more or less *heart-shaped, fine-toothed* leaves with *uneven* bases. Twigs and buds green to bright red; buds with only 2–3 visible scales; end bud false. Bundle scars more than 3 per leaf scar. Pith continuous and round in cross section; sap clear. Inner bark fibrous; outer bark dark and shallowly grooved when mature but often smooth grayish on the upper parts. Leaves 3"–10". Height 50'–80' (125'); diameter 2'–3' (4'). Flowers yellow, fragrant, June–Aug. Fruits small nutlets clustered beneath large leafy wings that act as spinning parachutes upon ripening, Aug.–Oct. Mostly in moist fertile soils. The basswoods are difficult to separate. The following key provides a tentative basis for identification, but see also the identification chart facing Pl. 26. In addition to our 3 native species, European and Asiatic imports occasionally escape from cultivation.

1. Grown leaves hairless:
    2. Leafstalks and flower stalks hairless. Northern states and Canada.   **American Basswood, Pl. 26.**
    2. Leafstalks and flower stalks hairy. Coastal Plain, southern.
                                                   Carolina Basswood.
1. Grown leaves hairy beneath:
    3. Leaf undersides green, hairs loose.   **Carolina Basswood.**
    3. Leaf undersides white-velvety. Mainly in Appalachians.
                                                   White Basswood.

American Basswood

SIMILAR SPECIES: In winter, Chestnut (Pl. 32) sometimes has more than 3 bundle scars per leaf scar and 2–3 bud scales per bud. The buds are brown, and the pith is irregular rather than round in cross section. It typically occurs on dry sites rather than moist ones. REMARKS: As with mulberries, elms, and some other species, the inner bark of basswoods, especially of roots, is tough and fibrous and can be twisted into cords, mats, and lines. Buds and fruits eaten by ruffed grouse, prairie chickens, bobwhite, squir-

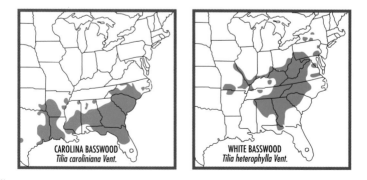

rels, and chipmunks; twigs eaten by deer and cottontails. Lumber is used in commerce. Important honey plants.

FLORIDA-ONLY TREES
Among the species on Pl. 26, Florida Trema and Sea Hibiscus may range into the Caribbean and/or other tropical regions. They occur in the eastern U.S. only in Florida.

POPLARS AND TALLOWTREE (PLATE 27)

The poplars, aspens, and cottonwoods are all members of the genus *Populus*. The leaves are mostly single-toothed and somewhat triangular, with 3–5 main veins meeting near the leaf base. The leafstalks of all poplars are unusually long. In some species the leafstalks are flattened so that the leaves flutter even in a slight breeze.

Poplar buds are unique among alternate-leaved trees with 3 bundle scars in that the lowermost bud scale is directly above the leaf scar. The end bud is true and may have more scales than side buds. The twigs are often sharply angled (somewhat ridged). Spur branches are frequent. Fruits of poplars are in long, clustered, caterpillarlike catkins, which often release "cottony" seeds. The sexes are separate. Male plants of White Poplar and Balm-of-Gilead (see Balsam Poplar) are unknown in our area. The bark of most species is a distinctively smooth greenish white when young and dark-furrowed when older (p. 28).

Distributed widely in the Northern Hemisphere, trees of the poplar group may form extensive forests on barren, burned, or cleared areas. Rapid-growing, short-lived species, they are of most value for paper pulp, though some of the soft lumber is used in construction work and in the manufacture of boxes and woodenware. Some kinds are of value as ornamentals and windbreaks. Seeds, buds, and twigs are important foods of numerous birds and mammals, including ruffed, spruce, and sharptail grouse, prairie chicken, whitetail deer, moose, beaver, porcupine, snowshoe hare, cottontail rabbit, and black bear.

Though not related, Tallowtree resembles aspens and is discussed here.

QUAKING ASPEN *Populus tremuloides* Michx. **PL. 27**
A medium-sized tree; leaves often *nearly round* and edged with 20–40 pairs of *fine teeth*. Leafstalk *flattened*. Twigs hairless and dark brown; end bud shiny, somewhat gummy, ¼"–⅜". Mature bark mostly *smooth, chalk white to yellow-green* (photo, p. 276). Leaves 2"–6", appearing earlier in spring than leaves of Bigtooth

QUAKING ASPEN

Quaking Aspen

Aspen. Height 20'–50' (75'); diameter 1'–2' (3'). **SIMILAR SPECIES:** (1) Bigtooth Aspen has fewer and larger leaf teeth, dull hairy buds, and more yellowish bark. (2) Lombardy Poplar has dark bark, yellowish twigs, and more heart-shaped or triangular leaves. (3) See also Eastern Cottonwood. (4) Tallowtree has smooth-edged leaves and milky sap. Often confused with (5) Paper Birch (Pl. 34), which has a streaked and peeling white trunk. **REMARKS:** Reproduction by root sprouts is frequent, and vegetative clones often spread over considerable areas. Botanists, combining radiocarbon dating with growth rate studies, have calculated some aspen groves to have lived 10,000 years, outclassing bristlecone pines, giant sequoias, and California redwoods in longevity. Widely known as Popple. Becomes golden yellow in autumn.

TALLOWTREE *Sapium sebiferum* (L.) Roxb.   **FIG. 17**
Resembling Quaking Aspen but unrelated. Of Chinese origin, planted and spread widely in the South. Leaves pointed at *both* ends and *not toothed* but may be wavy-edged. Leafstalks *not* flattened and with a pair of *glands* (use lens) at the leaf base. Sap is *milky* and *poisonous* if rubbed in the eyes or taken internally. Twigs *green* or brown; visible bud scales 3; bundle scars 3, indistinct. Leaves 2"–6". Height to 30'. Flowers small, yellow-green,

Fig. 17. Tallowtree.

2"–4" clusters at twig ends, spring. Fruits ¼" waxy capsules that split to expose 3 white seeds that cling to a central stalk. **SIMILAR SPECIES:** Aspens have toothed, square-based leaves and clear sap. Their mature twigs are not green. **REMARKS:** Introduced from Asia so that waxy fruits could be used in making soap and candles. Also called Popcorn-tree, from the white seeds, and Milktree, from the milky sap. Foliage red in autumn.

BIGTOOTH ASPEN *Populus grandidentata* Michx. PL. 27

A small to medium-sized tree with 5–15 pairs of *large* leaf teeth and flattened leafstalks. Leaves white-woolly beneath when young. Twigs hairless or slightly gray-silky; end bud *dull*, more than ⅜" long, decidedly *gray-hairy*. Bark mostly *smooth yellow-green*. Leaves 2"–6". Height 30'–40' (80'); diameter 1'–2'. **SIMILAR SPECIES:** (1) Quaking Aspen is similar but has fine-toothed leaves, shiny hairless buds, and often more whitish mature bark; its leaves appear earlier in the spring. See (2) Tallowtree.

EASTERN (COMMON) COTTONWOOD PL. 27
Populus deltoides Bart. ex Marsh

A tall tree with *coarse-toothed* leaves that have 2–3 small but obvious *glands* (use lens) at upper end of *flattened* leafstalks. Twigs

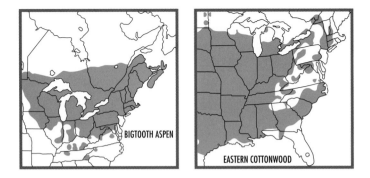

BIGTOOTH ASPEN

EASTERN COTTONWOOD

usually hairless, *yellowish,* sometimes four-angled on vigorous shoots. End bud ⅝"–1", quite *gummy* and with 6–7 scales. They are *not* spicy-fragrant when crushed. Side buds usually do not hug twig. Bark smooth, yellow-green when young but on mature trees dark and ridged. Leaves 2"–8". Height 40'–80' (100'); diameter 1'–2' (3½'). Bottomlands. **SIMILAR SPECIES:** Of the poplars with flattened leafstalks, only this species has glands on the stalks. (1) Lombardy Poplar trees have columnar growth form. (2) Balsam Poplar is more northern and has gummy end bud with fewer scales and a firlike fragrance when crushed. (3) Quaking Aspen has fine-toothed foliage and brown twigs. (4) Bigtooth Aspen has leaf teeth larger and end bud hairy. (5) Tallowtree has leafstalk glands, nonflattened leafstalks, leaves not toothed, greenish twigs, and milky sap.

LOMBARDY POPLAR *Populus nigra* var. *italica* Munchh.   **PL. 27**

An imported tall, thin, *steeple-like* tree (silhouette, p. 24) much used to border gardens and for windbreaks. Leaves are *fine-toothed;* flattened leafstalks *lack* glands. Twigs hairless, *yellowish;* end bud less than ⅜" long, not gummy; side buds usually pressed against

Bark of Eastern Cottonwood

twigs. Bark furrowed, rather dark. Leaves 2"–8". Height 30'–70' (100'); diameter 1'–2' (3'). May escape from plantings. **SIMILAR SPECIES:** (1) Typical Black Poplar (*P. nigra* L.) may occur locally; lacks peculiar thin spirelike shape but has same leaf, twig, and bud characteristics as this variety. In *P. nigra* form, it is unlike (2) Quaking Aspen in having dark bark, yellow twigs, and much more sharply triangular or even heart-shaped leaves.

BALSAM POPLAR *Populus balsamifera* L. PL. 27

A northern tree with *fine-toothed, narrowly heart-shaped* leaves and *rounded* (or occasionally slightly flattened) leafstalks. Leaves usually hairless but may be slightly hairy on veins beneath. May have 2 small glands at leaf base. Twigs dark brown and hairless. End bud *more than ⅝" long, gummy,* and *spicy-fragrant* when crushed; 5 bud scales. Side buds have 2 visible scales. Mature bark dark and grooved; gray-green and smooth on younger parts. Leaves 6"–10". Height 30'–80' (100'); diameter 1'–3' (6'). **SIMILAR SPECIES:** See (1) Eastern and (2) Swamp cottonwoods. **REMARKS:** This species along with a sterile form, possibly a hybrid with another *Populus* species, is frequently called Balm-of-Gilead. Sterile plants spread mainly by sprouts and may have leaf undersides, leafstalks, and twigs somewhat *hairy.*

SWAMP COTTONWOOD *Populus heterophylla* L. PL. 27

Mainly a southern tree with *fine-toothed* and *broadly heart-shaped* leaves with *rounded* leafstalks. Leaves and dark brown twigs *white-woolly* or hairless; end bud ⅜"–⅝", hairless or white-hairy toward base and *somewhat gummy.* Bark dark and deeply ridged. Leaves 6"–10". Height 40'–60' (90'); diameter 1'–2' (3'). **SIMILAR SPECIES:** No other poplar has gummy end buds less than ⅝" long. See Balsam Poplar.

WHITE POPLAR *Populus alba* L.

European but widely naturalized, especially in the North. A tall tree with *white-woolly* leaves, twigs, and buds. Leaves with a few large blunt teeth or shallow to deep *lobes*, often somewhat leathery. Leafstalks rounded or flattened. Bark smooth and whitish above, often thick and dark at base. Spreads by means of root suckers. Leaves 2"–6". Height 60'–80' (100'); diameter 2'–3' (4'). Thickets. **SIMILAR SPECIES:** No other tree is as silvery white in all aspects. (1) Bigtooth Aspen leaves may be somewhat white-hairy, but they are many-toothed. When foliage lobed, not to be confused with (2) maples (Pl. 11), which have opposite leaves.

OAKS I–IV (PLATES 28–31)

The oaks are usually tall trees and have great and diversified values. Group identification points are: true end buds clustered at tips of twigs, more than 3 bundle scars per leaf scar, and acorn fruits. Only a very few other plants have clustered end buds — principally Fire or Pin Cherry (Pl. 36) and Corkwood (Pl. 45) — and they lack the other characteristics. Male flowers appear in May and early June as slender drooping clusters of long catkins. Female blossoms are inconspicuous. Acorns begin development shortly thereafter, becoming green at first and finally brown.

In the eastern United States, the genus *Quercus* is generally divided into 2 sections: the red (or black) oaks and the white oaks. Red oaks differ from white in that the (1) leaves or their lobes or teeth have hairlike bristle tips, (2) broken brown acorn shells (not cups) have hairy inner surfaces, and (3) acorns require 2 years to mature. Thus on mature trees in summer, both tiny first-year and larger second-year acorns are often present on twigs and branchlets, respectively. White oaks have leaves that lack bristle tips and have hairless inner acorn shells and acorns that mature in 1 year. These grow only on the twigs.

Acorns of red oaks are yellow, bitter, and usually inedible; those of some white oaks are white, relatively sweet, and often edible. The bark of many red oaks is dark in color; that of white oaks is mostly light. Within the white oak group, however, the chestnut oaks are a distinctive subdivision. They have wavy-edged or toothed leaves, mostly bitter and inedible acorns, and often dark, frequently deeply ridged bark. The 34 tree-sized species of the eastern U.S. include 13 white and 21 red oaks.

To provide for more simple identification, the oaks are here divided into groups primarily according to whether the leaves are lobed, wavy-edged, or neither. Though variable, most oaks can be identified in season by their leaf shapes alone, as shown on the plates. Exceptions are the Scarlet–Pin Oak group and hybrids between species. Additional foliage data appear below for each species. As an aid to winter identification, see the identification charts on pp. 282–283.

Where a species is listed as having hairy twigs, the degree of hairiness is often slight. An adequate magnifying lens should be used to determine whether twigs or buds are hairy. Twigs taken for identification from unknown specimens should be carefully selected for their full, mature growth.

Acorns and their cups are often of assistance in identifying oak species. If none is growing on the tree, look for old ones on the ground (but try to verify that they fell from the tree being examined). Acorns always grow partly enclosed in basal growths universally called "cups," but the cups are nevertheless nearly always described as saucerlike, bowl-like, goblet-shaped, or otherwise uncuplike.

Not every oak specimen can be identified with certainty by the amateur. Even professional botanists are frequently puzzled by apparent hybrids and variants. Winter identifications are often especially difficult.

Oaks provide about half the annual production of hardwood lumber in the United States. They are slow-growing, long-lived, and relatively disease- and insect-resistant. Bark of several oaks is rich in tannin used in curing leather.

By grinding the nuts and pouring hot water through the flour to leach out the tannic acid, Native Americans converted even the acorns of red oaks into staple articles of diet. In ancient England, oak forests were valued highly for fattening swine, and laws provided that anyone wantonly injuring or destroying an oak should be fined according to the size of the tree and its ability to bear fruits.

Extensive browsing on early spring foliage occasionally causes livestock to be poisoned. Acorns are eaten by nearly all herbivorous birds and mammals. The list of species eating these nuts in our area includes many songbirds as well as the ruffed and sharp-tail grouse, prairie chicken, bobwhite, wild turkey, pheasant, mourning dove, wood duck, whitetail deer, black bear, red fox, gray fox, raccoon, opossum, gray squirrel, and fox squirrel. Deer, cottontail rabbits, and snowshoe hares browse twigs; porcupines eat the growing layer beneath bark.

Text continues on p. 284

All oaks have clustered end buds and produce acorns. Distributions given are the areas where each species is most common; see maps in text for full ranges.

SPECIES AND REMARKS	End buds over ¼"	End buds sharp	End buds hairy[1]	End buds angled[2]	Twigs hairy	Acorn cup shape[3]	White (W) or Red (R) Oak	Major distribution[4]	Plate number
BLACKJACK OAK (P. 291) Twigs angled, dull; bark blocky.	+	+	+	+	+	B	R	E	28
EASTERN BLACK OAK (P. 288) Twigs angled, shiny; bark ridged.	+	+	+	+	−	B	R	E	28
TURKEY OAK (P. 290) Southern Coastal Plain. End buds thin, ¼–½".	+	+	+	−	−	B	R	S	28
SHUMARD OAK (P. 287) Southern lowlands.	+	+	−	+	−	S	R	S	28
CHESTNUT OAK (P. 298) Trunk dark; deep furrows. Uplands.	±	+	−	−	−	B	W	A	30
BASKET OAK (P. 297) Trunk light, flaky. Southern lowlands.	±	+	−	−	−	B	W	S	30
ENGLISH OAK (P. 294) Acorn stalks 1 "–3 " long. Trunk dark.	+	−	−	±	−	B	W	w	29
SOUTHERN RED OAK (P. 289) Bark dark, furrowed. Uplands.	±	+	+	−	+	S	R	S	28
BLUEJACK OAK (P. 300) Trunk blocky, dark or gray. Southeast.	±	+	+	−	±	S	R	S	31
SCARLET OAK (P. 284) Buds white-tipped. Appalachians.	±	±	+	−	−	B	R	A	28
NORTHERN RED OAK (P. 288) Trunk dark; shiny ridges.	±	±	−	−	−	S	R	E	28
WATER OAK (P. 299) Buds often white-tipped. Southern Coastal Plain.	−	+	+	+	−	S	R	S	31
NUTTALL OAK (P. 286) Acorn cups stalked. Southern Mississippi Valley.	−	+	+	−	−	B	R	S	28
SHINGLE OAK (P. 299) Acorn cups not stalked. North-central.	−	+	+	+	−	B	R	M	31
WILLOW OAK (P. 300) Southern uplands. Not evergreen.	−	+	−	+	−	S	R	S	31

SPECIES AND REMARKS	End buds over ¼"	End buds sharp	End buds hairy[1]	End buds angled[2]	Twigs hairy	Acorn cup shape[3]	White (W) or Red (R) Oak	Major distribution[4]	Plate number
ARKANSAS OAK (P. 298) Scattered; nw. Fla. to sw. Ark.	−	+	−	−	+	S	R	S	31
PIN OAK (P. 284) Lowlands. Low branches slope down.	−	+	−	−	−	S	R	M	28
JACK OAK (P. 285) Northern uplands. Cups taper. Trunk dark.	−	+	−	−	−	B	R	M	28
CHINKAPIN OAK (P. 296) Uplands. Trunk gray. Midwest.	−	+	−	−	−	B	W	M	30
DURAND OAK (P. 295) Buds globular. Southern.	−	−	+	−	−	S	W	S	30
OGLETHORPE OAK (P. 300) Stone Mt., Ga., and nearby.	−	±	−	−	−	B	W	S	31
BUR OAK (P. 294) Slender stipules among end buds.	−	−	+	−	±	U	W	M	29
POST OAK (P. 293) Small trees. Dry soils. South.	−	−	+	−	+	B	W	S	29
BEAR OAK (P. 291) Appalachians to New England.	−	−	−	−	+	B	R	A	28
CHAPMAN OAK (P. 296) S.C. to Fla.	−	−	−	−	±	B	W	C	30
OVERCUP OAK (P. 294) Buds chestnut brown. South.	−	−	−	−	−	U	W	S	29
SWAMP OAK (P. 297) Acorn stalks 1"–3". North-central.	−	−	−	−	−	B	W	N	30
EASTERN WHITE OAK (P. 292) Buds red-brown. Widespread.	−	−	−	−	−	B	W	E	29
GEORGIA OAK (P. 291) Scattered; S.C., n. Ga., n. Ala.	−	−	−	−	−	S	R	S	28
LAUREL OAK (P. 301) Southern lowlands. Often evergreen.	−	+	−	+	±	S	R	S	31

[1] Use lens.
[2] In cross section.
[3] B = bowl-shaped, deep; S = saucer-shaped, shallow; U = unique (see text).
[4] A = Appalachians, C = Coastal Plain, E = East, M = Midwest, N = North, S = South, w = widespread.

All species on this plate are members of the red oak group.

SCARLET OAK *Quercus coccinea* Muenchh. **PL. 28**

A medium-sized tree with leaves *deeply lobed* (over halfway to the midrib) and either hairless or with tufts of hair in angles of veins beneath. Twigs hairless; end buds *scraggly-hairy,* nearly ¼" long, blunt or sharp, often *whitish tipped.* Trunk dark, finely grooved. Acorn cup brownish, hairless or nearly so (use lens); more than ¼" deep, *bowl-like,* and ⅝"–⅞" in diameter. Leaves 3"–6". Height 40'–50' (80'); diameter 1'–2' (3'). Dry soils. **SIMILAR SPECIES:** The next 4 species all have foliage similar to that of Scarlet Oak; best identified by acorn cups (see Figs. 18–21). Of these, Pin Oak has drooping lower branches and occurs on moister sites. Among others in the group, (5) Northern Red Oak and (6) Eastern Black Oak have leaves not so deeply lobed.

PIN OAK *Quercus palustris* Muenchh. **ACORN, FIG. 18**

Similar to Scarlet Oak, but end buds *hairless,* small, sharp. Twigs hairless. Lower branches characteristically *slope downward* (sil-

Scarlet Oak

SCARLET OAK

PIN OAK

Bark of Pin Oak

houette, p. 27); many stubby pinlike branches usually present. Acorn cup brownish and hairless but shallow and *saucerlike*, only ⅜"–⅝" in diameter, and less than ¼" high. Leaves 3"–7"; dead leaves tend to *remain* on tree in winter. Height 70'–80' (110'); diameter 2'–3' (5'). Bottomlands. **SIMILAR SPECIES:** See (1) Scarlet Oak. (2) Jack Oak is more northern, occurs on dry soils, and has deeper, more tapered acorn cups.

JACK OAK   *Quercus ellipsoidalis* E. J. Hill   **ACORN, FIG. 19**
Similar to Pin Oak but more northern and growing on uplands. Acorn cup bowl-shaped and somewhat *conical*, with sides sloping

Fig. 18. Pin Oak.   *Fig. 19. Jack Oak.*

Fig. 20. *Nuttall Oak.*   Fig. 21. *Shumard Oak.*

gradually. Cups finely *gray-hairy;* mostly less than ½" across. Buds small, red-brown, sharp, hairless. Leaves 3"–7". Height 60'–70'; diameter 2'–3'. **SIMILAR SPECIES:** See (1) Pin Oak. (2) Nuttall Oak and (3) Shumard Oak also have gray-hairy acorn cups. Nuttall Oak occupies a more southern range and acorn cups, if cone-shaped, have a basal constriction. Shumard Oak is also more southern; leaves and acorns generally larger. **REMARKS:** Also known as Northern Pin and Hill's Oak.

NUTTALL OAK   *Quercus texana* Buckl.   **ACORN, FIG. 20**
Similar to the more northern Jack Oak but with conspicuous tufts of hair at the vein angles on leaf undersides, and the acorn cup usually constricted to form a *distinct* basal portion. Acorn cup varies from cone- to bowl-shaped, is ⅝"–¾" across, with a con-tracted scaly basal portion ⅟₁₆"–¼" long. The acorn scar within the cup is ⁵⁄₁₆"–½" in diameter. End buds less than ¼" long, pointed, *not* angled, with *hairless* scales. Leaves 4"–8". Height to 120'; diameter to 3'. Lowlands, s. Mississippi Valley. **REMARKS:** Formerly named *Q. nuttallii* Palmer.

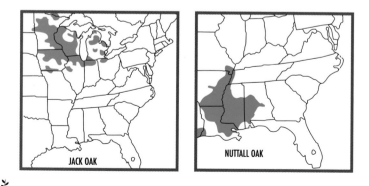

JACK OAK   NUTTALL OAK

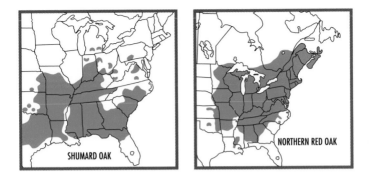

SHUMARD OAK

NORTHERN RED OAK

BUCKLEY OAK *Quercus buckleyi* Nixon & Dorr **NOT ILLUS.**
Now separated from Nuttall Oak, Buckley Oak may be recognized by an *absence* of hair tufts at the vein angles on the leaf undersides and by the acorn scar ⅛"–⁵⁄₁₆" across. Distributed north-south from cen. Okla. to s.-cen. Texas.

SHUMARD OAK *Quercus shumardii* Buckl. **ACORN, FIG. 21**
Resembles Scarlet Oak, but mature leaves mostly more than 6" long. End buds clay- or straw-colored, *more* than ¼" long, pointed, *hairless,* and *angled.* Twigs hairless. Acorn cup *gray,* shallow, *saucerlike,* ¾"–1" in diameter. Leaves 6"–8". Height 70'–100' (120'); diameter 2'–3' (6'). Bottomlands, mostly Coastal Plain. **SIMILAR SPECIES:** (1) Scarlet, (2) Pin, (3) Jack, and (4) Nuttall oaks have smaller leaves. Also see the winter identification chart on p. 282.

Northern Red Oak

NORTHERN RED OAK *Quercus rubra* L.   PL. 28

A large tree. Leaves *moderately lobed* (not more than halfway to the midrib), hairless, thin, *dull above.* Twigs hairless; end buds ³⁄₁₆"–⁵⁄₁₆", sharp or blunt, *hairless, not angled.* Acorn cup flat and *saucerlike,* ¾"–1¼" across. Trunk dark, furrowed, often laced with *broad, shiny strips.* Leaves 4"–10". Height 70'–80' (150'); diameter 3'–4' (5'). Woods. **SIMILAR SPECIES:** Best separation point between this and Eastern Black Oak is the buds, which are hairless and smaller in Northern Red Oak. Mature buds usually not available between May and Aug., during which period leaf textures (and possibly acorn cups) are helpful. **REMARKS:** Established and spreading in w. Europe.

EASTERN BLACK OAK *Quercus velutina* Lam.   PL. 28

Similar to Northern Red Oak but with leaves somewhat *thickened,* generally *glossy* above and mostly hairless beneath. Twigs angled, hairless; end buds ¼"–½", pointed, densely *gray-hairy* and *sharply angled.* Trunk dark, mostly *without* shiny ridges. Orange inner bark, often relied upon as an identification mark of Black Oak, frequently seems to be similar to that of Northern Red Oak. Acorn cup *bowl-shaped* and finely gray-hairy; edge rough with fringelike scales. Leaves 4"–10". Height 70'–80' (100'); diameter

Bark of Eastern Black Oak

EASTERN BLACK OAK

3'–4' (5'). Dry soils. **SIMILAR SPECIES:** (1) Shumard Oak has leaves more deeply lobed and acorn cups shallow, not fringed. See (2) Northern Red Oak.

SOUTHERN RED (SPANISH) OAK   PL. 28
Quercus falcata Michx.

A moderate-sized to tall tree; leaves *variable*, usually with 3 *main lobes* toward tip. Leaf bases *rounded*. Leaf undersides and twigs gray-hairy. End buds ³⁄₁₆"–⁵⁄₁₆", *hairy*, sharp-pointed but not angled. Acorn cup flat, gray-hairy, saucerlike. Bark dark, somewhat furrowed. Leaves 4"–12". Height 70'–80' (100'); diameter 2'–3' (5'). Sandy uplands. **SIMILAR SPECIES:** Three-lobed leaves are distinctive. (1) Cherrybark Oak has wider leaves with 7–11, mostly single-pointed, lobes (Fig. 22). (2) Turkey Oak has more prominent basal leaf lobes, forming a "turkey track" shape (Fig. 24). (3) A form of Water Oak (Pl. 31) has deeply three-parted leaf tips, but they are not as sharp-pointed and are nearly hairless beneath.

CHERRYBARK OAK   *Quercus pagoda* Raf.   LEAF, FIG. 22
Though formerly classified as a variety of Southern Red Oak, the leaves are wider, resembling those of Northern Red Oak, but with 7–11 lobes that are often *single-pointed*. If the leafstalk is pointed

Bark of Southern Red Oak

SOUTHERN RED OAK

Fig. 22. Cherrybark Oak.

skyward, the angled lobes of the upside-down leaf are reminiscent of the several overlapping roofs of an oriental pagoda. Leaf bases *angled* or rounded. Bark may resemble that of Black Cherry (Pl. 36). Floodplains. **REMARKS:** Sometimes called Swamp Red Oak or Pagoda Oak.

TURKEY OAK *Quercus laevis* Walt.   **ACORN, FIG. 23; LEAF, FIG. 24**
Leaves and buds of this small *southern* tree most closely resemble Southern Red Oak. Leaves leathery, hairless, often three-lobed, with central and lower lobes all *narrow,* resembling turkey tracks in outline. Twigs more or less hairless; end buds *slender, pointed,* ¼"–½", somewhat fine-hairy. Trunk *blue-gray,* furrowed. Acorn cups about ¾" in diameter, deeply *bowl-shaped,* gray-hairy, with scale tips loose at the cup edges. Leaves 4"–10". Height 15'–20' (60'); diameter 1'–2'. Sandy Coastal Plain soils. **SIMILAR SPECIES:** Southern Red Oak has smaller buds, hairy twigs, and shallow acorn cups.

Fig. 23. Turkey Oak acorn.

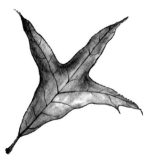

Fig. 24. Turkey Oak leaf.

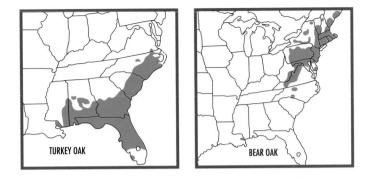

BEAR (SCRUB) OAK *Quercus ilicifolia* Wangenh.   **PL. 28**
    A thicket-forming shrub or small tree with leaves also *small* and
    white-hairy beneath. Twigs *hairy:* end buds small, blunt, hairless,
    not angled. Acorn less than ⅜" long and cup *bowl-shaped.* Bark
    dark. Leaves 2"–5". Height 3'–9' (18'). Northeastern Appalachian
    Mts. **SIMILAR SPECIES:** See Georgia Oak.

GEORGIA OAK *Quercus georgiana* M.A. Curtis   **ACORN, FIG. 25**
    A small tree of rocky soils in northern *Georgia* and nearby por-
    tions of South Carolina. Leaves and buds resemble those of Bear
    Oak but leaves somewhat *glossy* above and *hairless* beneath. Twigs
    hairless. Bark light brown. Acorn cup *shallow,* saucerlike, ½".
    Leaves 2"–5". Height to 25'.

BLACKJACK OAK *Quercus marilandica* Muenchh.   **PL. 28**
    A low to medium-sized tree. Leaves thick, *leathery, shallow-lobed,*
    brownish-scaly or hairy beneath. Twigs angled, *hairy;* end buds

Fig. 25. Georgia Oak.

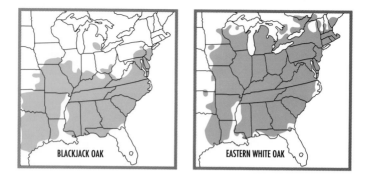

BLACKJACK OAK

EASTERN WHITE OAK

large, hairy, sharp-pointed, angled. Dark trunk bark broken into *squarish blocks.* Acorn cup somewhat hairy, *deep,* with a narrowed base, somewhat goblet-shaped. Cup scales appear loosely attached. Leaves 4"–8". Height 40'–50' (70'); diameter 1'–2' (4'). **SIMILAR SPECIES:** (1) Eastern Black Oak may have leathery leaves, but the sinuses are deeper; foliage and twigs are hairless. (2) Post Oak (Pl. 29) also has leathery foliage and often grows with Blackjack, but leaves more deeply lobed and not bristle-tipped.

OAKS II: LEAVES FEATHER-LOBED WITHOUT BRISTLE TIPS (PLATE 29)

The species on this plate are all members of the white oak group.

EASTERN WHITE OAK *Quercus alba* L. PL. 29

A tall tree with rather *evenly lobed, hairless* leaves that may be

somewhat whitened beneath. Lobes 7–11. Twigs hairless; end buds red-brown, small, blunt, hairless, and not angled. Bark light gray, slightly furrowed to scaly. Acorn cup bowl-shaped, covering ⅓ or less of acorn. Leaves 3"–9". Height 60'–80' (150'); diameter 2'–3' (5'). Dry to moist

Eastern White Oak

POST OAK

Bark of Post Oak

woods. **SIMILAR SPECIES:** (1) Overcup and (2) Bur Oak leaves usually have deeper divisions; their acorn cups are unique. In winter, the end-bud stipules of Bur Oak help to differentiate that species. (3) Swamp Oak (Pl. 30) has 1"–3" acorn stalks, and leaves may have shallow lobes. See also (4) Bluff Oak (Pl. 30).

POST OAK *Quercus stellata* Wangenh.   **PL. 29**

A small tree with *often leathery* leaves and 3–5 lobes usually arranged so that they *resemble a Christian cross.* Leaves often shiny above and gray or *yellowish-hairy beneath.* Twigs *gray-hairy;* end buds less than ¼" long, blunt and rather hairy. Bark brownish, broken by long shallow cracks and often divided into rectangular blocks. Bowl-shaped acorn cups cover ⅓–½ of acorn. Leaves 3"–8". Height 50'–60' (100'); diameter 1'–2' (3'). Dry soils. **SIMILAR SPECIES:** See (1) Blackjack Oak (Pl. 28). In winter, unique acorns, terminal stipules, and often-winged branchlets distinguish (2) Bur Oak. **REMARKS:** With twigs hairless and leaves less regularly crosslike, Dwarf Post Oak (*Q. margaretta*) is now accepted as distinct. It grows to 40' tall and is distributed from se. Va. and w. Okla. to cen. Fla. and cen. Texas. Swamp Post Oak (*Q. similis*) also has been separated. Ranging from S. Carolina and Ga. to Ark. and La., it has hairy twigs and leaves scarcely crosslike.

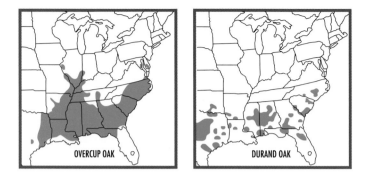

OVERCUP OAK   DURAND OAK

OVERCUP OAK *Quercus lyrata* Walt.   **PL. 29**
 A moderate-sized tree mainly of Coastal Plain bottomlands.
Leaves vary (may even resemble White Oak somewhat) but generally have *deep indentations* near base and narrow basal lobes; *fine-
hairy* and often whitened beneath. Twigs and end buds as in
White Oak except that buds are chestnut brown. Bark light, broken by shallow cracks. Rough acorn cup is unique, *enclosing
nearly all of globular nut;* only very tip visible. Leaves 3"–10".
Height 50'–80' (100'); diameter 2'–3' (4'). Swamp forests. **SIMILAR
SPECIES:** (1) Bur Oak leaves have deep sinuses more centrally located. Acorn cups of both species distinctive. (2) White Oak has
shallower leaf sinuses with wider basal lobes; its acorn cup is
bowl-like.

BUR (MOSSYCUP) OAK *Quercus macrocarpa* Michx.   **PL. 29**
 A tall tree with variable foliage, usually marked by a *narrow waist*
that divides the leaves into 2 or more portions. Leaves often leathery and shiny above, usually somewhat *hairy and whitish beneath.*
Twigs yellow-brown, variably hairless to rather hairy; end buds
hairy, blunt, not angled, with slender *stipules* commonly present.
Branchlets sometimes have *corky wings* like those of Sweetgum
(Pl. 25). Acorn cups bowl-shaped, with a peculiar "bur" or
"mossy" *fringe* of elongate scales. Bark light gray, shallowly
grooved. Leaves 4"–10". Height 70'–80' (170'); diameter 2'–3'
(7'). **SIMILAR SPECIES:** See (1) White and (2) Overcup oaks.

ENGLISH OAK *Quercus robur* L.   **PL. 29**
 A handsome imported tree. Leaves *small,* hairless, with 7–11
lobes. Leaf bases *"eared."* Twigs mostly hairless; end buds *more
than ¼"* long, blunt, hairless, often somewhat angled. Acorns on
1"–3" *stalks,* cups deep. Leaves 3"–5". Trunk bark *dark.* Height to

BUR OAK

Bur (Mossycup) Oak

150' in Britain. Spreading from upland plantings in a few northern localities. **SIMILAR SPECIES:** (1) Eastern White Oak foliage is not "eared" and has fewer lobes. (2) Swamp Oak (Pl. 30) also has 1"–3" acorn stalks, but the leaf edges are merely wavy. (3) Virginia Live Oak (Pl. 31) is evergreen with acorn stalks to 1".

OAKS III: LEAVES WAVY-EDGED OR TOOTHED (PLATE 30)

The species of this plate are all members of the white oak group with leaves mostly V-based and (except Swamp Oak) acorn stalks no longer than the leafstalks.

DURAND OAK *Quercus sinuata* Walt.   PL. 30

A medium-sized tree that grows on fertile soils of the southeastern Coastal Plain. Foliage variable, from shallow lobes to merely wavy-edges. Leaves glossy above, hairless to silver-hairy beneath. Twigs more or less hairy; buds small and nearly *globular*. Bark light gray. Acorns ½"–¾" long, in a *saucerlike* cup, sometimes on a ¼" stalk. Leaves 3"–8". Height 60'–90'; diameter 2'–3'. Damp to dry sites. **REMARKS:** Formerly named *Q. durandii*.

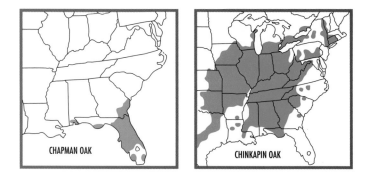

CHAPMAN OAK

CHINKAPIN OAK

BLUFF OAK *Quercus austrina* Small.   **NOT ILLUS.**
Though with leaves shaped much like those of Water Oak (Pl.
31), this tree lacks the red oak characteristics of that species. It
differs from Durand Oak in having essentially hairless foliage and
a deeply bowl-shaped acorn cup. Height to 75'. Lowland forests,
S. Carolina and Ga. to cen. Fla. and cen. Ala. **REMARKS:** Also known
as Bastard White Oak. Bluff Oak is the preferred common name,
however, of Godfrey (1988) and other southern botanists.

CHAPMAN OAK *Quercus chapmanii* Sarg.   **PL. 30**
A shrub or small tree of sandy Coastal Plain soils from S. Carolina to s. Florida. Leaves *wavy-edged,* hairless, mostly leathery,
mostly U-based, and often *notched* at the tip. The nearly evergreen leaves are shiny above but dull beneath (see Myrtle Oak, Pl.
31). They may he held late in the year. Twigs variably hairy. Buds
small, *blunt,* more or less hairless. Bark light gray. Acorns ½"–1"
long, cup bowl-shaped. Leaves 2"–5". Height to 25'. Dry soils.

CHINKAPIN OAK *Quercus muehlenbergii* Engelm.   **PL. 30**
A medium-sized *upland* tree whose leaves usually have 10 or
more pairs of *sharp* teeth. Leaf undersides fine-hairy. Twigs hairless. End buds narrow, *sharp,* hairless, not angled, and mostly
about ³⁄₁₆" long. Bark *light gray* and often flaky, not ridged. Acorn
cup bowl-shaped, less than 1" across, with tight scales free only at
the tips. Leaves 4"–9". Height 20'–50' (160'); diameter 6"–24"
(4'). **SIMILAR SPECIES:** (1) Chestnut Oak has dark, ridged bark. (2) A
mostly 3'–10' shrub, Dwarf Oak (Dwarf Chinkapin Oak—*Q. pri-
noides* Willd.) also has sharp leaf teeth, but leaves are white-
woolly, smaller, and with 5–9 tooth pairs. (3) Virginia Live Oak
(Pl. 31) may have some leaves with sharp teeth, but foliage is
leathery and evergreen. **REMARKS:** Also spelled Chinquapin.

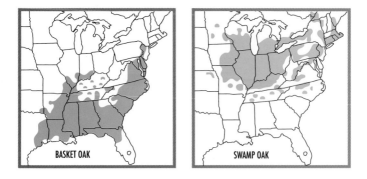

BASKET OAK

SWAMP OAK

BASKET OAK *Quercus michauxii* Nutt.   **PL. 30**

A southern tree whose leaves are *velvet-hairy* beneath and have 7–16 pairs of mostly *rounded* teeth. Twigs hairless. Buds *to* about ¼" long, hairless, and pointed. Trunk bark *light gray,* rough, and flaky like Chinkapin Oak. Acorn cup similar to that of Chestnut Oak but *broader* (1"–1¼" in diameter) and bowl-shaped, with scales attached *only at base.* Leaves 4"–8". Height to 100'; diameter to 4'. Coastal Plain *bottomlands.* **SIMILAR SPECIES:** See Swamp Oak. **REMARKS:** Also known as Swamp Chestnut Oak.

SWAMP OAK   **PL. 30**
Quercus bicolor Willd.

A more northern species with only 4–6 pairs of *large, rounded teeth* (occasionally sharp-toothed and sometimes forming shallow lobes). Foliage is shiny above, more or less hairless, often whitened beneath. Twigs are hairless. End buds chestnut brown, *small, blunt,* and hairless. Acorn cup bowl-shaped, with *stalks 1"–3".* Bark

Bark of Swamp Oak

light gray, ridged or flaky. Leaves 4"–9". Height 60'–70' (100'); diameter 2'–3' (8'). Wet woods. SIMILAR SPECIES: (1) Basket Oak is more southern and has hairy leaf undersides, 7–16 pairs of leaf teeth, and often larger buds. (2) Chestnut Oak, also with more leaf teeth, has dark and deeply ridged trunk bark. (3) English Oak, also with long acorn stalks, has lobed foliage and dark trunk bark. REMARKS: Also known as Swamp White Oak. The lumber not distinguished from that of White Oak.

CHESTNUT OAK *Quercus montana* Willd.   PL. 30
An *upland* tree whose leaves have 7–16 pairs of *rounded teeth* (sometimes sharp). Foliage somewhat leathery, glossy above and slightly hairy beneath. Twigs and buds resemble those of Basket Oak, but trunk bark *dark, deeply ridged,* quite distinctive. Acorn cups deeply bowl-shaped, less than 1" across, with tight scales free only at the tips. Leaves 4"–9". Height 60'–70' (100'); diameter 3'–4' (7'). Dry woods. SIMILAR SPECIES: Other trees of this group have light gray trunk bark. Chestnut (Pl. 32) lacks clustered end buds and has sharp leaf teeth. REMARKS: Also known as *Q. prinus* L.

OAKS IV: LEAVES TYPICALLY SMOOTH-EDGED (PLATE 31)

Though these oaks usually lack leaf lobes, teeth, or wavy edges, some specimens of several species rarely may have such leaf edges. Oglethorpe Oak and Virginia Live Oak are white oaks; all others on this plate are in the red oak group.

ARKANSAS OAK *Quercus arkansana* Sarg.   PL. 31
Resembling Blackjack Oak (Pl. 28) but with *smaller* and less leathery leaves, *saucerlike* acorn cups and a more restricted and

CHESTNUT OAK

ARKANSAS OAK

scattered *southern* range. The leaves are without teeth and *wide*, with several bristle points typical of the red oak group. Foliage *hairless*, sometimes slightly three-lobed. Twigs hairy; end buds small, sharp, hairless, and not angled. Acorns small, ¼"–⁷⁄₁₆" long, with shallow cups. Trunk bark dark, thick, furrowed. Leaves 2"–4". Height to 50'. Sandy soils.

WATER OAK *Quercus nigra* L.   PL. 31

A *southern* tree with *wedge-shaped* hairless leaves that are *broadest near tip*. Leaves bristle-tipped. Leaf tips sometimes three-parted. Twigs hairless; end buds narrow, sharp, quite *hairy* and *angled*, often white-tipped. Acorn cup flat, saucer-shaped, ⅜"–⅝" across. Trunk dark and rather smooth. Leaves 2"–5". Height 50'–60' (80'); diameter 2'–3' (4'). Lowlands. SIMILAR SPECIES: (1) Chapman Oak (Pl. 30) also has leaves wider near the tip, but it is a white oak species with foliage wavy-edged, leathery, and mostly U-based. (2) Durand Oak (Pl. 30) also is wavy-edged and has small, blunt, hairless buds. See (3) Shingle Oak and, if leaf tips are deeply three-lobed at tips, also (4) Southern Red Oak (Pl. 28).

SHINGLE OAK *Quercus imbricaria* Michx.   PL. 31

A mainly *midwestern* tree whose leaves *lack* either teeth or lobes but whose single bristle tip shows it to belong to red oak group. Foliage *shiny* above and densely *hairy beneath*. Twigs hairless; end buds small, sharp, angled, and more or less *silky*; bud-scale edges hairy. Acorn cup *bowl-shaped*, covering ⅓–½ of acorn and ⁹⁄₁₆"–¹³⁄₁₆" across. Trunk dark, irregularly grooved. Leaves 4"–10". Height 50'–60' (100'); diameter 2'–3' (4'). Fertile forests. SIMILAR SPECIES: Shingle Oak leaves average wider than those of most other non-evergreen oaks in this group. Water and Arkansas oaks have leaves that are wider near the tips.

WATER OAK   SHINGLE OAK

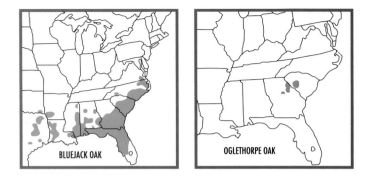

BLUEJACK OAK

OGLETHORPE OAK

BLUEJACK (SAND) OAK *Quercus incana* Bartr. **PL. 31**

A small tree or shrub of the *southeastern* states with somewhat *leathery but not evergreen* leaves, shaped like those of Shingle Oak but narrower and occasionally wavy-edged. Foliage shiny and bristle-tipped and with *fine, whitish woolliness* beneath. Twigs densely woolly to nearly hairless; buds ($\frac{3}{16}$"–$\frac{5}{16}$") *longer* than those of others in this group, sharp, hairy, and not angled. Acorn cup saucer-shaped, $\frac{3}{8}$"–$\frac{5}{8}$" across. Trunk black or gray, bark divided into squarish blocks. Leaves 2"–5". Height to 35'. Dry Coastal Plain soils. **SIMILAR SPECIES:** Shingle Oak has larger and thinner leaves, hairless twigs, and bowl-shaped acorn cups.

OGLETHORPE OAK *Quercus oglethorpensis* Duncan **PL. 31**

A local tree of the *white oak* group. Known *only* from bottomlands in extreme w. South Carolina and adjacent ne. Georgia. Leaves thin, narrow, *blunt-tipped* and pale *yellow-hairy* beneath. Twigs and buds hairless, the buds pointed or not, and not angled. Acorns small, $\frac{3}{8}$", in a *bowl-shaped* cup. Trunk bark gray and flaky. Leaves 3"–5". Height to 45'. Named for Oglethorpe County, Georgia, and General James Oglethorpe, founder of Georgia.

WILLOW OAK *Quercus phellos* L. **PL. 31**

A tall tree with thin, *narrow, bristle-tipped* leaves that are shiny and *hairless* above, dull and sometimes gray-hairy beneath. Twigs hairless; end buds narrow, sharp, hairless, somewhat angular, mostly less than $\frac{1}{8}$" long. Acorns to $\frac{1}{2}$" long, cups very *shallow* and saucerlike, $\frac{3}{8}$"–$\frac{1}{2}$" across. Trunk dark and shallowly grooved. Leaves 2"–5". Height 70'–80' (100'); diameter 2'–3' (4'). Lowlands. **SIMILAR SPECIES:** (1) Shingle Oak has wider leaves and deeper acorn cups; (2) Bluejack Oak has leaf undersides and twigs more or less woolly. (3) Laurel and (4) Darlington oaks have leaves

Willow Oak

somewhat shiny beneath, thicker, nearly evergreen. **REMARKS:** Not related to willows. Widely used in street and park plantings in the South.

LAUREL OAK   PL. 31
Quercus laurifolia Michx.

A large, mostly deciduous tree with leaves *thin, V-based,* and intermediate in shape between Shingle and Willow oaks, somewhat *shiny* and *hairless* except for tufts in angles of veins beneath. Twigs hairless or slightly hairy. End buds sharp, hairless, *angled,* ⅛"–³⁄₁₆" long. Acorns nearly globular, to 1" long; cups saucer-shaped, ⅝"–⅞" across. Trunk *gray,* scaly. Leaves 3"–6". Height to 100'. Coastal Plain swamps. **SIMILAR SPECIES:** See Willow Oak. **REMARKS:** Laurel and Darlington oaks, once viewed as probably one species, are now separated.

WILLOW OAK   LAUREL OAK

DARLINGTON OAK *Quercus hemisphaerica* Bart.   **NOT ILLUS.**
Like Laurel Oak but with leaves *more or less leathery* and bases
U-shaped or obtusely angled. It flowers two weeks later than Lau-
rel Oak and favors dry sites.

MYRTLE OAK *Quercus myrtifolia* Willd.   **PL. 31**
An *evergreen* shrub or small tree of Coastal Plain soils in Florida
and nearby states. Leaves *leathery,* often shiny on both sides, and
quite veiny above, but nearly *hairless* beneath. The edges are
rolled under. Some may lack a bristle tip. Twigs usually *hairy;* end
buds *pointed,* hairless and not angled. Trunk light gray, rather
smooth. Leaves 1"–2". Height to 40'. Acorns to ¼", nearly globular, stalks *short, cups saucerlike.* Dry soils.

VIRGINIA LIVE OAK *Quercus virginiana* Mill.   **PL. 31**
A spreading southern *evergreen* tree of the *white oak* group, with
leathery leaves 2"–4" long. Leaves sometimes have moderately
rolled edges, shiny above and mostly gray- or white-hairy beneath.
Some may be sharply toothed in part. Leaves *not* bristle-tipped.
Twigs hairless, rarely gray-hairy; end buds small, hairless, *blunt;*
not angled. Acorns are on ¾"–1" *stalks,* and cup *bowl-shaped.*
Trunk dark, bark somewhat broken into squares. Leaves 1"–4".
Height to 60'; diameter to 8'. **SIMILAR SPECIES:** Any evergreen oak
species may be called a live oak. There are many kinds, especially
in the West. In our area, only the next species also has leathery,
smooth-edged leaves, small blunt buds, and sometimes long
acorn-stalks. Where toothed leaves occur on Virginia Live Oak,
they are shaped unlike leaves of other oaks of Pl. 30.

SAND LIVE OAK
Quercus geminata Small
NOT ILLUS.
Much like Virginia Live Oak
but the leaves are cupped umbrellalike, the edges are strongly rolled under, and veins on
the upper surface are deeply
imbedded. To 15' tall. Mainly
on deep Coastal Plain sands
from S.C. to Ala. and s. Fla.

Virginia Live Oak

VIRGINIA LIVE OAK

MYRTLE OAK

TREES WITH ALTERNATE COARSE-EDGED LEAVES (PLATE 32)

These species have coarse-toothed or conspicuously scalloped foliage. All have 3 bundle scars per leaf scar. They *lack* the end clusters of leaves and buds present in oaks.

AMERICAN CHESTNUT   PL. 32
Castanea dentata (Marsh.) Borkh.

Originally a large tree, but now there are only occasional new plantings plus a few survivors sprouting from old stumps. Leaves *large but narrow,* hairless; undersides somewhat paler, *coarse-toothed.* Buds blunt, with only 2–3 visible scales and end bud false. Bundle scars 3, occasionally more. Bark smooth and gray when young, dark with numerous wide-topped, shiny ridges when mature. Leaves 5"–8". Height 60'–80' (100'), now mostly less than 25' high; diameter 2'–4' (17'). Flowers June–Aug., male blossoms small, in catkins 6"–8" long. Fruits nuts, *several* to each *spiny* husk, each nut *flattened* on 1 or more sides, edible. Sept.–Oct. SIMILAR SPECIES: Species name should not be confused with that of the compound-leaved and unrelated Horsechestnut (Pl. 6). (1) Chestnut Oak (Pl. 30) has leaves and buds clustered at twig tips: buds have more scales. (2) Beech has shorter leaves and long, slender buds. See (3) Ozark, (4) Eastern, and (5) Florida chinkapins. In winter, basswoods (Pl. 26) also have only 2–3 bud scales. Their branchlets, however, have tough inner bark and the twigs are mostly red or green. REMARKS: The American Chestnut not very long ago was a dominant tree in dry forests throughout much of our region. Soon after 1900, however, a fungus bark disease believed to be of Asiatic origin became epidemic and in less than a human generation completely eliminated our Chestnut as

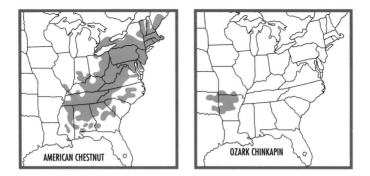

AMERICAN CHESTNUT

OZARK CHINKAPIN

an important forest tree. Sprouts may continue from some old stumps, and these may flower and produce fruits. As soon as these shoots attain a moderate size, however, the bark-shattering blight usually girdles them near their bases. Blight-resistant strains are being developed, and planted specimens may be encountered.

Chestnut lumber was quite valuable. It was used for furniture, musical instruments, interiors, caskets, and fences. Tannin was derived from the bark, and the nuts were once a staple food of Native Americans and settlers. Bobwhite quail, passenger pigeons, wild turkeys, squirrels, and whitetail deer are among the many forms of wildlife that once fed on the nuts. Chestnuts sold commercially are mostly fruits of the Spanish or Sweet Chestnut (*C. sativa* Mill.). Hybrids between American Chestnut and various foreign species are being studied.

ALLEGHENY CHINKAPIN

FLORIDA CHINKAPIN

OZARK CHINKAPIN *Castanea ozarkensis* Ashe   PL. 32

Similar to American Chestnut but smaller and with leaves *white-downy* beneath. Leaf teeth coarse. Twigs and buds fine-hairy. The edible nut occurs *singly.* Nut *not* flattened. Leaves 5"–8". Height to 65'. The next species has more woolly leaves and twigs. Dry woods in the Ozarks region.

ALLEGHENY (EASTERN) CHINKAPIN   PL. 32
Castanea pumila Mill.

Similar to Ozark Chinkapin but with smaller leaves and *white-woolly* twigs and leaf undersides. Twigs *woolly.* Leaves 3"–5". Height to 40'. Flowers June; fruits single. Dry woods of Appalachia and the Southeast.

FLORIDA CHINKAPIN *Castanea alnifolia* Nutt.   PL. 32

A shrub or small tree of the southeastern Coastal Plain. Leaves *small,* resembling those of Beech. Leaves and twigs hairless; buds *short,* hairless or somewhat hairy. Leaves 2"–4". Height to 20'. Nuts single in a husk that is spiny but less so than that of other Chinkapins. Dry soils. **REMARKS:** Sometimes considered a form of Allegheny Chinkapin.

Bark of Beech

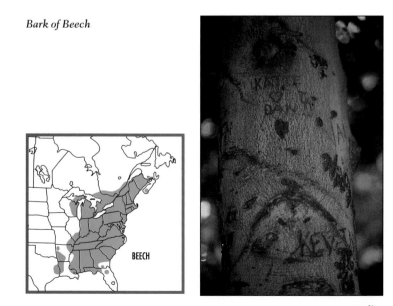

BEECH

BEECH *Fagus grandifolia* Ehrh.   **PL. 32**

A tall tree with distinctive *smooth gray bark and long, slender, many-scaled buds*. Leaves are elliptic or egg-shaped and *coarse-toothed*. The teeth are small or lacking in trees of some, mostly southern, areas. Twigs hairless or somewhat long-hairy, *encircled* or almost encircled by stipule scars at each leaf scar. End bud true. Leaves 3"–6". Height 60'–80' (120'); diameter 2'–3' (4'). Flowers April–May. Fruits small, *triangular* nuts enclosed in somewhat spiny bracts, Sept.–Oct., edible. Fertile woods. **SIMILAR SPECIES:** (1) European Beech (*F. sylvatica* L.), often planted, has similar bark and buds but wavy-edged foliage. (2) Red Maple (Pl. 11) and (3) Yellowwood (Pl. 21) also have beechlike bark, but the former has opposite lobed foliage, and the latter (not common) has compound leaves. See also (4) American Chestnut and (5) Florida Chinkapin. **REMARKS:** An important timber species. Quality of wood only fair but used for cheap furniture, tool handles, veneer, shoe lasts, and fuel. Beeches are planted widely for ornament. Fruits eaten by ruffed grouse, wild turkey, bobwhite, pheasant, black bear, raccoon, red and gray foxes, whitetail deer, cottontail rabbit, many squirrels, porcupine, and opossum.

COMMON WITCH-HAZEL *Hamamelis virginiana* L.   **PL. 32**

A shrub or small tree with *wavy-toothed, uneven-based* leaves. Leaves and twigs typically hairless but rarely hairy and leathery. Buds are *without scales, hairy,* and somewhat stalked at the base. End bud true. Some pairs or tight groups of stubby, four-parted seed pods can usually be found at any time of year. Bark smooth or rough in patches, often with some cross-stripes. Leaves 3"–6". Height 10'–25' (30'); diameter 2"–10" (14"). Flowers with narrow yellow petals, Sept.–Nov. Fruits Aug.–Oct. **SIMILAR SPECIES:** The only other species with naked buds and 3 bundle scars are the buck-

COMMON WITCH-HAZEL

GROUNDSEL-TREE

thorns (Pl. 43). They have even-based, sometimes toothed, and more egg-shaped leaves and buds without narrowed bases. **REMARKS:** Colloquial names Winter-bloom and Snapping-alder indicate peculiarities of this plant. In late autumn, after the leaves drop and the old fruit pods pop their seeds up to 20' away—and sometimes even after snow is on the ground—the straggly blossoms appear. An extract of the bark has long been used for medicinal purposes. Branches are used as "divining" or "witching" rods in efforts to locate underground water. Witch-hazel seeds, buds, or twigs are dietary items of pheasant, bobwhite, ruffed grouse, whitetail deer, cottontail rabbit, and beaver. A shrubby relative, Springtime Witch-hazel (*H. vernalis* Sarg.), occurs in the Ozark Plateau in Mo., Ark., and Okla.; bearing its flowers Dec.–March.

GROUNDSEL-TREE *Baccharis halimifolia* L.   **PL. 32**

A shrub or small tree with *green, ridged* twigs. Wedge-shaped leaves of lower portions of plant have large and often deep teeth; those of upper portions often lack teeth. Buds two- to three-scaled; end bud false. Leaves 1"–3". Height to 15'. Flowers Aug.–Sept. Fruits small, dry, white, silky, Sept.–Dec. Coastal regions and nearby inland areas. **SIMILAR SPECIES:** No other tree with 3 bundle scars has green, ridged twigs.

STRAWBERRY-TREE *Muntingia calabura* L.   **PL. 32**

A fast-growing *evergreen* Caribbean species occurring also in cen. and s. Florida. Leaves narrow, toothed, pointed, and hairy beneath with 3 *main veins* meeting at the very *uneven* base. Twigs and buds *hairy;* end bud false. Leaves 2"–4". Height to 25'. Flowers white. Fruits reddish or yellowish, fleshy. The bark is fibrous and is used in making rope and baskets. Moist soils and pine woods. See Pl. 26 for other fan-veined trees and Pl. 33 for elms also with uneven-based foliage and fibrous inner bark.

ELMS AND WATER-ELM (PLATE 33)

Elms (except Siberian and Chinese [plus some Cedar] elms, and Water-elm) have double-toothed leaves, mostly with *uneven* bases and sharp tips. Buds are many-scaled, with scales in 2 vertical rows; end bud is false. Leaf scars are unusually smooth; the 3 bundle scars are sunken. Trunk bark grayish, with vertical, often cross-thatched ridges. Flowers are inconspicuous, mostly appearing before the leaves in spring, and giving rise to small, flat, papery-winged, oval to circular fruits. Birches (Pl. 34) have even-based leaves, buds with only 2–3 scales, and trunks with many narrow cross-stripes. The several double-toothed plants illus-

American Elm

trated on Pl. 35 can be separated from elms by their distinctive buds and other characteristics.

Water-elm, or Planer-tree, is included as a close relative of the true elms, although it is in a different genus. It differs in having fruits that are small, wingless, soft-spiny nuts. Leaves are single-toothed.

Inner bark of branches and roots is generally tough and fibrous and can be twisted into rope, fishline, nets, and snares. This feature can also aid identification. The wood is difficult to split. Fruits are eaten by many game and songbirds and by squirrels. Twigs and foliage are consumed by rabbits, deer, and muskrats.

AMERICAN ELM *Ulmus americana* L. PL. 33
Full-sized wild trees are becoming rare as a result of disease. When growing in the open as a large tree, however, trunk divides near the ground into large limbs, giving a *unique vase-shaped form* (silhouette, p. 24). Leaves variable, more or less smooth or sand-papery above, hairless or somewhat hairy beneath. Twigs hairless or barely hairy; branchlets *without* corky "wings." Buds more than ¼" long, with light brown but *dark-edged* scales. Leaves 4"–6". Height 80'–100' (125'); diameter 2'–5' (10'). Flowers March–May. Fruits ⅜"–½", hairless except for hairy margin, deeply

notched, long-stemmed, April–May. Principally bottomlands. **SIMILAR SPECIES:** Other elms have small leaves and/or distinctive buds. See Rock Elm. **REMARKS:** Seeds are eaten by bobwhite, European partridge, ruffed grouse, prairie chicken, gray and fox squirrels, and opossum. Cottontail rabbit, snowshoe hare, and whitetail deer browse twigs. Like American Chestnut (p.303) in an earlier generation, this beloved

SLIPPERY ELM

species has been decimated by disease. Wild trees old enough to display a vase-shaped form are scarce. Stands of dead trees continue to expand and occupy lowland sites in many places. "Dutch" elm disease is a fungus spread by a beetle.

SLIPPERY ELM *Ulmus rubra* Muhl. PL. 33

A medium-sized tree with either single or divided trunk. Leaves are *hairy-edged,* quite *sandpapery* above and somewhat woolly beneath. Twigs *rough-hairy;* buds prominently *red-hairy* and more than ⅛" long. Leaves 4"–8". Height 40'–60' (70'); diameter 1'–2' (3'). Flowers March–May. Fruits ½", nearly circular, hairless except for centers of each side, slightly notched, and tightly bunched, May–June. Fertile uplands. **SIMILAR SPECIES:** No other elm has rough-hairy twigs and red-hairy buds. **REMARKS:** The common name of this coarse-textured tree refers to the slimy and reddish inner bark, once well known as a scurvy preventative when ground into flour or chewed piecemeal. It was reportedly also chewed to allay thirst and hunger. Cottontail rabbits and deer eat the twigs. Porcupines may eat the growing layer beneath bark. English Elm (*U. procera* Salisb.), established locally, lacks hairy leaf edges and may show branchlet "wings."

WINGED ELM *Ulmus alata* Michx. PL. 33

A small, single- or divided-trunk tree, usually bearing some branchlets with *wide corky "wings."* Leaves only 1"–3" long, hairy beneath, *smooth* to rough-hairy above. Leafstalks *short,* less than ¼" long, often nearly lacking. Twigs and buds hairless or nearly so; buds less than 3/16" long; bud scales with dark borders. Height 40'–50' (60'); diameter 1'–2'. Flowers March. Fruits ¼"–⅜" long, deeply notched, hairy or not, with fringed edges and pointed tips, long-stemmed, March–April. Bottomlands. **SIMILAR SPECIES:** (1)

WINGED ELM

Bark of Winged Elm

Rock Elm has drooping lower branches, larger leaves, longer leaf-stalks, hairy twigs, and larger fruits. (2) Cedar Elm has sandpapery leaves, narrow wings, hairless twigs, and fruits in autumn. (3) September Elm has hairless twigs, bud scales without dark edges, and flowers in fall. (4) Sweetgum (Pl. 25) and (5) Bur Oak (Pl. 29) are the only alternate-leaved woody plants besides elms that regularly possess corky "wings." Sweetgum has star-shaped leaves and a true end bud; Bur Oak has feather-lobed leaves and clustered end buds.

ROCK ELM *Ulmus thomasii* Sarg.   **PL. 33**
A single-trunked tree, usually with *corky "wings"* on some branch-lets and often with strongly *drooping* lower branches. Leaves hair-less, with leafstalks ¼" long. Twigs and buds somewhat *hairy.* Buds more than ¼" long; brown, with *dark* scale edges. Leaves 2"–4". Height 60'–80' (100'); diameter 2'–3' (4'). Flowers April–May. Fruits ⅜"–⅝" long, not circular, with a *moderate* notch, fringed margins, long-stemmed, May. Upland sites. **SIMILAR SPECIES:** (1) When corky wings are present, see Winged Elm. (2) When wings are lacking, smaller leaves, hairy twigs and buds, columnar trunk, and upland habitat distinguish it from American Elm. (3) Slippery Elm buds are red-hairy.

ROCK ELM

CEDAR ELM

CEDAR ELM *Ulmus crassifolia* Nutt.   PL. 33

A *small-leaved, fall-flowering* tree of the lower Mississippi Valley with *sandpaper-surfaced* foliage, sometimes with single teeth. *Narrow* corky wings may occur on the branchlets. Twigs and buds hairless; buds ⅛"–³⁄₁₆"; bud scales *without* dark borders. Leaves 1"–2". Height to 70'; diameter 1'–2'. Flowers Aug.–Oct. Fruits ³⁄₁₆"–½", deeply notched and white-hairy, Sept.–Oct. Bottomlands. **SIMILAR SPECIES:** See Winged and September elms.

SEPTEMBER ELM *Ulmus serotina* Sarg.   NOT ILLUS.

A rare, mostly southern-midwest species which, like Cedar Elm, may have corky branchlet wings and flowers and fruits in the *fall* of the year. Its leaves are *larger* and *not* sandpapery. Twigs and buds hairless; buds ³⁄₁₆"–⁵⁄₁₆" and scales *not* dark-edged. Leaves 2"–4". Height to 65'. Flowers Sept. Fruits ½" long, deeply notched, edges hairy, Oct.–Nov. Floodplains.

SIBERIAN ELM *Ulmus pumila* L.   NOT ILLUS.

A hardy shrub or small tree introduced from Asia and established widely. The 1"–3" leaves are ¾"–1⅜" wide and *single-toothed.* Twigs and buds nearly hairless; twigs without wings and buds small, *dark,* and *blunt.* Fruits more or less hairless, winged, nearly circular, ⅜"–⅝" long and deeply notched. **SIMILAR SPECIES:** Water-elm (below) occurs eastward. **REMARKS:** Also known as Chinese Elm, but that species (*U. pumila* L.) has small foliage less than ¾" wide and seeds not winged.

WATER-ELM *Planera aquatica* J. F. Gmel.   PL. 33

A small *southern* tree with egg-shaped, *single-toothed,* somewhat rough-surfaced but nearly hairless leaves. Twigs not winged; twigs and buds *hairless,* the latter mostly less than ⅛" long and *pointed.*

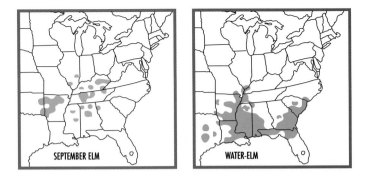

SEPTEMBER ELM

WATER-ELM

Trunk bark more scaly than in true elms. Leaves 2"–4". Height 40'–50'; diameter 18"–20". Flowers April. Fruits *wingless nuts* covered with irregular protuberances, April–May. Coastal Plain swamps. See map, above. **SIMILAR SPECIES:** In this group, only Siberian and Chinese (plus some Cedar) elms also have single-toothed leaves. Ranges, fruit, and bud shapes, however, are dissimilar. **REMARKS:** Fruits eaten by mallard, black, and ringneck ducks and by squirrels.

BIRCHES (PLATE 34)

Birches are trees and shrubs of mostly northern distribution. The leaves are double-toothed, more or less egg-shaped or triangular, and with bases mostly *even*. The mature bark of most species often will, by itself, identify the tree. Typically, bark of birches (and most cherries) is marked by numerous *cross-streaks*. In some birches, it tends to separate into papery sheets. Birch buds have only 2–3 scales, and there are 3 bundle scars. Short spur branches of densely clustered leaves and leaf scars are usually *present*. The end bud is false except on spurs.

Native birches that possess dark bark might be confused with some cherries (Pl. 36). Birches differ in that (1) bud scales are fewer, (2) leaves are double-toothed and usually do not taper at the base, (3) leafstalks do not have glands, (4) broken twigs lack the sour odor of cherry twigs but may have a strong wintergreen odor, and (5) the bark of many birches can be separated into papery sheets. Though the blossoms and fleshy fruits of a few cherries occur in lengthened clusters, the flowers of birches are always in caterpillarlike catkins that become lengthened clusters of small dry fruits. Male catkins are often present in winter.

Birch lumber is of value in cabinetmaking and interior finishing. It is also used in the manufacture of agricultural implements, spools, clothespins, etc. The bark of some species was once used in making canoes. In several birches the curling older bark is highly flammable, providing excellent tinder even when damp. The fermented sap of some birches has been used in beverages. Seeds and buds are eaten by numerous song and game birds. Several mammals consume the twigs and bark.

PAPER (AMERICAN WHITE) BIRCH PL. 34
Betula papyrifera Marsh.

White birches grow from small saplings with brownish bark to be small to medium-sized trees with *white* trunks. The white, *peeling bark* of mature trees readily separates into *papery layers* and is marked by narrow *horizontal streaks*. Dark, chevron-shaped trunk markings are few. Leaves have *9 or fewer* pairs of side veins, and the tips, though more or less tapered, make up only 1/10–1/6 of the blade. Twigs slightly rough-warty, if at all, and without wintergreen odor. Buds blunt, hairless. Some local varieties have brown bark in maturity, drooping twigs, or heart-shaped leaves. Leaf blades 1"–4". Height 70'–80' (120'); diameter 1'–3' (4'). Flowers spring. Fruiting catkins drooping, *slender,* 1"–2", Aug.–Sept. Open woods and cutover areas. **SIMILAR SPECIES:** (1) Gray Birch

Bark of Paper Birch

PAPER BIRCH

GRAY BIRCH

Bark of Gray Birch

leaves are more triangular and more extensively long-pointed. Its white trunk is non-peeling and marked by large black chevrons at the bases of most branches. Its twigs, too, are conspicuously rough-warty, and the fruiting catkins are shorter and less slender. See (2) Heartleaf Birch and (3) Weeping Birch. See also (4) Quaking Aspen (Pl. 27). **REMARKS:** Bark layers have been used by Native Americans for canoes and shelter coverings (tied in place with White Spruce rootlets), boxes, cups, makeshift shoes, and emergency snow goggles. They, as well as the early French-Canadian voyageurs, reportedly used the springtime sap as a refreshing drink and also boiled it into a sweet syrup. Leaves have been used for tea but are not as good as those of Sweet and Yellow birches. Paper Birch lumber is used for woodenware, pulp, and fuel. Seeds and buds eaten by ruffed and sharptail grouse. Twigs are cropped by moose, deer, and snowshoe hare.

HEARTLEAF BIRCH *Betula cordifolia* Regal   **NOT ILLUS.**
Much like Paper Birch but leaves with *heart-shaped bases* and *9–12* pairs of lateral veins. Mature trunk bark pinkish white to tan or bronze. Twigs mostly roughened with resin-glands. Height to 65'. Distributed from Hudson Bay and Wisc. east to the Atlantic Coast and south to n. Ga.

GRAY BIRCH *Betula populifolia* Marsh. PL. 34

A one- to many-stemmed small tree mainly of New England and the Maritime Provinces with *chalky white* bark and *triangular, long-tapering* leaves (see silhouette, p. 28). The leaf tips extend *about half* the length of the leaf blade. Twigs are *rough-warty* and without wintergreen odor. Trunks are marked by *many dark chevrons* (shallow, inverted Vs) at bases of branches as well as by narrow horizontal marks. Bark does *not* peel or readily separate into layers. Leaf blades 1"–4". Height 20'–30' (40'); diameter 10"–18". Flowers April–May. Fruiting catkins drooping, *sturdy,* ¾"–1¼" long. Sept. Mixed woods. **SIMILAR SPECIES:** Long-pointed leaves; hairless, rough-warty twigs; and chalk-white, non-peeling, chevron-marked bark are distinctive. **REMARKS:** Gray Birch used mainly for fuel and charcoal. Seeds and buds eaten by ruffed grouse and several songbirds. Twigs browsed by whitetail deer.

WEEPING BIRCH *Betula pendula* Roth NOT ILLUS.

Like Gray Birch with long-tapered leaf tips. The twigs, however, are *pendent* and the trunk bark is *glossy* white and *black-fissured at the base,* reported sometimes to peel in lengthy strips. Leaves 1"–3" long and more or less *hairless.* Twigs *hairless* and smooth, or with small resin-dots. Height to 75'. A landscape tree naturalized in the ne. U.S., in Washington state, and perhaps elsewhere. Also known as European White Birch.

SWEET (BLACK) BIRCH *Betula lenta* L. PL. 34

A tall, straight, brown- or *black-barked* tree, mainly of Appalachian forests. Young trunk bark tight, marked by thin horizontal stripes. Older bark often cracked. Leaves short-pointed. Main side veins may be *branched.* Broken twigs have delightful spicy *wintergreen* odor. Buds and twigs *hairless,* or lower bud scale

SWEET BIRCH

VIRGINIA BIRCH

alone is fringed with sparse hairs. Leaves 1"–6". Height 50'–70' (80'); diameter 2'–3' (5'). Flowers April–May. Fruiting catkins cylindrical, erect, fruits Aug.–Oct. Moist forests. **SIMILAR SPECIES:** (1) A mature Yellow Birch normally has distinctive yellow- to silver-gray bark, but small specimens look and smell like Sweet Birch and may grow side by side with it. Sometimes branched leaf veins plus hairless twigs and buds help identify this species. See (2) Virginia Birch. **REMARKS:** Sweet Birch wood is hard and heavy and is frequently made into furniture. Rare "curly" and "wavy" grain woods are especially valuable. Oil of wintergreen is obtainable from sap and leaves. Fermented sap may be an ingredient of birch beer. Buds and seeds eaten by ruffed and sharptail grouse; twigs browsed by whitetail deer, moose, and cottontail rabbit. Also known as Cherry Birch.

VIRGINIA BIRCH *Betula uber* (Ashe) Fern.   **NOT ILLUS.**
A small birch with dark bark, hairless twigs and foliage, and nearly circular, 1"-long, toothed leaves. Broken twigs have a wintergreen odor. Growing to 30' tall, it is classified as an endangered species. **REMARKS:** Found in the mountains of Smyth County, sw. Virginia, it is little known and may be only a variety of Sweet Birch. Also called Roundleaf Birch.

Bark of Yellow Birch

YELLOW BIRCH

YELLOW BIRCH *Betula alleghaniensis* Britton
PL. 34

A tall tree, often growing with Sweet Birch and Hemlock. Bark *shiny yellow to silver-gray* with narrow horizontal lines and *peeling* in small thin curls. Broken twigs give off *wintergreen* odor like that of Sweet Birch but a bit weaker. Leaves short-pointed, with main side veins *unbranched*. Twigs and buds (at least scale edges) somewhat *hairy*. Leaves 1"–5". Height 70'–80' (100'); diameter 2'–3' (4'). Flowers spring. Fruits Aug.–Oct.; fruiting catkins somewhat egg-shaped and more or less upright. Moist northern and mountain forests. **SIMILAR SPECIES:** Mature Yellow Birch is usually distinctive, but see Sweet Birch. **REMARKS:** Oil of wintergreen occurs in sap and leaves. Wood important in commerce; often stained for cherry or mahogany finishes. Ruffed and sharptail grouse, prairie chicken, whitetail deer, moose, cottontail rabbit, and red squirrel use the plant for food.

RIVER BIRCH *Betula nigra* L.
PL. 34

A *shaggy-barked* tree of streambanks; most *southern* of our birches. Bark varies from smooth and *red-brown* on youngest branches to *orange* and *peeling* and to rough, near-black plates on trunk. Leaf bases widely *V-shaped*. Undersides of leaves whitish and sometimes velvety. Leafstalks, twigs, and buds hairy. Twigs some-

Bark of River Birch

RIVER BIRCH

times rough-warty. Buds narrowed at base. Leaves 1"–5". Height 60'–80' (90'); diameter 2'–3' (5'). Flowers April–May. Fruiting catkins more or less cylindrical, erect; fruits mature over winter, June–Sept. **SIMILAR SPECIES:** The only other streamside tree birches have white bark when mature. **REMARKS:** Ruffed grouse and wild turkeys sometimes eat the seeds.

WATER BIRCH *Betula occidentalis* Hook.   **NOT ILLUS.**
A birch with *red-brown, shiny* trunk marked by *white* transverse streaks and seldom peeling. Leaves 1"–3" long, *short-pointed,* often heart-shaped, and with 4–5 pairs of side veins. Twigs *rough-warty, hairless.* Height to 40'. Local throughout mountains of w. North America; in Canada extending east to w. Ontario. **SIMILAR SPECIES:** A shrubby dwarf birch, *B. minor* (Tuck.) Fern., with similar bark and only minor difference in catkin scales, extends throughout e. Canada to n. New England and New York.

OTHER TREES WITH MOSTLY DOUBLE-TOOTHED LEAVES AND/OR SMALL WOODY CONES (PLATE 35)

These species and the birches (Pl. 34) make up a group that is related to the willows, poplars, oaks, and other plants whose flowers and fruits also occur in catkins. Catkins are usually evident as caterpillarlike dangling strands of small flowers; in a few instances they may be short, inconspicuous clusters. The mature female catkins of alders are usually present and resemble tiny pine cones.

Plants of this plate (except Seaside Alder) have double-toothed leaves. All have 3 bundle scars per leaf scar and *lack* spur branches. While elms and birches also have double-toothed leaves, elms have uneven-based leaves and bud scales in 2 rows, while birches have even-based leaves, spur branches present, and only 2–3 bud scales per bud.

IRONWOOD *Carpinus caroliniana* Walt.   **PL. 35**
A small tree whose smooth gray trunk has a distinctly *muscular* appearance. The trunk has a deeply rippled and sinewy look. Leaves egg-shaped, double-toothed, and sometimes long-pointed, with U-shaped bases. Side veins tend to be parallel and *not forked.* Twigs variably hairy or not. Buds brown, *somewhat square* in cross section, with numerous scales in 4 rows; end bud false. Leaves 1"–5". Height 20'–40'; diameter 10"–24". Flowers April, male catkins *not* present in winter. Fruits tiny nuts attached to three-pointed leafy bracts, Aug.–Oct. Bottomlands and rich soils.

IRONWOOD

Bark of Ironwood

SIMILAR SPECIES: Trunk and bark are unique. Angled buds and non-forked parallel veins help separate small specimens from those of Eastern Hornbeam. **REMARKS:** Nearly all botany books published during the past generation name this plant Blue-beech and the next one Ironwood. Yet *Carpinus* (which is not in the same family as the true Beech) is still commonly called Ironwood in many areas because of the strong muscular appearance of the trunk. Conversely, *Ostrya* appears no stronger than most small trees. The result is a confusion of 2 "ironwoods," further complicated by the alternate names "American Hornbeam" and "Hop Hornbeam," which are applied to these two species, respectively.

Wood of this tree is heavy and tough but, surprisingly, decays rapidly upon contact with the ground. Charcoal made from Ironwood was reportedly once used in manufacture of gunpowder. The fruits are eaten by many birds, including ruffed grouse, bobwhite, pheasant, and wild turkey, and by gray squirrels. Cottontail rabbit and whitetail deer nip the shoots.

EASTERN HORNBEAM *Ostrya virginiana* (Mill.) K. Koch **PL. 35**
A small tree with foliage and twigs much like those of Ironwood but trunk bark brownish, grooved, and *shreddy.* Some of the parallel side veins of the leaves are usually *forked.* Buds greenish,

Eastern Hornbeam

round in cross section; end bud false. Bud scales 6–8, finely *grooved* (use lens), and not arranged in rows. Leaves 1"–5". Height 20'–30' (40'); diameter 6"–12" (24"). Flowers April–May, male catkins usually *present* in winter. Fruits small, bladder-enclosed nuts, Aug.–Oct. Fertile woods. **SIMILAR SPECIES:** Ironwood has a gray, *muscular* trunk, squarish buds, and parallel leaf veins that are not forked. See note under Ironwood concerning confusion over the common name. **REMARKS:** Related European trees were originally used in yoking oxen and were known as Yoke-elms, or Hornbeams. Seeds eaten by ruffed and sharptail grouse, bob-white, pheasant, and ptarmigan. Deer and cottontail rabbits browse twigs.

ALDERS

PL. 35

These trees and shrubs grow mostly on streamside and other moist sites. Our species have unique 2–3 scaled buds that are smooth, reddish, and *stalked* (narrow-based). End buds are true. Alders also usually have woody female catkins which, when mature, resemble 1" pine cones. Male catkins usually present in winter. The dark trunk generally has short, horizontal, whitish, barlike markings.

SMOOTH ALDER *Alnus serrulata* (Ait.) Willd. **PL. 35**

A shrub or small tree forming thickets along watercourses. Leaves variably hairless or velvety beneath, bases *wedge-shaped* or only slightly rounded. Leaf edges *finely* single- or double-toothed and somewhat wavy. Dark trunk usually *lacks* speckles or may have some of the white barlike markings of Speckled Alder, but these are shorter and fewer. Leaves 2"–5". Height 6'–12' (25'); diameter 1"–2" (4"). Flowers Feb.–May; only slender male catkins droop. Fruit cones on 1/16"–1/4" stalks and more or less erect. **SIMILAR SPECIES:** Wedge-shaped leaf bases, fine-toothed leaf edges, and relatively unspeckled bark and non-drooping cones distinguish this species from (1) Speckled Alder. (2) Seaside Alder has single-toothed, sharply pointed leaves and separated bud scales. **REMARKS:** Hybridizes with Speckled Alder. Deer eat twigs, but they are not a favorite food. The bark yields a brown dye.

SPECKLED ALDER **PL. 35**
Alnus incana (L.) Moench. subsp. *rugosa* (Du Roi) Claus.

Similar to Smooth Alder but more northern. Leaves egg-shaped, sometimes leathery, edges *coarsely* double-toothed and not wavy. Leaf bases *rounded* to somewhat heart-shaped. Leaf undersurfaces typically green and hairless. Dark bark plentifully *speckled* with transverse white warty lenticels. Fruit cones *droop*. Leaves 2"–5". Height 6'–12' (25'); diameter 1"–2" (4"). **SIMILAR SPECIES:** See Smooth Alder. **REMARKS:** Ptarmigan and sharptail grouse feed on buds; muskrats, cottontail rabbits, deer, and moose browse twigs. Sometimes called Black Alder, not to be confused with the next species or with Common Winterberry Holly (Pl. 40), both also sometimes given that name. Also termed Tag Alder in some areas. Formerly named *A. rugosa* (DuRoi) Spreng.

SMOOTH ALDER

SPECKLED ALDER

EUROPEAN (BLACK) ALDER
Alnus glutinosa (L.) Gaertn.

An upright tree with *wide, blunt-tipped,* sometimes notched, and usually double-toothed leaves. Leaf bases *rounded.* Twigs and young leaves *gummy.* Buds, as in most alders, smooth, few-scaled, reddish, narrow-based. Bark of stout trunk *dark,* with numerous short warty stripes. Leaves 2"–5". Height 20'–50' (70'); diameter 1'–2'. Flowers March–May. Fruit cones on *long* (½"–⅞") slender stalks. Introduced and established in the northern states and e. Canada. **SIMILAR SPECIES:** (1) Speckled Alder leaves are more short-pointed, the cones have shorter stalks, and the plant is less tall. (2) Seaside Alder has single-toothed, pointed leaves and separated bud scales. **REMARKS:** Common Winterberry Holly (Pl. 40) is sometimes also called Black Alder but is unrelated.

SEASIDE ALDER *Alnus maritima* (Marsh.) Muhl. ex Nutt. **PL. 35**
A shrub or tree of restricted distribution. Leaves single-toothed, egg-shaped to elliptic, with tips *sharp,* bases mostly *wedge-shaped,* and upper surface *glossy.* Bud scales narrow and *distinct,* the edges not joining. Stem bark smooth. Leaves 2"–5". Height to 30'; diameter to 6". Flowers in *late summer,* Aug.–Sept. See Smooth Alder. Pond and streambanks; coastal districts of Maryland and Delaware; also reported from the Red River, Oklahoma. Distribution probably affected by Pleistocene glaciers.

CHERRIES AND PEACH (Plate 36)

The cherries, plums, and peach are all members of the genus *Prunus,* in the rose family. Only some of the first 2 groups are native to the U.S. Those illustrated on this plate are thornless species, with a true end bud and fine-toothed leaves.

All 3 groups are alike in having the trunk marked with numerous cross-streaks; leaves *mostly single-toothed,* narrow-based (except Mahaleb Cherry), and frequently with long-pointed tips; buds with more than 3 scales; fruits fleshy; and twigs that when broken emit a peculiar odor. The "almond" or "sour" scent of the broken twigs is difficult to describe but, once learned (by testing a known plant), is a reliable aid to the identification of many group members, especially cherries. Flowers and *single-seeded* fruits are borne on short spur branches when these are present (Pl. 36). Remnants of the calyx, the circle of sepals located just beneath the flower petals, persist above the fruits of some species.

The leaves of most *Prunus* species are toothed, and their leaf-stalks bear small but evident glands at or near the leaf base. The leathery leaves of Carolina Laurelcherry (Pl. 43) and West Indies

Cherry (Pl. F-46C), however, lack teeth. These evergreen species lack leafstalk glands, as may three plums (Pls. 23, 37).

Although the fruits of most cherries are edible, the leaves, twigs, and seeds often contain hydrocyanic acid, believed to lend the characteristic odor to their broken twigs. Depending, apparently, upon the reaction of the stomach juices, the kind of feed previously consumed, and the condition of the plant when eaten, horses and cattle may die, become ill, or remain unaffected after browsing the potentially dangerous foliage of cherries. No plums have been listed as dangerous to livestock.

Wood of the larger cherries is of commercial value. Fruits of all species are eaten by a large number of birds and mammals.

CHOKE CHERRY *Prunus virginiana* L. PL. 36

A shrub or small tree with *egg-shaped* and bristly *sharp-toothed* leaves, the midribs *hairless* and 8–11 pairs of side veins present. Winter buds hairless, *more than ¼" long*; bud scales *rounded* at tips. Bark gray-brown and *smooth*. Only this cherry and the next 2 have blossoms and fruits in *long clusters* and have spur branches *lacking*. Leaves 2"–5". Height 6'–20' (30'); diameter 2"–6" (8"). Flowers white, April–July. Fruits purplish, *lacking* calyx lobes, July–Oct. Young woods and thickets. SIMILAR SPECIES: See (1) Black Cherry and (2) European Bird Cherry. (3) Sweet, (4) Sour, and (5) Mahaleb cherries have spur branches and short-clustered fruits. Common names are similar, but chokeberries are shrubs of a different genus (*Pyrus*, or *Aronia*). REMARKS: The tart fruits can be made into delicious jellies and are used for pies. A great number of songbirds, the ruffed grouse, sharptail grouse, prairie chicken, bobwhite, pheasant, raccoon, black bear, red fox, whitetail deer, cottontail rabbit, and gray squirrel regularly consume the fruits.

BLACK CHERRY *Prunus serotina* Ehrh. PL. 36

A small to large tree whose leaves typically are long and *narrow*, with *incurved or blunt teeth* and *more than 13 pairs* of lateral veins. Also (especially in the North), the midrib is *prominently fringed beneath* with brown to whitish hairs. Buds *less than ³⁄₁₆"* long, hairless; bud scales *pointed*; spur branches *lacking*. Mature trunk has a *rough dark* outer bark marked with short horizontal

Bark of Black Cherry

lines and often exposing the red-brown underbark where cracked. Reddish bark is characteristic of smaller branches. Leaves 2"–6". Height 60'–80' (100'); diameter 2'–3' (5'). Flowers white, in slender clusters, May–June. Fruits blackish, usually *retaining* calyx lobes; June–Oct. Woods and thickets. **SIMILAR SPECIES:** (1) Only other tree cherry with regularly narrow leaves is Fire Cherry, with non-hairy leaves, spur branches, short flower clusters, and buds clustered at twig tips. (2) Choke Cherry leaves are wider, with hairless midribs, bristly-sharp teeth, and fewer side veins. Buds are somewhat longer, with rounded scale tips; remnants of calyx lobes are not retained on fruits. See also (3) European Bird Cherry. In winter, the trunk bark of mature (4) Sweet Birch (Pl. 24) is similar, but its broken twigs are spicy-scented. **REMARKS:** One of the largest cherries, this species is of value for lumber and as food for humans and wildlife. The bitter fruits are often used for jelly. Bark has been used as flavoring. Fruits and twigs eaten by much the same animals as listed for Choke Cherry. Wood hard and close-grained; used for furniture and interior furnishing.

EUROPEAN BIRD CHERRY *Prunus padus* L.   **NOT ILLUS.**
Similar to and with elongate flower clusters like the preceding 2 cherries. Bud scales are pointed, flower petals are longer (¼"–⅜"), and seeds *irregularly grooved*. Fruits without persistent calyx. Se. Canada and ne. U.S. Ornamental; rarely escapes to wild.

PEACH *Prunus persica* Batsch   **PL. 36**
Occasionally the cultivated peach, a native of Asia, escapes to thickets. Very long, *narrow, hairless,* sharp-toothed leaves. Twigs are hairless; spur branches present; buds more than ¼" long,

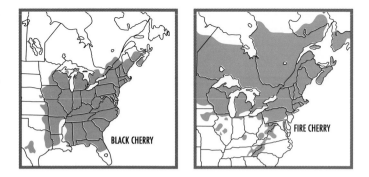

BLACK CHERRY

FIRE CHERRY

hairy, blunt-scaled, and not clustered at twig tips. Leaves 4"–9". Flowers single or paired, pink; fruits yellow and *velvet-hairy,* seeds *pitted.*

FIRE (PIN) CHERRY *Prunus pensylvanica* L. f.   PL. 36

Growing either as a shrub or small tree, this cherry has *narrow, sharp-toothed,* hairless leaves and clusters of nearly hairless buds at or *near ends* of red twig tips (as well as on spur branches). Buds are short, with *pointed* scales. Short white flower clusters are *umbrellalike,* as in all remaining species of cherries and plums. Bark red-brown and smooth. Trunk marked with crossbars; spur branches present. Leaves 2"–5". Height 10'–30' (40'); diameter 2"–10" (12"). Flowers white, March–July. Fruits red, ¼" across, July–Sept. Thickets and young forests, especially after burns or land clearing. **SIMILAR SPECIES:** (1) The only other native cherry with narrow leaves is Black Cherry, but that species lacks clustered end buds, spur branches, and red fruits. (2) Peach does not have clustered end buds. See also (3) Sweet and (4) Sour cherries. **REMARKS:** Known also as Bird Cherry. Sour fruits eaten raw or used in jellies and cough mixtures. Consumed by bobwhite, ruffed and sharptail grouse, ptarmigan, prairie chicken. Deer, moose, cottontail rabbit, beaver, and chipmunk browse the twigs.

SWEET CHERRY *Prunus avium* (L.) L.   PL. 36

A rather tall tree with *single* main trunk and *red-brown smooth* bark prominently marked with horizontal stripes and often peeling. Leaves egg-shaped; rather sharply *double-toothed;* 10–14 *pairs* of veins; *dull-surfaced* and hairless. Buds slender, light brown, more than ¼" long, and scales pointed. Flowers or fruits may be clustered on *leafless* spur branches. Leaves 2"–6". Height 30'–50' (75'); diameter 1'–2' (3'). Flowers white, April–May.

Fruits red to black, sweet, with *persistent* calyx, June–July. Cultivated, occasionally escapes to wild. SIMILAR SPECIES: (1) Sour Cherry is the only other of this group with double-toothed leaves and a persistent calyx. It usually lacks a central trunk and has leaves more or less shiny, 6–8 pairs of leaf veins, rough bark, and leafy fruiting spurs. (2) Mahaleb Cherry has single leaf teeth and hairy twigs. (3) Choke Cherry has long flower clusters and lacks spur branches. (4) Fire Cherry has much narrower leaves. REMARKS: This European species, known also as Mazzard Cherry, is the parent of many of the sweeter garden cherries. A few ornamental varieties possess variegated foliage. Fruits attractive to many songbirds and to squirrels.

SOUR CHERRY *Prunus cerasus* L. PL. 36

A tree usually *lacking* a central trunk. *Grayish* bark, at least of older trunks, *much cracked* and broken, sometimes scaly. Leaves like Sweet Cherry but more or less *shiny* above and with 6–8 *pairs* of veins. Buds stout, dark brown, and more than ¼" long. White flowers and fruits clustered on *leafy* spur branches. Leaves 2"–5". Height 20'–30'; diameter 10"–12". Flowers May–June. Fruits red, sour, with *persistent* calyx. May escape from cultivation. SIMILAR SPECIES: See Sweet Cherry. REMARKS: Believed to have originated in western Asia. Many cultivated varieties, principally those with tart flavor, are derived from this stock.

MAHALEB CHERRY *Prunus mahaleb* L. NOT ILLUS.

Similar to Sour Cherry but with *hairy* twigs and small but wide, *almost circular, hairless* leaves, which may be heart-shaped at base. Twigs *velvety*. Flowers white, in short clusters; fruits black, *without* persistent calyx. Established locally; New England and s. Ontario southward to Delaware, Indiana, and Kansas. REMARKS: Mahaleb, or Perfumed, Cherry was imported from Europe and the Caucasus for grafting stock. The fruits are inedible but yield a violet dye. Oil from seeds is used to fix perfumes. Aromatic wood is fashioned into pipes and walking sticks.

THORNLESS PLUMS (PLATE 37)

Though also members of the genus *Prunus,* the plums differ from several cherries in having flowers and fruits in rounded or flat-topped clusters and from all cherries in that the end bud is false. Leaves are mostly single-toothed (except in Mexican Plum). Spur branches are present except in Hortulan Plum. Leafstalk or leaf-base glands may be present (though they are sometimes absent

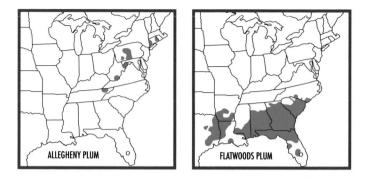

ALLEGHENY PLUM   FLATWOODS PLUM

from Allegheny and Flatwoods plums). Bundle scars 3. Fruits are fleshy and marked with lengthwise ridges. A single large and usually flattened stone contains the seed. As in cherries, the bark is usually marked with horizontal lines.

Broken twigs may have the "almond" odor characteristic of cherries, but whether this character is consistent for all plums is not certain. Occasionally, these species bear some thorns. See Pl. 23 and pp. 258–259 for plums that are regularly thorny.

ALLEGHENY PLUM *Prunus alleghaniensis* Porter   **PL. 37**
A northeastern shrub or small tree with *hairy* twigs and narrow to egg-shaped, *sharp-toothed,* gradually *long-pointed* leaves, often somewhat hairy beneath. Leafstalk glands usually present. Occasionally twig tips are spiny. Leaves 2"–5" long, ¾"–1¼" wide. Height to 17'; diameter to 8". Flowers *as* leaves appear, April–May. Fruits *purple,* about ⁷⁄₁₆" in diameter, stone pointed at both ends, Aug.–Sept. Mountain thickets. **REMARKS:** The tart fruits are used for jelly and pies. They are eaten by bears, songbirds, and other wildlife.

FLATWOODS PLUM *Prunus umbellata* Ell.   **PL. 37**
Like the Allegheny Plum, this small tree or shrub has *sharp* leaf teeth, twigs, and leafstalk glands sometimes absent. The leaves, though, are *short*-pointed. Leaves 1"–3" long, 1"–1½" wide. Height to 20'; diameter 6". Flowers early spring, *before* leaves appear. Fruits *black,* about ⅝" in diameter, Aug.–Sept., stone pointed at both ends. Southeast Coastal Plain.

MEXICAN PLUM *Prunus mexicana* Wats.   **PL. 37**
Like the previous 2 species a *sharp-toothed* plum, but with wider (to 2"), *double-toothed* leaves, and twigs *not* hairy. Leafstalk

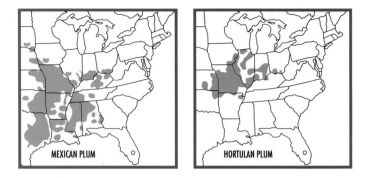

MEXICAN PLUM

HORTULAN PLUM

glands usually *present*. Leaves are mostly short-pointed. Twigs hairless. Leaves 2"–4". Height to 25'; diameter to 10". Flowers March. Fruits red to purple; stone nearly spherical, *not* pointed. Midwestern thickets and bottomlands. **REMARKS:** Despite the name, this species occupies a wide range in the Mississippi Valley as well as in northern Mexico.

HORTULAN (GOOSE) PLUM *Prunus hortulana* Bailey **PL. 37**
  A shrub or small tree with narrow to egg-shaped, *blunt-toothed* leaves that are hairless or nearly so. Leafstalk glands *present*. The only thornless plum *lacking* spur branches. Twigs hairless. Leaves 3"–6". Height 10'–20' (30'); diameter 4"–10" (12"). Flowers March–May. Fruits yellow or red, stone pointed at *both* ends. Aug.–Oct. Fertile soils. **SIMILAR SPECIES:** Wildgoose Plum has spur branches and stones not pointed at both ends. **REMARKS:** Grown by horticulturists, this native species has given rise to numerous cultivated varieties.

WILDGOOSE (MUNSON) PLUM **PL. 37**
Prunus munsoniana Wight and Hedr.
  A close relative of the Hortulan Plum. Has longer, quite narrow, long-pointed and blunt-toothed leaves that may appear to be sharp because of tiny reddish glands. Leafstalk glands also present. Twigs hairless. Fruiting spurs short but usually present. Fruits bright red, rarely yellow; stone pointed *at one* end. A native parent of horticultural varieties. Thickets.

GARDEN PLUM *Prunus domestica* L. **PL. 37**
  A small cultivated tree that has escaped to the wild in some localities in the n. U.S. and s. Canada. Leaves are somewhat hairy beneath, with leaf teeth *rounded*. Leafstalk glands usually pre-

sent. Twigs hairless. Leaves 2"–4". Height to 25'. Flowers spring. Fruits purple, to 1½" in diameter. **REMARKS:** Marketed fresh and dried as prunes. Originally native in e. Europe and w. Asia. Bullace Plum (p. 260) is sometimes considered to be a thorny variety of this species.

WILDGOOSE PLUM

WILLOWS I–II (Plates 38 and 39)

Many willows, but not all, are easily recognized as such by the slender leaves. The single scale of the willow bud, however, forms a complete hoodlike covering and, although not obvious except on close examination (use lens), is distinctive among plants with 3 bundle scars. Many willows are only shrubs, some far northern and high-altitude species being only a few inches tall.

The tree willows are divided here into those (Pl. 38) with leaves narrow (8–15 times longer than wide) or of medium width (5–7 times longer than wide) and those (Pl. 39) with wide leaves (only 2–4 times longer than wide). On the vigorous shoots of some species there are also small, somewhat leaflike stipules on the twigs at the bases of leafstalks. The stipules are useful in identification but may drop early. When stated to be large, they are reasonably leafy; when reported to be small, they are not evident except upon close examination. Tiny leafstalk or leafbase glands may be present (use lens).

Mature buds are listed as small when they are less than ⅛" long, large if they are more than ¼", and medium-long if they are in between. Twigs are said to be brittle at the base if they are easily detached, as Gordon (1960) says, "with a flick of the finger or by high winds." Frequently galls that resemble pine cones grow on the twigs. The end bud is false in willows. The bark of tree willows is mostly yellow-ridged. Flowers and fruits are small, dry, and occur in catkins.

Identifying willows is often a difficult task even for the professional botanist. Individual variation, minute identification marks, and hybridization are complicating factors. Winter characteristics

Text continues on p. 331

Only willows have buds with a single caplike bud scale combined with leaf scars containing 3 bundle scars. Twigs mostly slender; end bud false. All species bear catkins and grow on moist, sunny sites. Winter characteristics need further investigation.

SPECIES AND REMARKS	Twigs hairy	Twigs brittle-based[1]	Twigs yellowish[2]	Buds blunt	Bud size[3]	Major distribution[4]	Text page
COASTAL PLAIN WILLOW Se. U.S., local in Midwest.	+	+	–	–	–	S/N	334
OSIER WILLOW Twigs long, slender, limber.	+	–	–	–	+	N	333
BEBB WILLOW Twigs gray-woolly.	+	–	–	+	±	N	337
SILKY WILLOW	±	+	–	+	+	N/S	335
SANDBAR WILLOW Dead leaves short-stalked (⅛").	±	–	±	+	±	N/S	332
PUSSY WILLOW Opening catkins furry.	±	–	–	+	+	N	336
WHITE WILLOW[5] Twigs hairless to silky.	±	–	–	+	±	N/S	334
CRACK WILLOW[5] Buds sticky.	–	+	–	+	+	N	334
WEEPING WILLOW[5] Twigs long, hang limp.	–	+	–	+	±	N/S	333
SHINING WILLOW Twigs glossy.	–	+	–	+	±	N	335
BLACK WILLOW Trunks clustered.	–	+	–	–	–	N/S	331
PEACHLEAF WILLOW Twigs shiny, orange-brown.	–	–	+	–	–	N	336
BASKET WILLOW[5] Many buds nearly opposite.	–	–	–	+	±	N	337
BROADLEAF WILLOW Twigs white-powdered.	–	–	–	±	+	N	336
MEADOW WILLOW Twigs clustered at branchlet ends.	–	–	–	–	±	N	332
SATINY WILLOW Twigs white-coated.	–	–	–	–	±	N	335
BALSAM WILLOW Twigs and buds reddish, aromatic.	–	–	–	–	±	N	337
FLORIDA WILLOW Local; s. Ga.–cen. Fla. only	–	+	–	–		S	338

[1] Twigs easily detached at the base "with a flick of the finger or by high winds" (Gordon 1960).

[2] Twigs yellowish rather than brown or reddish.

[3] Bud sizes: large (+) = over 1/4"; small (–) = 1/8" or less; medium (±) = 1/8"–1/4".

[4] Distribution: N = n. U.S. and (often) adjacent Canada; S = s. U.S.

[5] Old World species, introduced and established in the wild.

are incompletely known. Those that seem most suitable, however, have been assembled in the winter identification chart on p. 330. For identification of leafless, *non-shrubby* willows, see that chart. Since final identification of willows frequently depends on examination of the tiny flowers and fruits, some uncertain specimens may have to be identified professionally or accepted merely as willows. Though Willow Oak (Pl. 31) has narrow and willowlike leaves, it has clustered, scaly end buds and bears acorns.

As pioneer species invading moist soils, willows are valuable in controlling streambank and mountainside erosion. Stakes of green branches will often sprout if they are merely driven into damp ground. Several willows provide long twigs used in basketmaking. A great many are valued as ornamental plants. The wood of tree species is of some commercial value but is generally used only for fuel, charcoal, and posts. Willow bark provides tannin and a medicinal substance, salicin, the basis for aspirin.

Willow leaves, twigs, and buds are of importance as browse for livestock. The many birds and mammals eating willow twigs, buds, leaves, or fruits include ruffed and sharptail grouse, willow and rock ptarmigan, elk, whitetail deer, moose, beaver, muskrat, snowshoe hare, and porcupine.

Russian-olive (*Elaeagnus angustifolia* L.), also known as Oleaster, has been introduced from Eurasia and planted widely as a windbreak on the western plains and for ornamental landscaping in the East. The leaves are narrow (occasionally egg-shaped) and willowlike. Though dark green above, the foliage of Russian-olive, unlike that of willows, is covered beneath with silvery scales. The twigs, too, are silvery, sometimes with thorns. Branchlets are brown. The buds differ from willows in having 2–4 silvery scales. Fruits silvery-red, juicy. Bundle scar 1. Other narrow-leaved trees include Willow Oak (Pl. 31), Peach (Pl. 36), and bayberries (Pl. 43).

WILLOWS I: LEAVES VERY NARROW TO MEDIUM IN WIDTH (PLATE 38)

BLACK WILLOW *Salix nigra* Marsh.   PL. 38

A shrub or tree with narrow, *long-pointed* leaves that are *green* on both sides and have wedge-shaped or rounded bases. Foliage fine-toothed and hairless. Leafstalks *short* (less than ⅙" long). The hairless twigs are *brittle* at the base and have small sharp buds. Stipules usually conspicuous. Trunks often clustered. Leaves 3"–6". Height 10'–40' (120'); diameter 2"–24" (96"). Flowers April–June. **SIMILAR SPECIES:** Meadow Willow has longer leafstalks, leaves whitened beneath, and no stipules.

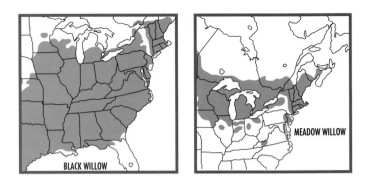

MEADOW WILLOW

MEADOW WILLOW   **PL. 38**
Salix petiolaris J. E. Smith

Leaves narrow, *long-pointed,* toothed, shiny green above, *whitish*
and hairless beneath. Leafstalks ¼"–½" long. Young leaves become
black on drying. Twigs dark, hairless, and *not* brittle at base. Typically, twigs are clustered at the branchlet ends. Buds of medium
length, pointed. Stipules *absent* or very small. Leaves 2"–4".
Height to 25'. Flowers May–June. **SIMILAR SPECIES:** See (1) Black
Willow. (2) Sandbar Willow has very short leafstalks and leaves
that often lack teeth.

SANDBAR WILLOW   **PL. 38**
Salix exigua Nutt.

A species with leaves variably toothed and/or hairy beneath. Distinguished, however, by *short-stalked* (about ⅛"), *narrow, long-
pointed* foliage that either lacks teeth or has *widely spaced,* tiny,

sharp teeth. Leaves are variably whitened or green beneath. Stipules are minute or lacking. Twigs are yellowish to brownish, hairy or not, and not brittle-based. Buds of medium length, *blunt.* Leaves 2"–6". Height to 20'. Flowers May–June. **SIMILAR SPECIES:** When the narrow leaves are without teeth, (1) Osier Willow has longer leaves, and (2) Satiny Willow has wider, thicker, short-pointed leaves. (3) Bebb and (4) Basket willows (Pl. 39) have wide leaves that sometimes lack teeth.

OSIER WILLOW *Salix viminalis* L. PL. 38
Similar to Sandbar Willow but leaves *very* long, narrow, long-pointed, *toothless,* and *silvery-hairy* beneath. Twigs *very long* and flexible, more or less silky-hairy, not brittle at the base; buds *large,* pointed. Stipules small or lacking. Leaves 4"–10". Height to 25'. Flowers April–June. A European import escaped from cultivation, ne. U.S. and se. Canada. **REMARKS:** The long twigs (osiers) are employed in making baskets and wickerware. Also called Basket Willow, but this is the common name also for *S. purpurea* (p. 337).

WEEPING WILLOW *Salix babylonica* L. PL. 38
An Old World tree with *extremely long,* brittle-based twigs and branchlets that *hang vertically,* often sweeping the ground or overhanging a lake or stream (silhouette, p. 29). Leaves moderately narrow, hairless or silky, fine-toothed, long-pointed, whitened beneath. Small leafstalk *glands* may be present. Twigs *dark,* buds of medium length, blunt. Stipules small or lacking. Leaves 3"–7". Height 30'–50' (60'); diameter 1'–3' (5'). Flowers April–May. Se. Canada to Georgia and Missouri. **SIMILAR SPECIES:** Brownish twigs and extreme weeping characteristics distinguish

this willow from other (yellow-twigged) cultivated forms with weeping growth habits. See White Willow.

COASTAL PLAIN (WARD) WILLOW   PL. 38
Salix caroliniana Michx.

Mainly a southern tree. Leaves toothed, moderately narrow, long-pointed, *hairless*, and *whitened* beneath. The leafbase is *U-shaped* and the stalks are *without glands*. Twigs somewhat hairy, reddish, and *brittle* at base. They do *not* droop. Buds are small and sharp. Leafy stipules *conspicuous* if present. Leaves 2"–7". Height to 35'. Flowers May–June. **SIMILAR SPECIES:** (1) Crack, (2) White, and (3) Silky willows also have long-pointed foliage, but their leaves have V-shaped bases and their buds are blunt.

CRACK WILLOW *Salix fragilis* L.   PL. 38

This European tree has hairless, *long-pointed, medium-width* leaves whitened or pale beneath and V-based. Leafstalks bear *glands*. Buds large, blunt, and somewhat *sticky*; twigs hairless, very *brittle* at base. Stipules small or lacking. Leaves 3"–6". Height 50'–70' (80'); diameter 2'–3' (4'). Flowers April–June. Established from Newfoundland and S. Dakota to Virginia and Kansas. **SIMILAR SPECIES:** Other willows with leaves medium-wide have foliage hairy beneath and often short-pointed.

WHITE WILLOW *Salix alba* L.   PL. 38

This naturalized and moderately fine-toothed European tree is our only willow with leaves that are often white-hairy *above and below*. Leafstalk glands may be present. Twigs olive-brown, nearly hairless to silky, sometimes drooping, not brittle at base; buds of medium length. Stipules mostly lacking. Leaves 2"–6". Height to 80'. Flowers April–May. Se. Canada to Georgia and Missouri.

SILKY WILLOW

ONTARIO WILLOW

SILKY WILLOW   *Salix sericea* Marsh.

A tree or shrub with *short-pointed,* medium-width, fine-toothed leaves, *dark green* above, *very* white-silky beneath, and lacking leafstalk glands. Young leaves become *black* on drying. Twigs brown, hairless or nearly so, and *brittle* at base; buds large and blunt. Stipules usually drop early but are sometimes obvious on vigorous shoots. Leaves 2"–5". Height to 15' (24'). Flowers March–May. **SIMILAR SPECIES:** Both this species and the next have medium-width leaves that are not long-pointed. Satiny Willow has leaves not toothed and buds pointed.

SATINY WILLOW
Salix pellita Anderss. ex Schneid.

A large shrub to small tree of the far north with leaves *not* toothed, thick, of medium width. Foliage *short-pointed, whitened, and silky-hairy beneath.* Leaf undersides and twigs covered with *white powder.* Twigs hairless; buds of medium size and pointed. Stipules small or lacking. Leaves 2"–5". Height to 30'. Flowers May–June. **SIMILAR SPECIES:** The only tree willow with medium-width, short-pointed leaves that are not toothed. (1) Osier and (2) Sandbar willows have narrow, long-pointed foliage. See (3) Bebb and (4) Basket willows (Pl. 39). **REMARKS:** Also called Ontario Willow.

WILLOWS II: LEAVES RELATIVELY WIDE (PLATE 39)

This group has relatively wide leaves, only 2–4 times as long as broad. Most have U-shaped leaf bases and at least some teeth.

SHINING WILLOW   *Salix lucida* Muhl.
The somewhat wide, *long-pointed* leaves are *shiny* on both sides,

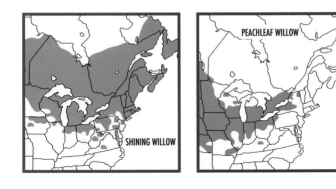

PEACHLEAF WILLOW

SHINING WILLOW

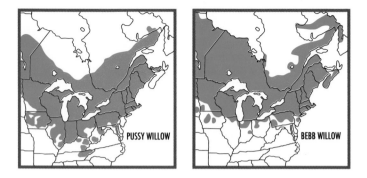

hairless, fine-toothed, green beneath, and often rather leathery. Leafstalks have heavy *glands* near or at leaf bases. Twigs *dark, hairless, brittle-based;* buds blunt, of medium size. Stipules usually large. Leaves 2"–7". Height 10'–15' (25'); diameter 1"–6" (12"). Flowers April–June. **SIMILAR SPECIES:** Peachleaf Willow also has long-pointed leaves but they are dull above, whitened beneath, and lack leafstalk glands and stipules.

PEACHLEAF WILLOW *Salix amygdaloides* Anderss. **PL. 39**
    A shrub or small tree with leaves *long-pointed, not shiny,* fine-toothed, hairless, somewhat leathery, *whitened* beneath. The *shiny,* hairless, *red-brown or orange,* flexible twigs droop moderately. Buds small, sharp. Stipules *small or lacking.* Leaves 3"–7". Height to 40'. Flowers April–June. **SIMILAR SPECIES:** See Shining Willow.

PUSSY WILLOW *Salix discolor* Muhl. **PL. 39**
    A shrub or tree. Leaves elliptic, whitened beneath, hairless, short-pointed, *wedge-based,* and toothed *mainly above the middle.* Leafstalks more than ¼" long. Twigs generally hairless; buds medium-long. Stipules often large. Leaves 2"–5". Height to 30'. Flowers Feb.–May, opening catkin buds very *furry.* **SIMILAR SPECIES:** Basket Willow also has leaves toothed mainly above the middle, but its leaves and buds are mainly opposite, and the leaf bases are U-shaped.

BROADLEAF WILLOW *Salix glaucophylloides* Fern. **PL. 39**
    A shrub or small tree of ne. U.S. and e. Canada. Leaves hairless, semileathery, fine-toothed *to the base,* shiny dark green above, whitened beneath; bases *broad,* sometimes heart-shaped. Young leaves become *black* on drying. Twigs dark, hairless, and white-

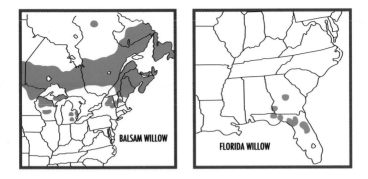

BALSAM WILLOW

FLORIDA WILLOW

powdered. Buds pointed or not. Stipules usually present and conspicuous. Leaves 1"–6". Height to 17'. Flowers May–June. **SIMILAR SPECIES:** Balsam Willow, also fine-toothed to the leaf base, has foliage aromatic when crushed.

BEBB WILLOW *Salix bebbiana* Sarg.   PL. 39

A variable shrub or small tree with leaves wide and *coarse-toothed,* less commonly nearly without teeth. Foliage *tapered* at both ends, dull above, *grayish woolly* and *veiny* beneath. Leafstalks short, less than ⅜" long. Twigs *gray-woolly*; buds medium-long, blunt. Stipules small or lacking. Leaves 2"–4". Height to 25'; diameter to 8". Flowers April–June. **SIMILAR SPECIES:** The only tree willow with wide, coarse-toothed, and gray-hairy leaves with wedge-shaped tips and bases. When leaf teeth are lacking, Basket Willow has more or less opposite and hairless foliage.

BASKET WILLOW *Salix purpurea* L.   PL. 39

A tall shrub or small tree with narrow leaves that have small teeth *only near tips* or not at all. Leaves usually opposite or *nearly opposite* each other, hairless, whitened beneath, and usually with *rounded* bases. Twigs *purplish* and hairless; buds often nearly opposite and of medium length. Leaves 1"–5". Height to 20'. Flowers April–May. Northern states and se. Canada. Introduced. **SIMILAR SPECIES:** Leaf type and nearly opposite leaves and buds are distinctive. See (1) Sandbar (Pl. 38) and (2) Bebb willows. **REMARKS:** Osier Willow (p. 333) is also sometimes called Basket Willow.

BALSAM WILLOW *Salix pyrifolia* Anderss.   PL. 39

A shrub or small tree with fine-toothed, mostly hairless, broad, thin leaves on long slender stalks. Foliage is dark green above and *whitened* beneath, with a pleasant, *firlike aroma* when crushed. ⚑

Twigs and buds *reddish* and hairless. Buds pointed, of intermediate length. Stipules small or lacking. Leaves 1"–5". Height to 20'. Flowers May–Aug. **SIMILAR SPECIES:** See Broadleaf Willow.

FLORIDA WILLOW *Salix floridana* Chapm.　　　**PL. 39**

Found scattered locally from s. Georgia to cen. Florida, this is a rather rare species. It grows only to small-tree size, mainly on *limestone* soils. The short-pointed leaves are up to 2" across, dark green, and hairless above and *white-hairy* beneath. Leaf teeth are small, and leaf bases are broadly rounded. Twigs brittle-based. Leaves 5"–6". Height to 20'. Flowers spring.

HOLLIES (Plates 40 and 41)

Hollies as a group are difficult to identify. No readily apparent characteristic occurs throughout. They are, however, our only trees with *spur branches* common and a *single* bundle scar. Minute black, pointed *stipules* are reported to be characteristic of hollies. These flank the leaf scars or, more often, are evident at the twig bases. They are difficult to see, however, and may drop off with age.

　　Leaf blades of most hollies are pointed, single-toothed, and wedge-based. Buds are commonly more numerous near tips of

the twigs. There may be more than 1 bud above each leaf scar. Hollies usually have 1 pair of bud scales, but sometimes 4–6 are present. The end bud is true. Holly bark is usually smooth. The small white or greenish male and female flowers may occur on different plants, being produced in the leaf angles or along the twigs. The several small nutlets in the fleshy red or dark fruits are either smooth or grooved on the outside surface, varying with the species.

Possumhaw Holly

The hollies are divided here into those with thin, deciduous (non-evergreen) leaves (Pl. 40) and those with thicker evergreen foliage (Pl. 41).

DECIDUOUS HOLLIES (PLATE 40)

Deciduous trees drop their leaves seasonally. These hollies have leaves rather thin and pointed at *both* ends (except Juneberry Holly). Leaves are alternate on fast-grown twigs and clustered on spur branches. Twigs are hairless with side buds often obscure. Fruits are red or orange, mostly short-stalked (under ½"), about ¼" in diameter, and shiny.

POSSUMHAW (DECIDUOUS) HOLLY   **PL. 40**
Ilex decidua Walt.

Shrubby or growing to small-tree size, this non-evergreen holly has variable narrow to egg-shaped leaves, generally thin but sometimes somewhat thickened. Leaf tips *blunt,* edges *wavy-toothed*, and undersides sometimes hairy. Twigs *stiff;* side buds somewhat *pointed.* Leaves 2"–3". Height 10'–20' (30'); diameter 2"–6" (10"). Flowers April–May. Fruits red, nutlets grooved. Sept.–March. Wet sites. **SIMILAR SPECIES:** Yaupon (Pl. 41) leaves are also wavy-edged, but smaller and evergreen. **REMARKS:** Fruits eaten by several birds, including bobwhite. Sometimes called Possumhaw, but note also Possumhaw Viburnum, p. 213.

LARGELEAF HOLLY *Ilex montana* Torr. & Gray   **PL. 40**

A tall shrub or tree with leaves *large* for a holly. Leaves narrow to elliptic, long-pointed, sharply toothed. Side twigs not especially stiff. Twigs green to reddish, lateral buds somewhat *pointed.* Leaves 4"–6½". Height 6'–20' (40'); diameter 2"–10" (12"). Flow-

POSSUMHAW HOLLY

LARGELEAF HOLLY

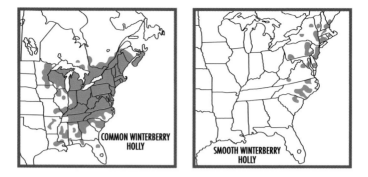

COMMON WINTERBERRY HOLLY

SMOOTH WINTERBERRY HOLLY

ers June. Fruits red, ½" in diameter, nutlets grooved, Oct.–Nov. and remaining into winter. Fertile soils. **SIMILAR SPECIES:** No other deciduous holly has leaves over 4" long or fruits ½" in diameter. **REMARKS:** An alternate name, Mountain Holly, should not be confused with the non-toothed Mountain-holly, *Nemopanthus mucronata* (L.) Trel, a shrub.

COMMON WINTERBERRY HOLLY   PL. 40
Ilex verticillata (L.) Gray

A shrub or small tree whose leaves are usually wide but vary from narrow to nearly circular. Leaves mostly *dull* above, with more or less *coarse* teeth; may be thin or thickish, somewhat *hairy* beneath, short-pointed, and with leaf bases *V-shaped.* Buds *blunt* with broadly pointed scales. Leaves 2"–4". Height to 25'. Flowers June–Aug. Fruits red, rarely yellow, nutlets *smooth,* Sept.–Oct. or later. Wet sites. **SIMILAR SPECIES:** The dull upper leaf surfaces, coarse

leaf teeth, and often hairy leaf undersides separate this species from the next. Large-leaf Holly has big leaves and fruits as well as grooved nutlets. **REMARKS:** Also called Black Alder (see *Alnus,* Pl. 35).

Common Winterberry Holly

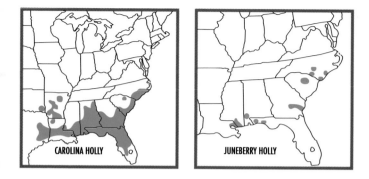

CAROLINA HOLLY   JUNEBERRY HOLLY

SMOOTH WINTERBERRY HOLLY   PL. 40
Ilex laevigata (Pursh) Gray
Similar to but less variable than the preceding; foliage may never-theless be narrow to elliptic. Leaves usually *shiny* above, *hairless* or nearly so beneath, and rather *fine-toothed.* Buds blunt but with *sharp-pointed* scales. Leaves ½"–4". Height to 20'. Flowers May–July. Fruits red, rarely yellow, nutlets smooth, Sept.–Jan. Wet sites.

CAROLINA HOLLY *Ilex ambigua* (Michx.) Torr.   PL. 40
Leaves *fine-toothed,* usually somewhat hairy beneath; bases usu-ally V-shaped. Twigs hairy or not. Buds pointed. Leaves 2"–3". Height to 20'. Flowers April–June. Fruits short-stalked, red, with grooved seeds, Aug.–Sept. Upland woods.

GEORGIA HOLLY *Ilex longipes* Chapm. ex Trel.   PL. 40
A large shrub or small tree with sharply toothed leaves similar to those of Carolina Holly but sometimes rather leathery. Side buds mostly pointed. Leaves ½"–4". Height to 20'. Flowers May–June. Fruits with slender stalks ½"–1" long, red, nutlets grooved, Oct. Southeastern states; streamsides and wooded slopes. **SIMILAR SPECIES:** All other deciduous hollies have short-stalked fruits except Juneberry Holly, which has rounded leaf bases.

JUNEBERRY HOLLY *Ilex amelanchier* M. A. Curtis   NOT ILLUS.
A rare small tree of southern swamps. The only deciduous holly with U-based leaves and long-stalked fruits. Foliage resembling that of some juneberries (Pl. 42). Leaves with fine teeth or none, somewhat oblong, and slightly hairy beneath. Buds pointed. Nut-lets grooved. Fruits dull red and on stalks ½"–⅞" long. Leaves 1"–3". Height to 15'. **SIMILAR SPECIES:** (1) Georgia Holly. (2) Juneber-

ries (p. 344) have U- or heart-shaped leaf bases and 3 (not 1) bundle scars per leaf scar.

EVERGREEN HOLLIES (PLATE 41)

These hollies have leathery leaves mostly with the edges smooth and rolled under or with a limited number of pointed teeth. The foliage of Yaupon Holly and some leaves of Tawnyberry Holly, however, are wavy-edged.

YAUPON HOLLY *Ilex vomitoria* Ait. **PL. 41**
A distinctive plant whose red-fruited branches are often gathered for decorative purposes. Evergreen leaves *small,* blunt-tipped, and *wavy-edged.* A strong medicinal "black drink" once brewed by Indians is believed to have been made from Yaupon leaves. The caffeine-containing dried leaves reportedly make a desirable tea. Leaves ½"–1½". Height 5'–15' (30'); diameter 2"–4" (12"). Flowers May–June. Fruits red, berrylike, nutlets grooved, Sept.–Oct. Sandy Coastal Plain. **SIMILAR SPECIES:** Possumhaw Holly (Pl. 40) has wavy-edged leaves, but these are thin and non-evergreen.

MYRTLE HOLLY *Ilex myrtifolia* Walt. **PL. 41**
Sometimes regarded as a variety of the next species, this southern shrub or small tree has small, pointed leaves only ½"–1½" long. Foliage is either *smooth-edged* or few-toothed above the middle. Side twigs stiff. Height to 25'. Flowers spring. Fruits red with grooved nutlets, late fall. Wet soils. **SIMILAR SPECIES:** (1) Yaupon Holly has small, wavy-edged leaves. (2) Dahoon Holly has larger leaves.

YAUPON HOLLY

MYRTLE HOLLY

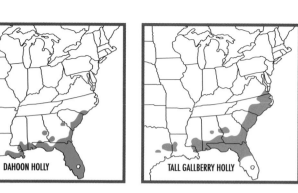

DAHOON HOLLY   TALL GALLBERRY HOLLY

DAHOON HOLLY *Ilex cassine* L.   PL. 41
Similar to Myrtle Holly but with leaves 2"–4" long. Twigs may be *hairy*. Flowers May–June. Fruits red or orange, seeds grooved. Oct.–Nov. or longer. Bottomlands.

TALL GALLBERRY HOLLY   PL. 41
Ilex coriacea (Pursh) Chapm.
A southern shrub or tree whose leaves may have sharp teeth near the pointed tips or may lack teeth. Leaves often marked with fine *black dots* beneath (use lens). Twigs hairless or sticky. Leaves 2"–3". Height to 20'. Flowers May. Fruits *black*, juicy, sweet; nutlets *smooth,* Sept.–Oct. Swamps and sandy soils. **REMARKS:** Called "tall" in contrast to the shrubby Low Gallberry Holly (*I. glabra*), which has blunt leaf tips and dry, bitter fruits.

AMERICAN HOLLY *Ilex opaca* Ait.   PL. 41
One of the most universally recognized eastern trees. The *prickly* evergreen leaves are distinctive. Leaf bases are U-shaped. Buds minute. Leaves 2"–4". Height 10'–40' (100'); diameter 6"–24" (48"). Flowers May–June. Fruits are *red,* rarely yellow, Aug.–June; nut-

American Holly

AMERICAN HOLLY

lets are grooved. Bottomlands. **REMARKS:** This is the Christmas holly. The collection of foliage sprays has become a sizable business, and because of over-harvesting, this decorative plant is less common than for-merly in some areas. Holly lumber, peculiarly ivory white, is in demand for special prod-ucts such as piano keys, ship models, and inlays. Though reported to be toxic to some animals, the fruits are eaten by numerous songbirds, bobwhite, and wild turkey. English Holly (*I. aquifoliium* L.) is often planted. Its leaves are only ¾"–1½" long and quite shiny.

TAWNYBERRY HOLLY *Ilex krugiana* Loes   **PL. 41**

A Caribbean holly found in this country *only* near Miami, Florida. Young plants may have toothed leaves; foliage of older ones *lacks* teeth but has *wavy* edges. Dropped leaves turn *black*. Leaves 3"–5". Fruits red, turning black. **SIMILAR SPECIES:** In this group, no other species has leaves that turn black, and only the prickly American Holly also has U-shaped leaf bases. The broken twigs and crushed leaves of West Indies Cherry (Pl. 46C) have the dis-tinctive "almond" odor of cherries.

MISCELLANEOUS TREES WITH ALTERNATE TOOTHED LEAVES (PLATE 42)

All of the following miscellaneous species have true end buds, except Sourwood.

JUNEBERRIES   **PL. 42**

These are shrubs or small trees with the leaves toothed and often blunt-tipped. The buds are pink to reddish, slender, with scales dark-tipped and usually somewhat twisted. Bundle scars are 3 per leaf scar. The trunk bark is usually tight and rather dark, with low, vertical, twisting ridges.

Known variously as serviceberries, shadbushes, shadblows, and sarvis, the amelanchiers make up one of the "difficult" groups within the rose family. Whether there are few or many species

Downy Juneberry

depends upon the botanist consulted. The species are quite variable, and some apparently hybridize. Marks of identification in winter have not been determined for all species. Fine-toothed species have 14–30 leaf teeth per inch, while coarse-toothed plants possess only 6–12 teeth per inch.

Though the group is composed mostly of shrubs, small-tree juneberries are often prominent in the forest understory. In the early spring, before the leaves develop, the terminal drooping white flower clusters are quite attractive. In the eastern states near tidal rivers, the name Shadbush alludes to the appearance of the flowers as the shad ascend coastal streams to spawn.

The small, several-seeded, applelike fruits of the juneberries are eaten by some people. Heavy crops are rare because numerous birds and mammals are quick to take advantage of any fruits that mature. When available, they are delicious in jams, jellies, and pies. They are eaten by many songbirds, wild turkeys, ruffed and sharptail grouse, bobwhites, mourning doves, striped skunks, red foxes, raccoons, black bears, red and gray squirrels, and chipmunks. Cottontail rabbits, beaver, whitetail deer, and moose browse the twigs.

Juneberry Holly (p. 341) has only 1 bundle scar per leaf scar.

DOWNY JUNEBERRY

Amelanchier arborea (Michx. f.) Fern

Leaves fine-toothed, usually *heart-shaped* at base, *short-pointed,* white-hairy beneath, at least along veins and leafstalk. Leaves 3"–5", with slender stalks more than ¼" long. Height 20'–40' (50'); diameter 8"–16" (24"). Flowers March–June. Fruits reddish purple, *dryish, not tasty,* June–Aug. Woods. **SIMILAR SPECIES:** (1) Bartram Juneberry is also fine-toothed and has short-pointed foliage but the leaves are short-stalked and the blossom clusters have few flowers. (2) Oblongleaf Juneberry has blunt-tipped foliage. **REMARKS:** Wood heavy, hard, close-grained. Sometimes used for tool handles.

BARTRAM JUNEBERRY

Amelanchier bartramiana (Tausch) M. J. Roem.

Rather than having flowers in long clusters, this species is alone among our juneberries in having small *groups of 1–4* flowers scattered in the leaf angles. Leaves are fine-toothed, *short-pointed,* and unlike those of other juneberries in that they have *short, stout* stalks (less than ¼" long) and leaf blades that tend to be pointed *at both ends.* Leaves 2"–3". Mostly shrubby, but reported as small trees in Nova Scotia. Flowers May–Aug. Fruits blackish, July–Sept. Northern woods. **SIMILAR SPECIES:** See Downy Juneberry.

OBLONGLEAF JUNEBERRY

Amelanchier canadensis (L.) Medic.

An upright tall shrub or small tree growing in clumps. Leaves *oblong, fine-toothed,* mostly *rounded* at tips, and toothed nearly to base. Although white-woolly when growing, leaves soon become nearly hairless. Leaves 1"–3". Height to 25'. Flowers March–June. Fruits blackish, June–July. Coastal Plain thickets, se. Que-

ROUNDLEAF JUNEBERRY

ALDERLEAF JUNEBERRY

bec to se. U.S. **SIMILAR SPECIES:** Downy Juneberry has larger leaves, mostly heart-shaped at the base and with pointed tips.

ROUNDLEAF JUNEBERRY PL. 42
Amelanchier sanguinea (Pursh) DC.

Leaves *coarse-toothed* and at least somewhat *pointed,* toothed to the base or nearly so, hairy beneath when young but soon hairless except for leafstalk; shape somewhat oblong to nearly circular. Plant clumped or not, *rarely* spreading by underground stems. Twigs reddish. Leaves 1"–3". Height to 9' (23'). Flowers May–June. Fruits purple, July–Aug. Woods. **SIMILAR SPECIES:** Also coarse-toothed, Alderleaf Juneberry is very similar but mainly western, though reported to occur locally in s. Ontario and se. Quebec. Its leaves are blunt- to square-tipped and it regularly spreads by underground runners.

ALDERLEAF JUNEBERRY NOT ILLUS.
Amelanchier alnifolia (Nutt.) Nutt.

A clumped upright shrub or small tree principally ranging from w. Minn. to n. Calif. and Alaska. Leaves *coarse-toothed,* often *square-tipped,* yellow-hairy when young but nearly hairless when mature; *nearly circular,* heart-shaped at base, and toothed mainly *above* the middle. This species normally spreads by *underground runners.* Leaves 1"–3". Height to 22'. Flowers May. Fruits, June–Aug. Thickets. **SIMILAR SPECIES:** See Roundleaf Juneberry. **REMARKS:** Also known as Western Serviceberry and Saskatoon Juneberry.

MOUNTAIN PEPPERBUSH *Clethra acuminata* Michx. PL. 42

A shrub or tree of southern mountains, with usually *hairy* twigs, a *large* true end bud with loose or shedding hairy outer scales as long as the bud, and *long-pointed,* fine-toothed leaves. Bundle

MOUNTAIN PEPPERBUSH

SOURWOOD

CAROLINA SILVERBELL

LITTLE SILVERBELL

scar 1, oval, protruding. Outer bark red-brown, separating into loose strips. Leaves 3"–6". Height to 18'. Flowers small, white, bell-like, at twig ends in dense, slender spikes that are *not* one-sided, July–Aug. Fruits small, dry, *three-parted* capsules. Mountain woods. **SIMILAR SPECIES:** Pepperbushes are the only plants with 1 bundle scar that have large end buds (much bigger than side buds) whose outer scales are as long as the buds. They are the only upright non-evergreen, heathlike plants with dry fruits and a true end bud that also have hairy twigs. Leaves of this species larger and more long-pointed than those of the shrubby Coast Pepperbush (C. *alnifolia* L.).

SOURWOOD *Oxydendrum arboreum* (L.) DC.   **PL. 42**
The only full-sized tree with long, slender, dry fruit clusters. Leaves fine-toothed, *narrow* to egg-shaped, with a sour taste and often somewhat leathery texture. Twigs hairless. Buds small; end bud *false*. Bundle scar single and U-shaped. Bark dark and furrowed. Leaves 4"–8". Height 20'–50' (70'); diameter 18"–20". Flowers small, white, bell-like, in slim, drooping, *one-sided clusters* at twig ends, June–July. Fruits small, dry capsules, *five-parted*. Rich woods. **SIMILAR SPECIES:** The only tall non-evergreen tree with 1 bundle scar and toothed simple leaves. Sourgum (Pl. 44), with a similar common name, has leaves without teeth and chambered pith. **REMARKS:** Highly ornamental at all seasons but especially so when in flower or in crimson autumn color. Deer eat twigs.

CAROLINA SILVERBELL *Halesia carolina* L.   **PL. 42**
A southeastern tree with beautiful bell-shaped white blossoms. Leaves toothed, egg-shaped, somewhat hairy beneath. Twigs hairless to hairy. Bundle scar 1, more or less U-shaped. Buds reddish, *sharp*, and often one above the other; pith *chambered*. Flowers

TWO-WING SILVERBELL

LOBLOLLY-BAY

produced along the twigs; *showy*, hanging, with 4 *shallowly notched* petals, each ½"–1" long. Fruits dry, *broadly four-winged*, 1"–2". Young bark with pale *vertical streaks*. Leaves 2"–7". Height 10'–20' (90'); diameter 6"–12" (3'). Hilly woods. **SIMILAR SPECIES:** (1) Sweetleaf (Pl. 43) and (2) Persimmon (Pl. 44) also have chambered pith and single bundle scars, but they have dark buds. Sweetleaf has few teeth, and Persimmon has none. See (3) Little Silverbell. **REMARKS:** In May, Carolina Silverbell is in full bloom in Great Smoky Mountains National Park and Blue Ridge Parkway, Va. and N.C.

LITTLE SILVERBELL *Halesia parviflora* Michx.   **NOT ILLUS.**
Similar to the Carolina Silverbell but with leaves 2"–4", buds more *blunt*, pith less definitely chambered, flower petals *shorter* (¼"–½" long), and fruits about 1" long, *narrowly* four-winged. Height to 30'. Coastal Plain woods. **SIMILAR SPECIES:** See (1) Carolina and (2) Two-wing silverbells.

TWO-WING SILVERBELL *Halesia diptera* Ellis   **PL. 42**
Like the other silverbells, but leaves 3"–5", flower petals *deeply lobed*, and fruits 1¼"–2" long, with only 2 wings. Wet woods.

LOBLOLLY-BAY *Gordonia lasianthus* (L.) Ellis   **PL. 42**
A small *evergreen* tree of the southeastern Coastal Plain with large, dark, shiny, *leathery, wedge-based* leaves and large *showy* blossoms. Leafstalks may be winged near the leaf base. Buds broad-based and *hairy;* bundle scar single. Leaves 3"–6". Height to 65'. Flowers white, fragrant, 2"–3" across, with stalks 1"–3" long, at the leaf junctions, July–Sept. Fruits dry, hairy, 5-parted, egg-shaped capsules. Sept.–Oct. Wet woods. **SIMILAR SPECIES:** Relatively few broadleaf evergreen trees have toothed leaves. Over

most of its range, the large, toothed, leathery leaves of this species are distinctive. **REMARKS:** Franklinia, apparently surviving only in gardens, has thin deciduous leaves, shorter leaf and flower stalks, and spherical fruits. Like Franklinia and the stewartias, Loblolly-bay is a member of the tea family. About a dozen other members of the genus *Gordonia* occur in se. Asia. It is presumed that this species became isolated from its relatives in earlier geologic times.

FRANKLINIA *Franklinia alatamaha* Bartr. ex Marsh.   **NOT ILLUS.**
Evidently extinct in the wild. Similar to Loblolly-bay but with leaves that are *thin*, neither leathery nor evergreen, and with flower stalks *less than* ¾" long. Flowers white, in leaf angles, 3"–3¾" in diameter, summer. **REMARKS:** Found along the Altamaha River in coastal se. Georgia in 1765, the plant has not been seen in the wild since 1790 (Elias 1980; Little 1980). Thought by some to have been exterminated when the original plants were transplanted, the species still survives in cultivation. Perhaps wild specimens will be rediscovered.

VIRGINIA STEWARTIA (SILKY CAMELLIA)   **PL. 42**
Stewartia malachodendron L.
A shrub or tree with thin, elliptic leaves, soft-hairy beneath, with *U-shaped* bases and somewhat winged leafstalks. Buds slender, less than ⅛" long, *hairless* to slightly hairy. Twigs may be fine-hairy. Trunk bark smooth, peeling, *much mottled.* Leaves 2"–4". Height to 15'. Flowers white, 2"–3" across, at junctions of the leaves, June. Fruits ½" long, dry, 5- to 10-seeded, round, *short-pointed.* Moist forests. **SIMILAR SPECIES:** Only a few trees have toothed leaves, showy blossoms, and winged leafstalks. (1) Loblolly-bay leaves are thick and leathery. (2) Mountain Stewartia

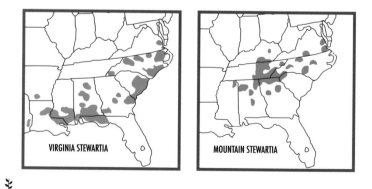

VIRGINIA STEWARTIA   MOUNTAIN STEWARTIA

has non-mottled trunk bark, larger leaves, and buds that are more hairy and more hidden by enfolding leafstalk wings. The (3) snowbells (Pl. 43) have buds without scales. **REMARKS:** Closely related to cultivated camellias.

MOUNTAIN STEWARTIA
(MOUNTAIN CAMELLIA)   *Stewartia ovata* (Cav.) Weath.

Similar to Virginia Stewartia, but leaves 5"–6" long; buds *hairy*, more than ⅛" long; trunk bark dark, *smooth*; fruits *long-pointed*. Flowers May–Aug. Bottomland forests.

MISCELLANEOUS TREES WITH ALTERNATE LEAVES SOMETIMES TOOTHED (PLATE 43)

BAYBERRIES

Of the several plants of this group, the first four are related species of the bayberry or waxmyrtle family. These species are among the few outside the several pea-related (legume) families that enrich the soil through nitrogen-fixing bacteria contained in root nodules. The crushed foliage has a pleasant aroma. The short-stalked leaves and usually the twigs are marked with tiny yellow resin dots. The dots, ordinarily not visible except when magnified, are good identification marks. End bud true; bundle scars 3. The flowers and whitish, waxy fruits are small and clustered in short, stout catkins. (Odorless Bayberry of Pl. 46 lacks resin dots and is not aromatic.)

SOUTHERN BAYBERRY   *Myrica cerifera* L.

An *evergreen southern* shrub or tree. Leaves *narrow*, leathery, *wedge-based*, toothed or not toward the sometimes blunt tip, hairless, with resin dots on *both* surfaces and edges often rolled

SOUTHERN BAYBERRY

EVERGREEN BAYBERRY

ALTERNATE SIMPLE LEAVES   **351**

under. Twigs sparsely hairy or hairless. Buds yellowish and globular. Leaves 2"–3" long, to ½" wide. Height 10'–30' (40'); diameter 3"–10" (12"). Flowers April–June. Fruits ⅛", wax-covered nuts, Aug.–Oct. Wet sandy soils. **SIMILAR SPECIES:** (1) Evergreen and (2) Northern bayberries have resin dots numerous only on the leaf undersides. **REMARKS:** The wax is collected for making scented candles. A pound of nutlets immersed in hot water yields 4 ounces of wax. The root bark is reported to be astringent and emetic. Fruits are eaten by many birds, including bobwhite and wild turkey. Also known as Common Waxmyrtle.

EVERGREEN (BLACK) BAYBERRY   PL. 43
Myrica heterophylla Raf.
    Similar to Southern Bayberry but leaves dull, 1"–2" wide, somewhat *leathery* with edges often rolled under, and resin dots almost entirely on leaf *undersides*. Twigs *black-hairy*. Leaves 2"–5". Height to 15'. Flowers April–June. Fruits *hairless*, waxy, ⅛"–³⁄₁₆", Aug.–Oct. Coastal Plain wet soils.

NORTHERN BAYBERRY   *Myrica pensylvanica* Mirbel   PL. 43
    Non-evergreen, with egg-shaped, shiny, *thin* leaves *to* 1" wide. Resin dots few or lacking on the often somewhat hairy upper sur-

Northern Bayberry

NORTHERN BAYBERRY

face. Twigs *gray-hairy*; buds whitish. Leaves 1"–5". Height to 15'; diameter to 6". Flowers May–July. Fruits hairy, becoming wax-covered, more than ¾₆" across. June–April. Damp sandy soils. **SIMILAR SPECIES:** (1) Southern and (2) Evergreen bayberries have more leathery, evergreen leaves. The former has resin dots on both leaf surfaces. **REMARKS:** Many songbirds (notably myrtle warbler) and also ruffed grouse, bobwhite, and pheasant eat the fruits.

CAROLINA BUCKTHORN *Rhamnus caroliniana* Walt.   PL. 43

This tree and the next species are our only trees with alternate simple leaves, 3 bundle scars, and *naked buds that are not stalked.* This species taller. Leaves prominently parallel-veined, either few-toothed or with rounded teeth, and either hairless or hairy beneath. End bud false. Twigs *fine-hairy.* Leaves 2"–6". Height to 40'. Flowers on *branched* stalks at the leaf angles, tiny, greenish, May–June. Fruits red to black, fleshy, 3-*seeded*, Aug.–Oct. Open fertile sites. **SIMILAR SPECIES:** (1) Snowbells, also without bud scales, have only 1 bundle scar. (2) Common Buckthorn (Pl. 12) has thorny twig ends, opposite leaves, and scaly buds. See (3) European Buckthorn and (4) Witch-hazel (Pl. 32).

EUROPEAN BUCKTHORN *Rhamnus frangula* L.   NOT ILLUS.

Escaped from cultivation. Similar to Carolina Buckthorn but not as tall. Leaves hairy beneath and *rarely toothed.* Twigs hairy. Flowers/fruits on individual unbranched stalks. Leaves 1"–3". Height to 20'. Flowers pale yellow, May–July. Fruits black, 2-*seeded.* Fencerows. Ne. U.S. and se. Canada.

BIGLEAF SNOWBELL *Styrax grandifolius* Ait.   PL. 43

A shrub or small tree with few-toothed, egg-shaped leaves, *white-hairy* beneath. Buds with *no* scales, blunt and brown-hairy, often

CAROLINA BUCKTHORN

BIGLEAF SNOWBELL

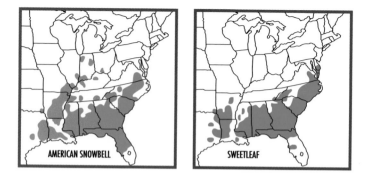

AMERICAN SNOWBELL   SWEETLEAF

one above the other; end bud false. Bundle scar *single*, sometimes somewhat broken. Twigs very *hairy* or scaly. Leaves 2"–8". Height to 40'. Flowers white, showy, in 2"–6" elongate clusters at twig ends. Fruits dry, one-seeded, Sept.–Oct. Rich woods. **SIMILAR SPECIES:** Only Snowbells have naked buds and single bundle scars. See (1) American Snowbell and (2) Carolina Buckthorn.

AMERICAN SNOWBELL *Styrax americanus* Lam. **NOT ILLUS.**
Similar to Bigleaf Snowbell but more shrubby and with *smaller* leaves that are nearly *hairless*. Twigs also *hairless* or nearly so. Leaves 1"–4". Height to 15'. Flowers in 1"–2" clusters.

SWEETLEAF *Symplocos tinctoria* (L.) L'Her. **PL. 43**
A large shrub or small tree mainly of the Coastal Plain. Leaves narrow to egg-shaped, often with yellowish midribs and hairy beneath, usually at least partially toothed. Foliage semileathery, often remaining until spring; *sweet* to the taste. Buds dark with several scales. Pith *chambered*. Bark grayish smooth, often with shallow vertical cracks. Leaves 3"–7". Height to 40'; diameter to 10". Flowers yellow, April–May. Fruits fleshy but becoming dry, reddish, single-seeded, about ⅜", clustered in leaf angles, Aug.–Sept. Damp places. **SIMILAR SPECIES:** Of species with chambered pith and single bundle scars, (1) the silverbells (Pl. 42) have reddish buds, while (2) the dark buds of Persimmon (Pl. 44) have only 2 scales.

WATER TUPELO *Nyssa aquatica* L. **PL. 43**
Leaves pointed, frequently with 1–3 or more large teeth, sometimes somewhat hairy beneath; rarely heart-shaped at base. Leafstalks 1"–3" long. Twigs *hairless* or nearly so. Pith tends to be *chambered*, with cross-plates at intervals. Buds broad and pressed

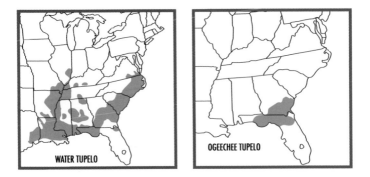

WATER TUPELO

OGEECHEE TUPELO

against twigs; end bud true. Bundle scars 3. In swamps, the trunk base is often swollen. Leaves 4"–13". Height to 100'; diameter to 4'. Flowers greenish, April–May. Fruits single, near the twig ends, more than 1" long, thinly fleshy, dark *purple* with a single ribbed stone. Coastal Plain swamps. **SIMILAR SPECIES:** (1) Ogeechee Tupelo has blunt leaves, velvety twigs, and red fruits. (2) Sourgum (Black Tupelo) has leaves not toothed, twigs not hairy, buds not pressed against the twigs, and fruits in 2's and 3's (see Pl. 44).

OGEECHEE TUPELO *Nyssa ogeche* Bartr. ex Marsh. **NOT ILLUS.**
Like Water Tupelo but with leaves often narrow and usually blunt-tipped. Twigs *velvety-hairy,* and fruits *red* with a narrowly winged stone. Leaves 3"–6" with stalks ½"–1" long. Height to 60'. Flowers January–May. Coastal Plain swamps.

DOMESTIC APPLE *Malus (Pyrus) sylvestris* (L.) Mill. **PL. 43**
The apple and pear are the only species on this plate that usually have short *spur branches* of crowded leaves and leaf scars. Apple is a *round-topped* small tree. Leaves egg-shaped, more or less *round-toothed,* usually somewhat white- or *gray-hairy* beneath; may be heart-shaped at base. Twigs short, stiff, sometimes with thorny tips; usually somewhat *hairy.* Leaf scars somewhat raised; short lines leading downward at sides. Buds usually blunt and woolly; end bud true. Bundle scars 3. Bark scaly and brownish. Leaves 1"–4". Height 20'–30' (50'); diameter 6"–18". Flowers white or pinkish, clustered on spur branches, April–June. Fruits more than 1" across, Sept.–Nov. Hedgerows and old farms, south to Georgia and Missouri. **SIMILAR SPECIES:** (1) The 3 crabapples (Pl. 23) are almost always thorny, with pointed leaf teeth and buds. (2) The Domestic Pear is mostly hairless, more often thorny, and usually has long, not round, fruits, which contain grit cells. A pear

tree has 1 or several strong upright branches, giving the tree a narrowly pointed silhouette rather than the round-topped crown shape of the apple. In winter, the apple has hairier twigs, blunter buds, and leaf scars more raised than the pear. **REMARKS:** The exact origin of the apple is lost in antiquity, but the etymology of the name indicates that it originated in the w. Himalayas and traveled westward by way of n. Persia, Asia Minor, the Caucasus, and the Mediterranean countries. The apple of the Bible is believed to have been not our northern fruit but the apricot, still common in the Holy Land. The Domestic Apple persisting in old orchards or locally gone wild is an important food of deer, pheasant, mourning dove, gray fox, and many other animals. Also called *Pyrus malus* L. and *Malus pumila* Mill.

DOMESTIC PEAR *Pyrus communis* L.　　　　　　　　PL. 43
Similar to Domestic Apple but usually with several strong upright branches, making a *narrow-topped* tree. Thorns sometimes present. Leaves and twigs nearly *hairless*. Fruits *elongate, fleshy,* and containing *grit* cells. Leaves 1"–3". Height 20'–35' (60'); diameter 6"–15". Flowers white, early spring. Fruits green, autumn. Hedgerows and abandoned farms throughout our area.

CAROLINA LAURELCHERRY　　　　　　　　　　　　　PL. 43
Prunus caroliniana (Mill.) Ait.
A southern *evergreen* cherry whose shiny, *leathery* leaves sometimes bear a few sharp teeth. Foliage and twigs *hairless*. Buds reddish brown, sharp-pointed, and *hairless*; bundle scars 3. Leaves 2"–5". Height to 40'. Flowers white, in slender clusters 1"–2" long at the leaf angles, March–April. Fruits single-seeded, ½"

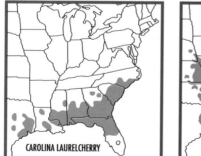

CAROLINA LAURELCHERRY

COMMON PAWPAW

across, nearly spherical, dry, *black,* inedible, clustered in leaf angles, usually remaining all winter. Moist lowlands. **SIMILAR SPECIES:** (1) When leaf teeth are present, this leathery-leaved species can be separated from similar hollies (Pl. 41) by the 3 bundle scars (rather than 1) and the single-seeded fruit. Otherwise, it may resemble (2) plants of Pl. 46. Those of the same leaf length differ in flowers and fruits and have only a single bundle scar. (3) Cyrilla and (4) Odorless Bayberry also have leaves wider toward the tip; (5) crushed Redbay foliage is spicy. In extreme s. Fla., also see (6) West Indies Laurel cherry (Pl. F-46C). **REMARKS:** Sometimes used in hedges and other landscape plantings. Partially wilted foliage, like that of other cherries, contains hydrocyanic acid and may poison livestock.

GEIGER-TREE *Cordia sebestena* L. **NOT ILLUS.**
A shrub or small tree of peninsular and tropical Florida. Leaves *evergreen, broad* (2"–4"), more or less heart-shaped, *sandpaper-rough* above, usually hairy beneath, with widely spaced teeth or none. Twigs hairy; buds without scales. Leaves 4"–6". Height to 30'; diameter to 6". Flowers *orange-red,* clustered at twig ends, tubular, to 1¼" across, all year. Fruits 1"–2" long, white, somewhat pointed, with a large seed. Poor soils, seashores. **REMARKS:** Reportedly named after John Geiger, an early ship captain in the Florida Keys. Sometimes planted as an ornamental.

TREES WITH LEAVES NEITHER TOOTHED NOR EVERGREEN (Plate 44)

The foliage of Persimmon and Sourgum may occasionally be somewhat leathery but not to the extent seen in the evergreen species of Pl. 46. Except for Persimmon, the end bud is true.

COMMON (TALL) PAWPAW *Asimina triloba* (L.) Dunal **PL. 44**
A shrub or small tree with *large, toothless* leaves and a long, *naked, deep brown-hairy* or reddish-hairy end bud. Side buds shorter, also hairy. Twigs and young leaves often hairy, like buds. Bundle scars 5–7. Pith usually, but not always, partitioned by transverse woody diaphragms. Bark dark, smooth or somewhat broken. Leaves 6"–12". Height 6'–20' (40'). Flowers on the previous year's growth, purplish, more than 1" across, April–May. Fruits large, fleshy, green, *somewhat bananalike,* seeds flattened, Aug.–Oct. Bottomlands. **SIMILAR SPECIES:** Dark naked end bud plus (usually) chambered pith are unique among plants with more than 3 bundle scars. (1) Magnolias (Pl. 45) have similar leaves, but twigs are encircled by stipule scars at each leaf scar. (2) See

next species. **REMARKS:** A northern representative of the tropical custard-apple family. Fully ripened fruits difficult to find, since they are eaten by opposum, squirrels, raccoon, foxes, etc. People may enjoy them raw or made into desserts.

SMALLFLOWER (DWARF) PAWPAW   NOT ILLUS.
Asimina parviflora (Michx.) Dunal
Similar to Common Pawpaw but with leaves less than 7" long, flowers less than 1" across, seeds plump. Dry woods, southeastern states.

AMERICAN SMOKETREE   *Cotinus obovatus* Raf.   PL. 44
One of the rarest American trees, this relative of the sumacs is found in only a few areas (see range map). Leaves wide, usually *blunt-tipped*; side buds small, with 2–4 scales, and long-pointed. Wood *yellow* and odorous, sap gummy. Bundle scars 3. Name alludes to *foot-long* hazy end sprays of small feathery sterile flowers that resemble puffs of smoke. Leaves 3"–6". Height 6'–25' (35'); diameter 1"–12" (14"). Flowers greenish yellow, April–May. Fruits June–Sept. Dry slopes. Foliage becomes a brilliant red in autumn. European Smoketree (*C. coggygria* Scop.) is used in landscaping.

ALTERNATE-LEAF DOGWOOD   PL. 44
Cornus alternifolia L. f.
Among the dogwoods (see Pl. 14), this small tree or shrub is the only species that does not have opposite leaves or raised twig leaf scars. Leaf veins tend to *follow leaf edges*. Leaves long-stalked, abruptly tipped, sometimes crowded (some may be opposite or whorled) toward tips of hairless, *greenish yellow* twigs. Pith white.

AMERICAN SMOKETREE

ALTERNATE-LEAF DOGWOOD

Buds have only 2 scales. Leaf scars narrow and raised; bundle scars 3. Leaves 2"–5". Height to 25'. Flowers May–July. Fruits small, fleshy, clustered at twig ends, blue-black with red stems, and with 1–2 somewhat rounded seeds, July–Sept. Streambanks and pondsides. **REMARKS:** Fruits eaten by many birds, including ruffed grouse. Twigs are browsed by deer and rabbits.

CORKWOOD *Leitneria floridana* Chapm. **PL. 44**

A shrub or small tree related to poplars and other catkin-bearing plants but peculiar enough to be classified in a family by itself. Leaves narrow to elliptic, gray-hairy beneath. Twigs *hairy*. End buds *clustered;* much larger than some side ones. Bark smooth and, as in many other swamp trees, trunk swollen at base. Wood more buoyant than cork; local fishermen are said to use Corkwood blocks for net floats. Leaves 3"–6". Height to 25'. Flowers on the previous year's growth, March. Fruits leathery, ½"–1", 1-seeded, brown, May. **SIMILAR SPECIES:** Its *swamp* habitat, swollen trunk base, and 3 bundle scars separate this species from the several oaks that also have clustered end buds and smooth-edged leaves (Pl. 31). **REMARKS:** Reportedly, a yellow dye can be made from the wood.

COMMON PERSIMMON *Diospyros virginiana* L. **PL. 44**

A tree with distinctive *dark thick* bark, typically broken into *small, squarish blocks.* Leaves somewhat thickened, egg-shaped. Twigs typically hairless. Buds *very dark with 2 overlapping scales.* End bud *false.* Pith solid or sometimes divided into chambers by *weak* partitions. Bundle scar 1. Leaves 2"–5". Height 30'–50' (130'); diameter 10"–12" (7'). Flowers yellowish, in the leaf angles, May–June. Fruits are slightly larger than cultivated cherries,

CORKWOOD

COMMON PERSIMMON

Bark of Common Persimmon

orange-colored, with several large, flat seeds, edible when ripe, Aug.–Oct. or later. Uplands. **SIMILAR SPECIES:** No other tree has the combination of toothless leaves, dark buds, and regularly cracked bark. Bark of (1) blackhaw viburnums (Pl. 12) and Flowering Dogwood (Pl. 14) is similar, but those plants have opposite leaves. (2) Sweetleaf (Pl. 43) has chambered pith and dark bark, but there are more than 2 bud scales, and some leaves may bear teeth. (3) See Sourgum, below. **REMARKS:** The green fruit is astringent and causes the mouth to "pucker" for some time after being tasted. Cool, ripe persimmons that are soft and fully colored, however, are delicious. They are eaten by nearly all birds and mammals, from songbirds to turkeys and from dogs to deer. The Common Persimmon, a member of the ebony family, has strong, heavy, close-grained wood that has occasionally been used for shoe lasts and shuttles.

SOURGUM *Nyssa sylvatica* Marsh. **PL. 44**
A tree with dark, deeply *checkered* bark. Leaves shiny, hairless or nearly so, egg-shaped to elliptic (less commonly roundish), often somewhat leathery; scarlet in autumn. Pith *distinctly chambered.* Spur branches common. Brown buds stand out from twigs; bud scales several. Bundle scars 3. In southern swamps, trunks growing in water are swollen at base. Leaves 3"–6". Height 40'–60' (125'); diameter 1'–2' (5'). Flowers greenish, April–June. Fruits in 2's and 3's along the twigs, fleshy, less than ¾", bluish, single-seeded, Aug.–Oct. **SIMILAR SPECIES:** (1) Plain foliage and checkered bark are most like Persimmon, but chambered pith rather than

Bark of Sourgum

the usually solid pith, triple rather than single bundle scars, and lowland rather than upland habitat characterize this species. (2) Water Tupelo has leaves toothed, twigs hairy, buds pressed against the twigs, and fruits single (see Pl. 43). Sourwood (Pl. 42) should not be confused because of the similarity of names. It has toothed leaves and solid pith. (3) Also see Persimmon (above). **REMARKS:** Lumber of Sourgum, also called Black Gum or Black Tupelo, is useful for furniture, boxes, crates, veneer, and paper pulp. Fleshy bitter fruits are relished by black bear and by over 30 species of birds, including ruffed grouse, prairie chicken, pheasant, and wild turkey.

CRAPEMYRTLE *Lagerstroemia indica* L.   **PL. 44**

An Asiatic plant possibly not spreading to grow wild but commonly planted in southern towns and found around abandoned homesites. Leaves and buds are in both alternate and opposite patterns, with the alternate arrangement predominant on the upper branches. Leaves short-stalked and pointed or somewhat rounded. Twigs *four-lined* or four-winged; buds with 2 scales; bundle scar 1. Bark flakes to leave smooth greenish surface; trunk has vertical fluted ridges. Leaves 1"–3". Height to 35'. Flowers *showy*, pink or white, in terminal clusters. Fruits dry, ½" capsules.

Crapemyrtle

ELLIOTTIA   *Elliottia racemosa* Muhl. ex Ell.   **PL. 44**
   Very *rare* in e. Georgia (and formerly in adjacent S. Carolina), this
   member of the heath (rhododendron) family also has elliptical
   leaves. Buds with 2–3 scales; bundle scar 1. Leaves 2"–6". Height
   to 30'. Flowers in end clusters, white, August. Fruits small, dry,
   nearly spherical capsules. Coastal Plain dry ridges. **REMARKS:**
   Reported to be so scarce that cross-pollination between plants is
   unlikely. Plant patches may spread only through rootstock
   growth.

MAGNOLIAS (PLATE 45)

   The magnolias are distinctly marked plants of tropical appearance and with southern and Appalachian affinities. Several
   species occur in Great Smoky Mountains National Park, N.C.-
   Tenn. The ranges of a number extend into the northern states,
   however, especially in the mountains. The leaves are smooth-
   edged and often *large*; twigs are *ringed* by stipule scars, buds are
   covered by a *single* scale; the true end bud is especially large, and
   bundle scars are many. The leaf scars are crescent-shaped (but U-
   shaped in Cucumber Magnolia). Some have pith chambered; sev-

eral have leaves/buds crowded near the twig tips. Magnolias are frequently cultivated for their large leaves and showy terminal white flowers. Their large, brownish, conelike fruit clusters are frequently ornamental when ripe. They release bright red seeds on silky threads from many slitlike openings.

Among deciduous (non-evergreen) trees, only the magnolias, Sycamore, and Tuliptree have ringed twigs and more than 3 bundle scars per leaf scar. Sycamore (Pl. 25) has peculiar mottled bark as well as buds surrounded by leaf scars; Tuliptree (Pl. 25) has notched leaves, buds spicy when crushed, and chambered pith; it is a member of the magnolia family. Beech (Pl. 32) has ringed twigs, but the leaves are toothed and bundle scars are only 3. Common Pawpaw and other plants (Pl. 44) have foliage much like the magnolias but lack stipular rings. In peninsular and s. Florida, see also Pl. F-46A to F-46D.

EVERGREEN (SOUTHERN) MAGNOLIA   PL. 45
Magnolia grandiflora L.

A *leathery-leaved* evergreen tree whose thick foliage is *shiny* above and *rusty-hairy* beneath. Leaves are *rounded* at the base and not crowded at the twig tips. Twigs and buds *rusty-hairy;* end bud is less than 1 " long. Pith *chambered.* Leaves 6"–8". Height 60'–80'; diameter 2'–3'. Flowers 6"–8" across, white, fragrant, May–June. Cones 3"–4", egg-shaped, Sept.–Oct. Moist forests. **SIMILAR SPECIES:** See Sweetbay Magnolia. **REMARKS:** Frequently planted in parks and gardens.

SWEETBAY MAGNOLIA *Magnolia virginiana* L.   PL. 45

A large shrub or small tree with thin but *somewhat leathery,* elliptic leaves that may be evergreen in the South. Leaf bases mostly V-shaped. Foliage *spicy* when crushed, *hairless and whitish beneath.* End bud green, *hairy,* and less than 1 " long; twigs often hairless. Pith *chambered.* Leaves 4"–6". Height to 50' (rarely 70'); diameter to 2' (rarely 3'). Flowers 2"–2½", white, fragrant,

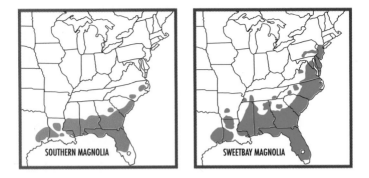

SOUTHERN MAGNOLIA

SWEETBAY MAGNOLIA

May–July. Cones 1"–2", egg-shaped, Sept.–Oct. Wet soils. **SIMILAR SPECIES:** Only Evergreen Magnolia also has both leathery leaves and chambered pith. Its leaf undersides are brown, however, and the crushed foliage is not spicy-scented.

CUCUMBER MAGNOLIA *Magnolia acuminata* (L.) L.   **PL. 45**
A hardy magnolia of tree size with large, *thin,* egg-shaped leaves that are *green, pale,* slightly hairy beneath, *U-shaped* at base, and not crowded at the twig tips. Twigs brown, hairless; pith *not* chambered. Buds *hairy;* end bud whitish green and up to ¾" long; leaf scars *U-shaped.* Trunk bark dark and furrowed, much like that of ashes. Leaves 4"–10". Height 40'–70' (90'); diameter 1'–2' (3'). Flowers green or green and yellow, with unpleasant odor at close range, May–June. Cones dark red, and cucumberlike when young, 2"–3", Aug.–Oct. Moist soils. **SIMILAR SPECIES:** Among non-evergreen magnolias, (1) Bigleaf and (2) Ashe Magnolia also have

hairy buds, but leaves and end buds are larger, and leaves are crowded at the twig tips. (3) Sweetbay Magnolia, also with end bud small and hairy, has spicy, more or less evergreen foliage and chambered pith. **REMARKS:** Wood is of some value for interiors and cabinetmaking. Twigs eaten by deer.

Cucumber Magnolia

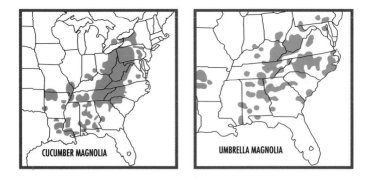

CUCUMBER MAGNOLIA

UMBRELLA MAGNOLIA

UMBRELLA MAGNOLIA *Magnolia tripetala* (L.)   **PL. 45**
Similar to Cucumber Magnolia but with leaves larger and *crowded* at twig tips. Leaf bases *V-shaped.* End bud *hairless,* purplish, ¾"–1⅛" long. Twigs *stout;* pith *not* chambered. Trunk bark *brown* and smooth. Leaves 10"–24". Height 20'–30' (40'); diameter 10"–12" (18"). Flowers 7"–10", white, odor *not* pleasant, May. Fruits candle-shaped, 3"–4", Sept.–Oct. Moist mountain forests.

EARLEAF MAGNOLIA *Magnolia fraseri* Walt.   **PL. 45**
The only magnolia with leaf bases *deeply "ear-lobed."* Leaves usually large and *crowded* near twig tips. Leafstalks often *more than* 3" long. Leaves, buds, and slender twigs *hairless.* Purplish end buds 1½"–2" long. Pith often *faintly* chambered. Trunk bark smooth, *gray.* Leaves 8"–15". Height 20'–30' (40'); diameter 10"–12" (18"). Flowers 8"–10" across, white, fragrant, May. Fruits cylindrical, 3"–4", Sept.–Oct. Moist mountain forests. Nice floral displays in May along Blue Ridge Parkway, Va.-N.C.

EARLEAF MAGNOLIA

PYRAMID MAGNOLIA

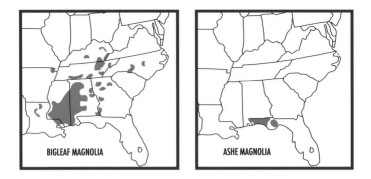

BIGLEAF MAGNOLIA   ASHE MAGNOLIA

PYRAMID MAGNOLIA *Magnolia pyramidata* Bartr.　**NOT ILLUS.**
Similar to Earleaf Magnolia but more southern, with leaves
smaller, less deeply "ear-lobed," and leafstalks *less than* 3" long.
Leaves 5"–9". Height 30'–40'; diameter 1'. Flowers 4", white,
spring. Fruits 1½"–2½", fall. Moist Coastal Plain soils.

BIGLEAF MAGNOLIA *Magnolia macrophylla* Michx.　**PL. 45**
A small southern tree with the *largest* simple leaves of any tree
north of the tropics. Leaves often clustered near twig tips; *white
and hairy* beneath, bases often shallowly "ear-lobed." Twigs and
buds greenish, *hairy;* end bud 1½"–2"; pith not chambered. Trunk
bark smooth, grayish. Leaves 20"–30". Height 20'–50' (100');
diameter 12"–24" (30"). Flowers white with purple spots, often
12" across, fragrant, May–June. Fruits *egg-shaped,* reddish,
2"–3", Sept.–Oct. Moist forested slopes; uncommon. **SIMILAR
SPECIES:** See Ashe Magnolia.

ASHE MAGNOLIA *Magnolia ashei* Weatherby　**NOT ILLUS.**
Sometimes regarded only as a variety of Bigleaf Magnolia. Foliage
and blossoms smaller. Rare and local in nw. Florida. Leaves
14"–22". Height to 30', often shrubby. Fruiting cones 2"–3",
candle-shaped. Upland slopes.

TREES WITH LEATHERY EVERGREEN LEAVES MOSTLY NOT TOOTHED (PLATE 46)

These are mainly southern plants—only Mountain Laurel and
the rhododendrons extend their ranges along the Appalachians
into the North. Myrtle and Virginia Live oaks (Pl. 31) plus several
trees on Pls. 43 and 45 may also have evergreen leaves not

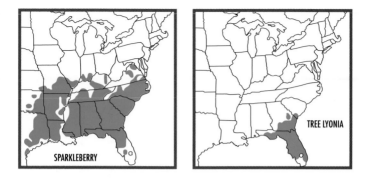

SPARKLEBERRY

TREE LYONIA

toothed. In Florida, many tropical and semitropical trees have foliage of this type; see Tawnyberry Holly (Pl. 41) and Pls. F-46A to F-46D.

SPARKLEBERRY (FARKLEBERRY)   PL. 46
Vaccinium arboreum Marsh.

Shrubby or a small crooked tree, a member of the blueberry genus. Leaves elliptic, 1"–2" long, *short-stalked,* sometimes fine-toothed, hairless, and with a slender *tip.* Twigs hairy or not. End bud false. Height to 30'. Flowers white, bell-shaped, in slender drooping clusters at the leaf angles, April–June. Fruits fleshy, edible but not tasty, black, Sept.–Oct.

TREE LYONIA (STAGGERBUSH)   PL. 46
Lyonia ferruginea (Walt.) Nutt.

A straggling shrub or small tree. Leaves *small,* edges often finely wavy and rolled under, tips mostly pointed, stalks normal. Twigs and leaf undersides *rusty-hairy.* End bud false. Bundle scar 1. Leaves 1"–3". Height to 20'. Flowers white, bell-shaped, in open clusters at the leaf angles, May–June. Fruits dry, urn-shaped, 5-parted capsules, Sept.–Oct. or later.

BUCKWHEAT-TREE   PL. 46
Cliftonia monophylla (Lam.) Britton ex Sarg.

Leaves *crowded* near the twig tips; the *small* leaves are mostly wedge-based, short-stalked, and with rolled edges and *rather pointed* tips. Twigs hairless; end bud true. Leaves 1"–2" long and ½"–¾" wide. Flowers white, often erect, in elongate clusters at twig *tips,* Feb.–May. Fruits small, *four-winged,* buckwheatlike, June–winter. **REMARKS:** Also called Titi (see Cyrilla). A source of honey.

CYRILLA (TITI) *Cyrilla racemiflora* L. **PL. 46**

Resembles Buckwheat-tree but with leaves 2"–4" long, ¾"–1½" wide, and mostly crowded near the twig ends. Flowers in clusters 3"–8" long at twig *bases,* June–July. Fruits small, dry capsules, *not* winged, Aug.–winter. Height to 35'. Bottomlands and damp places. **REMARKS:** Related to Buckwheat-tree. Colorful in autumn. Bark at tree base said to be astringent, useful in controlling minor bleeding. Despite its natural occurrence only in the South, it is reported (Elias 1980) that the species can tolerate temperatures as low as -10 degrees F. A useful honey plant.

ODORLESS BAYBERRY *Myrica inodora* Bartr. **PL. 46**

Our only bayberry to *lack* both resin dots and a fragrant scent (see Pl. 43), this small tree ranges only in a narrow coastal belt from sw. Georgia to se. Louisiana. It differs from its relatives also in its leathery leaf texture (but see Evergreen Bayberry, p. 352) and in its lack of leaf teeth. Foliage shiny, wedge-based, with rolled edges and short, stout leafstalks. Leaves usually *not* crowded near the twig tip. Twigs hairless. Bark whitish. Leaves 2"–4" long, ¾"–1⅜" wide. Height to 25'. Flowers are *inch-long* catkins at *leaf angles,* the sexes on separate plants. Fruits whitish, wax-covered, in short clusters. Wet places. **SIMILAR SPECIES:** Best distinguished by the fruits, but in their absence, Cyrilla has leaves narrow and regularly clustered near the twig tips.

MOUNTAIN LAUREL *Kalmia latifolia* L. **PL. 46**

A gnarled shrub or small tree. Leaves pointed or blunt, light green beneath, hairless, edges *not* rolled, and often crowded near the twig ends (sometimes a few are opposite). Twigs hairless. Large flower buds of the rhododendron type lacking; side buds minute, silky. Leaves 2"–5". Height to 10', rarely to 35'. Flowers showy,

BUCKWHEAT-TREE

CYRILLA

Mountain Laurel

medium-sized, white to purple, clustered, with (pollen-bearing) stamens tucked into *pockets* in the fused petals, May–July. Fruits *rounded* dry capsules. Mainly mountain and hill slopes. **SIMILAR SPECIES:** (1) See Catawba Rhododendron. (2) Devilwood has leaves that are regularly opposite. **REMARKS:** When a bee lights on the flower, one or more stamens spring out of their pockets and slap the insect. Leaves poisonous to cattle, sheep, and deer but mostly not eaten when better foods are available.

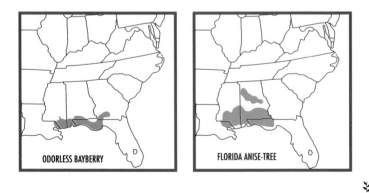

ODORLESS BAYBERRY

FLORIDA ANISE-TREE

FLORIDA ANISE-TREE *Illicium floridanum* Ellis. **PL. 46**

Leaves slender, with veins *indistinct,* pointed at both ends, and crowded toward the twig tips. Twigs hairless. Flowers and bruised foliage have an unusual but generally *unpleasant* odor. Leaves 3"–6". Height to 25'. Flowers showy, star-shaped, dark red, at twig *tips,* March. Fruits dry, *star-shaped,* summer. Wet areas. Gulf Coast from nw. Florida to e. Louisiana.

REDBAY *Persea borbonia* (L.) Spreng. **PL. 46**

A Coastal Plain tree. Leaves narrow, elliptic, shiny above, white or rusty-hairy beneath, veins *distinct,* edges rolled under, and tips pointed or somewhat blunt. Crushed foliage with a *spicy* odor. Twigs greenish, with hairs *pressed close* to surface, and *angled.* Bark dark reddish, deeply grooved. Leaves 3"–7". Height to 50' or 70'; diameter to 3'. Flowers May–July, with stalks *shorter* than nearby leafstalks. Fruits blue or black, fleshy, single-seeded, in red-stemmed clusters *along* the twigs, Aug.–Sept. **SIMILAR SPECIES:** (1) Swamp Redbay (*P. palustria* [Raf.] Sarg.) grows on wetlands over about the same range, with *erect* hairs and flower/fruit stalks *longer* than nearby leafstalks. (2) Silk Bay (*P. humilis* Nash), in Florida, has leaves less than 3" long. **REMARKS:** Leaves sometimes used in place of commercial bay leaves.

CATAWBA RHODODENDRON **PL. 46**
Rhododendron catawbiense Michx.

A dense thicket-forming shrub or small tree, mostly of the mountains. Leaves *large, thick, rounded* at base, and broadly pointed at tip, edges *rolled,* lighter green beneath. Twigs hairy. Flower buds large, at twig ends. Flowers large, pink to purple, in large clusters, May–June. Fruits *elongate* capsules, *rusty-hairy.* Leaves 3"–8".

REDBAY

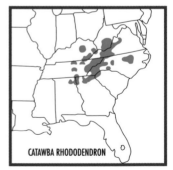

CATAWBA RHODODENDRON

Height to 30' or 40'; diameter to 10' or 12'. **SIMILAR SPECIES:** The two rhododendrons, along with Mountain Laurel, form almost impenetrable tangles on mountain slopes. (1) Great Rhododendron has narrow leaf bases. (2) Mountain Laurel has smaller leaves without rolled edges. **REMARKS:** A rhododendron-covered slope in full bloom is beautiful. Frequently cultivated for ornament. The hard wood may be used for tool

GREAT RHODODENDRON

handles, decorative objects, and fuel. Leaves sometimes poisonous to cattle and deer but usually avoided by them.

GREAT RHODODENDRON *Rhododendron maximum* L. **PL. 46**
Like the preceding but more northern and with *wider, hairless* leaves. Leaf bases and tips *pointed.* Leaves often somewhat *hairy and whitish* beneath. Leaves 3"–8". Height to 20'. Flowers large, rose-purple, clustered, June–July. Fruits elongate capsules, *not* rusty-hairy. Damp slopes and streamsides.

CAMPHORTREE *Cinnamomum camphora* (L.) J. S. Presl. **PL. 46**
Escaped from cultivation in a few southern areas. Some leaves may be opposite, but all leaves are short- or long-pointed and have a *camphor odor* when crushed. *Glands* occur in the vein angles on leaf undersides. There are 3 main veins from the leaf base. Leaf edges sometimes curled and wavy. Twigs *green.* Leaves 2"–6". Height to 40'; diameter to 2'. Flowers small, yellow, 1"–3" clusters, spring. Fruits blue-black, one-seeded, in a greenish cup. **REMARKS:** A native of Asia. Distillation of the leaves and wood produces the oil used in medicine and industry. Often planted in the South for shade.

VI

PALMS, CACTI, AND YUCCAS
(PLATES 47–48)

The palms, yuccas, and cacti are distinctive and recognizably different from other woody plants. The first 2 groups have evergreen, parallel-veined leaves. In the palms, these are long-stalked and clustered at the ends of the stems.

Palms from all over the world have been imported and planted over much of Florida. Only the species native to the U.S. are considered here. Most have single unbranched trunks, but the leafy fronds of palms are of 2 types. They are either fan-shaped, with

Fig. 26. Leaves of palms, yuccas, and cacti.

segments radiating from the end of a central leafstalk or a quite short "partial midrib" (Pl. 47), or long and featherlike, with a central midrib (Pl. 48). The fan-leaved species range north to the Carolinas and west to the Mississippi Valley; the feather-leaved palms grow wild only in Florida.

The end bud, or "heart of palm," grows at the top of the tree. It is eaten as a delicacy in salads and also can be cooked or dried into flour. Removing this bud, however, kills the plant.

Yuccas have long, sword-shaped, and usually sharp-pointed leaves whose bases clasp the stem in dense abundance. They range widely in coastal districts of the Southeast. A tree-sized pricklypear and giant cactus are included in this group for convenience. Their unique succulent and spiny stems are like those of no other trees. They occur only in s. Florida.

FAN-LEAVED PALMS (PLATE 47)

Fan-leaved palms are southern trees which, like the feather-leaved palms on Pl. 48, have large evergreen leaves whose segments show parallel veins. The leaf blades of the fan-leaved palms, however, are nearly circular. For most species, the leafstalk ends at the base or barely enters the leafy portion of the frond. Cabbage Palm differs in having the leafstalk extend almost through the leaf (especially evident as viewed from the leaf underside), essentially forming a midrib. Dwarf Palmetto leafstalks also penetrate the leaf blade but only slightly. The other fan-leaved palms have leafstalks merely attached strongly to the edge of the leaf blade. Also unusual is the occasional branching of the Saw-palmetto. This is the only native palm that may have a branched trunk. The Cabbage Palm and palmettos are distributed more widely than our other native palms.

CABBAGE PALM *Sabal palmetto*   **PL. 47**
(Walt.) Lodd. ex J. A. & J. H. Schult.
The 2 *Sabal* species have leafstalks that continue into the leaf blade. In this palm, it extends almost *completely* through the frond. At the trunk end, the leafstalk base is *forked*. The leafstalk bases often remain *attached*, especially on the upper portions of the trunk, after the leaves die and drop off. Leaves 4'–6' plus leafstalk 6'–7'. *Loose fibers* occur at the edges of leaf segments. Height 40'–50' (90'); diameter 2' (3'). Flowers yellowish white, in *loose* clusters to 6' long, June. Fruits ¼", spherical, becoming black. **SIMILAR SPECIES:** (1) The leafstalk of Dwarf Palmetto barely penetrates the leaf blade, and the leaf segments are not filamentous. (2) Saw-palmetto has saw-edged leafstalks. **REMARKS:** The

CABBAGE PALM

Cabbage Palm

pulp of ripe fruits can be eaten raw. Native Americans also pounded both the dried fruits and the pith of the upper trunks into flour for making bread. The Cabbage Palm is the state tree of Florida.

DWARF PALMETTO *Sabal minor* (Jacq.) Pers. **PL. 47**
Like Cabbage Palm but with leafstalks shorter and extending into the leaf blade for *only* 2″ or so, leafstalk bases *not* split, and edges of leaf segments *without* loose filaments. Usually shrubby in the eastern portions of its range but often developing a trunk westward. Leaves 3′–5′ plus leafstalks of equal length. Height 5′–15′; diameter to 12″. Flower clusters *narrow, to* 3′ *long*; fruits ⅕″–⅓″ wide.

SAW-PALMETTO *Serenoa repens* (Bartr.) Small **PL. 47**
Often creeping and thicket-forming with underground stems but sometimes one or *several* trunks stand upright, occasionally *branched*. The leaves are up to 3′ across, with segments radiating from the ends of the leafstalks. The leafstalk does *not* extend into the leaf blade and is *saw-edged* with tiny (⅒″) spines. Old leaf bases cover the trunk. Height to 20′. Flowers small, white; clusters as long as the leaves. Fruits fleshy, ¼″–¾″ in diameter, blue-black.

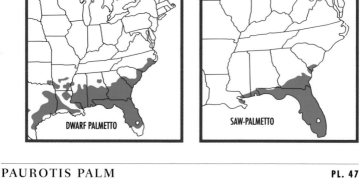

DWARF PALMETTO

SAW-PALMETTO

PAUROTIS PALM   PL. 47
Acoelorrhaphe wrightii (Griseb. & H. Wendl.) H. Wendl. ex Becc.
> Known also as Everglades Palm, this s. Florida plant grows in
> clumps. Usually several trunks, each covered with *fibrous* matting
> and slender leafstalk bases. Leafstalks 2' long, not penetrating the
> blade, and edged with stout orange curved *thorns* ³⁄₁₆"–¼" long.
> Leaves 2'–3' in diameter. Height to 25'; diameter to 6". Flowers
> greenish, in 2'–3' clusters. Fruits ¼"–½" in diameter, orange to
> black. Swamps.

FLORIDA THATCHPALM   PL. 47
Thrinax radiata Lodd. ex J. A. & J. H. Schult.
> The Thatchpalms are slender trees. This species has leaves 3'–4'
> in diameter and pale *yellow-green* beneath. The 2'–3' leafstalks do
> *not* penetrate the leaf blade and bases are *forked* or split where
> they attach to the trunk. Trunk may have some fibrous matted
> covering. Height to 35'. Flowers white on short *stems* and in 3'–4'
> clusters. Fruits white, ¼" globes on ¼" stalks, dry. Coasts, s. Flor-
> ida. **REMARKS:** Once used for thatching.

KEY THATCHPALM   *Thrinax morrisii* H. Wendl.   PL. 47
> Like the preceding species but with leaves 2'–3' in diameter, *sil-
> very-white* beneath, and flowers *stemless,* in clusters 4'–7' long.
> Fruits white, only ⅛" diameter, without stalks. Coasts, s. Florida
> north to Broward County.

FLORIDA SILVERPALM   PL. 47
Coccothrinax argentata (Jacq.) Bailey
> A small tree of limestone soils that is similar to the Thatchpalms
> but has leaves 1'–2' in diameter, with thin and deeply divided seg-
> ments that are dark green above and quite *silvery* beneath. Leaf-

stalks 2'–3' and *not* forked at the base. Trunks often covered with fibrous matting. Flowers white, in 8'–9' clusters. Fruits purple to *black,* fleshy spheres to ¼"–¾". Fla. Keys north to Palm Beach Co.

FEATHER-LEAVED PALMS, TREE-CACTI, AND YUCCAS (PLATE 48)

These feather-leaved palms are native in s. Florida and have ring-scarred trunks free of old leafstalk bases. Their leafstalks are not thorny. The only tree cacti in the eastern U.S. occur in s. Florida. The yuccas range more widely.

FLORIDA ROYALPALM *Roystonea elata* (Bartr.) F. Harper **PL. 48**
The smooth, cement-colored and *bulging* lower trunk topped by a smooth *bright-green crownshaft* cylinder is distinctive. Ring scars *faint.* Fronds 15' or longer. Frond segments do *not* lie flat but grow *all around* the midrib. Height to 125'. Flowers greenish white, developing from a spearlike green spathe at the *base* of the 5'–6' long crownshaft. Fruits blue to purple, ¼" in diameter, leathery. Rich soils, hammocks (swamp islands).

COCONUT PALM *Cocos nucifera* L. **PL. 48**
Ranging along tropical coastlines throughout the world, the wild form of this palm characteristically has a brownish *leaning* trunk with *prominent* ring scars and usually a swollen base. The *feather-shaped* leaves may be over 15' long, the frond segments tending to *lie flat.* There is *no* crownshaft. A clothlike fiber *matting* occurs at the bases of the leafstalks. Height to 65'. Flowers in sheathed clusters up to 5' long, in leafstalk angles. Fruits to 1', more or less

Coconut Palm

three-sided, heavy, green maturing to brown, clustered. **REMARKS:** One of the most useful trees worldwide. The seeds (coconuts) are nearly globular, 5"–10" in diameter, and hollow, with a nutritious liquid center and a lining of tasty white copra "meat." In tropical communities, the thick husk surrounding the coconut is removed by pounding the hand-held fruit against a sharpened stake. The brownish material of the husk is sold as a commercial fiber. Dried copra (white coconut meat) is exported widely for use in candies, cakes, cookies, etc. The "green" or soft copra is more often eaten by residents in the tropics. There are many cultivated varieties of coconuts, including a dwarf Malaysian strain with gold-colored fruits. This variety is reported to be resistant to the increasingly serious lethal yellowing disease of coconuts.

BUCCANEER PALM   PL. 48
Pseudophoenix sargentii H. Wendl. ex Sarg.

Rare in the U.S., growing naturally only on the upper Florida Keys and largely destroyed there by real estate development. The grayish trunk is topped by a 1'–3' crownshaft leading to feather-like leaves 8'–9' long. Fronds folded *V-like*. Height to 25'. Flowers yellow-green, at the *top* of the crownshaft. Fruits 1"–2" in diameter, orange-red. **REMARKS:** An endangered species requiring strict protection. Also called Florida Cherrypalm or Sargent's Cherry-palm. *Phoenix* is the generic name of the date palm; the Bucca-neer Palm with similar foliage is a "false date" named after Charles Sprague Sargent, an eminent botanist of the late 1800s and early 1900s.

BRAZIL PRICKLYPEAR   PL. 48
Opuntia brasiliensis (Willd.) Haw.

An introduced upright succulent and prickly cactus of s. Florida. The cylindrical trunk gives rise to *rounded* branches with *flat-tened* joints. Stem and flat pads armed with sharp, slender, white, brown-tipped spines up to ¾" long as well as with numerous tiny, sharp bristles. Leaves not readily evident as such. Height to 15'. Flowers yellow, 2" long. Fruits 1"–1½", nearly spherical, *yellow*, fleshy, edible. Dry disturbed sites.

INDIANFIG PRICKLYPEAR   NOT ILLUS.
Opuntia ficus-indica (L.) Mill.

Like the Brazil Pricklypear, this cactus may become treelike. It has *only* flattened joints, which may bear short barbed bristles or none. Spines usually absent. Ranging widely throughout the world tropics, this importation has become established locally in s. Florida. Height to 13'. Flowers yellow, 3"–4" long. Fruits 2"–4", *red,* edible. **REMARKS:** This plant was reportedly brought to Europe by Columbus, who called it Indianfig and offered it as proof of his landing in Asia.

KEY GIANT-CACTUS **NOT ILLUS.**
Cereus robinii (Lem.) L. Benson

Either polelike or branched and with a *vertically grooved* succulent stem, this relative of the western giant saguaro cactus is now rare on the Florida Keys. Trunk and branches 9–13 *ribbed,* leafless, gray- or blue-green and covered with clusters of short spines. Leaves absent. Height to 30'. Flowers single, 1"–2" long, *greenish.* Fruits fleshy, *reddish.*

ALOE YUCCA (SPANISH BAYONET) **PL. 48**
Yucca aloifolia L.

A unique shrub or small tree covered with live green (and usually over lower portions of the tree, with dead brown), *sword-shaped,* and pointed leaves, each 1'–3' long. Leaves with numerous tiny marginal *teeth* and sharp, brown tips. Height to 16'. Flowers showy, white, 1"–2" long, in prominent erect end clusters 1'–3' tall. Fruits 3"–4" long, green to black, somewhat leathery. Coastal areas, N. Carolina to Alabama and the Florida Keys. **SIMILAR SPECIES:** Moundlily Yucca is a somewhat similar plant with smooth-edged leaves. **REMARKS:** Yuccas are woody plants related to lilies and often planted for ornament. The species name refers to the aloes of s. Africa, which have similarly thickened leaves.

MOUNDLILY YUCCA *Yucca gloriosa* L. **PL. 48**
Like Aloe Yucca but with shorter, *smooth-edged* leaves and fruits with 6 prominent ridges. Height to 12' or so. Occurs along the Atlantic Coast from N. Carolina to n. Florida.

SPANISH BAYONET   MOUNDLILY YUCCA

TREES FOUND
ONLY IN FLORIDA

Florida is home to nearly half as many native and naturalized tree species as occur in all other eastern states and provinces together. Including six species (Chalk Maple, Sand Pine, Wingleaf Soapberry, Florida Torreya, Florida Willow, and Florida Yew) that scarcely cross the Florida border to enter Alabama and/or Georgia, 133 native trees occur naturally only in Florida. The complex genus of hawthorns (*Crataegus*) is omitted in this tally (see p. 256). Three other species that attain tree size only in Florida but occur as shrubs in other states are also not counted here. Species like Florida Chinkapin, Florida Forestiera, and Florida Maple, which also occur well outside Florida, are excluded from this count despite their names.

Persons attempting to identify a tree in the states and provinces north and west of Florida could be confused if all of Florida's species were discussed and illustrated along with the more northern plants. In consequence, it seemed wise to separate most of those plants which are found only in the Sunshine State. Only readers *in* Florida need consider the many Caribbean species that occur there, often only in certain parts of the state.

Thirty-six Florida-only trees receive more or less full treatment in the main body of the text. Mostly these are illustrated on the color plates or by drawings in the text. Ninety-seven Florida-only trees, however, are identified in the final plate section starting on p. 130.

To identify a tree found growing in Florida, first use the main plates (numbers 1–48) and text to see whether it is one of the many species that occur *both* in Florida and elsewhere in the eastern U.S. and Canada. Plants of n. or n.-cen. Florida are especially likely to be distributed also in other states and provinces. If the identity of the unknown tree is still uncertain, then review the plants on the F-plates starting on p. 130. These show the tropical and subtropical trees of s. and cen. Florida that have not been illustrated earlier in the Plates section. Many of them will have thickened, leathery, evergreen leaves. A nice collection of labeled specimens of local trees grows just outside the visitor center at Everglades National Park.

As a guide to Florida-only species found throughout the book, the following key will serve as an index. If needed, notes on p. 387 describe how to follow this key. Please refer to Fig. 4, p. 17 and cross-references in order to avoid poisonous plants.

1. Palms and tree-cacti. **Pls. 47–48**
1. Leaves needlelike (conifers and coniferlike species). **2**
1. Leaves with broad blades (broadleaf trees). **4**
    2. Needles short, flat.   **Florida Yew and Florida Torreya, Pl. 4**
    2. Needles long, slender. **3**
3. Needles bound in clusters of 2.   **Sand Pine, Pl. 2**
3. "Needles" of jointed, fine-grooved segments.
        Casuarinas (Australian-pine, Brazilian Beefwood), p. 172
    4. Broadleaf trees with leaves opposite. **5**
    4. Broadleaf trees with leaves alternate. **7**
LEAVES OPPOSITE
5. Leaves opposite compound.   **Torchwoods, etc., Pl. F-7**
5. Leaves opposite simple. **6**
    6. Seashore trees, often in salt water.   **Mangroves, Pl. 13**
    6. Mainly upland tropical trees.   **Pls. F-13A, F-13B**
LEAVES ALTERNATE
7. Leaves compound. **8**
7. Leaves simple. **14**
    8. Plants thorny, aromatic.   **Prickly-ashes, etc., Pl. F-15**
    8. Plants not thorny. **9**
9. Leaves once-compound. **10**
9. Leaves twice-compound. **13**
    10. Midribs not winged. **11**
    10. Midribs winged. **12**
11. Leaflets triangular, with black spots. *Poisonous!*
        Florida Poisonwood, Pls. 20, F-21A
11. Leaflets otherwise; not poisonous.
        Scrub Hickory, etc., Pls. 19, F-21A, and F-21B
    12. Leaflets 3"–5", not aromatic.
        Wingleaf Soapberry, Pl. 21
    12. Leaflets 1"–3", turpentine-scented.
        Brazilian Peppertree, Pl. F-21A

13. Minor leaflets more than ¾" long.

Lebbek, Pl. 22

13. Minor leaflets less than ¾" long.

Mexican Leadtree, etc., Pl. F-22

LEAVES ALTERNATE SIMPLE

14. Plants thorny.
Saffron-plum Bumelia, Tallowwood, *Citrus* species, Pl. 24

14. Plants not thorny. 15

15. Leaves fan-lobed.
Papaya* and Castorbean,* p. 269

15. Leaves not lobed. 16

16. Leaves fan-veined. 17

16. Leaves feather-veined. 18

17. Leaves triangular or heart-shaped.
Tremas, Sea Hibiscus, Portiatree, Pl. 26

17. Leaves narrow. 18
Strawberry-tree, Pl. 32

18. Leaves sandpapery above.
Geiger-tree, p. 357

18. Leaves smooth, not sandpapery: 19

19. Leaves fine-toothed, narrow; bud scale single; n. Fla.
Florida Willow, Pl. 39

19. Leaves not toothed. 20

20. Tree of nw. Fla.
Ashe Magnolia, p. 366

20. Trees of cen. and s. Fla.
Pls. F-46A–D

COMPLETE SCIENTIFIC NAMES
OF TREES FOUND ONLY IN FLORIDA

Because of lack of space, the identification charts facing the plates of Florida-only species do not name the authorities (authors) who assigned the Latin names. Complete scientific names, including the species authors, appear here for these 97 Florida-only trees, followed by the corresponding plate number. The 36 additional Florida-only species (see p. 379) described in the main text are not repeated here.

SCIENTIFIC NAME	COMMON NAME AND PLATE
Acacia choriophylla Benth.	Cinnecord, Pl. F-22
Acacia macracantha Humb. & Bonpl. ex. Willd.	Longspine Acacia, Pl. F-15
Acacia tortuosa (L.) Willd.	Huisachillo, Pl. F-15
Alvaradoa amorphoides Liebm.	Mexican Alvaradoa, Pl. F-21 B
Amphitecna latifolia (Mill.)	Black-calabash, Pl. F-46D
Amyris balsamifera L.	Balsam Torchwood, Pl. F-7
Amyris elemifera L.	Small Torchwood, Pl. F-7

* Growing to tree size only in Florida but occurring elsewhere as shrubs.

Annona glabra L.	Pond-apple, Pl. F-46B
Annona squamosa L.	Sugar-apple, Pl. F-46B
Ardisia escallonioides Schiede & Deppe ex Schlecht. & Cham.	Marlberry, Pl. F-46B
Asimina obovata (Willd.) Nash	Bigflower Pawpaw, Pl. F-46A
Bourreria ovata Miers	Bahama Strongbark, Pl. F-46C
Bourreria radula (Poir.) G. Don	Rough Strongbark, Pl. F-46D
Bursera simaruba (L.) Sarg.	Gumbo-limbo, Pl. F-21A
Byrsonima lucida DC.	Locustberry, Pl. F-13B
Caesalpinia pulcherrima (L.) Sw.	Flowerfence Poinciana, Pl. F-15
Calyptranthes pallens Griseb.	Pale Lidflower, Pl. F-13B
Calyptranthes zuzygium (L.) Sw.	Myrtle-of-the-river, Pl. F-13B
Canella winterana (L.) Gaertn.	Cinnamon-bark, Pl. F-46C
Capparis cynophallophora L.	Jamaica Caper, Pl. F-46B
Capparis flexuosa (L.) L.	Limber Caper, Pl. F-46A
* *Casasia clusiifolia* (Jacq.) Urban	Seven-year-apple, Pl. F-13A
Chrysobalanus icaco L.	Cocoplum, Pl. F-46A
Chrysophyllum oliviforme L.	Satinleaf, Pl. F-46A
Citharexylum fruticosum L.	Florida Fiddlewood, Pl. F-13A
Clusia rosea Jacq.	Florida Clusia, Pl. F-13B
Coccoloba diversifolia Jacq.	Pigeon-plum, Pl. F-46B
Coccoloba uvifera (L.) L.	Seagrape, Pl. F-46A
Colubrina arborescens (Mill.) Sarg.	Coffee Colubrina, Pl. F-46D
Colubrina cubensis (Jacq.) Brongn.	Soldierwood, Pl. F-46C
Colubrina elliptica (Sw.) Briz. & Stern	Nakedwood, Pl. F-46D
Conocarpus erectus L.	Buttonwood, Pl. F-46A
Crossopetalum rhacoma Crantz	Florida Crossopetalum, Pl. F-13B
Cupania glabra Sw.	Florida Cupania, Pl. F-21B
Dipholis salicifolia (L.) A. DC.	Willow Bustic, Pl. F-46C
Dodonaea viscosa Jacq.	Varnishleaf, Pl. F-46B
Drypetes diversifolia Krug & Urban	Guiana-plum, Pl. F-46B
Drypetes laterifloria (Sw.) Krug & Urban	Milkbark, Pl. F-46D
Eugenia axillaris (Sw.) Willd.	White Stopper, Pl. F-13A
Eugenia confusa D.C.	Redberry Stopper, Pl. F-13B
Eugenia foetida Pers.	Boxleaf Stopper, Pl. F-13A
Eugenia rhombea (Berg) Krug & Urban	Red Stopper, Pl. F-13A
Eugenia uniflora L.	Surinam-cherry, Pl. F-13A
Exostema caribaeum (Jacq.) Roem. & Schult.	Princewood, Pl. F-13B
Exothea paniculata (Juss.) Radlk.	Inkwood, Pl. F-21A
Ficus americana Aublet	West Indies Laurel Fig, p. 384
Ficus aurea Nutt.	Strangler Fig, Pl. F-46B
Ficus benghalensis L.	Banyan Fig, p. 384
Ficus benjamina L.	Weeping Fig, p. 384
Ficus carica L.	Common Fig, p. 384
Ficus citrifolia Mill.	Shortleaf Fig, Pl. F-46B

Ficus elastica Roxb. ex. Hornem.	India-rubber Fig, p. 384
Ficus microcarpa L. f.	Indian Fig, p. 384
Ficus religiosa L.	Sacred Fig, p. 384
Flacourtria indica (Burm. f. Merr.)	Governor's-plum (not shown)
Guaiacum sanctum L.	Roughbark Lignumvitae, Pl. F-7
Guapira discolor (Spreng.) Little	Longleaf Blolly, Pl. F-13A
Guettarda elliptica Sw.	Elliptic-leaf Velvetseed, Pl. F-13B
Guettarda scabra (L.) Vent.	Roughleaf Velvetseed, Pl. F-13B
Gyminda latifolia (Sw.) Urban	False-boxwood, Pl. F-13B
Gymnanthes lucida Sw.	Crabwood, Pl. F-46C
Hamelia patens Jacq.	Scarletbush, Pl. F-13A
Hippomane mancinella L.	Manchineel, Pl. F-46C
Hypelate trifoliata Sw.	White Ironwood, Pl. F-21A
Illicium parviflorum Michx. ex Vent.	Yellow Anise-tree, Pl. F-46A
Jacquinia keyensis Mez	Joewood, Pl. F-13A
Krugiodendron ferreum (Vahl) Urban	Leadwood, Pl. F-13A
Leucaena leucocephala (Lam.) de Wit	Leadtree, Pl. F-22
Licaria triandra (Sw.) Kosterm.	Florida Licaria, Pl. F-46C
Lysiloma latisiliquum (L.) Benth.	Bahama Lysiloma, Pl. F-22
Mangifera indica L.	Mango, Pl. F-46B
Manilkara bahamensis (Baker) Lam & Meeuse	Wild-dilly, Pl. F-46C
Manilkara zapota (L.) v. Royen	Sapodilla, Pl. F-46B
Masticodendron foetidissimum (Jacq.) H. J. Lam	Mastic, Pl. F-46B
Maytenus phyllanthoides Benth.	Florida Mayten, Pl. F-46A
Melaleuca quinquenervia (Cav.) S. T. Blake	Cajeput-tree, Pl. F-46A
Myrcianthes fragrans (Sw.) McVaugh	Twinberry Stopper, Pl. F-13A
* *Myrsine floridana* A. DC.	Myrsine, Pl. F-46A
Nectandra coriacea (Sw.) Griseb.	Lancewood, Pl. F-46B (F-13A)
Picramnia pentandra Sw.	Bitterbush, Pl. F-21A
Piscidia piscipula (L.) Sarg.	Jamaica-dogwood, Pl. F-21A
Pisonia rotundata Griseb.	Pisonia, Pl. F-13B
Pithecellobium guadalupense (Pers.) Chapm.	Guadeloupe Blackbead, Pl. F-15
Pithecellobium unguis-cati (L.) Benth.	Catclaw Blackbead, Pl. F-15
Prunus myrtifolia (L.) Urban	West Indies Cherry, Pl. F-46C
Psidium guajava L.	Guava, Pl. F-13A
Psidium longipes (Berg) McVaugh	Longstalk Stopper, Pl. F-13B
Reynosia septendrionalis Urban	Darling-plum, Pl. F-13B
Rhodomyrtus tomentosa (Ait.) Hassk.	Downy-myrtle, Pl. F-13A

*Name does not follow Little (1979) but has been accepted for a forth-coming five-volume *Flora of Florida*.

Savia bahamensis Britton	Maidenbush, Pl. F-46D
Schaefferia frutescens Jacq.	Florida-boxwood, Pl. F-46D
Schinus terebinthifolia Raddi.	Brazilian Peppertree, Pl. F-21A
Schoepfia chrysophylloides (A. Rich.) Planch.	Graytwig, Pl. F-46A
Simarouba glauca DC.	Paradise-tree, Pl. F-21B
Solanum erianthum D. Don	Potato-tree, Pl. F-46D
Suriana maritima L.	Bay-cedar, Pl. F-46A
Swietenia mahagoni Jacq.	West Indies Mahogany, Pl. F-21B
Tamarindus indica L.	Tamarind, Pl. F-21B
Tecoma stans (L.) H.B.K.	Yellow-elder, Pl. F-7
Terminalia catappa L.	India-almond, Pl. F-46D
Tetrazygia bicolor (Mill.) Cogn.	Florida Tetrazygia, Pl. F-13B
Zanthoxylum coriaceum A. Rich.	Biscayne Prickly-ash, Pl. F-15
Zanthoxylum fagara (L.) Sarg.	Wild-lime Prickly-ash, Pl. F-15
Zanthoxylum flavum Vahl.	Satinwood, Pl. F-21B

Guide to figs *(Ficus)* introduced from Asian and the West Indies and now established as trees in extreme s. Florida (based on the key devised by Wunderlin, in Morin 1997). Leaves are mostly evergreen and without teeth; the end bud is enclosed by large smooth, deciduous stipules; twigs are ringed by stipule scars; sap is milky. Some "strangling-fig" species grow on and around the trunks of other trees, eventually surrounding them. SEveral, too, have aerial roots that descend from branches; these often become stout supplementary trunks. Most have leathery evergreen leaves. (To read key, see p. 387.)

1 . Leaves with 3–5 lobes, hairy, deciduous.   **Common Fig. F. carica**
1 . Leaves not lobed, mostly hairless, evergreen. 2
   2 . Long-pointed leaf tip = 50% of blade.   **Sacred Fig F. religiosa**
   2 . Leaf tip, if prolonged, then much shorter. 3
3 . Leaves fan-veined; twigs/fruits hairy.   **Banyan Fig F. benghalensis**
3 . Leaves feather-veined; twigs/fruits hairless. 4
   4 . Leaf veins regularly spaced, more than 10 pairs. 5
   4 . Leaf veins unevenly spaced, mostly less than 10 pairs. 6
5 . Stipules ± 1" long, fruits round, leaf blade ± 2" (4") long.
                     Weeping Fig F. benjamina
5 . Stipules 1"–4" long, fruits egg-shaped, leaf blade 4"–12" long.
                     India-rubber Fig F. elastica
   6 . Fruit stalks mostly ⅜"–⅝". 7
   6 . Fruit stalks 0–³⁄₁₆" long. 8
7 . Leafstalks ¼"–2½" long, fruits spotted, leaf base ± U-shaped.
                     Shortleaf Fig F. citrifolia
7 . Leafstalks ¹⁄₁₆"–⁷⁄₁₆" long, fruits unspotted, leaf base ± V-like.
                 West Indies Laurel Fig F. americana
   8 . Fruits ± ¼" wide, leaf blade 1"–4" long. **Indian Fig F. microcarpa**
   8 . Fruits ¼"–⁹⁄₁₆" in diameter, leaf blade 2"–6" long.
                 Strangler Fig F. aurea

APPENDIXES
GLOSSARY
REFERENCES
PHOTO CREDITS
INDEX

APPENDIX A
KEY TO LEAFLESS TREES

See drawings (Fig. 4, p. 17) and learn the characteristics of our few poisonous plants before handling unknown specimens.

1. Coniferous trees whose needles fall in winter, fruits mostly dry cones, swamps and wet soils (Section I). **2**
1. Broad-leaved trees (fruits of some—alders, magnolias—called "cones" but not coniferlike), sites various. **3**
   2. Stubby spur branches numerous on branchlets, northern. **Larches, Pl. 1**
   2. Small "leaf scars" (actually twig scars) but no spurs present, southern. **Baldcypresses, Pl. 4**
3. Leaf scars opposite (Sections II and III). **4**
3. Leaf scars alternate (Sections IV and V). **19**
   4. Trees with thorns. **5**
   4. Trees thornless. **6**
5. Twigs silver-scaly, inner bark not yellow. **Silver Buffaloberry, Pl. 14**
5. Twigs not silvery, inner bark yellow. **Common Buckthorn, Pl. 12**
   6. Twigs four-angled or four-lined, bundle scar 1. **7**
   6. Twigs otherwise, bundle scars 1 or more. **8**
7. Broken twigs spicy-scented, gray-hairy. **Chastetree, Pl. 6**
7. Broken twigs not spicy, twigs green or red. **Burningbush, Pl. 12**
   8. Twigs stout, inflexible; end bud mostly more than ½" long, sometimes gummy. **Buckeyes, Pl. 6**
   8. Twigs slender to moderately stout; end bud less than ⅜" long, not gummy. **9**
9. Central end bud missing, a single pair of buds present at the twig tip; bundle scars 4 or more. **10**
9. One or 3 buds present at twig tip, bundle scars variable. **11**

10. Leaf scars circular or nearly so.   **Princess-tree, etc., Pl. 10**
10. Leaf scars 4-sided to crescent shaped.
                                  Bladdernut, etc., Pl. 7
11. Buds with a single caplike scale.   **Basket Willow, Pl. 39**
11. Buds with 2 or more scales. **12**
    12. Twigs only moderately slender, rather stiff. **13**
    12. Twigs slender, flexible. **14**
13. Twigs green or purplish, leaf scars meeting in raised points, bundle scars 3.   **Ashleaf Maple, Pl. 9**
13. Twigs mostly grayish, leaf scars not meeting in raised points, bundle scars 4 or more.   **Ashes, Pls. 8, 9**
    14. Bundle scar single. **15**
    14. Bundle scars 3. **16**
15. Buds short, somewhat ball-shaped.   **Forestieras, Pls. 12, 13**
15. Buds longer than broad.   **Fringetree, etc., Pl. 14**
    16. Buds with only a pair of scales. **17**
    16. Bud scales 4 or more.   **Maples, Pl. 11**
17. Twig leaf scars raised.   **Dogwoods, Pl. 14**
17. Twig leaf scars not raised. **18**
    18. Buds stalked; fruits dry, winged.   **Maples, Pl. 11**
    18. Buds not stalked, fruits fleshy.   **Viburnums, Pls. 12, 13**

LEAF SCARS ALTERNATE (SECTIONS IV AND V OF TEXT):
  19. Twigs silvery, branchlets brown, sometimes thorny.
                                    Russian-olive, p. 331
  19. Twigs not silvery, branchlets variable. **20**
    20. Trees thorny or bristly. **21**
    20. Trees thornless. **27**
21. Thorns paired. **22**
21. Thorns not paired. **23**
    22. Twigs hairy, usually green, one thorn larger, southern.
                                    Jujube, Pl. 23
    22. Twigs otherwise, some northern.
              Black Locust, Mountain-ashes, etc., Pl. 15
23. Sap milky in broken twigs (if not too cold).
                     Bumelias, Osage-orange, Pl. 24
23. Sap not milky. **24**
    24. Thorns on short, bud-bearing branches.
                       Crabapples, Plums, Pl. 23
    24. Thorns mostly without buds. **25**
25. Trunk and twigs with many prickles, twigs stout, leaf scars large, bundle scars 20 or more.   **Hercules-club, Pl. 15**
25. Trees otherwise. **26**
    26. Buds ball-shaped, fruits like small apples.   **Hawthorns, Pl. 23**
    26. Buds various, fruits pealike pods or small oranges.
                                 Locusts, etc., Pl. 15

27. Buds encircled, or nearly so, by O-, U-, or V-shaped leaf scars. **28**

27. Buds located above leaf scars. **30**

    28. Leaf scars with 3–5 bundle scars.   **Hoptree, Yellowwood, Texas Sophora, Pl. 21**

    28. Leaf scars with numerous bundle scars. **29**

29. Buds often woolly, with several scales; bundle scars sometimes in 3 groups.   **Sumacs, Pl. 20**

29. Buds not woolly, with only 1 caplike bud scale.   **Eastern Sycamore, Pl. 25**

    30. Leaf scars large, triangular or shield-shaped; twigs stout, relatively inflexible; bundle scars 4 or more, sometimes in 3 groups. **31**

    30. Leaf scars narrow, twigs mostly slender, bundle scars various. **38**

31. Buds with a single caplike bud scale, twigs encircled by narrow lines (stipule scars).   **Magnolias, Pl. 45**

31. Buds with more than 1 bud scale, twigs not ringed. **32**

    32. Fruits small, white, dry clusters; twigs hairless; wet or damp sites.   **Poison-sumac, Pl. 20**

    32. Fruits otherwise, twigs various, upland sites. **33**

33. Pith chambered.   **Walnuts, Pl. 16**

33. Pith continuous, solid. **34**

    34. Fruits 4-parted nuts, end bud usually larger.   **Hickories, Pls. 17–19**

    34. Fruits otherwise, end bud not much larger. **35**

35. Buds often several at each leaf scar, above one another. **36**

35. Buds single, 1 per leaf scar. **37**

    36. Buds embedded in bark, twigs whitish, pith pink.   **Coffeetree, Pl. 22**

    36. Buds raised, twigs not whitish, pith whitish.   **Soapberries, Pl. 21**

37. Leaf scars three-lobed, bundle scars in 3 groups.   **Chinaberry, Pl. 22**

37. Leaf scars deeply triangular, bundle scars scattered.   **Tree-of-heaven, Pl. 16**

Leaf scars narrow

    38. Twigs nearly or completely encircled by narrow lines (stipule scars) beneath buds. **39**

    38. Twigs without encircling stipule scars. **41**

39. Buds with only 1 caplike bud scale.   **Magnolias, Pl. 45**

39. Buds with more than 1 bud scale. **40**

    40. Buds blunt, two-scaled, spicy when crushed; pith chambered.   **Tuliptree, Pl. 25**

    40. Buds long-pointed, many-scaled, not aromatic; pith continuous.   **Beech, Pl. 32**

41. Buds clustered at twig tips. **42**
41. Buds not clustered at twig tips. **44**
    42. Bundle scars many.   **Oaks, Pls. 28–31**
    42. Bundle scars 3. **43**
43. End buds much larger than side buds, southern states.
                                  Corkwood, Pl. 44
43. End buds about same size as side buds, northern states and Canada.   **Fire Cherry, Pl. 36**
    44. Pith chambered or at least partitioned at leaf scars. **45**
    44. Pith solid, continuous. **51**
45. Trunk bark divided into small squares. **46**
45. Trunk bark not checkered. **47**
    46. Bundle scar 1, buds dark, two-scaled.   **Persimmon, Pl. 44**
    46. Bundle scars 3, buds brown, four-scaled.   **Sourgum, Pl. 44**
47. Bundle scar 1, end bud true, southern trees. **48**
47. Bundle scars 3–5, end bud false. **49**
    48. Buds dark.   **Sweetleaf, Pl. 43**
    48. Buds reddish.   **Silverbell, Pl. 42**
49. Growing on periodically flooded sites in South, trunk bases often swollen, bundle scars 3.   **Tupelos, Pl. 43**
49. Growing on upland sites, widespread. **50**
    50. Bundle scars 3, twigs hairless.   **Hackberries, Pl. 26**
    50. Bundle scars 5, twigs rough-hairy.   **Paper-mulberry, Pl. 25**

PITH CONTINUOUS, SOLID

51. Buds without scales. **52**
51. Buds with scales. **54**
    52. End bud much larger than side buds, bundle scars 5–7.
                                  Pawpaws, Pl. 44
    52. End bud about the same size as side buds, bundle scars 1–3. **53**
53. Buds narrowed at the base (stalked), bundle scars 3.
                              Witch-hazel, Pl. 32
53. Buds not stalked, bundle scar 1.   **Snowbells, Buckthorns, Pl. 43**
    54. Bud scale single.   **Willows, Pls. 38, 39**
    54. Bud scales more than 1. **55**
55. Twigs green. **56**
55. Twigs not green. **60**
    56. Twigs ridged or lined lengthwise. **57**
    56. Twigs without lengthwise ridges or lines. **58**
57. Twigs with many fine ridges.   **Groundsel-tree, Pl. 32**
57. Twigs four-lined or four-angled.   **Grape-myrtle, Pl. 44**
    58. Broken twigs spicy-scented, twigs forked, bundle scar 1.
                                    Sassafras, Pl. 25
    58. Broken twigs not spicy scented. **59**

59. Bundle scar single or indistinct, buds brown-hairy.
Chinese Parasoltree, p. 267
59. Bundle scars 3, buds not hairy, two-scaled.
Alternate-leaf Dogwood, Pl. 44

Twigs not green
    60. Sap milky in broken twigs (if weather not too cold). **61**
    60. Sap not milky. **62**
61. Buds tiny (1/16"); fruits dry, white, at twig ends.
Tallowtree, p. 276
61. Buds larger (1/4"); fruits fleshy, along twigs.   **Mulberries, Pl. 25**
    62. Inner bark of branches peels in fibrous strips when cut. **63**
    62. Inner bark not especially fibrous. **64**
63. Buds red or green, with 2–3 scales.   **Basswoods, Pl. 26**
63. Buds brown, many scales in 2 rows.   **Elms, Pl. 33**
    64. Bundle scar 1. **65**
    64. Bundle scars more than 1. **69**
65. Spur branches usually present; fruits fleshy, berrylike; tiny black stipules may flank leaf scars (use lens).   **Hollies, Pl. 40**
65. Spur branches lacking, fruits and stipules various. **66**
    66. Buds blackish, with 2 scales; fruits fleshy.
Persimmon, Pl. 44
    66. Buds otherwise, fruits dry. **67**
67. Buds more than 1/4" long, end bud true.
Mountain Pepperbush, Stewartias, Pl. 42
67. Buds less than 1/8" long; twigs hairless; fruits small, dry capsules at twig ends; end bud false. **68**
    68. Fruits in one-sided clusters, widespread in South.
Sourwood, Pl. 42
    68. Fruits in rounded clusters, rare—only in Georgia.
Elliottia, Pl. 44

Bundle scars 3 or more
    69. Bundle scars 4 or more. **70**
    69. Bundle scars 3. **71**
      70. Leaf scars narrow, bundle scars in a curved line.
Mountain-ashes, Pl. 16
      70. Leaf scars oval or triangular, bundle scars not in a line.
Chestnuts, Pl. 32
71. Buds blunt, with a narrow base (stalked), reddish; woody, conelike catkins usually present.   **Alders, Pl. 35**
71. Buds without a constricted base. **72**
    72. Twigs with small yellow resin dots (use lens).
Bayberries, Pl. 43
    72. Twigs without resin dots (use lens). **73**

73. Buds with the lowermost scale centered directly above leaf scar, bark often smooth and greenish on young trunks and branches. **Poplars, Pl. 27**

73. Buds with lowermost scale not centered directly above leaf scar. **74**

    74. Buds long-pointed, reddish, scales often twisted with black notched tips, second bud scale usually less than half length of bud. **Juneberries, Pl. 42**

    74. Buds relatively short and stout, blunt to sharp but not long-pointed. **75**

75. Older bark usually with narrow cross-stripes, spur branches often present. **76**

75. Older bark without cross-stripes, buds with 4 or more scales. **78**

    76. Buds with 2–3 scales, broken twigs with or without a peppermint odor. **Birches, Pl. 34**

    76. Buds with 4–6 scales, broken twigs usually with almond or sour odor. **77**

77. End bud true, fruit usually with a rounded stone. **Cherries, Pl. 36**

77. End bud false, fruit usually with a flattened stone. **Thornless plums, Pl. 37**

    78. Spur branches present, end bud true. **79**

    78. Spur branches absent, end bud as indicated. **80**

79. Bud scales about 6, hairy-fringed (use lens); branchlets often with corky wings. **Sweetgum, Pl. 25**

79. Bud scales about 4, not hairy-fringed (use lens); branchlets not winged. **Domestic Apple, Domestic Pear, Pl. 43**

    80. Buds tiny, brownish, with 2–4 paired pointed scales, end bud true. **American Smoketree, Pl. 44**

    80. Buds otherwise, end bud false. **81**

81. Leaf scars raised, with 2 or 3 obvious lines leading down, upper edge often hairy-fringed, some buds narrow at base (stalked). **Redbud, Pl. 26**

81. Leaf scars not raised or at least without obvious lines leading from them. **82**

    82. Twigs somewhat zigzag and often angled, beanpod fruits often present. **Silktree, Lebbek, Pl. 22**

    82. Twigs and fruits otherwise. **83**

83. Buds four-angled, scales in 4 rows, trunk smooth, gray, "muscular." **Ironwood, Pl. 35**

83. Buds not angled, rounded, scales finely grooved (use lens) and not in regular rows. **Hornbeam, Pl. 35**

APPENDIX B
PLANT RELATIONSHIPS

Field identification does not require a knowledge of major classification groups or even of family or scientific names. Yet it is often
desirable to know the general relationships of the various plant
species. The following list indicates the family relationships of
the genera of the trees within our area. This classification is that
of Gleason & Cronquist (1991). All major and many minor botanical subdivisions are based on flower and fruit structures. Family
names tend to be standardized by the ending *-aceae*, orders by
-ales, subclasses by *-idae*, classes by *-opsida*, and divisions by
-ophyta.

KINGDOM PLANTAE
SUBKINGDOM EMBRYOBIONTA
DIVISION PINOPHYTA
CLASS PINATAE
SUBCLASS PINIDAE

Order Taxales
Family Taxaceae: *Taxus, Torreya*

Order Pinales
Family Pinaceae: *Abies, Cedrus, Larix, Picea, Pinus, Tsuga*
Family Taxodiaceae: *Taxodium*
Family Cupressaceae: *Chamaecyparis, Juniperus, Thuja*

DIVISION MAGNOLIOPHYTA
CLASS MAGNOLIOPSIDA
SUBCLASS MAGNOLIIDAE
Order Magnoliales
Family Magnoliaceae: *Liriodendron, Magnolia*
Family Annonaceae: *Annona, Asimina*
Family Canellaceae: *Canella*

Order Laurales
Family Lauraceae: *Cinnamomum, Licaria, Nectandra, Persea, Sassafras*

Order Illiciales
Family Illiciaceae: *Illicium*

SUBCLASS HAMAMELIDAE
Order Hamamelidales
Family Platanaceae: *Platanus*
Family Hamamelidaceae: *Hamamelis, Liquidambar*

Order Urticales
Family Ulmaceae: *Celtis, Planera, Trema, Ulmus*
Family Moraceae: *Broussonetia, Ficus, Maclura, Morus*

Order Leitneriales
Family Leitneriaceae: *Leitneria*

Order Juglandales
Family Juglandaceae: *Carya, Juglans*

Order Myricales
Family Myricaceae: *Myrica*

Order Fagales
Family Fagaceae: *Castanea, Fagus, Quercus*
Family Betulaceae: *Alnus, Betula, Carpinus, Ostrya*

Order Casuarinales
Family Casuarinaceae: *Casuarina*

SUBCLASS CARYOPHYLLIDAE
Order Caryophyllales
Family Nyctaginaceae: *Guapira, Pisonia*
Family Cactaceae: *Cereus, Opuntia*

Order Polygonales
Family Polygonaceae: *Coccoloba*

SUBCLASS DILLENIIDAE
Order Theales
Family Theaceae: *Franklinia, Gordonia, Stewartia*
Family Clusiaceae: *Clusia*

Order Malvales
Family Tiliaceae: *Tilia*
Family Sterculiaceae: *Firmiana*
Family Malvaceae: *Hibiscus, Thespesia*

Order Violales
Family Flacourtiaceae: *Flacourtia, Muntingia*
Family Tamaricaceae: *Tamarix*
Family Caricaceae: *Carica*

Order Salicales
Family Salicaceae: *Populus, Salix*

Order Capparales
Family Capparaceae: *Capparis*

Order Ericales
Family Cyrillaceae: *Cliftonia, Cyrilla*
Family Clethraceae: *Clethra*
Family Ericaceae: *Elliottia, Kalmia, Lyonia, Oxydendrum, Rhododendron, Vaccinium*

Order Ebenales
Family Sapotaceae: *Bumelia, Chrysophyllum, Dipholis, Manilkara, Mastichodendron*
Family Ebenaceae: *Diospyros*
Family Styracaceae: *Halesia, Styrax*
Family Symplocaceae: *Symplocos*

Order Primulales
Family Theophrastaceae: *Jacquinia*
Family Myrsinaceae: *Ardisia, Myrsine*

SUBCLASS ROSIDAE
Order Rosales
Family Rosaceae: *Amelanchier, Crataegus, Malus, Prunus, Pyrus, Sorbus*
Family Chrysobalanaceae: *Chrysobalanus*
Family Surianaceae: *Suriana*

Order Fabales
Family Mimosaceae: *Acacia, Albizia, Leucaena, Lysiloma, Prosopis, Pithecellobium*
Family Caesalpiniaceae: *Caesalpinia, Cercis, Gleditsia, Gymnocladus, Parkinsonia, Tamarindus*
Family Fabaceae: *Cladrastis, Erythrina, Piscidea, Robinia, Sophora*

Order Proteales
Family Eleagnaceae: *Eleagnus, Shepherdia*

Order Myrtales
Family Lythraceae: *Lagerstroemia*
Family Myrtaceae: *Calyptranthes, Eugenia, Melaleuca, Myrcianthes, Psidium, Rhodomyrtus*

Family Melastomataceae: *Tetrazygia*
Family Combretaceae: *Conocarpus, Laguncularia, Terminalia*

Order Rhizophorales
Family Rhizophoraceae: *Rhizophora*

Order Cornales
Family Nyssaceae: *Nyssa*
Family Cornaceae: *Cornus*

Order Santalales
Family Olacaceae: *Schoepfia, Ximenia*

Order Celastrales
Family Celastraceae: *Crossopetalum, Euonymus, Gyminda,*
  Maytenus, Schaefferia
Family Aquifoliaceae: *Ilex, Nemopanthus*

Order Euphorbiales
Family Euphorbiaceae: *Drypetes, Gymnanthes, Hippomane,*
  Ricinus, Sapium, Savia

Order Rhamnales
Family Rhamnaceae: *Colubrina, Krugiodendron, Reynosia,*
  Rhamnus, Ziziphus

Order Polygales
Family Malpighiaceae: *Byrsonima*

Order Sapindales
Family Staphyleaceae: *Staphylea*
Family Sapindaceae: *Cupania, Dodonaea, Exothea, Hypelate,*
  Sapindus
Family Hippocastanaceae: *Aesculus*
Family Aceraceae: *Acer*
Family Burseraceae: *Bursera*
Family Anacardiaceae: *Cotinus, Mangifera, Metopium, Rhus,*
  Schinus, Toxicodendron
Family Simaroubaceae: *Ailanthus, Alvaradoa, Picramnia,*
  Simarouba
Family Meliaceae: *Melia, Swietenia*
Family Rutaceae: *Amyris, Citrus, Poncirus, Ptelea, Zanthoxylum*
Family Zygophyllaceae: *Guaiacum*

Order Apiales
Family Araliaceae: *Aralia*

SUBCLASS ASTERIDAE
Order Solanales
Family Solanaceae: *Solanum*

Order Lamiales
Family Boraginaceae: *Bourreria, Cordia*
Family Verbenaceae: *Avicennia, Citharexylum, Vitex*

Order Scrophulariales
Family Oleaceae: *Chionanthus, Forestiera, Fraxinus, Ligustrum,
    Osmanthus*
Family Bignoniaceae: *Amphitecna, Catalpa, Paulownia, Tecoma*

Order Rubiales
Family Rubiaceae: *Casasia, Cephalanthus, Exostema, Guettarda,
    Hamelia, Pinckneya*

Order Dipsacales
Family Caprifoliaceae: *Sambucus, Viburnum*

Order Asterales
Family Asteraceae: *Baccharis*

CLASS LILIOPSIDA
SUBCLASS ARECIDAE
Order Arecales
Family Arecaceae: *Acoelorraphe, Coccothrinax, Cocos, Pseudo-
    phoenix, Roystonia, Sabal, Seronoa, Thrinax*

SUBCLASS LILIIDAE
Order Liliales
Family Agavaceae: *Yucca*

GLOSSARY

See also diagrams and text (pp. xvi–xvii and 1–15) in "How to Use This Book."

Aerial rootlet (vine). Small, rootlike organs along stems of some climbing vines. See Poison-ivy, p. 17.

Alternate (leaves, buds). Not opposite but arranged singly at intervals along twigs.

Angled (twig, bud). With evident ridges; not smoothly rounded.

Aromatic. Having a distinctive odor, at least when crushed.

Base (leaf). The lower portion, toward the leafstalk.

Berry (fruit). Strictly speaking, a fleshy fruit that contains small seeds (such as a grape). "Berry" or berrylike fruits are mentioned, indicating fleshy fruits that are not true berries.

Blade (leaf). The broad, expanded portion.

Bloom (twig, leaf, fruit, etc.). A whitish powdery coating.

Bract. A somewhat leaflike, petal-like, or woody structure occurring beneath a flower or fruit or their clusters.

Branchlet. Except for the twig, the youngest and smallest division of a branch. See **Twig**.

Bristle. A stiff hair, sometimes pricklelike.

Bundle scars. Tiny dots or lines within the leaf scar, caused by the breaking of bundles of ducts leading into the leafstalk. Sometimes elongate or curved.

Capsule. A dry fruit that splits partly open at maturity.

Catkin. A cluster of tiny flowers or fruits, usually fuzzy and caterpillar-shaped, often drooping. It occurs in willows and relatives. Where there are flowers of only 1 sex, male catkins usually are larger.

Chambered (pith). Pith divided crosswise by numerous plates or membranes. Term is here used broadly to include all types of segmented and transversely divided pith (diaphragmed, partitioned). When the twig is cut lengthwise, such a pith looks ladderlike. See **Partitioned.**

Coarse-toothed (leaf edge). With large teeth; dentate, serrate.

Compound (leaf). Divided into leaflets, each of which usually has the general appearance of a leaf. See pp. xvii and 3.

Continuous (pith). Smoothly pithy, the twig center neither chambered nor hollow.

Deciduous (leaf, stipule, bud scale, etc.). Falls off seasonally, usually in autumn or dry periods.

Double-toothed (leaf edge). Each tooth bearing smaller teeth.

Egg-shaped (leaf). Broader near the base than at the tip, the base broadly rounded (but leaf tip is sharper than apex of an egg); ovate.

Elliptic (leaf). Widest in the middle and tapering evenly to both ends like the cross section of an American football.

End bud (twig). True end bud or sometimes several, clustered, located at the precise end of the twig. False end bud occurs in some species when the end bud is shed and a nearby side bud acts as end bud. A scar marks the site of the shed bud and lies beside the false end bud. See drawing, p. 6.

Fan-compound (leaf). A compound leaf with leaflets radiating from a point; palmate-compound.

Fan-lobed (leaf). Major lobes radiating from a point; palmate-lobed.

Fan-veined (leaf). Main veins radiating from a point; palmate-veined.

Feather-compound (leaf). Midribs of main leaflets branching from a central main midrib at several points in a featherlike pattern; pinnate-compound.

Feather-lobed (leaf). The main lobes more or less at right angles to the midrib, not radiating from a central point; pinnate-lobed.

Feather-veined (leaf). The main veins more or less at right angles to a main midrib; pinnate-veined.

Fine-toothed (leaf edge). With small teeth; denticulate or serrulate.

Fluted (trunk). With rounded, vertical, columnlike segments.

Form. Used in this volume to include all populations of plants of the same species which vary slightly from the typical, whether such variation is limited geographically (see Variety) or not; forma.

Four-lined (twig). With 4 more or less equidistant lines running lengthwise along the twig.

Four-sided (twig; bud). Approximately square in cross section.

Fruit. The seed-bearing portion of a plant with its associated structures. The term does not imply that it is either fleshy or edible.

Genus. A group of species sufficiently closely related to be given the same generic name.

Gland. Strictly speaking, a surface or protuberance that secretes a substance, but generally any small knob or wart that is a normal part of the plant and has no other known function.

Glandular-toothed (leaf). Having teeth that bear glands. See Tree-of-heaven, Pl. 16.

Hairy. Covered with hairs; pubescent, hirsute, etc.

Heart-shaped (leaf). The shape of the valentine heart; cordate.

Hollow (pith). Twig actually without pith but with the space present.

Hybrid. The offspring of a cross between 2 species.

Involucre. A circle or cluster of bracts beneath flowers or fruits.

Lateral (bud). To the side rather than at the end of twig or branchlet.

Leaf scar. The mark left on the twig at the point of attachment of a leafstalk when the leaf falls.

Leaflet. A leaflike subdivision of a compound leaf.

Leafstalk. The stalk supporting a leaf; petiole.

Leathery (leaf). Of a smoothly tough texture; coriaceous.

Legume. A plant of the pea family or the one- to many-seeded podlike fruit of a pea-family plant.

Lenticel. A corky spot on the bark originating as a breathing pore and either circular or somewhat stripelike (see Cherries).

Lobed (leaf, flower petal, sepal). Divided into incompletely separated sections, often rounded.

Long-pointed (leaf). The tip gradually tapering to a point; acuminate.

Midrib (leaf, leaflet). The central rib or main vein.

Naked (bud). Without bud scales.

Narrow (leaves). Shaped like the top view of a canoe; slender and pointed at each end. Often slightly wider near the base; lanceolate.

Net-veined (leaf). With a network of veins.

Node. The place, sometimes swollen, on a stem or twig where a leaf is attached or a bud or leaf scar occurs.

Oblong (leaf). Longer than broad, with the longer sides somewhat parallel.

Once-compound (leaf). A compound leaf with a single set of undivided (major) leaflets (see **Twice compound**).

Opposite (leaves, leaf scars, buds). Two at a node; in opposing pairs.

Ovary. The ovule-bearing (egg-bearing) portion of the flower.

Ovule. See **Ovary.**

Palmate. See various **Fan** prefixes.

Parasitic (plant). Growing on another plant and deriving food from it.

Partitioned (pith). The pith divided crosswise by woody plates, usually near the leaf scars.

Pendent: Hanging from a stem.

Persistent (scales, fruits, leaves). Remaining attached.

Petal (flower). One of a circle of modified leaves immediately outside the reproductive organs; usually brightly colored. See **Sepal.**

Petiole. See **Leafstalk.**

Pinnate. See various **Feather** prefixes.

Pith. The spongy or hollow center of twigs or some stems. See **Chambered, Continuous,** and **Hollow.**

Pod. The dryish fruit of some plants, especially legumes, containing one to many seeds and usually flattened, splitting down 1 or both sides; see **Legume.**

Prickle. A small, sharp outgrowth involving only the outer epidermal layer; generally more slender than a thorn. But in this book no stress is placed on the technical distinctions between prickles and thorns. See also **Bristle, Thorn, Spine.**

Prostrate. Flat on the ground.

Reclining (stem). The lower portion somewhat flattened along the ground but the upper parts curving upward.

Resin-dot. Tiny circular or globular yellow spots, usually not obvious except under magnification.

Ridged (twig). Angular, with lengthwise lines.

Ringed (twig). With narrow encircling stipule scars at nodes.

Rolled (leaf edge). Curled under; revolute.

Scale (bud, leaf, twig). (1) A thin, membranelike covering of the bud or twig base, or (2) a fine, grainlike surface material.

Seed. That portion of the ripened fruit which contains the embryo and its closely associated essential coats.

Sepal (flower). One of the outermost circle of modified leaves surrounding the reproductive organs; usually green. See **Petal.**

Sheath (conifer needle). Thin tissues present at needle bases and binding the needle bundles.

Short-pointed (leaf tip). Abruptly constricted and sharply pointed; not gradually tapering.

Shreddy (bark). Dividing into fragile, thin, narrow sheets or flakes.

Shrub. A woody plant usually growing with several equally strong stems and less than about 1 5 feet maximum height.

Side (buds). In a lateral, not end, position.

Simple (leaf). Composed of only a single blade, though sometimes lobed.

Single-toothed (leaf edge). Bearing only a single set of teeth. See also **Double-toothed.**

Sinus (leaf). The space between 2 leaf lobes.

Solid (pith). See **Continuous.**

Species. For practical purposes here: populations whose individuals freely breed with one another and vary only slightly from one another.

Spicy-scented. Aromatic, with a spicy odor.

Spike (flowers, fruits). A cluster with a narrow, fingerlike shape, the individual flowers or fruits without separate stalks or with only very short ones.

Spine. See **Thorn.**

Spur branch. A stubby branchlet with densely crowded leaves and leaf scars. See drawing, p. 6.

Stalked (buds). Having a narrow necklike base.

Sterile (flower). Infertile, unproductive.

Stipule. A growth at the base of the leafstalk, usually small and in pairs, leaving scars on the twig when they drop. See also **Ringed.**

Straggling. Semi-upright.

Thorn (twig, branchlet, branch, stem). A stout, sharp, woody outgrowth of the stem. Technically, prickles and spines are of different origins, but this book does not require a distinction to be made.

Thrice-compound (leaf). Divided into major leaflets that in turn are divided into minor leaflets, which are further divided into subleaflets; an uncommon type.

Tip (leaf). The apex.

Tree. A woody plant with a single main stem at least 3 inches in diameter at breast height ($4\frac{1}{2}'$) and growing more than 1 3 feet tall.

Trunk. The main stem of a tree.

Tubular (flower). With the basal portion hollow and tubelike.

Tundra. Vegetation type of very cold climates, especially in far north, overlying permafrost and consisting of lichens, sedges, mosses, grasses, and low woody plants.

Twice-compound (leaf). With the major leaflets divided into minor leaflets.

Twig. The end subdivision of a branch; the current year's growth. See **Branchlet.**

Undulant (leaf edge). With minor up and down (vertical) waviness. See **Wavy-edged.**

Variety. That portion of a species which in a certain geographic area differs slightly from the remainder of the species elsewhere. See **Form.**

Wavy-edged (leaf edge). With shallow, rounded undulations in a flat plane. See **Undulant.**

Wavy-toothed (leaf edge). Wavy-edged but with more toothlike projections; crenate.

Wedge-shaped (leaves, leaf bases, leaf tips). With narrow, tapering, V-shaped bases or, less often, tips (cuneate, acute).

Whorled (leaves, leaf scars). Arranged in circles around the twigs.

Winged (leafstalk, twig). With projecting thin flat membranes or corky outgrowths.

Woody plant. With the stems and limbs containing lignin (wood).

REFERENCES

Argus, George W. 1986. *The Genus Salix (Salicaceae) in the Southeastern United States.* Syst. Bot. Monog. 9, American Society of Plant Taxonomists.

Barnes, Burton V., and Warren H. Wagner. 1981. *Michigan Trees.* Univ. Mich. Press, Ann Arbor, Mich.

Blackburn, Benjamin. 1952. *Trees and Shrubs in Eastern North Amer-ica.* Oxford Univ. Press, New York.

Blackwell, Will H., Jr. 1976. *Guide to the Woody Plants of the Tri-state Area.* Kendall Hunt, Dubuque, Iowa.

Brown, Clair A. 1945. *Louisiana Trees and Shrubs.* La. For. Comm. Bull. No. 1. Baton Rouge, La.

Brown, Claud L., and L. Katherine Kirkland. 1990. *Trees of Georgia and Adjacent States.* Timber Press, Portland, Ore.

Clark, G. Thomas. 1981. *Winter Twigs of Arkansas.* Rose, Little Rock, Ark.

Clewell, Andre F. 1985. *Guide to the Vascular Plants of the Florida Panhandle.* Univ. Presses of Fla., Tallahassee.

Core, Earl L., and Nelle P. Ammons. 1958. *Woody Plants in Winter.* Boxwood Press, Pittsburgh.

Cronquist, Arthur. 1981. *An Integrated System of Classification of Flowering Plants.* Columbia Univ. Press, New York.

Davis, Donald E., and Norman D. Davis. 1975. *Guide and Key to Alabama Trees.* Kendall Hunt, Dubuque, Iowa.

Elias, Thomas S. 1980. *The Complete Trees of North America.* Van Nostrand Reinhold, New York.

Fernald, M. L. 1950. *Gray's Manual of Botany,* 8th ed. Amer. Book, New York.

Gleason, Henry A., and Arthur Cronquist. 1991. *Manual of Vascular Plants of the Northeastern United States and Adjacent Canada,* 2nd ed. New York Bot. Garden, Bronx.

Godfrey, Robert K. 1988. *Trees, Shrubs and Woody Vines of North-*

ern Florida and Adjacent Georgia and Alabama. Univ. of Ga. Press, Athens.

Gordon, Robert B. 1960. *A Winter Field Key to Willows of Pennsylvania.* Proc. Penn. Acad. Sci. 34:10–14.

Graves, Arthur Harmount. 1952. *Illustrated Guide to Trees and Shrubs.* Published by the author, Wallingford, Conn.

Gupton, Oscar W., and Fred C. Swope. 1981. *Trees and Shrubs of Virginia.* Univ. Press of Virginia, Charlottesville, Va.

Harlow, William M., and Elwood S. Harrar. 1958. *Textbook of Dendrology.* McGraw Hill Book Co., New York.

Harrar, Ellwood S., and J. George Harrar. 1962. *Guide to Southern Trees*, 2nd ed. Dover, New York.

Hicks, Ray R., Jr., and George K. Stephenson. 1978. *Woody Plants of the Western Gulf Region.* Kendall Hunt, Dubuque, Iowa.

Hosie, R. C. 1969. *Native Trees of Canada.* Canadian Forestry Service, Ottawa.

Hough, Romeyn Beck. 1947. *Handbook of the Trees of the Northern States and Canada.* Macmillan, New York.

Krugman, Stanley L., and James L. Jenkinson. 1974. *Pinus* chapter in *Seeds of Woody Plants in the United States.* Agric. Handbook No. 450, Forest Service, U.S. Dept. Agric., Washington, D.C.

Kurz, Herman, and Robert F. Godfrey. 1962. *Trees of Northern Florida.* Univ. Florida Press, Gainesville.

Lakela, Olga, and Richard P. Wunderlin. 1980. *Trees of Central Flor-ida.* Banyan Books, Miami, Florida.

Little, Elbert L., Jr. 1971. *Atlas of United States Trees. Vol. 1: Conifers and Important Hardwoods.* U.S. Dept. Agric. Misc. Publ. 1146.

———. 1977. *Atlas of United States Trees. Vol. 4: Minor Eastern Hardwoods.* U.S. Dept. Agric. Misc. Publ. 1342.

———. 1978. *Atlas of United States Trees. Vol. 5: Florida.* U.S. Dept. Agric. Misc. Publ. 1361.

———. 1979. *Checklist of United States Trees (Native and Naturalized).* Agric. Handbook 541, Forest Service, U.S. Dept. Agric., Washington, D.C.

———. 1980. *The Audubon Society Field Guide to American Trees.* Alfred A. Knopf, New York.

Long, Robert W., and Olga Lakela. 1971. *A Flora of Tropical Florida.* Univ. Miami Press, Coral Gables, Florida.

Miller, Howard A., and H. E. Jaques. 1972. *How to Know the Trees.* Wm. C. Brown, Dubuque, Iowa.

Morin, Nancy R. (ed.) 1993, 1997. *Flora of North America,* Vols. 2, 3. Oxford Univ. Press, New York and Oxford.

Morton, Julia F. 1971. *Plants Poisonous to People in Florida and Other Warm Areas.* Hurricane House, Miami, Florida.

Muenscher, W. C. 1950. *Keys to Woody Plants.* Comstock, Ithaca, New York.

Oosting, H. J. 1956. *The Study of Plant Communities.* Freeman, San Francisco.

Petrides, George A. 1972. *A Field Guide to Trees and Shrubs,* 2nd ed. Houghton Mifflin, Boston.

Radford, Albert E., Harry E. Ahles, and C. Ritchie Bell. 1968. *Manual of the Vascular Flora of the Carolinas.* Univ. North Carolina Press, Chapel Hill.

Sargent, Charles Sprague. 1965. *Manual of the Trees of North Amer-ica.* Dover, New York.

Schopmeyer, C. S. 1974. *Seeds of Woody Plants in the United States.* Agric. Handbook No. 450, Forest Service, U.S. Dept. Agric., Washington, D.C.

Scurlock, J. Paul. 1987. *Native Trees and Shrubs of the Florida Keys.* Laurel Press, Pittsburgh, Penn.

Small, John Kunkel. 1933. *Manual of the Southeastern Flora.* Published by author, New York.

Stevenson, George B. 1969. *Trees of Everglades National Park and the Florida Keys.* Everglades Natural History Assoc.

Symonds, George W. D. 1958. *The Tree Identification Book.* William Morrow, New York.

———. 1963. *The Shrub Identification Book.* William Morrow, New York.

Tomlinson, P. B. 1980. *The Biology of Trees Native to Tropical Florida.* Harvard Univ., Allston, Mass.

Trelease, William. 1931. *Winter Botany.* Dover, New York.

Van Dersal, William R. 1938. *Native Woody Plants of the United States: Their Erosion Control and Wildlife Values.* Misc. Publ. 303, U.S. Dept. Agric., Washington, D.C.

Vines, Robert A. 1977. *Trees of East Texas.* Univ. Texas Press, Austin, Texas.

Wagner, W. H., Jr. 1974. Dwarf Hackberry (Ulmaceae: *Celtis tenuifolia*) in the Great Lakes Region. *Mich. Botanist* 13:73–99.

Wharton, Mary E., and Roger W. Barbour. 1975. *Trees and Shrubs of Kentucky.* Univ. Press of Kentucky, Lexington.

Wunderlin, Richard P. 1982. *Guide to the Vascular Plants of Central Florida.* Univ. Presses of Fla., Gainesville.

Photo Credits

DAVID CAVAGNARO: Nannyberry, Tree-of-Heaven, Shagbark Hickory, Coffeetree, American Plum, Scarlet Oak, Bur Oak, American Elm, Downy Juneberry.

KATHY ADAMS CLARK: Rusty Blackhaw, Buttonbush, Honey Locust, Southern Prickly-ash, Post Oak, Winged Elm.

PRISCILLA CONNELL/PHOTO/NATS: Sassafras.

DEREK FELL: White Pine, White Spruce, Horsechestnut, White Ash, Northern Catalpa, Red Maple, Sugar Maple, Red Mangrove, Pecan, Pignut Hickory, Smooth Sumac, Silktree, Osage-orange, Tuliptree, Redbud, American Basswood, White Oak, Willow Oak, Virginia Live Oak, Common Winterberry Holly, American Holly, Evergreen Magnolia, Cucumber Magnolia, Cabbage Palm, Coconut Palm.

CHARLES MARDEN FITCH: Sugar Maple bark, Black Locust, Staghorn Sumac, Northern Red Oak, River Birch.

CARL HANNINEN/PHOTO/NATS: Jack Pine.

LYNNE HARRISON: Loblolly Pine.

ARTHUR LEE JACOBSON/PHOTOGARDEN: Hornbeam.

JOHN A. LYNCH/PHOTO/NATS: Eastern Cottonwood.

STEPHEN G. MAKA/PHOTO/NATS: Northern Bayberry.

JERRY PAVIA: Tamarack, Eastern Hemlock, Ashleaf Maple, Flowering Dogwood, American Mountain-ash, Quaking Aspen.

GEORGE A. PETRIDES: Pine cones: Slash, Longleaf, Loblolly, Shortleaf pines; Scotch Pine, Austrian Pine, Red Pine, Shortleaf Pine, Baldcypress, Eastern Redcedar, Striped Maple, Black Walnut, Butternut, Yellowwood, Eastern Sycamore, Northern Hackberry, Pin Oak, Black Oak, Southern Red Oak, Swamp Oak, Beech, Paper Birch, Gray Birch, Yellow Birch, Ironwood, Black Cherry, Weeping Willow, Persimmon.

BEN PHILLIPS/PHOTO/NATS: Possumhaw Holly, Crapemyrtle.

PHOTOSYNTHESIS: Northern White-cedar, Common Juniper, Princesstree.

INDEX

Page references in *italics* refer to illustrations in the text. Entries in **boldface** type refer to the color and black-and-white plates beginning on p. 33.

THE PETERSON SERIES ®

PETERSON FIELD GUIDES ®

BIRDS

FISH

INSECTS

MAMMALS

ECOLOGY

PLANTS

EDIBLE WILD PLANTS (23) Eastern and central North America 31870-X
EASTERN TREES (11) North America east of 100th meridian 90455-2
FERNS (10) Northeastern and central North America, British Isles and
    Western Europe 19431-8
MEDICINAL PLANTS (40) Eastern and central North America 92066-3
MUSHROOMS (34) North America 91090-0
PACIFIC STATES WILDFLOWERS (22) Washington, Oregon, California, and
    adjacent areas 91095-1
ROCKY MOUNTAIN WILDFLOWERS (14) Northern Arizona and New Mexico to
    British Columbia 18324-3
TREES AND SHRUBS (11A) Northeastern and north-central U.S. and south-
    eastern and south-central Canada 35370-X
WESTERN TREES (44) Western U.S. and Canada 90454-4
WILDFLOWERS OF NORTHEASTERN AND NORTH-
    CENTRAL NORTH AMERICA (17) 91172-9
SOUTHWEST AND TEXAS WILDFLOWERS (31) 36640-2

EARTH AND SKY

GEOLOGY (48) Eastern North America 66326-1
ROCKS AND MINERALS (7) North America 91096-X
STARS AND PLANETS (15) 91099-4
ATMOSPHERE (26) 33033-5

REPTILES AND AMPHIBIANS

EASTERN REPTILES AND AMPHIBIANS (12) Eastern and
    central North America 90452-8
WESTERN REPTILES AND AMPHIBIANS (16) Western North America, including
    Baja California 38253-X

SEASHORE

SHELLS OF THE ATLANTIC (3) Atlantic and Gulf coasts
    and the West Indies 69779-4
PACIFIC COAST SHELLS (6) North American Pacific coast, including Hawaii
    and the Gulf of California 18322-7
ATLANTIC SEASHORE (24) Bay of Fundy to Cape Hatteras 31828-9
CORAL REEFS (27) Caribbean and Florida 46939-2
SOUTHEAST AND CARIBBEAN SEASHORES (36) Cape Hatteras to the Gulf Coast,
    Florida, and the Caribbean 46811-6

PETERSON FIRST GUIDES®

PETERSON FIELD GUIDE COLORING BOOKS

PETERSON NATURAL HISTORY COMPANIONS

AUDIO AND VIDEO

EASTERN BIRDING BY EAR
cassettes 50087-7
CD 71258-0

WESTERN BIRDING BY EAR
cassettes 52811-9
CD 71257-2

EASTERN BIRD SONGS, Revised
cassettes 53150-0
CD 50257-8

WESTERN BIRD SONGS, Revised
cassettes 51746-X
CD 51745-1

BACKYARD BIRDSONG
cassettes 58416-7
CD 71256-4

MORE BIRDING BY EAR
cassettes 71260-2
CD 71259-9

WATCHING BIRDS
Beta 34418-2
VHS 34417-4

PETERSON'S MULTIMEDIA GUIDES: NORTH AMERICAN BIRDS
(CD-ROM for Windows) 73056-2

PETERSON FLASHGUIDES™

ATLANTIC COASTAL BIRDS 79286-X
PACIFIC COASTAL BIRDS 79287-8
EASTERN TRAILSIDE BIRDS 79288-6
WESTERN TRAILSIDE BIRDS 79289-4
HAWKS 79291-6
BACKYARD BIRDS 79290-8
TREES 82998-4
MUSHROOMS 82999-2
ANIMAL TRACKS 82997-6
BUTTERFLIES 82996-8
ROADSIDE WILDFLOWERS 82995-X
BIRDS OF THE MIDWEST 86733-9
WATERFOWL 86734-7
FRESHWATER FISHES 86713-4

WORLD WIDE WEB: http://www.petersononline.com

PETERSON FIELD GUIDES can be purchased at your local
   bookstore or by calling our toll-free number, (800) 225-3362.

When referring to title by corresponding ISBN number,
preface with 0-395.